›Becoming a
GREEN BUILDING
PROFESSIONAL

Holley Henderson

WILEY

John Wiley & Sons, Inc.

Library of Congress Cataloging-in-Publication Data:

Henderson, Holley, 1971-
  Becoming a green building professional : a guide to careers in sustainable architecture, design, development and more / Holley Henderson.
     p. cm.
  Includes index.
  ISBN 978-0-470-95143-9 (pbk.); 978-1-118-30028-2 (ebk); 978-1-118-30030-5 (ebk); 978-1-118-31037-3 (ebk); 978-1-118-31038-0 (ebk); 978-1-118-31039-7 (ebk)
  1. Sustainable architecture. 2. Architects—Training of. 3. Architecture—Study and teaching. 4. Sustainable buildings—Design and construction. 5. Buildings—Energy conservation. I. Title.
  NA2542.36.H46 2012
  720'.47023—dc23

                                                                    2011047550

Printed in the United States of America

10 9 8 7 6 5 4 3 2 1

For my mother, Nora Ellen

CONTENTS

FOREWORD

A Human Design Revolution

by

*Anthony D. Cortese, Sc.D. President, Second Nature; Organizer,
American College & University Presidents' Climate Commitment*

Humanity and Higher Education at an Unprecedented Crossroads

Because of the extraordinary and exponential growth of population and of the technological/
economic system, human beings have become pervasive and dominant forces in the health and
well-being of the Earth and its inhabitants. The sum of humanity and the expansive dynamic of industrial capitalism constitute a planetary force comparable in disruptive power to the Ice Ages and
the asteroid collisions that have previously redirected Earth's history. While the Earth's population
has grown from 1 billion to 6.7 billion in the last two centuries, energy consumption has risen 80
times, and economic output has risen 68 times. Most of that has occurred in the last half-century.
Despite the impressive array of environmental protection laws and programs established in the
industrialized countries since 1970, all living systems (oceans, fisheries, forests, grasslands, soils,
coral reefs, wetlands) are in long-term decline and are declining at an accelerating rate, according
to all major national and international scientific assessments. Some (e.g., major ocean fisheries,
coral reefs, forests) have collapsed, and more are moving rapidly to total collapse. Human beings
and the rest of nature are burdened by a staggering array of persistent, toxic natural and manmade
chemicals, as well as air and water pollution, that are affecting our health and the viability of large
ecosystems.

At the same time, we are not succeeding in many health and social goals: 3.2 billion people
are without sanitation and earn less than $2.50/day; over a billion have no access to clean drink-
ing water. The gap between the richest 20 percent of the world and the poorest 20 percent has
jumped from 28:1 to 85:1 since 1960. Even in the U.S., the gap is the greatest since the Gilded
Age of the late nineteenth and early twentieth centuries. We have a worldwide economic recession

and international conflicts and wars over resources such as oil and water that are destabilizing world society. This is happening with 25 percent of the world's population consuming 70–80 percent of the world's resources.

And the challenge that will accelerate all the negative trends is human-induced global warming, primarily from the burning of fossil fuels that is now destabilizing the Earth's climate and most of its other life-supporting systems. Despite what we may read or hear in the news media (especially in the U.S.), human-induced climate disruption is real and is already affecting us: It is worse and happening faster than predicted by the most conservative scientists just five years ago in 2007. What most people do not understand is that destabilizing the Earth's climate can undermine modern civilization. As Dianne Dumanoski asserts in her recent book, *The End of the Long Summer:*

> Our way of life depends on a stable climate. The cores of ice drilled from the ice sheets on Greenland and Antarctica tell us we live at a truly extraordinary time within the Earth's volatile climate history. Through most of our species' 200,000-year existence, our ancestors had to cope with a chaotic climate marked by extreme variability, a climate that could not support agriculture. The world as we know it, with agriculture, civilization, and dense human numbers, has only been possible because of a rare interlude of climatic grace—a "long summer" of unusual climatic stability over the past 11,700 years. The human enterprise has become a risky agent of global change. The gargantuan size of our modern industrial civilization is now disrupting our planet's very metabolism—the vast overarching process that maintains all of earthly life. Because of humanity's planetary impact, this exceptional moment on Earth is drawing to a close. What lies ahead is a time of radical uncertainty.[1]

While this may (and should) make us uncomfortable, it is current reality and leads to the central question for the future of humanity.

> How will we ensure that all current and future human beings will have their basic needs met, will live in thriving, secure communities, and will have economic opportunity in a world that will have nine billion people and that plans to increase economic output 3–4 times by 2050, on a planet whose capacity to support life is more precarious every day?

The consensus among Earth systems scientists is that if everyone lived like the average American, we would need four to five planets (three planets for a European lifestyle) to continu-

1 Dumanoski, Dianne. *The End of the Long Summer: Why We Must Remake Our Civilization to Survive on a Volatile Earth* (New York: Crown Publishers, 2009), p. 2.

ally supply all our resources and provide critical ecosystem services, including conversion of waste products into useful substances. At the same time, Asia, Africa, and Latin America are expanding economically at unprecedented rates to lift 3 billion people out of poverty and create a higher quality of life for all of their people. The challenge is not just an environmental one, it is arguably the greatest civilizational, moral, and intellectual challenge that humanity has ever faced. It is not about saving the planet. The planet has survived five major biological extinctions, the last being 65 million years ago in the age of the dinosaurs, and it will survive the sixth being caused by human beings. The goal is to create a thriving civilization for all of humanity. The goal is built on the understanding that all human activities and human survival are completely dependent on the Earth for all of their resources and key ecosystem services, including converting waste products into useful substances.

A Change in Mindset

How did we get here? The cultural operating instructions of modern industrial society are that, if we just work a little harder and smarter and let the market forces run society, all these challenges will work themselves out.

But the routine business of our civilization is threatening its own survival, and by putting Earth's living system in jeopardy, it also risks foreclosing on the conditions for any civilized life. In the industrialized world, we are guided by a myth of human separateness from and domination of nature for our purposes, and of continuing "progress" fueled by economic growth, because this model has worked in the last three centuries to create a modern society offering spectacular increases in the quality of life for a significant portion (though still a minority) of the world's population. This guiding myth contains an implicit assumption that the Earth will be the gift that keeps on giving—providing the resources and converting our wastes into useful substances—ad infinitum, irrespective of the size of the population or the level of its material desires. The guiding myth assumes that human technological innovation will allow us to ignore planetary limits.

We need a *transformative shift* in the way we think and act. As Einstein said, "We can't solve today's problems at the same level of thinking at which they were created." We currently view the array of health, economic, energy, political, security, social justice, environmental, and other societal issues we have as separate, competing, and hierarchical, when they are really *systemic* and *interdependent. We have a de facto systems design failure.*

For example, we don't have environmental problems *per se.* We have negative health and environmental consequences of the way in which we have organized society economically, socially, and technologically. The twenty first century challenges must be addressed in a systemic, integrated, and holistic fashion, with an emphasis on creating new and more desirable ways of helping society succeed. We need, for example, buildings that foster the health and productivity of their occupants, use as little energy as possible and get their energy from renewable sources, are constructed of renewable and ecologically friendly materials, live within and sustain local ecosystems, support strong local and regional social networks, allow for easy access through sustainable transportation, and constantly educate us about how to live sustainably.

Remaking the Built Environment

When we look at the scale of human impact and needs, it is clear that remaking the nature and the location of the built environment must be a top priority. Buildings have a significant impact on the environment and human health, accounting for *one-sixth* of the world's freshwater withdrawals, *one-quarter* of its wood harvest, and *two-fifths* of its material and energy flows (*70 percent* of electricity), with very large negative impacts on the environment and health. Structures also impact areas beyond their immediate location, affecting watersheds, air quality, and transportation patterns of communities—*over four-fifths* of all transportation is from one building to another. Moreover, people in developed countries spend nearly *90 percent* of their lives indoors, making the quality of the indoor environment key to good health. The resources required to create, operate, and replenish this level of infrastructure are enormous and are diminishing. By all accounts, we will have to replace *three-quarters* of the existing building stock and *double* the built environment in the next 40 years, to accommodate the demand. This is not possible without a radical change in the design, construction, operation, and location of buildings.

Design Principles

Here is what we know about living sustainably over the long run:

- Use as little resources and energy as possible; power the economy with renewable energy.
- Move from the linear "take, make, waste" model to a circular industrial production in which the concept of "waste" is eliminated because every waste product is a raw material or nutrient for another industrial activity.
- Live off nature's interest, not its capital—use natural resources only at the rate that they can self-regenerate—by following the ideas embodied in sustainable forestry, fishing, and agriculture.

This is the concept of *biomimicry*—learning from and imitating nature, which has figured out what works and survives after 3.4 billion years of experimentation.

These principles afford the best chance that all current and future generations will be able to pursue meaningful work and have the opportunity to realize their full human potential, both personally and socially. A growing consensus of business, government, labor, and other leaders believe that a clean, green economy based on these principles is the only way to restore American economic leadership, create millions of jobs, and help solve global health and environmental problems. Ray Anderson, the late chairman and founder of Interface, Inc.—the world's largest modular carpet manufacturer, with annual sales of $1.2 billion, and one of the world's leading companies dedicated to economic, social, and ecological sustainability—says:

> At Interface, the business case for sustainability (as a core purpose of our business) is crystal clear. A capitalist to the core, I can't think of a better business case than lower costs, better products, higher morale, loyal employees and goodwill in the marketplace. Our costs are down, not up, dispelling the myth that sustainability is expensive. Our first initiative—zero-tolerance waste—has netted us $433 million in saved or avoided costs, more than paying for all capital investments and other costs associated with sustainability. Our products are the best they've ever been. Sustainability is a wellspring of innovation; our product designers have been particularly successful using "biomimicry" as a guide, nature as inspiration. Our people are galvanized around our mission and a shared higher purpose—Maslow at his best: self-actualization that comes when people commit to something bigger than themselves, a type of top-to-bottom and bottom-to-top alignment that sustainability has fostered. The goodwill of the marketplace is tremendous, winning business for Interface because customers want to be aligned with a company that is trying to do the right thing. No amount of marketing, no clever advertising campaign, could have created the kind of customer loyalty that we have experienced.[2]

Transforming Our Thinking, Values, and Actions

These principles must be a foundation of learning and practice. Higher education must lead this effort because it prepares most of the professionals who develop, lead, manage, teach, work in, and influence society's institutions, including the most basic: elementary, middle, and secondary schools. Higher education has been a crucial leverage point in making a modern, advanced civilization possible for an unprecedented number of people in almost every important way, and it will be even more important in a world that is rapidly expanding and becoming more interdependent. In addition, college and university campuses are microcosms of the rest of society—they are like mini cities and communities that mirror society.

2 Ray C. Anderson. "Editorial: Earth Day, Then and Now." *Sustainability: The Journal of Record.* April 2010, 3(2): 73–74. doi:10.1089/SUS.2010.9795,

Unfortunately, the current education system is, by and large, reinforcing the current unsustainable paradigm. Indeed, it is the graduates of the world's best colleges, universities, and professional schools who are leading us down this path. For example, despite the growing number of architecture schools focusing on teaching sustainable design, most have yet to make sustainable design the default for education and practice. The same is true in the education for virtually every intellectual discipline and profession.

Why is this the case? Several structural aspects of the current system contribute to the problem. Interactions between population, human activities, and the environment are amongst the most complex and interdependent issues with which society must deal, as are the strategies, technologies, and policies for a secure, just, and environmentally sustainable future. These issues cross over the disciplinary boundaries that dominate the higher education learning framework. Moreover, much of higher education stresses individual learning and competition, resulting in professionals ill prepared for cooperative efforts.

What if higher education were to take a leadership role in helping to make sustainability a reality? *The context of learning* would make the human/environment interdependence, values, and ethics a seamless and central part of teaching of all the disciplines. *The content of learning* would reflect interdisciplinary systems thinking, dynamics, and analysis for all majors and disciplines, with the same *lateral rigor* across and *vertical rigor* within the disciplines. *The process of education* would emphasize active, experiential, inquiry-based learning and real-world problem solving *on the campus* and *in the larger community*. Higher education would *practice sustainability* in *operations, planning, facility design, purchasing, and investments* connected with the formal curriculum. It would form *partnerships with local and regional communities* to help make them sustainable, as an integral part of higher education's mission and the student experience. The latter is critical since higher education comprises anchor institutions of economic development, with annual operating expenditures of $320 billion. This is greater than the GDP of all but 28 countries in the world.

Beacons of Hope

There has been unprecedented, exponential growth in distinct academic programs related to the *environmental dimension* of sustainability in higher education, especially in the last decade. Exciting environmental (and now sustainability) studies and graduate programs in every major scientific, engineering, and social science discipline, and in design, planning, business, law, public health, behavioral sciences, ethics, and religion, are abundant and growing. Progress on campuses modeling sustainability has grown at an even faster rate. Higher education has embraced programs for energy and water conservation, renewable energy, waste minimization and recycling, green buildings and purchasing, alternative transportation, local and organic food growing, and "sustainable" purchasing—saving both the environment and money. *The rate of increase is unmatched by any other sector of society.* In the U.S., according to the U.S. Green Building Council,[3] the higher education sector has nearly 4,000 new buildings that are being designed or have been designed to meet advanced levels of sustainable design under the LEED system (Leadership in Energy and Environmental Design) in the last decade. The student environmental movement in the U.S. is the most well organized, largest, and most sophisticated student movement since the civil rights and anti-war movements of the 1960s. These developments represent one of most encouraging trends in higher education innovation since World War II.

Unfortunately, higher education is doing a poor job on the health, social, and economic dimensions of sustainability. And the educational efforts have not reached the majority of students, who know little about the importance of sustainability or how to align their personal and professional lives with sustainability principles. With a few exceptions, sustainability, as an aspiration for society, is not a central institutional goal, or *lens* for determining the success of higher education institutions.

One of the brightest beacons of light for systemic change in the U.S. is the American College & University Presidents' Climate Commitment (ACUPCC),[4] launched in January of 2007 by 12 college and university presidents, working with Second Nature, the Association for the Advancement of Sustainability in Higher Education (AASHE), and ecoAmerica. It is a high-visibility, joint and individual commitment to measure, reduce, and eventually neutralize campus greenhouse gas emissions, to develop the capability of students to help all of society do the same, and, importantly, *to publicly report on their progress.* Second Nature provides the ongoing support and organization of the ACUPCC Network.

As of January 2011, just under five years later, 675 colleges and universities in all 50 states and the District of Columbia have made this unprecedented commitment. They represent 5.9 million students—about 35 percent of the student population—and include every type of institution, from two-year community colleges to the biggest research universities. *This is unprecedented leadership. Higher education is the first and only major U.S. sector to have a significant number of its members commit to climate neutrality.* This is especially important given the inability of the international community and, in my experience, the U.S. Congress, to act. These schools are doing what is scientifically necessary, not what is easily doable within their current mode of operation.

Another beacon of hope is the efforts of the design, construction, and planning professions, through the professional schools, societies, and nongovernmental organizations (such as USGBC, Architecture 2030, and American Institute of Architects). Holley Henderson's book *Becoming a Green Building Professional* is an important contribution to this effort—combining a wide variety of perspectives and knowledge critical to the *teams* of design professionals that are necessary to create the building and community design revolution. It is written in a way that is useful to practicing professionals, faculty, and students in colleges, universities, and professional schools.

---

3 USGBC: U.S. Green Building Council, www.usgbc.org/, accessed July 15, 2010.
4 American College & University Presidents' Climate Commitment, www.presidentsclimatecommitment.org/, accessed January 2011.

While all these efforts are incredibly important, the scale of the challenge requires a quantum leap forward in our thinking, actions, and values. Most of the world's major international governmental, scientific, and nongovernmental institutions, as well as many business organizations, agree that the deep changes needed in individual and collective values and actions must occur within the next decade, if we are to avoid changes that will undermine the long-term viability of a complex human civilization.

Many argue that creating a healthy, just, and sustainable society is too hard or impossible. If we continue business as usual, today's students and their children will experience the worst effects of climate disruption, and of other large, unsustainable means of meeting human needs. They will find themselves in a world with greatly diminished prospects for a good quality of life, peace, and security. We are faced with the greatest intergenerational equity challenge in modern history. The Earth does not recognize how hard it is for us human beings to change. It will respond to the physical changes we cause on its own schedule and in its own ways. It doesn't have the cognitive ability to decide to wait for us to figure out how we can change to preserve our way of life and ourselves.

If we follow the principles in *Becoming a Green Building Professional*, future generations will have the kind of chance they deserve for a decent life.

PREFACE

PATH

When I was considering which career path to take, my inclination was an art-based field, so I found myself in the art of making space, as an interior designer. Have you ever found yourself doing something, and you know you can perform the tasks, but it's not your calling? This is where I found myself. So, on my mother's recommendation, I read a book called *Zen and the Art of Making a Living,* by Laurence G. Boldt. Two critical decisions came from this book:

- Investigate options.

- Ask myself: What is my purpose?

During my research of career options, I saw a presentation by Ray C. Anderson. I distinctly recall that he used overhead transparencies (old-school vintage presentation format that predates PowerPoint), and I was incredibly moved by his authentic story of a reformed businessman in search of zero impact solutions. My research, plus his inspiration, culminated in a very nervous, hand-trembling meeting with the president of the company I worked for at the time (tvsdesign), Roger Neuenschwander, FAIA. My pitch was simple: "Green building is the future, and I'm going in this direction." Without hesitation, he said, "Write a business plan, we'll back you." I thought, "What is a business plan?" This conversation was in LEED's infancy and the recent green building buzz. I had zero environmental training or education other than one enlightening environmental biology class in college. He and the firm were taking a chance. I ended up writing the business plan and helping them to begin a sustainable design practice; years later, I worked for Ray's company, InterfaceFLOR, and finally began a sustainable consulting company called H2 Ecodesign. After seven blessed years, I was invited to write this book.

I offer my circuitous path as a living example of what my meditation class facilitator, Teresa, often says: "You are exactly where you need to be, doing exactly what you need to be doing." While I questioned at points along the way if I was in the right place, each step (whether I knew it at the time or not) was filled with purpose. This book was written with purpose in mind—your purpose. No matter what career path you take in the building field, or in a completely different direction—such as accounting, practicing law, or teaching—environmental consciousness can be woven into the fabric of your career. Shelters or buildings house all of us, so their contribution to our society is important.

Here's what I learned in the early nodes and milestones along the path of my career search, and what I continue to acknowledge: Listen to wise advice, act on inspiration, go forward with courage, and ground yourself in the knowledge that each step on the path is purposeful. Seek your internal compass.

You may be beginning your first career search, transitioning to an eco-job position, or simply considering the green building profession. Regardless of where you start, green building careers may be a new adventure for you. With this in mind, we have gathered a unique perspective from a dynamic US Green Building Council (USGBC) group called Emerging Professionals. Emerging Professionals are typically out of school but, under thirty years old. You'll find their voices thread throughout the book and indicated with this icon: **EP**

For more information on the USGBC Emerging Professionals please visit: www.usgbc.org/DisplayPage.aspx?CMSPageID=116

ACKNOWLEDGMENTS

It is with overwhelming gratitude and deep appreciation that I'd like to acknowledge the multitudes that made this book possible.

Thank you to God for the ability to serve as a vessel for Your Word.

Heartfelt appreciation to my family—William for his service to our country; Irene for her talents, dedication, fire, and creativity; Ellen for being the most amazing mother and life coach in the universe (www.createyourlifecanvas.com); Lauren for being my dependable little sister; Steve, Lily, Cooper, Cecilia, Haley, Kent, Chip, Tonya, and Ronald.

Gregg Hinthorn—I love you. I am grateful for your keen insight and constant support.

Sir Winston Longfellow—the best dog in the world. Thank you for your patience with missed walks and long lonely days.

Precious friends who are the puzzle pieces to create the whole—those still here and those who have gone beyond. Special thanks for the constant support and teaching by Candace, Gaines, Ruth Ann, Teresa, and the meditation class.

In the creation of the book, thank you to John Wiley & Sons, Inc. for this opportunity, as well as the amazing support provided by Kathryn, Danielle, Doug, Penny, and the entire behind-the-scenes editorial, production, and marketing team. Thank you to John Czarnecki for your early vision.

Writing and editing has not been my day-to-day vocation. So, in the early formation of the book, Shannon Murphy and Kathryn (Kit) Brewer were instrumental in setting the infrastructure and providing amazing guidance. For the majority of the book, Amara Holstein performed editing and feedback that really contributed to the book as a whole. She is also a writer and can be found at: www.amaraholstein.com/. Amara—thank you for your insight, late nights, and weekends. Paula Breen, Lee Waldrup, and Michael Bayer—thank you for your early advice.

Appreciation sent to Lisa Lilienthal for your creative ideas and your introduction to Tony Cortese. Tony, I am grateful for your contribution to our society as a whole by forging the environmental education path, and for your willingness to lend your thoughts to this work.

Each interview and image was the collective work of hundreds of academics, photographers, practitioners, and marketing departments who were willing to offer their time, knowledge, and property in support of green building careers of the future—thank you to each and every one.

Our internal team at H2 Ecodesign rallied to support the book in an extraordinary display of dedication to the message. There are not enough words to express thanks to Sharlyn for her level of unparalleled commitment, complete with many sleepless nights. Deep appreciation to Yvonne for her attention to detail and follow-through; her writing can be found at: http://yswords.com/. Thank you to Melissa for her time in the final days. Margie and Lauren, I appreciate your assistance with the image coordination.

Thank you to the anonymous early peer reviewers of the book proposal. In the final stages, Jim Hackler provided an insightful peer review—thank you for your time and feedback. For more on Jim's work please visit: http://theurbaneenvironmentalist.com/.

I drank a lot of tea over these months provided by the amazing folks at Octane Coffee: www.octanecoffee.com.

Last, but not least, a thank-you to each of the challenges in my life—you know who you are. Adversity creates an important perspective, and I now know that those moments are rich growth points.

❯ Becoming a
GREEN BUILDING PROFESSIONAL

1 Why Build Green?

Unless someone like you cares a whole awful lot, nothing is going to get better. It's not.

— DR. SEUSS, *from* The Lorax *(Children's book on the environment)*

Our Place

Green building is a profession that seeks to give back more than it takes from our natural surroundings—the environment at large—and, ultimately, to help preserve the health of both people and our planet. It is a lofty goal, and one that inspires most people in this career field both personally and professionally. Yet there is no one right way to become a green builder, nor is there only one type of green building expert. The field is vast and diverse, full of numerous jobs and specializations, all working together toward the same ideal: to create buildings that are sustainable, and ultimately regenerative.

Consider the people who create a green building. It is not just one, or even two, sets of people or teams that come together to plan, design, erect, and maintain a building. Instead, it is a well-integrated group of individuals, all of whom have varying backgrounds and job titles. For green building, the roles include an environmental consciousness where realtors and land developers focus on the planned structure's return on investment and overall sustainable strategy. Architects draft and design the framework of the building itself; interior designers sculpt the healthy interior space; engineers fill in the efficient systems inside, from plumbing to electrical to mechanical. Contractors make sure all the eco-conscious elements are properly installed during construction; and facility managers keep the place green after the sawdust is cleared and the last window is installed.

Relaxation area at Nusta Spa,
Washington, DC (LEED CI Gold).
Firm: Envision Design. PHOTO:
ERIC LAIGNEL

This book seeks to introduce readers to the green building profession, to explain how to become part of this quickly growing career field—and also, importantly, to inspire. This job path is new and not easily mapped, but it is one that provides great rewards to those who persevere.

As renowned green architect William McDonough, FAIA once said, "Our goal is a delightfully diverse, safe, healthy and just world, with clean air, water, soil and power—economically, equitably, ecologically and elegantly enjoyed—period! Which parts of this don't you like?"[1]

THE NEED

All over the world, cities are becoming ever taller, ever bigger, and ever more architecturally innovative. From concrete and steel structures that hover more than 2,700 feet above the Earth to urban areas packed with more than twenty million people, humans have pushed inventiveness past the limits of what was ever thought possible.

But such innovation comes with a tradeoff, and much of that fallout is environmental. In the United States alone, according to the Energy Information Association, buildings account for more than 30 percent of the waste output of the country, up to half of the energy usage, and almost three quarters of the nation's electricity consumption.[2]

Large impacts abound, many of which are created—or contributed to, in large part—by the built environment. Three of these key issues are air pollution, energy consumption, and water scarcity.

Air Pollution

One can survive a few days without food or water, but only minutes without access to air. An easy problem to ignore by virtue of its typical invisibility, poor air quality in buildings often takes the form of fine particulates, toxic emissions, and mold. A common contributor to poor air quality is increased volatile organic compounds (or VOCs) are emitted as gases by everything from paints to building materials to furniture to cleaning supplies. Energy production, consumption, and leaching of toxic building materials can affect air quality as well. All of these air concerns can cause serious health problems, such as asthma, upper respiratory illnesses, developmental issues for children, and even cancers.

Academic Center at Georgia Gwinnett College, Lawrenceville, GA. Energy recovery systems maximize energy efficiency and make the building very economical to operate and maintain. A glass curtain wall partially faces south but is designed with glass that gives a high transmission of visible light yet a low transmittance of solar energy into the building. In areas that receive sunlight for most of the day, a frit has been applied to the third surface of the inner light of the glass to further reduce the amount of solar energy transmission. Firm: John Portman & Associates. PHOTO: COURTESY OF GEORGIA GWINNETT COLLEGE

Energy Consumption

Energy is central to the mechanics of most buildings. Air cooling and heating, lighting, cooking, and electrical needs all require energy to function. Environmental energy concerns range from the limited resource of fossil fuels to climate change impacts, which many have argued contribute to rising sea levels, changing food supplies, and the eventual specter of displacing millions of people.

Water Scarcity

Water is one of the most essential elements for human survival, used for everything from drinking and hygiene to cooking and tending crops. And indeed, a person can only live for two to ten days without water.[3] But the planet's supply of fresh water is rapidly dwindling, and our needs for it are quickly expanding. A 2009 report by consulting firm McKinsey & Company showed that global water needs will increase by 40 percent by the year 2030, while shrinking watersheds, droughts, and rising sea levels are at the same time resulting in decreasing worldwide supplies.[4]

Renaissance Schaumburg Convention Center Hotel, Schaumburg, IL. The nearly 3.5 acres of ponds have been developed with 100 percent native plantings. Firm: John Portman & Associates. PHOTO: JAMES STEINKAMP

A REASON TO CARE

As a collective group, human beings can—and should—be the solution leaders for a sustainable environment. As Anthony D. Cortese, Sc.D., president of Second Nature, explains:

> To make this a reality we must realize that *the road to sustainability is one of culture and values as much as it is about scientific and technological development.* It must be guided by the arts, humanities, social and behavioral sciences, religion and other spiritual inspiration as well as the physical and natural sciences and engineering, in other words, through the fundamental framework of learning and culture. It must also be guided by commitment to have all humans have their basic needs met and have the opportunity for a life of fulfillment.
>
> These ideas must be the *heart of the design principles* of a healthy, just and sustainable society—principles based on a human consciousness in which we apply the Golden Rule to our dealings with all current and unborn humans as well with the rest of life that evolved on earth. To work, these principles must become the basis for society's economic and governance framework and, therefore, a fundamental part of all education.
>
> Can this be done?
>
> Yes, because we must.[5]

As owners, planners, designers, engineers, constructors, and managers of our physical built environment that sits on the Earth, why wouldn't we be the instigators to a more sustainable future?

LEADERSHIP

A green building professional is not just a nine-to-five workhorse. Instead, as with politicians and pastors, one of the interesting things about green building professionals is that their personal life is often an integral part of their professional life. As leaders working toward a more sustainable world, green building professionals are accountable for their entire lifestyle and actions, rather than just what they do in their office hours. Everything green building professionals do is taken into account and carefully considered, including the following:

Region where they are located: Urban or suburban?

Preferred transportation methods: Walk, bike, train, drive, or fly?

Food sources: Local, seasonal, and organic?

Goods purchased: Fair trade, manufacturer values, and content of product?

Often these values and sustainable objectives are part of a green building professional's overall ethos and mindset—and green building professionals are always looking for areas of improvement

ASHRAE provides special parking areas for carpoolers and those with fuel-efficient vehicles (LEED NC Platinum). Firm: Richard Wittschiebe Hand. OWNER AND PHOTO: ASHRAE.

in making their green footprint even smaller. Perhaps an environmental speaker who flies often for business will decide to only ride his bike, in combination with mass transit, while he is at home; or an environmental consultant may become a vegetarian to reduce her carbon footprint. While no one can be environmentally perfect or lead a no-footprint life, efforts to reduce one's footprint are often noted by others in the field and outside green building, and these sustainable actions authenticate a dedication to eco-ideals.

FURTHER INCENTIVES

Should environmental issues not be enough to persuade one about the importance in going green, there are a myriad of business and financial benefits to take into consideration. Building owners can brag about their green credentials to an increasingly savvy (and demanding) consumer market, resulting in the ability to charge higher lease rates and therefore realize a higher return on investment, as well as a preferred market position and demonstrated leadership in their field. There is less need for expensive building upgrade costs when green regulation takes effect, and additional money is saved through reduced insurance costs, tax rebates, and incentives.

As for saving money through health-related issues? Better building health has been demonstrated, resulting in better inhabitant health, thereby reducing absenteeism for illness, increasing work productivity and test scores, and ensuring long-term retention.

Better for both the environment *and* the bottom line.

WORLD OF GRAY

Paper or plastic? It is a common question at the grocery store. Often, however, there is no easy answer. Questions of raw materials extraction, packaging, transportation, associated water/

energy use, health implications of the materials, reuse, and a variety of other factors come into play. Even if you say no to paper or plastic bags, and you hoist your own bag onto the counter, questions remain: Where did your bag come from? What is it made out of? Who made it? How will it be cleaned? The dilemma over even this seemingly straightforward decision can become overwhelming.

But there is a simple solution. When faced with an issue that seems grayer than a crisp black or white, one way to move forward is to use the precautionary principle. A decision-making tool, in its most basic form, this principle means "better safe than sorry." The precautionary principle helps one decide if an action should or should not be taken, when risks are unclear. This is a fundamental premise in the mindset of the green building professional. In other words, the precautionary principle maintains that if there is any suspicion of possible harm to the public or environment from taking a specific action or implementing a policy, the burden of proof falls on those taking the action to show that it is the least harm.

Taking all environmental issues into account, the built environment and the precautionary principle is where the nexus of green building occurs.

GREEN BUILDING

So who in the United States is responsible for green building? From a federal government perspective, it's the U.S. Environmental Protection Agency (EPA), the government agency begun in 1970 to create and enforce laws regarding human health and the natural environment.[6]

Green Building The definition of "green building" from the U.S. Environmental Protection Agency (EPA) is as follows:

Green building is the practice of creating structures and using processes that are environmentally responsible and resource-efficient throughout a building's life-cycle from siting to design, construction, operation, maintenance, renovation, and deconstruction. This practice expands and complements the classical building design concerns of economy, utility, durability, and comfort. Green building is also known as a sustainable or high performance building.[7]

HISTORY OF GREEN BUILDING IN THE UNITED STATES

Green building is not a new concept. For thousands of years, passive solar design (daylighting versus electrical lighting) and the use of local and regional materials have been incorporated into the creation of buildings, for practical reasons. More recently, what we know as the modern green building movement was instigated by the U.S. energy crisis in the 1970s, in which the cost of gasoline fuel dramatically spiked, calling attention to the need for energy-efficiency research and alternative fuels.

TIMELINE

Here is a brief historical timeline of the green building progress over the last 40 years:

- 1970 launched the U.S. Environmental Protection Agency.

- The green building field began to come together more formally in the 1990s. A few early milestones in the US include:

  - American Institute of Architects (AIA) formed the Committee on the Environment (1989).

  - The EPA and the U.S. Department of Energy launched the ENERGY STAR program (1992).

  - The first local green building program was introduced in Austin, TX (1992).

  - The U.S. Green Building Council (USGBC) was founded (1993).

  - The "Greening of the White House" initiative was launched by the Clinton administration (1993).

  - The USGBC launched its Leadership in Energy and Environmental Design (LEED) version 1.0 pilot program for new construction (1998).

- The USGBC LEED version 2.0 was adopted (2000).

- Ed Mazria published reports and brought together scientists and the building sector to focus on building impacts on climate change and greenhouse gas emissions, with the 2030 challenge (2002).

- The General Services Administration (GSA) mandated that all new federal construction must be able to be certified to a minimum of LEED Silver level (2003).

- The Energy Policy Act of 2005 included federal building sustainable performance standards (2005).

- The Federal Green Construction Guide for Specifiers was made available on the Whole Building Design Guide website (2006).

- The Office of the Federal Environmental Executive published The Federal Commitment to Green Building: Experiences and Expectations (2007).

- President Bush signed Executive Order 13423—Strengthening Federal Environmental, Energy, and Transportation Management, which includes federal goals for sustainable design and high-performance buildings (2007).

- The Energy Independence and Security Act of 2007 included requirements for high-performance green federal buildings (2007).[8]

- USGBC updated LEED to version 2009 (3.0), including a required energy- and water-monitoring agreement

- ASHRAE Standard 189.1, Standard for the Design of High-Performance, Green Buildings Except Low-Rise Residential Buildings, was published as the first green building code (2010).

- The GSA upgraded to a minimum of LEED Gold level certifiable on all new federal buildings and major renovations (2010).

- The International Green Construction Code (IgCC): Safe and Sustainable by the Book released (2012) incorporates Standard 189.1 (2011) as an optional path for a new code baseline.

- The U.S. Green Building Council releases the next version of LEED (Version 4.0 under development in 2012).

AT ALL LEVELS

Thanks in large part to increased green building activity in recent years—both top-down (government requirements/corporate incentives) and bottom-up (consumer demand)—sustainability has become a pervasive notion in day-to-day life. For the most part, when people say "green" these days, it doesn't indicate Crayola's latest crayon color, but is instead recognized as referring to an environmental attribute.

As referenced in the historical "Timeline" feature, green building was mandated from the "top" by the federal government for their buildings, and many state and city governments followed suit. From the grassroots bottom, greater consumer awareness calls for eco-action in local neighborhood communities, buildings and homes—and corporations, manufacturers, and government officials are taking note.

Additional eco-conscious tools are being added to the market that also help the cause of eco-consciousness, the best-recognized example perhaps being the U.S. Green Building Council's LEED program, an internationally recognized green building certification program. Such tools have provided the industry with a user-friendly vehicle for widespread adoption and rapid market transformation.

With this much activity, the need for a specific team player dedicated to the green building effort emerges: the green building professional.

WHAT IS A GREEN BUILDING PROFESSIONAL?

Because it involves so many different aspects, the green building career field includes everything from traditional careers such as architecture, landscape architecture, engineering, interior design, construction, facility management, or real estate—professions that can incorporate sustainability into their approach. It is also possible to specialize as a green building professional consultant, which is a relatively new field.

So what unifies this diverse group of building professionals and brings them together to be "green"? Regardless of each professional's role or specialization, all sustainable building experts use triple-bottom-line thinking in their approach.

A term coined by John Elkington in his 1998 book *Cannibals with Forks: the Triple Bottom Line of 21st Century Business*, "triple bottom line" simply means creating balanced decisions that take the following factors into account equally:

- Economic factors
- Social factors
- Environmental factors

These three elements are also referred to as profit/people/planet, or the three pillars.[9] Another commonly associated term used with the triple bottom line and green building is "sustainability."

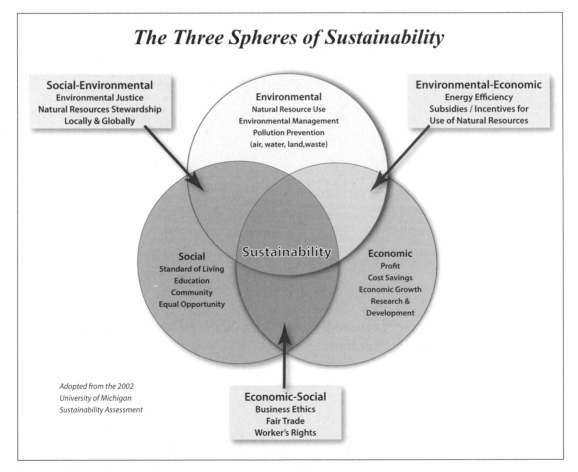

The Three Spheres of Sustainability

The term was originally defined in the Brundtland Commission of the United Nations in 1987 and generally means meeting current needs without impacts on the needs of future generations.[10] An example of sustainability would be producing food for the current population and ensuring that the land, water, and other resources necessary for food production remain for the upcoming generations.

Another term similar to sustainability is "regenerative"; however, it extends beyond human needs to all species and offers an opportunity for lost ecosystems to be regenerated. When first introduced to public discussion, some "green" terms may have had specific, separate meanings, but as more people have become involved and invested in environmental goals, many of these words have merged and become interchangeable in their usage. In that regard, the following terms in this book all attempt to describe and relate to a similar approach:

- Environmental
- Eco
- Earth-friendly
- Green
- Regenerative
- Sustainable

A green building professional integrates these principles of triple bottom line into all phases of a building's life, from inception to demolition. Here are just a few ways in which different green building professionals can foster better communities and buildings:

- Urban planners and developers consider urban context, community connectivity, and transportation.
- Civil engineers ensure that the building and site work well with the surrounding infrastructure, thereby minimizing ecological impact.
- Landscape architects design parks and vegetation to connect the natural and built environments.
- Architects and interior designers create healthy buildings and spaces that include efficient and well-considered resources.
- Mechanical engineers specify natural ventilation or high-efficiency filtering equipment, supplying fresh air to the occupants.
- Facility managers maintain the building with the highest-efficiency equipment and the lowest-impact maintenance program.
- Real estate professionals negotiate leases that create a win-win for both landlord and tenant.
- Green building consultants are generalists in all of these fields. Their typical specialty is in maximizing green building performance across all of these areas.

Green building professionals range in their scope and scale, creating a vast array of structures from commercial buildings to residential homes. This book, however, concentrates more specifically on communities and commercial buildings—including civic, office, education, healthcare, and hospitality—and explores how green building professionals can influence these buildings' design, construction, and operation.

LEGACY

When considering becoming a green building professional (or joining any profession), contemplate your ideal legacy.

> **leg·a·cy [lé-gə-sē] something from past:** something that is handed down or remains from a previous generation or time[11]

Some of the most respected workers in America are doctors, nurses, police officers, firefighters, government workers, lawyers, teachers, parents, business owners, nonprofit professionals, politicians, and scientists. In concept, the common thread in all of these fields is the desire to create a positive impact on health, safety, business, and science—on a varying scale from one individual (or animal) up to entire cities, states, or the country as a whole. A green building professional has the same common thread of helping in mind, and sews it into the fabric of our communities, buildings, homes, and ultimately, our lives.

> ### Why are you hopeful about the future of the environment in the United States in particular?

> ❯ Three weeks ago, each child in my daughter's Sunday school class had to come up with an 11th commandment. Twelve out of the thirteen children's 11th commandments were about the environment—recycling, picking up trash, conserving water. Yes, I am very hopeful!
>
> *Lynn N. Simon, FAIA, LEED AP BD+C, president, Simon & Associates, Inc.*

> ❯ There is no hope…but I might be wrong…
>
> *Peter Bahouth, executive director, U.S. Climate Action Network*

> ❯ I am hopeful. The reason I am hopeful is because I have the good fortune to know many young people, students currently in our K–12 education system, and these kids that I've been hearing from "get it." They understand that there is a monumental task before all of us to be more aware of how we use our natural resources and how we treat our natural environment. And they are up for the challenge. We have a lot of great minds working on these issues now, but change comes slowly in the beginning. With the rising of the "next generation" of leaders, I am confident great solutions will be seen.
>
> *Bryna Dunn, AICP, Associate AIA, LEED AP BD+C, director of sustainability planning and design, Moseley Architects*

Green building professionals create a legacy via regenerative, healthy spaces that house people in businesses, schools, health-care facilities, and homes. Buildings can be more than structures that shelter; they can enhance our day-to-day experiences, be a learning tool, and generate income. Next, let's look in detail at where green building professionals have such opportunities.

GREEN JOBS STATS

When thinking about a career path, it is useful to evaluate the future of the job market you are considering. By all accounts, the green building field will only get stronger over the coming years. One well-researched report was released in late 2009, prepared by the prestigious consulting firm Booz Allen, which was hired by the U.S. Green Building Council to better define where the market is headed.[12] The company looked specifically at jobs within the green building industry.

The results are extremely heartening. Booz Allen projected that the number of jobs in green building will increase fourfold by 2013, going from two million to nearly eight million jobs within just four years, which will generate more than $554 billion additional dollars in GDP, and more than $396 billion in earned wages. As for the USGBC, its LEED-related

Kiowa County Schools—Main Street. The primary circulation hallway in the school is called "Main Street." The wide, open hallway is a gathering space for students. It is daylit and clad with wood that came from salvaged cypress trees downed during Hurricane Katrina. Firm: BNIM. PHOTO: © ASSASSI

economic outlay has already supported 15,000 jobs—and is projected to support 230,000 jobs by 2013.[13]

As another example, an annual international survey called the Carbon Salary Survey released 2010 results on green jobs in a variety of fields. Of the 1,200 people surveyed, interesting findings included the facts that three-quarters of those in green jobs are satisfied with their work and 35 percent feel more secure in their positions than they did one year ago.[14] Moreover, the study found that green jobs are available across the world in the renewable energy field, perfect for those who want to work and live abroad.

GREEN AS IN "SALARY"

Income estimates for various green building professionals range widely and are updated frequently, so generally it is best to check reliable online sources and reputable annual surveys for the most current information. The Bureau of Labor Statistics has a website and associated tools dedicated specifically to the green building field. As a basic reference: in 2011, an environmental engineer is estimated by that site to make around $80,000 a year.[15] Another resource, PayScale, is a massive database of salary profiles for a variety of jobs, and it gives another good sense of current market salaries. This resource gives job seekers accurate numbers and negotiation leverage for interviews; average salaries for related building professionals in 2011 ranged from $76,000 for a mechanical engineer to $67,000 for an architect to $58,000 for a construction project manager.[16] These figures do vary, however; the Carbon Salary Survey found that the average salary for those they polled in the United States was $104,000.[17]

HOW TO GET INTO THE FIELD

Many different paths lead to the green building field, which means that each path may be custom-tailored or combined to fit specific needs and interests. These paths will be explored in greater depth in Chapter 3, but as a brief overview, here are the three main paths that can be taken: learn, involve, and collaborate.

Learn

The first path into the green building field is via educational knowledge and academic skills. This could be through formal higher education, training, hands-on experience, or competitions.

Involve

Another wide path to take could be volunteering at a local nonprofit organization, or a more formal mentoring or internship program where an experienced professional demonstrates how to incorporate green building principles.

Collaborate

One of the most important avenues to being hired in any profession is networking with existing and new relationships. Another form of collaboration is a formal engagement with a green recruiter that actively seeks an alignment between a candidate's skills and job opportunities. Lastly, a career coach can support those who know they want to enter the green building field but are unsure of their specific area of interest or how to transition into their chosen career.

What are your best tips for entry into the green building profession?

❯ DIVERSIFY. Learn all you can about economics, biology, business, systems thinking, and sociology. We need people who are able to bring deep knowledge and experience across all aspects of sustainability to address the real challenges and come up with truly innovative, effective solutions.

Mary Ann Lazarus, FAIA, LEED AP BD+C, senior vice president/global director of sustainable design, HOK

❯ Developing relationships through professional development and networking opportunities is vital for someone who wants to enter the green building profession. Green building is a collaborative process and it is through these relationships where true sustainability lies.

Lynn N. Simon, FAIA, LEED AP BD+C, president, Simon & Associates, Inc.

❯ There will be plenty of opportunity for folks with environmental degrees. However, I would recommend getting a building- or business-related education and augment it with deep environmental/sustainability knowledge (enthusiasm and idealism are great, but knowledge is critical). Also, just get involved. There are plenty of opportunities to get your feet wet, gain some experience, and meet lots of green building professionals.

Henning M. Bloech, LEED AP, executive director, GREENGUARD Environmental Institute

❯ Follow your heart and follow your passion. I decided in the third grade that I was going to major in biology and I was going to make the world a greener place. I did major in biology, and I also majored in environmental science. I earned a master's degree in environmental planning. But I still didn't know what I was going to be when I grew up, or how I was going to make the world a greener place. But I still knew that was what I wanted to do, and I wouldn't settle for any job that didn't give me that opportunity. When I heard the pioneering architect William McDonough speak about what he was trying to do with design, I finally knew how I wanted to put my education into practice. I have been working with architects for fifteen years now, helping to bridge that gap between the decisions we make every day about the built environment and how those decisions affect the natural environment. I hope that young professionals will discover their own nontraditional ways to also save the world in whatever part of the field that excites them—because if you're not having fun, you're not going to stay with it in the long term.

Bryna Dunn, AICP, Associate AIA, LEED AP BD+C, director of sustainability planning and design, Moseley Architects

Harness for Good

RICK FEDRIZZI
President, CEO, and Founding Chairman
United States Green Building Council

What does sustainability mean to you personally?

❯ To me, the definition of "sustainable" is simple: It means living my life today in a way that ensures my children, their children, and their children will be able to live as well as I did. It means laying the groundwork for a future that is more prosperous, more healthful, and more equitable than our present. It means that our habits—at a personal level as well as at a global level—don't lead to an inevitable depletion of resources that would disrupt our quality of life. Living sustainably means exactly what it says: that our lifestyles can be sustained, and that we don't prove to be our own worst enemies.

Why did you enter the field of green building, and how did you make the transition?

❯ I was fortunate enough to have worked for 25 years at United Technologies Corp. (UTC), an early

pioneer in what was then a fairly esoteric idea: that the unprecedented technological progress of our era could actually be harnessed for good. In other words, UTC recognized that true progress isn't about a decision between technological expansion or environmental quality; it is about embracing them both, and especially the places where they intersect and complement each other. It was the beginning of our understanding of the triple bottom line, and I knew I wanted to be part of it.

We hear so much about the negative impacts of human activity on the environment; tell us how, in your view, green building acts as an "antidote" to alleviate these negative impacts and/or creates positive impacts on the environment.

❯ Green building isn't about a laundry list of negative human behaviors that we shouldn't do; it's about all the innovative, exciting, and life-affirming things we can and should do that lead to an econ-

Kiowa County Schools: Courtyard. The building is organized around a courtyard gathering space, a hub of activity for all ages (LEED NC Platinum). Firm: BNIM. PHOTO: © ASSASSI

omy, an environment, and a social landscape in harmony with each other. It's about solutions, and the businessman in me knew that this was the key to making real change.

Green building's potential for truly transforming the way humans and our environment interact comes from one key concept: connectivity. Green building is focused not on a collection of gadgets and gimmicks but on maximizing the way all of a building's systems interact with each other. Those systems include the human beings who occupy the buildings and the communities that the buildings occupy. In the best buildings, better ventilation and natural daylight save energy while also nurturing the health and comfort of the people inside. Buildings located in walkable neighborhoods reduce greenhouse gases and also connect people to their neighbors and create a strong sense of place. Using less water also means less energy required for municipal water treatment. The use of local materials not only cuts back on transportation needs but also builds into the fabric of our homes, offices, schools, and communities a direct connection to our local economies. And when we spend our time in buildings that are designed, constructed, and operated with holistic sustainability at their core, our day-to-day behavior is affected and we all become part of the solution. In nature, we see how all creatures are intimately and inextricably connected with each other and with their ecosystems; green building ensures that humans interact with their environment in the same mutually beneficial way.

What have you seen as the biggest hurdles to the success of the green building field? How have these hurdles been overcome; or, if they remain, what do you see as potential solutions?

❯ As with every important change in human history, the biggest hurdle to success is the status quo.

When you begin talking about transformation, you are talking about a fundamental change in the way we do things. And when you talk about fundamental change, there will always be people who are nervous about that. They're nervous because they have found success in doing things the way they've "always been done," and they worry that change will upend their success. But green building has a built-in solution. The passion, innovation, and commitment of the people who have been driving this movement for the last two decades have systematically undermined any instinct to cling to the status quo and have disproved the notion that change is bad. Green building has been at the heart of the success of countless companies and professionals, whether they're the ones doing the designing or building, creating the products and materials used in those buildings, or owning and occupying the buildings. To start with, we have more than 16,000 companies whose membership in USGBC is a central component to their business strategies.

Which of the many positive impacts (environmental, social, economic, etc.) of green building do you think is the most exciting, and why?

❯ Each of the components of the triple bottom line is critical, and none is more important than the others because without one, you can't have the others. They are inextricably connected, and that is why green building works.

I am excited by this industry's economic promise because of its power to make green building devotees of people from all political and cultural walks of life.

Ours is a movement that is seamlessly pro-business, pro-environment, and pro-human, and that has been the key to our success.

Bio-Visionary

BILL BROWNING

Founder

Terrapin Bright Green

You have spoken before about seven ideas that you see as key to the sustainable thought process. Could you explain and describe the meaning and importance of these ideas?

❯ Biomimicry and biophilia provide the inspiration for thinking about design. Biophilic design reconnects humans with the natural world and leads to healthier, more fulfilling places. By asking nature for examples and proven experience, biomimicry gives us places to look for solutions to design challenges. By looking at the "deep ecological history" of a site, we can set a new level of performance standards tied to what the ecosystem of the site was capable of providing; it is a quantification of ecosystem services. "Node and network" then gives a way to scale and interconnect resilient green infrastructure systems; it is a way of connecting eco-districts. Net zero plus is a philosophy that then says not only should we strive for net-zero energy on a district scale, but we should also give them the capability to stand independently for extended periods. "Transcending the cost barriers" is an integrated approach to push for maximum efficiency that then allows downsizing or elimination of systems with the effect of lowering first cost. Net-zero and carbon-neutral projects are great goals, but sometimes it is not possible to get all the way there on site. "Engaged offsets" is a voluntary carbon-offset system that invests in localized energy-efficiency measures and renewable-energy systems.

All of these ideas are important. I am most focused on biophilic design as I believe that with increas-

ing urbanization, the need to connect with nature becomes stronger. Also, strongly biophilic buildings tend to be loved and maintained. Consider the Johnson Wax Administration Building designed by Frank Lloyd Wright; it is more than seventy years old, and it is still loved and used in its original configuration.

You have an undergraduate degree in environmental design from the University of Colorado, and a graduate degree in real estate development from MIT. Could you explain why you chose this educational path?

❯ Environmental design allowed me to explore architecture, landscape architecture, and town planning; this broad experience is not available in most design schools. I had intended to eventually go on to get an architectural degree, but ultimately came to the conclusion that developers were the ones shaping the decisions about what gets built. So I went to the MIT Center for Real Estate to learn the business of development.

From what work experience have you learned the most, and why?

❯ In many of our Terrapin projects we are paid to think, so each new one is exciting. Of the past work, the Greening of the White House project, starting in 1993, stands out as one of the early examples of how to tackle a really complex challenge with a truly integrated design process.

What is the most exciting new green technology or concept you have recently considered?

❯ We are using site-specific ecosystem metrics as the basis for goal setting—determining how much carbon a native ecosystem could capture on an annual basis and how much sunlight falls on a site and then is reradiated or captured through photosynthesis. What did the ecosystem do with water, how much was captured, how much was runoff, how much was evapotranspirated? How many species existed on the site? These become the performance metrics for the site, and the challenge is to see if we can meet or exceed the performance of the indigenous ecosystem. This is a much more interesting process than trying to save 30 percent of energy against some hypothetical standard.

What keeps you up at night regarding the environment?

I'm pretty horrified about how caring about the environment has become politicized.

What is one sustainable aspect from which international clients could learn from their American counterparts? Conversely, in what area could Americans follow the leads of their international colleagues?

American projects tend to "get" integrated design better. With some notable exceptions, in many other places green design tends to get trapped just on one issue. Social innovation around green developments is the next frontier for American projects.

Is there a new green trend that you find particularly intriguing?

Urban agriculture is important for reconnecting people to food production; even more important is the biophilic benefit and the experience of seeing a plant grow from seed.

THE POWER OF TWO

The next two interviews are with key green building leaders who happen to be married, and while they share an emerald-green building goal, they provide different yet overlapping roles as green building professionals—one focused on real estate and the other on architecture as well as interiors.

Experienced Passion

SALLY R. WILSON, AIA, LEED AP BD+C

Global Director of Environmental Strategy and Senior Vice President, Brokerage

CB Richard Ellis

Explain your professional background.

❯ I have a bachelor's degree in interiors and a master's degree in architecture. I practiced architecture for eighteen years—primarily focused on interiors.

I joined CB Richard Ellis as a tenant broker. Currently I hold titles of SVP in brokerage and Global Director of Environmental Strategy with CB Richard Ellis.

How and when did you know you wanted to be involved in green building?

❯ Green buildings have always been a focus of Ken's practice, and when I left the architecture profession (2003) he encouraged me to integrate green building principles in my services.

The first client we pitched green practices to was Toyota in 2004. It was a clear market differentiator for our team and we easily won the business. We are considered experts in green leasing practices. Clients have included USGBC, WWF, Greenpeace, Generation IM, Calvert, and numerous professional services firms and Fortune 500 companies with carbon reduction commitments.

In your work, how is green is involved in your day-to-day process?

❯ Tough questions because green has become so integral to our team's services offerings that I don't even think about it. Aside from the consulting work for CBRE around greening our enterprise and service offerings, I educate many clients and landlords on the benefits of sustainable buildings, practices, and processes.

Coming from different professional viewpoints, how do you and Ken inform each other's thoughts on green building?

❯ Ken is much more up on technology and practice. I'm more informed on market perception. My focus is to strategically position our clients so that others (such as Ken) can implement best practices.

As an early adopter, where do you see the trends for green building headed?

❯ Talk to anyone in their twenties or younger and they are concerned about climate change. The movement will only become stronger because we are building for them.

As past (first) chair of the board for GBCI (Green Building Certification Institute), what do you forecast in credentialing for the future?

❯ LEED is a market differentiator so I believe it will continue to grow. I also anticipate it will be an international standard. Even in the down economy, we have seen continued growth on both the certification and credentialing sides.

What has been your greatest learning experience along the way in becoming a green building professional?

❯ Participating in the carbon neutral process for CBRE. We have been working for the past four years to measure and minimize our footprint. This exercise has exposed me to carbon accounting and offset strategies as well as developing and implementing carbon reduction policies for a company with over 400 offices globally.

USGBC Headquarters: Entry, Washington, DC. Completed 2009 (LEED CI Platinum). Firm: Envision Design, PLLC. PHOTO: ERIC LAIGNEL

Green DNA

KEN WILSON, AIA, FIIDA, LEED FELLOW

Principal and Founder

Envision Design

Explain your professional background.

❯ I can trace my interest in architecture back to when I was in third grade. I went to my older brother's school science fair and saw some architectural models of houses built by some high school kids. I thought it was the coolest thing I had ever seen. My mom told me that was what an architect did, and from then on that's what I wanted to do for a career. Later, when I was about twelve, my mother took me to Taliesin West, which was an incredible experience.

I went to architecture school at Virginia Tech and graduated in 1981. I was able to spend my fourth year of school in England, and while I was there I was able to travel extensively in Europe and Scandinavia as well as throughout Great Britain. My travel in Europe and my work experience prior to finishing my final year were also extremely helpful to my education.

I worked in a variety of firms during the first nineteen years of my career and got to work on a wide variety of project types ranging from single-family houses to large commercial buildings. After about fifteen years of working in the field of buildings, I started working on interiors projects and found that I really enjoyed working with the part of a building that comes in direct contact with people. I started to think more about how building interiors can positively affect people's lives.

I also saw the effect that a recession can have on the architecture business and how work in interiors generally fares better in a down economy.

In the spring of 1999 I started my own firm, Envision Design, with the intention of creating a firm that was focused on client service and design excellence, and that could provide a range of services from architecture, to interiors, to product design and graphics. Our first project as a firm was to design the headquarters for Greenpeace USA, which was an incredible opportunity to become an expert at green design. That project completely changed our thinking from that point forward.

How and when did you know you wanted to be involved in green building?

❯ I always had a strong interest in the environment. I grew up in a small town in Arizona and loved to go camping and to be out in the wild. I liked architecture that was smart and not excessive. I like the idea of renovating existing buildings and being as energy efficient as possible. When we were hired to design the Greenpeace USA headquarters it all came together. I realized that I had been thinking green in many ways all along and the Greenpeace project allowed me to take that thinking to a much higher level.

Green became a market differentiator for Envision.

In the beginning, it didn't always work, but we kept trying and committed to introducing green design to every client.

Discuss how green is involved in your work, in your day-to-day process.

❯ After eleven years of owning my firm, green thinking is completely integral to our practice. It is just part of the way we do things. All of our professional staff are LEED APs and all of the LEED projects we currently have on the boards are seeking Platinum level certification. Our sample library has been completely vetted for non-green materials. Our boilerplate specifications are green regardless if the project is seeking LEED certification or not. Green thinking has become part of our DNA.

Coming from different professional viewpoints, how do you and Sally inform each other's thoughts on green building?

❯ Sally is typically dealing with sustainability at a much larger scale within her company. Because of her position at CBRE, she gets to network with her sustainability peers at other Fortune 500 companies, and sometimes I get to hear about what other large companies are doing to make their business more green. I have even gotten to tag along as a spouse to some high-level green conferences that wouldn't pay any attention to a twenty-person architecture firm such as Envision.

What do you think are the largest challenges we face today?

❯ There is still a long way to go in terms of educating the public to the benefits of green design. I am fortunate to work in Washington, DC, which is very progressive in terms of green thinking. There is a higher number of LEED-certified and LEED-registered projects in the Washington, DC, metropolitan area than anywhere else in the country.

You have provided headquarters to some of the most environmental nonprofits—Greenpeace, World Wildlife Fund, U.S. Green Building Council—what is the common thread among these projects, and what did you learn from these experiences?

❯ At the end of the day, green still doesn't trump everything. Even our environmental nonprofit clients still want space that is functional, efficient, and beautiful. They want their projects to run effectively and to be produced on time and on budget. Of course they want them to be green, but once we are hired and we have done our LEED charrette, our clients assume we are taking care of the green aspects of the project, and they focus their attention on the design and functionality of space. We constantly update our clients on the green aspects of a project, but it is not the most important part of regular meetings because there is a confidence that the sustainability issues are being addressed.

How do you bring green (or sustainability) home?

❯ We did a green renovation of our mid-century modern house in 2004 and we have continued to make improvements over the years. I drive a 2005 Prius, and Sally and I are pretty much homebodies on weekends. Our house is wind powered through green energy credits. We recycle everything that can be recycled and we compost organic waste. We try to set an example for our kids, and we talk as a family about issues of importance. Although they think their parents are weird, I think a lot of it has rubbed off on our boys.

Truth Seeker

NADAV MALIN

President

BuildingGreen

How and when did you know you wanted to be involved in green building?

❯ I've always cared about doing things in the best way I know how and about protecting the planet. I was building and remodeling homes in the early 1990s, but the market was tight and I was having trouble finding work, so I convinced Alex Wilson to hire me in his research and writing practice. At the time there was no field called "green building" but Alex had a vision of the need for it, which he shared with me. That's when I first discovered the idea, and it seemed just right at the time. Still does.

You have written chapters for several green books, as well as articles for magazines and journals— what have you learned in this process?

❯ I've learned that people are incredibly generous with their time and wisdom when you ask good questions and give them a soapbox from which to be heard. I've also learned that green building is as much about the connections between things as it is about the things themselves, and since everything is connected to everything else, it's hard to figure out how to organize the material!

The resources that are provided by BuildingGreen are some of the most respected in the industry— why do you think this is?

❯ I guess just sticking it out a long time earns us some respect. We have a consistent voice and perspective that leaders in the field have become famil-

iar with over the years, and they then recommend us to others. Of course, it doesn't hurt, in a field so rife with greenwashing, that we don't carry ads in our publications.

What is the best/worst part of your day-to-day job?

❯ The worst part is easy—figuring out what NOT to do. There are so many great projects we want to take on, and we get asked to work with people on many things. We just can't do all of it, but we're not so good at setting limits.

The best part of my job? I especially love learning new things, sharing ideas, and facilitating meetings of motivated, smart people.

What qualities do you look for when hiring a green building professional?

❯ Critical thinking skills come first—it's hard to gauge sometimes, but it really helps if people have a strong, effective BS detector. Attitude comes next— we need people to do a lot of different tasks, some of which can be tedious or challenging, so they have to be gung ho about doing whatever needs to be done!

Many can't wait until BuildingGreen's next Top 10 Green Building Products list hits the proverbial newsstand. Beyond there being such a vast array of products from which to select, what are the other challenges with creating this list?

❯ As with LEED and so many other things in the green building field, the challenge seems to be finding things that are ahead of the pack, but not so far ahead that the market doesn't know what to make of them. Some of our picks go on to be huge successes, but others fizzle out because not enough people recognized the value they bring.

On occasion, it seems you have to write "hard" articles or reviews that will be controversial. What motivates you to take the sometimes unpopular stand?

❯ People look to us for help interpreting and understanding complicated issues. Designers rarely have time to do the kind of research it takes to really dig in and understand things deeply—so that's a service we try to provide.

When things get controversial, we just try to follow our best sense of the truth, and trust that readers will appreciate that, even if they don't always agree with us. Most of all, though, we take the trouble to lay out the evidence and reasoning behind our ideas, so we are being as transparent as possible. That goes a long way toward easing people's concern about any specific position we take.

As an early adopter, where do you see the trends for green building headed?

❯ As I see it, the 1990s were about innovation—inventing the field. And the 2000s were, thanks largely to LEED, about getting the early adopters on board. That suggests that this decade of 2011 and beyond will be about the movement really going mainstream. As part of that trend, the push for more proof of actual performance benefits, as opposed to predictions based on modeling, will intensify.

What advice would you give someone embarking on a career in the green building professional field?

❯ This may sound strange coming from me, but the field is very different from what it was twenty years ago, when anyone could hang out a shingle. Now it's important to have solid professional credentials and a good education in architecture, engineering, or another design or construction profession. With that foundation, it's relatively easy to gain the green expertise needed to work on green buildings. It's all about connecting the dots....

Authentic Sustainability

L. HUNTER LOVINS

President and Founder

Natural Capitalism Solutions

How would you define a sustainability consultant?

❯ Sustainability consulting is the practice of helping companies, communities, and countries implement procedures, practices to operate in ways that enhance human and natural capital.

Most sustainability consultants came initially from careers of environmentalism or social justice. They were trying to get companies to do less harm to the environment and to people. Authentic sustainability means backing down from harmful practices and enhancing the natural world that sustains us. The work that I have been doing since 1968 has helped companies find ways to do this that are also more profitable because they are more sustainable.

This can be hard. In an economy in which unsustainable ways of doing business are subsidized, and are often the more familiar way of doing business, it takes creativity to make the business case that behaving in ways that are less wasteful can deliver savings that go right to the bottom line. Initially, and to some extent, still, some environmentalists attacked this approach. They believed that companies should do the right thing because it is the right thing. And some leading CEOs like Patagonia's Yvon Chouinard and Interface's Ray Anderson have profited enormously by taking this position. Yvon quotes my old mentor, David Brower, that you can't do business on a dead planet. Ray Anderson asked, "What's the business case for ending life on earth?"

I figured, that while these visionaries are right, waiting for their wisdom to pervade Wall Street would achieve the very outcome they were working against. If I can show CEOs a clear and present business case for using energy more efficiently, installing renewable energy, implementing genuinely more sustainable practices, pure greed might be a better motivator than morality.

For example, we just did a report for Boulder County, Colorado. It was a literature review on the science of

Sun Valley Branch, Los Angeles Public Library, Sun Valley, CA (LEED NC Gold). Firm: Fields Devereaux Architects & Engineers, James Weiner, AIA, LEED Fellow—design architect. An art glass window created by a local artist tells a narrative of the community that provides a focal point for the lobby. A tapered elliptical skylight well brings balanced light to the entry procession. PHOTO: © RMA PHOTOGRAPHY

genetically modified organisms (GMO), because the county has an ongoing debate as to whether farmers should be allowed to plant GMO sugar beets on publicly owned open space. It's interesting, because the science is all over the map. Our advice, therefore, is that it *isn't* a science issue, it's a policy issue. They need to determine what the people want the county to do, as the county is a steward for the people. That's not the sort of thing most people think of when considering sustainability, but is it important to ask whether GMOs are sustainable? Initially, they allow for the use of fewer herbicides and pesticides. But studies now emerging show real threats to human health. We looked through the span of literature about what others have said and came to the conclusion that it's an issue for the public to decide.

On the other hand, I was just in the Netherlands consulting for Royal Dutch Shell. Shell is trying to understand the nexus between energy, water, and food security, which opens a huge array of topics. A team of us was there helping them, including ecosystems scientist Eric Berlow. He talked about "ordered networks," or ways of organizing complex bodies of information. Folks were there from various universities, cities, and other businesses, such as Siemens and IBM, with their (IBM) Smarter Planet Initiative. The goal was to technically enable Shell to be a better-run and more profitable company, but we were there to use corporate might to achieve a better outcome for the Earth and its people. The details of your work depend entirely on who your client is, but the end game remains the same.

Given your experience with entities such as the World Economic Forum, the UN, and the major corporations, you have a broad, global view of the environment. What is your vision for the future?

❯ We're in a horse race between catastrophe and the creation of a whole new way of doing business, a new way of living on the planet, and treating each other. If you read Global Biodiversity Outlook 3, a great bit of research from Dr. Tom Lovejoy and a lot of scientists, you'll realize that all of the world's major ecosystems are in peril; three of them are tipping into collapse. Coral reefs, the first of these major ecosystems, will be gone by the end of the century if we continue the way we're going; these are the ocean's nurseries. The Amazon is collapsing. It is the world's lungs. Third, the oceans are acidifying. That could be game over for life as we know it. It's happening very rapidly, and it's scaring scientists badly. Indeed, it is written nowhere that humankind will endure. As comedian George Carlin pointed out, "Save the planet? The planet'll be fine, it's the people who need to be saved."

But those of us who think there's something noble and magnificent in this human experiment are working hard to ensure that future generations can enjoy a planet that's as beautiful as the one that's been given to us; that life as we know it can survive—because that's what's at stake, if you read the science literature. We're destroying it by the way we're doing business. We're facing formidable challenges: We're losing major species, we have economic instability, and we're almost certainly headed into a second major recession if not a global depression. We have volatile energy prices. Food is at record world prices. And Goldman Sachs now calls water the petroleum of the next decade.

At the same time, 24 separate studies from the big consulting houses show that the leading companies in sustainable policy have 25 percent higher stock values than their less-sustainable competitors. The companies with the fastest-growing stock values have market capitalization of $650 million more than their less-sustainable competitors and are well protected from value erosion even in a down economy. Something's going on here. We're helping companies understand that core business value is enhanced by behaving in more sustainable ways; that this enhances every aspect of shareholder value, even though it might not show up on their balance sheets. Given that a recent Accenture study said that 93 percent of Fortune 500 CEOs say sustainability will be extremely important in the coming decade, this is clearly a field with a big future.

What do you imagine will be the biggest shifts in the green building realm in the next five years?

❯ Focus on existing buildings and infrastructure will result in some breakthrough approaches to city planning revitalization.

Adaptation as a green building priority as we begin to see climate shifts having real impact, especially along the coasts (this is already happening in the UK).

Recognition of importance of water will begin to emerge in parallel with, and in some places, beyond, energy.

Mary Ann Lazarus, FAIA, LEED AP BD+C, senior vice president/global director of sustainable design, HOK

❯ Existing buildings, existing buildings, existing buildings—oh, did I say existing buildings!

Lynn N. Simon, FAIA, LEED AP BD+C, president, Simon & Associates, Inc.

❯ Interest in rating systems and systems of thought that go beyond LEED

Recognition that sustainability can be more thoroughly realized at a neighborhood or community scale than at a building scale

Alex Zimmerman, A.Sc.T., LEED AP BD+C, president, Applied Green Consulting Ltd., founding president of the Canada Green Building Council

❯ A much stronger focus on products and materials and their immediate impacts on occupants (chemical toxicity) and life-cycle impacts. I see us moving away from using single attributes and perceived singular environmental benefits (recycled content, rapidly renewable, PVC-free, etc.) to evaluate products toward EPDs (environmental product declarations) and more comprehensive impact assessments, which will lead to better purchasing decisions.

Henning M. Bloech, LEED AP, executive director, GREENGUARD Environmental Institute

❯ Climate change will change everything we do. If we decide to act in time it will have profound impact on siting, water, energy, transportation, materials, urban heat islands, mosquito control, and where our wine comes from.

Peter Bahouth, executive director, U.S. Climate Action Network

❯ I think the rapid changes in building codes, specifically the awareness now given to green building issues in the codes, is going to turn design and construction on its head. There is going to be a huge learning curve for those companies who haven't been paying attention.

Bryna Dunn, AICP, Associate AIA, LEED AP BD+C, director of sustainability planning and design, Moseley Architects

Rebuilding Bright Futures

KIOWA COUNTY SCHOOLS
Greensburg, Kansas
BNIM

Vision + Challenge:

Following the devastating tornado that destroyed their town and schools, Kiowa County USD (Unified School District) 422 chose a bold strategy to combine their schools into a single K–12 facility that would retain a distinct identity for each school function: elementary, middle, and high school. The design utilizes a highly flexible, sustainable approach that constantly maintains a student-centered focus.

In direct alignment with the town's Sustainable Comprehensive Master Plan, the school district decided to rebuild to LEED Platinum. This decision led the way for the city, which later mandated that all public buildings attain a Platinum rating. This K–12 facility combines the resources of three rural community school districts into a single facility, thereby right-sizing at a regional scale.

The district understood the importance of daylighting for increasing student academic performance/potential and focus, so the design optimizes daylighting and natural ventilation in all classrooms. Separate zones for kindergarten, elementary, middle, and high school grades allow students the unique learning and social opportunities that each age group requires. The design also integrates the students in key ways in order to build a sense of community, encourage mentorship, and instill a desire for achievement.

Strategy + Solution:

COMMUNITY

During the school design process, the town was implementing a community-wide Comprehensive Master Plan that heavily informed the school master plan. The new school's site was selected as part of an initiative to strengthen Greensburg's density and the fabric of development along Main Street. Other criteria served as even stronger influences: the ability to safely walk and bicycle between home and school; the availability of basic services within walking distance of the school; and the ability to share theater, meeting spaces, athletic fields, and other facilities with the larger community.

LAND

The team used a site master planning process to determine the best location for proper building orientation to maximize passive solar and wind opportunities for the school building, minimize site impact by maintaining the existing storm drainage flood path through the site, emphasize connection to the community, and provide a prominent location to support the shared use of the school facilities.

The site design for the school combines restoration of habitat with an infusion of native landscaping. A series of bioswales, constructed wetlands, restored wetlands, and walking trails re-create natural environment areas that also process stormwater. This environment reconnects students, staff, and visitors with vital ecosystems while protecting the land from erosion. It also creates a natural habitat for native species.

WATER

With Greensburg's low annual rainfall average amounts, increasing the efficiency of the building's water use safeguards water resources, as water becomes more costly and scarce. The City of Greensburg has no stormwater collection system, and the school site is bisected by a floodplain, so it became crucial to conserve and reuse whatever rainwater falls within school boundaries.

A variety of strategies mean that long-term water-saving goals will be met while helping to reduce the burden on municipal wastewater systems and reducing potable water demand. The building uses many efficiency strategies, such as low-flow plumbing fixtures, dual-flush valves, and waterless urinals.

To reduce potable water use, captured rainwater is stored in six cisterns to meet irrigation needs during dry months for the native, low-maintenance landscape. An on-site constructed wetland treats wastewater and returns it to the water table. The facility also captures condensation from HVAC equipment for reuse as make-up water in cooling towers.

ENERGY

One-hundred percent of Greensburg School's purchased electricity is from renewable energy sources. A 50-kilowatt wind turbine provides a portion of the electricity needs, while the remaining power is generated at the wind farm located outside of town.

HVAC (geothermal closed-loop ground source heat pump) systems isolate unavoidable sources of pollution, provide for adequate supply and filtering of fresh air and return air, and maintain the building and its equipment in clean condition. Controllability of systems, both temperature and supplemental task lighting, improves the comfort levels of the interior environment, promoting productivity and well-being.

The building envelope, orientation, lighting, and sun-control systems for the school buildings minimize the heating and air-conditioning loads for the building. Structural insulated panels were used to reduce thermal loading and create a high-performing building envelope. A rain screen cladding system improves resistance to moisture infiltration and reduces thermal loading. White and metallic silver roof finishes reduce thermal loading. In conjunction with high-efficiency chillers and modular air handlers, these strategies will reap substantial savings over an ASHRAE 90.1, 2004 minimum energy code baseline building.

MATERIALS

To avoid harvesting raw materials, products with recycled content were used throughout. Durable Kansas limestone, zinc, and reclaimed cypress were used on the exterior. Inside, raw materials such as polished concrete floors and concrete block were used in high-traffic areas, while reclaimed wood was used in tactile areas. Preference was given to materials manufactured within 500 miles, which conserved transportation energy while supporting local industry. An innovative limestone "shingle" skin came from a regional quarry 120 miles from the site.

To mitigate construction waste flow, the team incorporated reclaimed materials, from interior wood furring and paneling reclaimed from deconstructed warehouses to exterior furring, siding, and bridges from cypress salvaged from Hurricane Katrina.

The construction waste management plan diverted 95 percent of the construction waste from landfills to recycling. The school has an ongoing waste-recycling plan including a plan to compost kitchen waste for use in gardens.

LIGHT AND AIR

Daylighting and ventilation strategies shaped the building sections through placement of operable windows, sun-shading protection, and orientation to take advantage of passive lighting and air movement. The building's longest facades face the north and south to maximize daylighting and reduce heat gain from western sun. The gymnasiums, with sawtooth skylit roofs, are placed north of the classroom and administration areas to avoid blocking sun and air access to these areas. The classroom roofs are sloped in part to provide for the future placement of solar panels.

Kiowa County Schools: Lab. The design process first focused on daylight and the optimization of daylight in all occupied spaces. The significance of daylight in impacting academic achievement was a driving factor in the design solution (LEED NC Platinum). Firm: BNIM. PHOTO: © ASSASSI

Since daylighting optimization, ventilation, and indoor air quality have a great impact on student academic performance and the health and comfort of building occupants, these ideas became a central focus of the design. Daylighting and controls, operable windows, maximized views, classroom controls, outdoor classrooms and lunch areas, a courtyard playground, and shared learning spaces are all employed in the creation of a comfortable learning environment with a strong connection to the outdoors.

Expansive windows in the classrooms mean that they have views of the surroundings and can be entirely daylit during school hours. Exterior sun-shading devices reduce glare and heat gain. North-facing clerestories balance the light throughout the room and provide a path for natural ventilation that takes advantage of natural stratification and prevailing southwesterly breezes.

COLLECTIVE WISDOM AND FEEDBACK LOOPS
Engaging the community, students, and faculty in the full design process through large-scale workshops meant that there was buy-in to the design from the very beginning. The design team and school district worked with a child development specialist to help them better understand the learning and play opportunities for the outdoor spaces for the school. The entire collaborative process produced a building that meets the needs of the children, faculty, staff, and community, but furthermore, is a huge source of pride and is the heartbeat of the community.

ON THE HORIZON

The future is vast and exciting for people seeking to enter the ever-changing and expanding field of green building. As global demands increase on natural resources and people are striving to heal and restore the planet for future generations, the need for sustainability experts is great. Key to the solution of many current environmental problems, green building professionals have healthy job prospects, strong economic yields, and a plethora of resources to support the field. There is no better time than now to start the journey toward becoming a green building professional.

NOTES

1. William McDonough, "The Wisdom of Designing Cradle to Cradle," TED Talks, www.ted.com/index.php/talks/view/id/104, accessed September 30, 2011.

2. U.S. Environmental Protection Agency (EPA), "Buildings and Their Impact on the Environment: A Statistical Summary" (Revised April 22, 2009), www.epa.gov/greenbuilding/pubs/gbstats.pdf, accessed October 13, 2011.

3. U.S. Geological Services, USGS Water Facts Quiz, http://nd.water.usgs.gov/index/quiz.html, accessed October 2, 2011.

4. The 2030 Water Resources Group, McKinsey & Company, *Charting Our Water Future: Economic Frameworks to Inform Decision-Making,* 2009, page 11, www.mckinsey.com/App_Media/Reports/Water/Charting_Our_Water_Future_Exec%20Summary_001.pdf, accessed October 2, 2011.

5. Anthony D. Cortese, Sc.D. (October 2, 2010), *Presentation on the Urgent and Critical Role of Higher Education in Creating a Healthy, Just and Sustainable Society,* transmitted to the 2010 Presidents' Forum of Southeast and South Asia and Taiwan Universities at National Cheng Kung University, Tainan, Taiwan, www.secondnature.org/documents/cortese/cortese-SATU-october-2010.pdf, accessed October 13, 2011.

6. U.S. Environmental Protection Agency (EPA), "The Origins of EPA," www.epa.gov/aboutepa/history/origins.html, accessed October 2, 2011.

7. U.S. Environmental Protection Agency (EPA), "Definition of Green Building," www.epa.gov/greenbuilding/pubs/about.htm, accessed October 2, 2011.

8. U.S. Environmental Protection Agency (EPA), "Green Building History in the U.S.," www.epa.gov/greenbuilding/pubs/about.htm#4, accessed October 2, 2011.

9. John Elkington, *Cannibals with Forks: The Triple Bottom Line of 21st Century Business,* Oxford: Capstone Publishing, 1997; Hoboken, NJ: John Wiley & Sons, Inc., 1999.

10. United Nations General Assembly (March 20, 1987). *Report of the World Commission on Environment and Development: Our Common Future,* transmitted to the General Assembly as an Annex to document A/42/427—Development and International Co-operation: Environment, "Chapter 2: Towards Sustainable Development," Paragraph 1, www.un-documents.net/ocf-02.htm, accessed October 2, 2011.

11. Bing Dictionary, *Encarta® World English Dictionary* [North American Edition] © & (P) 2009 Microsoft Corporation. All rights reserved. Developed for Microsoft by Bloomsbury Publishing Plc., www.bing.com/Dictionary/search?q=define+legacy&qpvt=definition+of+legacy&FORM=DTPDIA, accessed October 2, 2011.

12. Booz Allen Hamilton and the U.S. Green Building Council, *Green Jobs Study,* 2009.

13. Ibid.

14. Acona and Acre Resources, *The Carbon Salary Survey,* 2010, page 25, www.carbonsalarysurvey.com/, accessed October 13, 2011.

15. U.S. Bureau of Labor Statistics, Occupational Employment Statistics: Occupational Employment and Wages, May 2010, "17–2081 Environmental Engineers," www.bls.gov/oes/current/oes172081.htm, accessed October 2, 2011.

16. Payscale, *2011–2012 College Salary Report,* "Best Undergrad College Degrees by Salary," www.payscale.com/best-colleges/degrees.asp, accessed October 2, 2011.

17. Acona and Acre Resources, *The Carbon Salary Survey,* 2010, pages 11–12, www.carbonsalarysurvey.com/, accessed October 13, 2011.

2 What Do Green Building Professionals Do?

People who work together will win, whether it be against complex football defenses, or the problems of modern society.

—Vince Lombardi *(an American football coach best known for winning the first two Super Bowls)*

IMAGINE A TYPICAL URBAN OFFICE BUILDING—a tall rectangle of steel and glass towering above city streets. Sunlight overheats the roof and inefficient wall of windows, triggering higher cooling needs and subsequent energy bills. Inside, workers are huddled under inefficient lights within tall workstations, cooled by stale air that pours in through air-conditioning vents. Headaches are common complaints, triggered by off-gassing of furniture and paint, and poor acoustics create constant distractions. At the end of the day, workers run to their cars, only to sit idling in bumper-to-bumper traffic during long commutes. It is hardly an ideal portrait of a work environment.

Now, picture a few changes to this building. Solar panels use the sun's rays, and turbines harness the wind to provide clean energy for the building. People picnic on rooftops and decks that are landscaped with grasses, trees, and flowers. Instead of cube farms inside, there are carefully planned office spaces with groupings of tables, all of which have access to daylight and views to the outdoors. Windows open to let in fresh air, a range of ambient and task lighting varies by workers' needs, and there is a pleasant hum throughout of muted activity and conversation. After work, people catch up on reading while sitting on buses or trains, or they enjoy the passing scenery on bicycles, skirting the traffic that clogs the freeways.

What makes the second scenario so much more appealing than the first? The difference is that green building professionals have been involved. Green building (sometimes called "sustainable building") is the practice of designing and constructing buildings in ways that are resource efficient, responsible to the environment, and protective of human health.

33

American Society of Hematology (LEED NC Platinum). Firm: RTKL. PHOTO © PAUL WARCHOL

For a structure to be truly green, all processes associated with its maintenance and operation, throughout the entire course of its life, should also strive for sustainable standards. In the end, when it is torn down or completely remodeled, all of its parts and materials should be reusable, recyclable, or contribute to regeneration.

Traditional building models focus on function, aesthetics, cost, and scheduling. Green building goes one step further, adding sustainable ideals to these imperatives. Though the processes, strategies, and technologies employed in building are constantly evolving and may be different in various climates and regions, there are a few core factors that green builders always take into consideration from design to operations, including:

■ Location, site features, and building orientation

■ Water conservation

■ Energy efficiency

■ Carbon accounting

- Material and resource selection/reduction
- Indoor air and environmental quality
- Toxin reduction / elimination

Sometimes, faced with budgetary, code, or other constraints, sustainability professionals must make trade-offs or compromise certain Earth-friendly features. After all, the overall goal is not simply to use green materials for every part of a building, but rather to create holistic systems—such as heating and sewage disposal—that integrate buildings into the environment and make lives healthier. When green features are included, inspiring examples abound of the results, from the alleviation of headaches for librarians who previously breathed in toxic fumes from off-gassing items on bookshelves to kindergarten students tending gardens and learning in sunlight-filled classrooms, then taking home lessons about being green to their parents. In ways such as these, green professionals change lives, not just buildings.

Common Principles

Anyone who dives into the pool of green building quickly realizes that the profession is more like an ocean. There is a wide array of green building characteristics and rating systems, and green building skills and professions seem almost unlimited. But despite this variety, two key principles define the green building profession today:

- Make minimum impact on the physical environment (including all species), communities, and economies.
- Provide health benefits to human occupants of the built environment.

These two principles serve as the basis for a common language and provide the overarching goals to which all green building professionals are committed. Medical doctors take a Hippocratic Oath to "do no harm";[1] architects take an oath to "provide health, safety, and welfare" to the public by means of the shelters they design.[2] The green building principles combine both of these imperatives and extend them to integrate care for individuals, families, and societies with care for Earth's resources and the built environment.

THE NATURAL STEP

In the late 1980s, Dr. Karl-Henrik Robèrt, a Swedish doctor and cancer scientist, drew a parallel between his cancer patients and how their families, in conjunction with care providers and the local community, came together across political lines and beliefs when focused on a higher goal of compassionate health. He sent a consensus paper out to numerous scientists and experts gathering their feedback, which culminated in a book called *The Necessary Step,* published in 1992. From this, The Natural Step Framework was created.[3]

The Natural Step Framework has taken people beyond the arguments of what is and is not possible; of what may be left or right wing. Instead, the Framework builds on a basic understanding of what makes life possible, how our biosphere functions and how we are part of the earth's natural systems. Rather than get lost in abstract definitions and causes, it builds on a platform of basic science and is designed to allow true interdisciplinary, cross sector cooperation for concrete and measurable change towards sustainability. After all, if you want to achieve 'success,' you have to first understand what this means in real terms before you can then take strategic steps to achieve it.[4]

The Natural Step Framework has four basic tenets of sustainability:

1. Eliminate our contribution to the progressive buildup of substances extracted from the Earth's crust (for example, heavy metals and fossil fuels).

2. Eliminate our contribution to the progressive buildup of chemicals and compounds produced by society (for example, dioxins, PCBs, and DDT).

3. Eliminate our contribution to the progressive physical degradation and destruction of nature and natural processes (for example, over harvesting forests and paving over critical wildlife habitat).

4. Eliminate our contribution to conditions that undermine people's capacity to meet their basic human needs (for example, unsafe working conditions).

At first glance, this list appears to suggest reducing development but, rather, it looks at the residual impacts from industrial progress. The fourth principle focused on meeting people's needs is based on the ideas of Chilean economist Manfred Max-Neef. His work identifies nine fundamental human needs that are consistent across time and cultures: subsistence, protection, affection, understanding, participation, leisure, creation, identity and freedom.[5]

Many major entities have incorporated the Natural Step Framework, including cities, states, colleges, and corporations such as IKEA, Nike, Panasonic, and Walmart.

With the Natural Step lens in mind, we can begin to look at how other metrics are important in the process of creating green buildings, organizations, and communities.

METRICS

A variety of measurement tools or metrics have been developed to support the principles of green building by quantifying and comparing the environmental impacts caused by building. Metrics are often complicated. To understand them, it is useful to begin by considering a common metric used to measure the health value of food.

The U.S. Food and Drug Administration (FDA) provides standards and guidelines to food producers and processors. Processors measure calories and nutrients and publish the numbers on the nutritional tables that are mandated for packaged foods.[6] As a result, when faced with a dazzling assortment of packaged foods, grocery shoppers can easily compare the health benefits of products by reading labels that detail everything from number of calories and grams of protein to micrograms of vitamins and minerals.

Therefore, just as food labels let consumers evaluate the dietary benefits of what they are eating, a wide array of assessment tools, strategies, and technologies let green building professionals assess the environmental impacts and health benefits of the structures they are creating. There's a popular adage: "You can't manage what you don't measure."[7] This concept is at the core of metrics. Metrics are numbers that indicate how a system or building is performing. These numbers give feedback to the user and contribute to the further evolution of holistic solutions to environmental and health challenges.

Standards

When determining how best to increase health benefits and reduce environmental impacts in architecture, green building professionals often use green building standards. Ideally, independent standards for green building are shaped locally, based on social and environmental concerns specific to particular places. As with the FDA requirements and guidelines for food products, some green building standards are mandatory international, national, or local codes; others are guidelines for voluntary compliance and certification. Examples of each follow.

Mandatory standards:

The U.S. Energy Policy Act of 2005 requires a water reduction in plumbing fixtures, such as sinks, showers, and toilets, in all newly constructed commercial buildings.[8]

Voluntary standards:

Responsible forest management is the guiding principle of the Forest Stewardship Council (FSC), a nonprofit organization that certifies wood products used in green building. Their

Cathedral City, CA: Store (LEED NC Gold). Firm: WD Partners. OWNER AND PHOTO: FRESH & EASY NEIGHBORHOOD MARKET

"chain of custody" shepherds wood from seed to tree to project site. It also protects the rights of the indigenous people and forest workers.

The evidence suggests that these standards are making a real difference in sustainable building practices. As just one example, in 1990, the FSC began as a small group of timber users, traders, and representatives of environmental and human rights organizations in California. Today, FSC standards protect over 357 million acres of forest worldwide.[9] That's an admirable achievement—especially given that participation in this program is purely voluntary.

Rating Systems

Similarly, governments issue codes, and nongovernmental organizations provide ratings systems and voluntary certifications to measure the green attributes of buildings and building processes. Many tools are available to assist green building professionals in their efforts to comply with standards. These tools are used in design and planning processes to determine the best ways to reduce environmental impacts and increase health benefits. Rating systems are one such tool that builders use to assess and publish the equivalent of the environmental "nutrition" information for a building. Where a nutrition label lists grams of fat or protein, for example, a "green label" might list water consumption or amount of energy harvested from the sun.

One important rating system is Leadership in Energy and Environmental Design (LEED). Developed by the U.S. Green Building Council and released in 1998, LEED provides building owners and operators with a concise framework for identifying and implementing practical and measurable green building design, construction, operations, and maintenance solutions.[10] Prior to the launch of LEED, environmental design had largely fallen off designers' radar screens. Today, LEED has transformed the green building market—and made sustainability prominent in the public eye. As of early 2012, there are over 11,000 buildings LEED-certified or over 1,765,000,000 square feet in 50 states and 43 countries, and over 150,000 LEED-credentialed professionals, the program has become a huge success.[11]

Beyond buildings, another noteworthy rating system, the GHG Indicator (Greenhouse Gas Indicator), was developed by the United Nations Environment Programme. It provides a method for converting easily obtainable information about fuel and energy use to a standardized estimate of greenhouse gas emissions.[12]

Green building professionals use these metrics to maximize the long-term success of their projects. They also use them to communicate with other community members, including government officials, project teams, and operations crews—and often with their clients and the general public.

LEED® Facts

[Your Project Here]
[City, State, County]

LEED for New Construction

Platinum	**100***
Sustainable Sites	26
Water Efficiency	10
Energy & Atmosphere	35
Materials & Resources	14
Indoor Environmental Quality	15

Out of a possible 100 points + 10 bonus points

Innovation & Design	6
Regional Credit	4

LEED for New Construction Scorecard.
IMAGE: U.S. GREEN BUILDING COUNCIL (USGBC)

INTEGRATED THINKING

Consider a single tree in a complex forest ecosystem. Air provides the tree with carbon dioxide for photosynthesis, wind spreads its seeds, soil provides it with nutrients, and water hydrates it. Each of these systems is essential, but it is their work together as an integrated whole that provides life to the tree.

In the same way, integrated thinking is a vital tool for green builders. All of the various sustainable approaches to creating a home, office, school, library, or any other structure require a comprehensive, team-oriented, holistic process. To find the best solution to a problem, the environmental or structural goal is outlined by the client and executed by a project team. All members of the team bring their own knowledge and skill sets to the project, but only by working together can they achieve the best possible final product.

For example, several green building professionals plan for water management at a building site. A civil engineer provides systems for reducing soil erosion caused by stormwater. A landscape architect provides ways to use surplus stormwater for irrigation in order to reduce use of municipal water. An architect offers ways to collect rainwater from the building's roof to be stored in a cistern. A plumbing engineer notes that the stored rainwater can be used for flushing toilets. Collectively, this integrated thinking process results in a holistic water efficiency plan for this green building and its site.

Houses
use unique strategies to collect, infiltrate, and cleanse rainwater.

150 Preserved Original Trees
(an estimated $1.5 million value) shape the location of pocket parks.

Swales
collect, absorb, and filter rainwater from streets and houses into ground.

Streets
slope to one side to direct rainwater into planted grass swales.

City Storm Drains
carry large flows of rainstorm water to the pond, which slowly realeases cleaner water into Longfellow Creek.

Yard Drains
direct rainwater to swales or a pipe.

High Point's innovative natural drainage system collects, infiltrates, and cleanses rainwater, while at the same time protecting a critical coho salmon habitat. High Point Community, Seattle, Washington (Built Green Three Star Rating). FIRM AND IMAGE: MITHUN

The alternative approach, whereby each professional considers solutions in isolation, results in an "unnatural," one-dimensional design. In the book *The Integrative Design Guide to Green Building,* 7group and Bill G. Reed describe in detail the evolution from "master builder"—responsible for all aspects of building—to the current "age of specialization."[13]

For the green builder with a highly specialized focus, the drawbacks of an isolated approach are clear. In such a model, for example, a designer might create a floor plan and ceiling design in isolation from the mechanical engineer designing the HVAC system. Without discussion and collaboration between the two specialists, problems would inevitably when the designs were put into practice without consideration for ceilings relative to mechanical ductwork shapes and sizes, resulting in a less than optimal finished space. As an antidote for this kind of

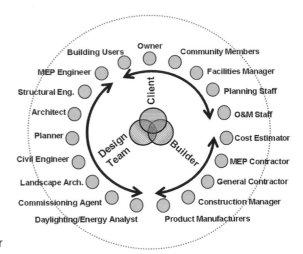

Composite Master Builder. IMAGE COURTESY OF BILL REED AND 7GROUP; ADAPTED FROM GRAPHIC BY BILL REED. REPRINTED WITH PERMISSION OF JOHN WILEY & SONS, INC.

Diagram of the Learning Wheel (applied). COURTESY OF ALEX ZIMMERMAN, ADAPTED FROM IDEAS PRESENTED IN PETER M. SENGE ET AL., *THE FIFTH DISCIPLINE FIELDBOOK: STRATEGIES AND TOOLS FOR BUILDING A LEARNING ORGANIZATION* (NEW YORK: DOUBLEDAY, 1994). REPRINTED WITH PERMISSION OF JOHN WILEY & SONS, INC.

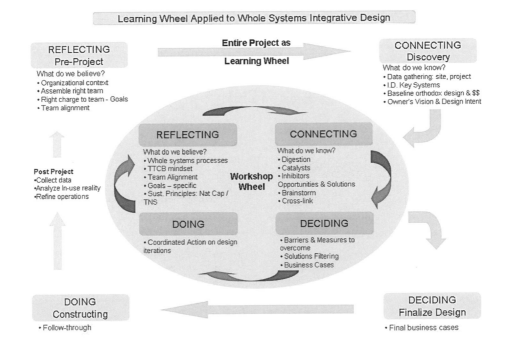

isolated approach, 7group and Reed give hands-on solutions for taking good to great by developing integrated thinking processes. The book states that "the Integrative Process can be described simply as a repeating pattern of Research/Analysis and Team Workshops." The diagram of the Learning Wheel, shown previously in this chapter courtesy of Alex Zimmerman, shows the process of learning in an integrative design session.[14]

MULTIFACETED PERSPECTIVE

We all wear many hats in our lives—student, teacher, employee, boss, child, parent, spouse, and friend. All of these "perspectives" shape the way we solve problems. One of the benefits of integrated thinking is the ability to be open to multiple viewpoints and solutions. The most successful green building teams are made up of individuals who recognize that their talents and skills are optimized when they integrate them with the talents and skills of others.

In one such instance, the building team for the Girl Scouts of Greater Atlanta's new headquarters—the building owner, donors who provided financing, a mechanical engineer, and a commissioning agent—worked together to develop the building's energy systems through an integrated thinking process. They began outside the building, first creating a series of on-site solar panels that convert sunshine to energy for the building. Inside, efficient heating, cooling, and lighting systems reduce the building's energy needs. At the end of the project, the systems were double-checked by the commissioning agent against the owner's original goals. The result of this team effort can be seen in the energy cost savings. This new headquarters received LEED Silver certification and the Girl Scouts created a podcast to celebrate (can be found at www.h2ecodesign.com). The podcast highlights the integrated process and building features.[15]

Each of the green building professionals profiled in this book brings a rich and complex perspective to green building, and all play multiple roles in the design and construction community. Together, principles, metrics, integrated thinking, a multifaceted perspective, and a high skill level in one or more green building specialties make up the basic aspects of the successful green building professional.

GREEN BUILDING PROFESSIONS

Academic	Environmental consultant
Architect	Facility manager
Building owner	Interior designer
Chief sustainability officer	Landscape architect
Civil engineer	Mechanical engineer
Commissioning agent	Nonprofit member
Contractor	Plumbing engineer
Electrical engineer	Real estate professional

What does a green building professional do?

❯ A green building professional incorporates sustainable practices into the typical building process. This means weighing the environmental implications for clients in addition to key issues like timing and economics. As a professional leasing buildings, I try to negotiate provisions whereby both the tenant and the landlord are incentivized to build, operate, and maintain their space and the building in an efficient and environmentally friendly manner.

Jennifer A. Ralph, LEED AP BD+C, Brokerage Services, CB Richard Ellis

❯ Answering what a green building professional does first requires a definition of what a green building professional is. A green building professional can fit into one of two categories:

1. Any of the "regular" activities related to the building industry, but with a sustainable or conservation twist. Examples: interior designer, architect, engineer, builder, or specialty contractor who utilizes conservation and sustainability methods and materials.
2. One of the emerging occupations in green building that are solely focused on a specific sustainable outcome. These occupations would not exist in great number without the growing trend of building more sustainably. Examples: building performance specialist, building certification consultant, energy manager, energy auditor, or building commissioning expert.

Jessica Rose, LEED Green Associate, chief navigator, Incite Sustainability

❯ A green building professional is involved in many different aspects of the built environment, but you ultimately always become an educator and teacher within the industry. You are responsible for leading a new industry that incorporates old practical principles with new innovative products. You are the person who will be asked to have a deeper understanding of how to blend people, profit, and planet concerns into buildings and developments.

Dan Donatelli, LEED-AP BD+C, sustainability director, Unisource Worldwide, Inc.

❯ A green building professional understands the importance of a team approach and recognizes that a building is a complex system. A green building professional brings everyone together early and often, and inspires and motivates the team to work collaboratively throughout the entire process, brainstorming innovations, evaluating synergies, and choosing strategies, materials, and technologies. He or she promotes and encourages continuous and open communication and is the facilitator of the entire process.

Liana Kallivoka, PhD, USGBC LEED Faculty, project manager and sustainability consultant, Austin Energy Green Building

❯ A green building professional understands and leverages the interdependence of green building science, technology, and the human need for beauty, function, and livability. The best green building professionals work at the intersection of these factors to develop structures and environments that support quality of life, protect the planet, and inspire others to do the same.

Michelle Bernhart, sustainability strategist, president, and founder, True Blue Communications LLC

❯ A green building professional is someone who is knowledgeable in environmentally responsible design and seeks to understand the connectedness between the multitude of green building issues, including health at three levels: for building occupants, local ecosystems, and the global environment. He or she is also committed to continued learning, willing to share knowledge, and demonstrates leadership and passion in the work.

Jean Hansen, FIIDA, CID, LEED AP BD+C, AAHID, EDAC, senior professional associate, sustainable interiors manager, HDR, Inc.

❯ A green building professional continually promotes the elevation of the bar that represents standard practice through research and benchmarking.

Samantha Harrell, LEED AP ID+C, LEED Certification Reviewer

❯ A green building professional continually learns how to improve the built environment to better serve its occupants and implements practices that better utilize the resources required to build, operate, and maintain structures.

Chad Pepper, LEED AP, president, Greek Key Services

❯ There are many skill sets within the green building industry. For those of us charged with communications regarding products and projects, a compelling story shares the learning of those directly involved and educates the broader marketplace about possible achievements. *How* can be as important as *what.* Whether new or existing structures, green building requires a holistic approach aimed at generating healthy interiors with limited impacts on the environment.

Nancy Rogers, founder, Green Earth PR Network

❯ The green design professional weaves the torn and frayed threads of the man-made and natural world. This new fabric is not a single all-encompassing design, but a construction of imagination and the celebration of life in all of its ancient and modern forms. In this place we dwell, reconnected to ourselves, our cultures, and the environment.

Rico Cedro, AIA, LEED AP BD+C, ID+C, director of sustainable design, Verdi Workshop

❯ It is my ultimate goal as a green building professional to reduce our industry's impact on the natural environment. To achieve this, I try to bridge the gap between our natural and built environments with green building strategies that are resource efficient and reduce greenhouse gas emissions. Gaining this knowledge and putting it into practice requires a constant learning process of analyz-

ing, scrutinizing, and disseminating the myriad of "green information" and providing encouragement to colleagues and clients to put this knowledge into everyday practice.

Cindy Davis, LEED BD+C, associate principal, Callison

❯ Sustainable design should reinvent itself every time you look at a new building problem. In today's environment of evolving products, systems, and strategies, all things are fluid. Going back to the last building problem solution is a disservice to mankind and the environment.

William (Bill) D. Abballe Jr., AIA, LEED AP BD+C, associate principal, tvsdesign

❯ A Green Building Professional is a client's trusted advisor in the full spectrum of the green building industry—from material selection to operations guidance to business strategy. She helps her clients reduce risk by communicating knowledge around pending regulation, as well as increase benefits from market offerings, such as funding mechanisms, incentives, and rebates.

Christine S. E. Magar, RA, AIA, LEED AP BD+C, Homes, Greenform

❯ We discover more and more each day that the green building concept engages multiple attributes of environmental responses that, in different combinations, produce extremely varying interpretations of "green building." Like traditional building, there is no perfect, one-size-fits-all sustainable design. Sustainable design must respond to and reflect the environmental, societal, and economic priorities of the individual user, owner, and affected community. Here's where green building professionals come into play. It is our job to help articulate, strategize, and execute these environmental priorities in a holistic, well-composed, and maintainable space.

Leslie Gage Ellsworth, Associate AIA, LEED AP BD+C, design associate, Monberg Wall Architects

What is a typical workday like for you?

❯ The majority of my time is spent working on specific projects, contracts, or guidance, which means participating in meetings or reviewing and writing documents to improve performance through green building issues. A large portion of my time is spent responding to inquiries through email or phone calls, providing advice, answers, resources, or pointing people in the right direction. I also try to reserve some time for reading newsletters, magazines, and list serves to learn about the latest issues, discussion topics and examples.

Don Horn, AIA, LEED AP BD+C, deputy director, Office of Federal High-Performance Green Buildings, U.S. General Services Administration

❯ Expect there to be no "typical workday." On any particular day you could be working in the office developing a LEED Commissioning plan, reviewing design or construction documents, or writing up reports. Or you could be meeting with a new client, generally a senior member of an organization, often the owner. You might be attending design or construction meetings, often on site to inspect or troubleshoot issues. Or you might be assisting clients, building operators, and tenants to understand how their building is intended to operate.

Robert (Jack) Meredith, P.Eng., LEED AP BD+C, founder and president, HGBC Healthy Green Building Consultants Ltd.

❯ When I'm in the office I spend about 20 percent of the time in office meetings, 20 percent in one-on-one meetings about specific projects, 20 percent on conference calls (generally volunteer responsibilities), 10 percent on administration and board coordination, and 30 percent on direct project work.

Gail Vittori, LEED AP BD+C, co-director, Center for Maximum Building Performance

❯ I spend part of the day in the office, reviewing design drawings, meeting with consulting engineers, and overseeing the work of the office. Often I am out at a construction site, answering questions from builders. I also spend a lot of time meeting and talking to prospective clients.

Muscoe Martin, AIA, LEED AP BD+C, M2 Architecture

❯ I try to avoid typical workdays. I like to make every workday different. Yes, there are regular ongoing activities that need to be attended to—emails and phone calls to return; research to be undertaken; proposals to be written; new materials, product standards and rating systems to review; project reports to be written—but the time, space, and place in which these occur vary tremendously. I am as likely to be found doing work from my home office, one of our office's conference rooms, the lobby of a convention center, the local Starbucks, a client's project office, the library, or the train and the bus as I am my assigned desk. I was a mobile worker long before the term was invented. It's delightful to be a trend before the trend exists!

Kirsten Ritchie, PE, LEED AP O+M, principal/director of sustainable design, Gensler

Lake View Terrace Library, Lake View Terrace, CA (LEED NC Platinum). Firm: Fields Devereaux Architects & Engineers, James Weiner, AIA, LEED Fellow, project architect. A lowered ceiling, curved bench, and bookshelf shape the children's story space. PHOTO: RMA PHOTOGRAPHY, INC.

What advice would you give to someone interested in becoming a green building professional?

❯ The more you learn about sustainability the more you understand how much there is yet to learn. Learn from experience and listen to others—attend conferences, read books, and participate in projects. Learn what more can be done from other green building projects and think of new possibilities. With sustainability there is always more to learn and do.

Don Horn, AIA, LEED AP BD+C, deputy director, Office of Federal High-Performance Green Buildings, U.S. General Services Administration

❯ Find your passion and pursue it. If you are having problems finding your passion, then be passionate about what you are doing until you find your passion.

Robert (Jack) Meredith, P.Eng., LEED AP BD+C, founder and president, HGBC Healthy Green Building Consultants Ltd.

❯ Ask questions! Don't assume that others know all the answers—there is much to be discovered. In the process, be willing to take risks and learn from mistakes.

Gail Vittori, LEED AP BD+C, co-director, Center for Maximum Building Performance

❯ Many architects claim they are green today, but it takes more than a LEED-certified project to become a green architect. I would recommend working in design or construction first before going to architecture school. Then read as much as you can about the impacts of construction on resources, water, energy, and land.

Muscoe Martin, AIA, LEED AP BD+C, M2 Architecture

❯ In addition to learning the technical aspects of the work, spend time learning skills such as group dynamics and facilitation, writing, and oral communication. In a green practice, architects, engineers, interior designers, and contractors don't work in a vacuum. Instead the successful practitioner excels at bringing together a team for each project and making sure that each team member is able to contribute his or her expertise and opinion. It's also important to be able to communicate about your work, since we are all learning from one another. Those who emerge as leaders often are good speakers and writers.

Most important, find people you respect and care for to be your colleagues, bosses, partners, and staff. Life and work are about people. Surround yourself with people who challenge you, help you to be your best self, teach you, and learn from you. Stay true to the values that attracted you to a green profession in the first place.

Joel Ann Todd, environmental consultant and chair of the USGBC LEED Steering Committee

❯ Start by figuring out how you can best leverage your current skill set and expertise. Intersect that with what you are absolutely passionate about—when you can say, "Yay! It's seven o'clock on Monday or midnight on Saturday and I get to work on this." Mix in the physical environment: "I love being in an office," or "I am really a jobsite person." With all that insight, you will be well positioned to pounce on the right opportunity when it presents itself. But that takes one more step: Finding the opportunities. You need to go and find them. Don't assume they will just come to you.

Kirsten Ritchie, PE, LEED AP O+M, principal/director of sustainable design, Gensler

Eye for Strategic Vision

DON HORN, AIA, LEED AP BD+C

Deputy Director, Office of Federal High-Performance Green Buildings
U.S. General Services Administration (GSA)

GSA is often called the federal government's "landlord" because it provides workspace and office services for almost every federal office and agency across our country—from courthouses to ports of entry. With 8,600 buildings and $500 billion in assets under its control, GSA is one of the largest property management organizations in the world.[16]
—SENATOR JOE LIEBERMAN, *February 1, 2010*

What are your daily roles and responsibilities?

My job is basically serving as a subject matter expert providing advice, guidance, and assistance to others in GSA and the federal government. I am working to transform the culture of the organization by incorporating sustainability into business practices and strategic thinking. This involves conceptualizing ways to improve performance through green building policies and operational practices.

What skills and attributes does a green building professional need in order to be successful?

I believe the most important skills for a green building professional today involve the ability to envision and communicate, including the capacity for whole systems thinking and change from standard practice and the abilities to convince others to think of greater possibilities, to influence others and their decision making, and to inspire ideas and a vision for change.

The field of green building is broad, and it includes many specialized professions. How would you recommend that someone new to the field narrow the options?

I would first ask, "What do you enjoy working with?" Are you interested in high-level, conceptual thinking or the more detailed, practical concerns of implementation, making things work, and products and materials?

There are limitless opportunities for green building professionals in practically any discipline, from designer solving problems to consultant/advisor identifying possibilities to consultant tracking documentation to manufacturer envisioning product improvements.

What are the largest growth areas for professionals in the green building field?

The greatest opportunities will be found by branching into disciplines that are slow to change or pick up green concepts. A new way of building is taking hold and there is a great need for individuals who understand how green building issues are changing basic services. These professions include code officials, inspectors, realty professionals, and anyone who can identify green characteristics that will save funds and improve effectiveness.

How did you enter the field of green building? Would you do it differently if you had it to do over again?

I wouldn't change a thing. In 1999, a new environmental division was formed in GSA's Public Buildings Service and an architect was needed to lead implementation of this new concept called "sustainable design." I jumped at the chance to take on the challenge. This opportunity brought together all of my interests: architecture, landscape architecture, historic buildings, reuse of resources, figuring out how things work, and a love of nature. The USGBC membership summit in the fall of 1999 was tremendously influential in laying the foundation for my green building career. I learned from listening to and talking with like-minded people who envisioned new ways of building and living on Earth in harmony with nature. Similar opportunities for personal dialogue and connection with others can still be found in local chapter meetings of various organizations and through events that offer discussion opportunities. Question, learn, and start making changes.

Skill Master

KIMBERLY HOSKEN, LEED AP O+M
Director, Green Buildings
Johnson Controls, Inc.

What are your daily roles and responsibilities?

Essentially, I have three objectives:

- Develop strategies, tools, processes, and teams to support our green building programs globally.
- Meet with internal and external customers.
- Forward sustainability at Johnson Controls globally.

Developing strategies, tools, resources, and processes involves understanding our customer needs and providing solutions. My role includes defining and outlining a strategic process for customers who want to pursue a greener, more sustainable culture and business.

How did you enter the field of green building?

I started in Lake Tahoe working for the Public Works Department. I was building erosion control projects to "protect the lake" and managing traffic to "improve air quality." I wasn't an environmentalist but a builder and construction manager. I am just a small part of a great effort to change how we do things—to create better ways to do things with better results on every level.

What skills and attributes does a green building professional need in order to be successful?

I believe that in order to be successful in any career you need an area of expertise and a specific skill set. You can be an architect or engineer, a property manager or facilities manager, or even a vice president of sales, but you need this type of skill first. I have so many young people with degrees in environmental science asking me for jobs. It isn't enough. I think this is so important for people in college to understand: You need to be able to add value and be able to contribute to an organization with a specific skill. Then learn how to green your particular area of expertise.

My own background is in construction; that is my area of expertise. I know how to build a building, how to manage a project. I added being green. I also went back to school for a master's degree in business so that I could understand more about the financial aspects of any business.

Also, the single most important skill that any professional has is the ability to communicate. I cannot stress this enough. Some people have this skill and do not need to learn it. If you are not one who is gifted with strong communication skills, there are

The use of vegetation and ground-covering plants: Trees, bushes, and ground-covering plants have been planted on rooftop and landscape areas to help reduce overall ambient temperature. Energy Complex, Bangkok, Thailand (LEED CS Platinum). Firm: Architect 49. Owner: Energy Complex Co., Ltd. PHOTO: 2011, ENERGY COMPLEX

tremendous resources and you can learn to be a better communicator.

Does your work allow you to travel frequently?

It is not unusual for my day to start or end on an airplane. I may be on our corporate shuttle heading from Milwaukee to Detroit, or I may be going to Istanbul, Cairo, Dubai, or Shenzhen. I am often asked to speak at green building conventions and conferences around the world, but I am also traveling to meet with customers. A typical day in Cairo recently involved a tour of three building sites, three days of design charrettes going through the LEED process, with evenings scheduled to meet with government officials, customers, and future customers.

What are the largest growth areas for professionals in the green building field?

I think long-term sustainability planning is what our customers need right now. They don't want just a green building; they want a green culture. This is a great opportunity for people from all aspects of a business or organization.

Lifelong Student

JOEL ANN TODD
Chair of USGBC LEED Steering Committee
Environmental Consultant

How did you enter the field of green building?

I was an environmental consultant with no background in architecture, engineering, or construction. In 1989, I was brought in by the American Institute of Architects (AIA) and the U.S. Environmental Protection Agency to man-

age the Life Cycle Assessment–based materials research and reports for the AIA's Environmental Resource Guide. I was lucky to work with some of the pioneers of green building on this project, and I learned so much from them. In these early days, most of us entered green building through a more specific interest, such as energy efficiency, green products, or indoor air quality. As we learned more, we realized that all of these specific topics were linked and interrelated and that we needed to understand it all. That message is still so important today, as we look at integrative approaches and regeneration.

What are the most important skills and attributes that a green building professional needs in order to be successful?

Good technical education, of course. The education should be as broad as possible—learn a little about all of the fields that relate to your specialty because you will be working with specialists in those fields.

Group facilitation and group dynamics, because you will be working in teams and leading teams.

Curiosity and love of learning.

Generosity of spirit and commitment to values. Keep these values at the heart of your practice.

The field of green building is broad. It includes many specialized professions. How should someone new to the field narrow the options?

First, follow your dream. What aspect of green building appeals to you most? Get some experi-

ence, and when you have an opportunity to participate in a project team, learn as much as you can about what the other team members do. Finally, don't focus on narrowing options too early. Get a broad background and you will find what really appeals to you.

A student works on a village planning exercise at Yestermorrow Design/Build School, Waitsfield, VT. PHOTO: 2011 MATTHEW RAKOLA

Communication by Design

PENNY BONDA, FASID, LEED AP ID+C

Partner Ecoimpact Consulting

Author of *Sustainable Commercial Interiors*

What was your path to becoming a green building professional (education, experience, mentors, etc.)?

In 1995, as the incoming national president of ASID, I attended an early USGBC membership meeting on its behalf. Going in I didn't even know

what a green building was. When I left I knew that I could no longer design interiors as I had been for the last twenty years without regard to occupant health or the health and survival of our planet.

At that meeting I met Bill Reed, an architect with a small practice in need of an interior designer. I needed a green education, and we made a deal—I'd work for him part-time while I served my term as ASID president, and he'd begin to teach me the basics of sustainability.

As a writer, interior designer, and sustainability consultant—how do the "three hats" you wear overlap and influence one another?

It has been eleven years since I have "practiced" interior design. I began writing a sustainable interiors column for *Interior & Sources* magazine in 2000, which led to my blogging for *Interior Design* magazine in 2005. I am now a monthly columnist for the Healthy Building Network.

I began speaking on green buildings as a member of the original LEED faculty for USGBC. Through both my writing and speaking I feel I have had a significant influence on the direction of interior design, and my ability to clearly communicate in designer-friendly terms has advanced sustainable building practices where they matter most to building occupants—in the interior.

Inspirational feature walls in transition corridors at the International Interior Design Association, Chicago, IL (LEED CI Gold). Firm: Envision Design. PHOTO: ERIC LAIGNEL

What do you forecast for the future of sustainability and/or the green building profession?

We are entering a new era of health and transparency where consumers will begin to expect buildings that protect, enhance, and sustain them and our planet. "Green buildings" must—will—become a redundant term. It is up to our profession to deliver this future.

The Call for Evangelist

KIRSTEN RITCHIE, PE, LEED AP O+M

Principal/Director of Sustainable Design

Gensler

What are your daily roles and responsibilities?

I am a sustainable materials expert, green building educator, and sustainable performance evangelist. I work for a wonderful, uniquely entrepreneurial, international design firm whose design portfolio ranges from a 6-centimeter wine label to a 600-meter tower. Daily I work with our clients and project teams around the world to improve the environmental and sustainable performance of our projects—whether a new social marketing campaign to foster sustainable behavior at a university or master planning a new city. To each of our projects I bring a particular sustainable, performance-based focus. I help the design team, the client, and the marketplace better understand the return on investment from a sustainable approach, whether in the form of improved brand perception, higher employee satisfaction, increased customer engagement, or lower life-cycle costs.

What do you see as the largest growth areas for professionals within the green building field, and why?

One growth area is smart grid deployment. Just a few of the emerging growth areas are distributed energy generation, smart appliances, community choice aggregation, an energy intranet, enabling electric vehicles, integrating renewables, consumer energy management, minimizing the impact of outages, and reducing distribution loss.

For the product designer and manufacturer, the new product market is green and clean tech. That's where the venture capital money is going in the U.S. However, there are also growing market pressures on all building product suppliers to improve the sustainable performance of their existing product lines, including reducing the carbon footprint, eliminating toxic components, improving the harvesting practices, minimizing the quantity of materials required to produce the products, and improving overall life-cycle energy efficiency. This will lead to many new professional opportunities for the green building enthusiast.

University of the Pacific: Breakout area seating (LEED NC Silver). Firm: Gensler. PHOTO: SHERMAN TAKATA

University of the Pacific: The Lair (pub), with a view to the stage (LEED NC Silver). Firm: Gensler. PHOTO: SHERMAN TAKATA

What are the most important skills/attributes a green building professional needs in order to be successful?

First and foremost, to be a successful green building professional you need to have your "beat," a particular area of green building expertise that defines you in the eyes of the marketplace.

Second, you need to have broad generalist knowledge.

Third, you need to be an effective collaborator/team player.

Fourth, you need to have a broad personal network.

Fifth, you need to be a great communicator.

Sixth, having a good sense of humor is a big help, particularly when you're dealing with arcane building requirements, recalcitrant engineers, or change-order-driven contractors.

And finally, seventh, you need to be a lifelong student.

If you had it to do over again, would you enter the field differently?

I would do it the same way. Entering the field while in college, working as a student intern, finding something I loved to do, becoming committed to fixing the problems our lifestyles were creating for our natural world, and knowing it was going to be a long, tough slog to convince the rest the world. It has been a fantastic journey and I am absolutely thrilled that now when I say, "I am a sustainable building evangelist," people reply, "Wow, that is so cool!" rather than just giving me a blank stare!

 As you embark on a career (or volunteer) in green building, what has surprised you the most about the field?

❯ How fast it is growing, especially in my area. It went from a virtually unheard-of laughable concept to an ideal that has generated a lot of interest and participation.

Stephanie Coble, RLA, ASLA, landscape architect, HagerSmith Design

❯ How new it is to everybody in the industry. The playing field is level for all; in what other industries can a young professional take their education upon themselves and be as knowledgeable in the technology and methods of green building as experienced members of the industry?

Mark Schrieber, LEED AP BD+C and Homes, project manager, The Spinnaker Group

❯ That money is the main driver for green building. This might change from region to region, but in my area, this seems to be the general way of thinking. Green buildings aren't seen as something that could bring one better health or help protect precious resources. It's about how it can save one money and be used as a status symbol in the community.

Lisa Lin, LEED AP BD+C, ICLEI, Local Governments for Sustainability

❯ There really is not one right or wrong solution to any one problem. Many, many variables to consider.

Stephanie Walker, interior designer, The Flooring Gallery

❭ It never ceases to amaze me how much "green-wash" there is. Deeper than that, and what is more surprising, is the fact that a lot of people who greenwash actually believe they are green. They are either misinformed, uneducated, or both. Some are actively stumbling through the learning process and getting themselves educated, which I applaud, but others choose to remain ignorant because it's "easier." Those choosing the "easy" path will be taking a very long road to catch up in the future.

Lindsey Engels, LEED AP BD+C, project coordinator, LPA, Inc.

❭ As I embarked on my career, the resistance to change is what surprised me the most. It seemed as though the decision makers were wary of the green building movement and its findings. However, after persistence, and let me reiterate, unyielding persistence, with the companionship of the United States Green Building North Florida Chapter we were able to pass a green building ordinance and have since built three LEED-certified buildings.

Brian C. Small, LEED AP BD+C, city planner, City of Jacksonville

❭ One of the most surprising facets of embarking in a green building field has been the recent realization that virtually anyone can be a "green building" professional, as long as the will to reduce our environmental impact is present and as citizens of our communities, we are willing to make changes to contribute to sustainability. Solving problems on the job also requires perspective from different professions and disciplines—engineers, architects, scientists, policy makers, and more.

Alessandra R. Carreon, PE, LEED AP O+M, Environ Holdings, Inc.

❭ How much work there still is to be done. I guess there is a little bit of naiveté that says that most of the world's problems have been solved and at best I can offer a contribution. Being involved in the green building movement, I've had an opportunity to see, firsthand, just how much opportunity there is to really do some impact work.

Ventrell Williams, Assoc. AIA, LEED AP O+M, Bank of America

❭ I am probably most surprised by the challenges that exist in driving change within the construction industry. I do a lot in my day-to-day job related to innovative construction materials and technologies, outside of green building, and we face the same kinds of challenges—the construction industry is very stuck in its ways and resistant to change. That said, it's been amazing to watch a new generation of builders and designers spur momentum and change when it comes to sustainability.

Will Senner, LEED AP BD+C, senior project manager, Skanska USA Building

❭ Stubborn engineers. This is perhaps the most frustrating for me and also the most rewarding when I do get to work with progressive engineering and energy consulting firms. If you are thinking of entering the engineering field, be sure to be very inquisitive of your prospective employer and how open they are to let you explore new innovative ideas on how to condition our buildings.

Michael Pulaski, PhD, LEED AP BD+C, project manager, Thorton Tomasetti/Fore Solutions

❭ Being green does not always require additional costs and in many cases can actually be a cost savings! In addition to having a positive impact on the environment, green building can even have a positive impact on the bottom line and operational costs of a business. This was definitely an eye opener for me.

Miriam Saadati, LEED AP, Tangram Interiors

❭ How disconnected end users and community organizations are from the crafters of sustainable policy and design. Bringing community to the table in discussions of policy and planning will contribute to a culture that accepts and understands sustainable design and lifestyle at a deeper level.

Katherine Darnstadt, AIA, LEED AP BD+C, CDT, NCARB, founder + principal architect, Latent Design

Noah's Ark Meets Green Design

SOUTHFACE ECO OFFICE
Atlanta, Georgia
Lord, Aeck & Sargent

Vision Challenge

The Eco Office project was intended to create versatile, highly productive work and educational space that would complement the existing Southface Resource Center and demonstrate small-scale sustainable, mixed-use commercial construction. As co-founder and executive director of Southface Energy Institute, Dennis Creech wanted to make the Eco Office into a demonstration facility for green building, so he came up with his now well-known "Noah's Ark" concept—the new building would feature at least two design solutions or technologies for every environmental challenge presented. The building's design evolved from strategies that were region-

ally appropriate and that most effectively addressed metropolitan Atlanta's most pressing environmental challenges, which included a significant urban heat island effect, poor urban air quality, and extremely limited potable water supplies together with booming population growth. The team also embraced "state-of-the-shelf" as a basis for its product and technology selections, ensuring the building accomplished its ambitious environmental goals while showcasing design strategies that could be duplicated by almost anyone who so desired.

Strategy & Solution

WATER
Rainwater harvesting and water-efficient plumbing fixtures were designed to achieve an 84 percent reduction in potable water use.

The Eco Office exhibits three water-efficient alternatives to the conventional 1.6-gallon-per-flush

View of the Eco Office from the south (LEED NC Platinum). Firm: Lord, Aeck & Sargent. IMAGE: COURTESY OF LORD, AECK & SARGENT

1. Existing Residential Resource Center
2. Atrium With Radiant Cooling
3. Classroom Level
4. Office Level
5. Outdoor Demonstration
6. Photovoltaic Array
7. Semi-Transparent Building-Integrated Photovoltaic System
8. Light Shelf
9. Daylight Glazing
10. Vision Glazing
11. Extensive Green Roof
12. Intensive Green Roof
13. Reflective Roof
14. Cistern
15. Raingarden

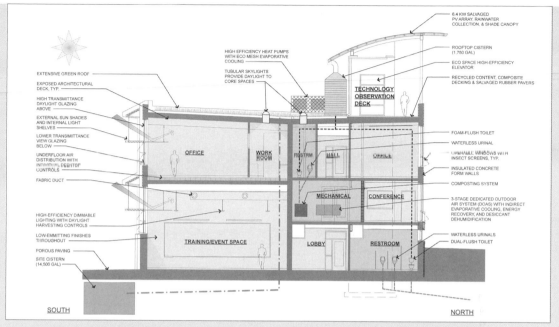

Green design features in Eco Office sectional diagram (LEED NC Platinum). Firm: Lord, Aeck & Sargent. IMAGE: COURTESY OF LORD, AECK & SARGENT

water closets currently in use in most conventional facilities. The public restrooms feature dual-flush water closets with controls that allow occupants to select either 1.6 gallons per flush for solid waste or 0.8 gallons per flush for liquid waste, and pressure-assisted 1.0-gallon-per-flush toilets.

Combined, these plumbing fixture strategies created a 56 percent reduction in water demand. Lord, Aeck & Sargent then directed their attention to meeting water demand with on-site resources in lieu of the municipal potable water system. As indicated earlier, Atlanta has abundant rainfall despite its limited municipal potable water supply. Its fifty-inch annual rainfall equates to approximately thirty gallons of runoff per square foot of roof each year.

Two systems were developed to capture this stormwater and meet the building's needs. A 1,750-gallon rooftop cistern captures rainwater as it flows off the photovoltaic array canopy and uses it for flushing toilets, dramatically reducing potable water con-

sumption. Approximately 43,000 gallons of harvested water are available annually to the Eco Office for toilet flushing, reducing its potable water demand, when compared to a conventional building, by 84 percent. The remainder of the rooftop cistern's captured water is put to good use irrigating the rooftop garden and cooling the HVAC equipment.

Native landscaping that requires no permanent irrigation also eliminates the demand for municipal water. A 14,500-gallon below-grade site cistern, constructed of modular rain tank boxes, captures runoff from the green roof as well as stormwater from the whole building site. This volume can be used for intermittent site irrigation during extended drought conditions. It can also supplement the rooftop cistern volume when needed, which further reduces the domestic water demand.

ENERGY

Lord, Aeck & Sargent first identified the building's largest energy uses, then identified ways to reduce them—for example, designing the building for optimum daylighting in order to eliminate energy-intensive overhead electric lights. Once the energy demand was reduced as low as it could go, then the focus shifted to greening the energy needed to meet the residual demands.

Lighting experts at Lord, Aeck & Sargent used computerized daylight models to optimize window glazing configurations and shading device design, with the goal of providing building occupants with uniform, glare-free illumination. In addition, the Eco Office includes automatic lighting controls that adjust artificial lighting when low daylight levels require it, and occupancy sensors turn off lighting in unoccupied spaces.

High-efficiency lighting further reduces the building's energy demands. Better still, these lighting design strategies also lower the building's cooling loads, as electric lights generate heat that must also be mitigated to maintain a comfortable inside building temperature. Together, this results in operational energy savings and allows a reduction in mechanical systems capacity and a corresponding first-cost savings.

Insulated concrete form wall construction, coupled with insulated, low-e window glazing, provides a high-performance thermal envelope, further reducing space conditioning demands. A combination of reflective roofing and extensive green roofing was used to help address the urban heat island effect, while providing the added benefit of reducing cooling loads associated with a conventional black roof. The resulting load demand is a fraction of that required by a conventional building.

In order to further address the need for comfort in Atlanta's hot, humid climate, they selected a dedicated outdoor air system (DOAS). The DOAS system decouples the sensible (temperature) and latent (humidity) loads, allowing each to be addressed independently while providing 100 percent outside air to the building occupants. The DOAS system features a series of three technologies: a dew-point evaporative cooler that preconditions the air, followed by a heat-recovery wheel that uses the building's exhaust air stream to further condition the incoming air stream, followed by a liquid

Eco Office green roof (LEED NC Platinum). Firm: Lord, Aeck & Sargent. IMAGE COURTESY OF LORD, AECK & SARGENT

desiccant dehumidification system, which completely removes excess humidity.

The building's latent load is met with high-efficiency air-to-air heat pumps fitted with a misting system that cools them to further boost efficiency. Inside the office, a raised-floor displacement ventilation system that features desktop controls lets individuals control the local temperature and air flow at their workstations.

A grid-tied, building-integrated photovoltaic array creates electricity from sunlight and greens the building's energy supply. Salvaged from a decommissioned BP gas station and doubling as a rooftop shade canopy and rainwater collection surface, the PV array provides further environmental dividends.

In combination, these measures resulted in a building that is projected to use 53 percent less energy than a conventional building.

PUTTING IT ALL TOGETHER

The Southface Eco Office sets a high but achievable bar for buildings everywhere. With clear goals and objectives for the facility from the outset, an integrated design process, a committed and talented design and building team, and readily available "state-of-the-shelf" technologies, Southface has proven that it is possible to produce healthy, regionally appropriate, high-performance workplaces that save significantly on operating costs and that reduce environmental burdens. The Eco Office is a world-class building, but the leadership was, without a doubt, all local!

NOTES

1. Michael North, translator, "The Hippocratic Oath," National Library of Medicine, National Institutes of Health, History of Medicine Division, 2002, www.nlm.nih.gov/hmd/greek/greek_oath.html, accessed October 2, 2011.
2. American Institute of Architects, AIA Continuing Education System: Health, Safety, Welfare, www.aia.org/education/ces/AIAB089080, accessed October 2, 2011.
3. The Natural Step, www.naturalstep.org/en/our-story, accessed October 20, 2011.
4. Ibid.
5. The Natural Step, www.naturalstep.org/the-system-conditions, accessed October 20, 2011.
6. U.S. Food and Drug Administration (U.S. FDA), "About FDA," www.fda.gov/AboutFDA/WhatWeDo/default.htm, accessed October 2, 2011.
7. Quote source is unknown. Quote origin options: http://answers.google.com/answers/threadview?id=139473.
8. U.S. Environmental Protection Agency, "Relevant Codes and Standards: Energy Policy Act of 2005," www.whdg.org/design/conserve_water.php, accessed October 2, 2011.
9. Forest Stewardship Council (FSC), "FSC by the Numbers," www.fscus.org/news/, from September 2011 Newsletter.
10. U.S. Green Building Council (USGBC), 2010, "Intro—What LEED Is," www.usgbc.org/DisplayPage.aspx?CMSPageID=1988, accessed February 2, 2012.
11. Provided via email from the U.S. Green Building Council on February 3, 2012.
12. United Nations Environment Programme, "GHG Indicator," www.unep.fr/energy/information/tools/ghg/, accessed November 3, 2010.
13. 7group and Bill Reed, *The Integrative Design Guide to Green Building: Redefining the Practice of Sustainability (Sustainable Design),* Hoboken, New Jersey: John Wiley & Sons, Inc., 2010, pages 1–9.
14. Ibid, page 35.
15. The Girl Scouts of Greater Atlanta, http://vimeo.com/10895684, accessed October 20, 2011.
16. Senator Joe Lieberman, "Lieberman Urges Confirmation of Martha Johnson," http://lieberman.senate.gov/index.cfm/news-events/news/2010/2/lieberman-urges-confirmation-of-martha-johnson, accessed October 2, 2011.

3 Green Building Education

If you want one year of prosperity, plant corn.
If you want ten years of prosperity, plant trees.
If you want one hundred years of prosperity, educate people.

—CHINESE PROVERB

IN MANY CAREERS, becoming a professional means following a predetermined path. If you wanted to be a doctor, for example, you would follow a specific set of steps, from taking certain classes in college to attending medical school to completing residency and medical boards. But if becoming a doctor is like taking the interstate from the premed onramp to the licensed medical professional exit, then becoming a green building professional is more akin to choosing from a vast array of back country roads—none of which is a direct route to your final destination, but all of which have different appealing views and compelling stops along the route. Though there can be challenges inherent in facing a less distinct road to success, the ability to forge your own way can make the rewards in the journey much richer.

Importance of Eco-Education

Education is key to creating a next generation of good green professionals. After all, only by learning the importance of sustainability can people discover how to better preserve our environment through smarter decisions, including building design. As the No Child Left Inside organization says, "The nation's future relies on a well-educated public to be wise stewards of the very environment that sustains us, our families and communities, and future generations. It is environmental education which can best help us as individuals make the complex, conceptual connections between economic prosperity, benefits to society, environmental health, and our own well-being. Ultimately, the collective wisdom of our citizens, gained through education, will be the most compelling and most successful strategy for environmental management."[1]

At the same time, getting a good "green" education is not about one class, one teacher, one curriculum, one degree, or even one school. Instead, it is a way of learning critical thinking and problem solving at an environmental level as well as within a social framework. And perhaps most importantly, it is a lifelong learning process that can start in early childhood.

Digital fabricated feature wall installation in the main internal stair at the Society for Neuroscience, Washington, DC. The installation is based on a sketch by Nobel Prize–winning scientist Santiago Ramón y Cajal (LEED CI Gold). Firm: Envision Design. PHOTO: ERIC LAIGNEL

Spanish Education Development Center, a 24,000-square-foot renovation of a 1940s-era Hahn's Shoes warehouse in Petworth, Washington, DC. This project was designed with water-efficient low-flow fixtures, aerators, and sensors that help teach young children concepts of water conservation. Firm: Hickok Cole Architects. PHOTO: B. DEVON PERKINS, AIA, LEED AP

A WELL-CONCEIVED PROCESS

So what is an eco-education? As discussed in Chapter 2, green building takes a holistic approach to design and construction. Only by working in integrated teams to look at the big picture can we achieve truly sustainable buildings that are harmonious with the environment and their surroundings.

David Orr, a renowned expert in the field of environmental studies and the Paul Sears Distinguished Professor of Environmental Studies and Politics and Special Assistant to the President of Oberlin College, writes in his book *Ecological Literacy:*

> Ecological design requires the ability to comprehend patterns that connect, which means looking beyond the boxes we call disciplines to see things in their larger context. Ecological design is the careful meshing of human purposes with the larger patterns and flows of the natural world; it is the careful study of those patterns and flows to inform human purposes. Competence in ecological design requires spreading ecological intelligence—knowledge about how nature works— throughout the curriculum. It means teaching students the basics of what they will need to know in order to stretch their horizons, to create a civilization that runs on sunlight; uses energy and materials with great efficiency; preserves biotic diversity, soils and forests; develops sustainable local and regional economies; and restores the damage inflicted on the earth throughout the industrial era.[2]

In other words, to learn and maintain a holistic view of green building, it is necessary to take an interdisciplinary approach to education, and not just focus efforts in one field.

The Environmental Protection Agency (EPA) provides a succinct outline of the components of an eco-education, as follows:

- Awareness and sensitivity to the environment and environmental challenges
- Knowledge and understanding of the environment and environmental challenges
- Attitudes of concern for the environment and motivation to improve or maintain environmental quality
- Skills to identify and help resolve environmental challenges
- Participation in activities that lead to the resolution of environmental challenges[3]

Higher Education

Since there is no one right way to become a green building professional, there is a plethora of choices and possible educational paths for anyone considering a career in sustainability. Thus, when you are contemplating higher education, there are two main ways to approach a college career. Either you can choose to enter a university with a focus on environmental education—as a broad multidisciplinary major or within a particular field (such as architecture or interior design)—or you may instead want to take a broader look at college and take a wide variety of classes with no particular regard to green building, and then hone your eco-savvy skills after graduation. There is no right answer of which path to choose, it is simply a matter of choice and available options.

DO YOU NEED AN "ENVIRONMENTAL" DEGREE?

The response to this question is twofold: "not necessarily" and "it depends." "Not necessarily" because there are many professionals currently working in the field who are self-taught by hands-on training. Twenty years ago, a student would have been hard-pressed to find a green building degree; few people taught energy efficiency and eco-literacy as part of the core curriculum.

"It depends" because, as with any career, the more specialized the practice, the more specific the education. For example, you can become a general practitioner of medicine, or concentrate your focus on fields such as neurosurgery or orthopedics, which requires specific classes on those topics. Therefore, if you have a key area of interest within the green building field, consider a focused environmental degree with the targeted classes that lead to your goal.

The following section will cover the myriad of options available to those pursuing a green building career, whether it be for a green building college degree, or a less formalized educational option. Regardless of the specific path chosen, everyone is in a perpetual process of learning, and the qualities of a successful green building "student" are universal.

Classroom at Paideia School (LEED NC Gold). Firm: Perkins + Will. PHOTO: DAN GRILLET

Academic Center at Georgia Gwinnett College, Lawrenceville, GA. Photocells in the building's interior spaces allow for up to two-thirds of the lights to be automatically shut off when the light level is adequately maintained through natural lighting. Firm: John Portman & Associates. PHOTO: MICHAEL PORTMAN

What are a few key characteristics/skills of a successful green building student?

 Environmental thinking: Ability to raise clear and precise questions, use abstract ideas to interpret information, consider diverse points of view, reach well-reasoned conclusions, and test alternative outcomes against relevant criteria and standards.

Investigative skills: Ability to gather, assess, record, apply, and comparatively evaluate relevant information within design and environmental coursework and design processes.

Ordering systems skills: Understanding of the fundamentals of both natural and constructed ordering systems and the capacity of each to inform design.

Applied research: Understanding the role of applied research in determining function, form, and systems and their impact on the environment, human conditions, and behavior.

Collaboration: Ability to work in collaboration with others and in multidisciplinary teams to successfully complete projects.

Human behavior: Understanding the relationship between human behavior, the natural environment, and the design of the built environment.

Sheri Schumacher, LEED AP, School of Architecture, Auburn University

〉 Creative, intelligent, team player, energetic, open-minded, persistent, organized

R. Alfred (Alfie) Vick, ASLA, LEED AP, associate professor, College of Environment & Design, University of Georgia

〉 Be open-minded. There are many perspectives and voices to be heeded when pursuing green building. It's not just about a building.

Be eager minded. There is a world of information to learn, and you should pursue it. Be judicious in what you consume, but be eager about acquiring knowledge.

Be community minded. Green buildings are successful because many people willingly share their time and expertise with one another to achieve a common goal of success. Green buildings are also successful because they are about more than simply the people that own them or inhabit them.

M. Shane Totten, AIA, IIDA, LEED AP BD+C, professor of interior design at Savannah College of Art + Design/CEO of OffGrid Studio

As befits green building, in which fields of study overlap and the importance of a holistic approach cannot be overstated, the qualities of good green building students reach across all disciplines. Select a field of study that focuses on your particular talents, interests, and long-term goals, then consider whether a formal eco-degree path feels appropriate or whether you would prefer to pursue your sustainability training after college.

BUILDING OR GREEN DEGREE?

For college students who know they want to become green building professionals, there are two routes to consider:

A building field degree

or

A focused environmental degree

Either of these routes may include coursework in sustainability, and it is certainly possible to incorporate green building ideas into the building degree path. Likewise, it is just as easy to include courses in architecture, design, and the other building professions into a focused environmental degree. Both paths also offer a variety of options for blending the two routes with areas of specialization, dual degrees, graduate degrees, and a number of other programs.

There are a variety of viewpoints on which path is better, although ultimately, there is no correct answer, and each student must decide which option suits him or her best.

> *Which approach would you recommend to a new college student wanting to embark on a green building career: a broader degree (liberal arts, business, engineering) with some environmental classes mixed in, or a specific environmental degree? Any specific courses that might help on this path?*

❯ My personal experience tells me that a degree in a particular field, with more of a specialization or focus on sustainability, is the smarter choice. I find that as a sustainability generalist you have less credibility than an engineer or an architect who focuses their work on sustainable design concepts and implementation. No matter what, take some business courses and overlay the rules/concepts/laws of sustainability on what you learn.

Susie Spivey-Tilson, LEED AP BD+C, director of sustainable design, tvsdesign

❯ I would recommend students pursue a broader degree so they are exposed to a variety of topics. Specialization can always come later in their undergraduate or graduate career. A broader degree may give students a better context for understanding green building.

Consider those courses that incorporate hands-on projects and focus on current issues facing the world. Learn about how policy, action, and the depleting natural resources in one area can have an impact on the rest of the world. Through education and policies courses, I learned about advocacy and community education, both critical components of advancing green building.

Meghan Fay Zahniser, LEED AP, STARS program manager, Association for the Advancement of Sustainability in Higher Education (AASHE)

❯ Although one may think an environmental degree would provide a student with the specifics in a green building career, I would still suggest getting a broader degree, such as engineering, architecture, interior design, etc., and mixing in a few environmental classes. A green building career is still part of the building industry, in which the coursework of the broader degrees is not able to be replaced. Think of the green building profession as a lawyer or doctor may—obtain your undergraduate degree with your general base focus, and then continue your specialty through additional courses with a minor or even a graduate degree.

In terms of coursework: interior space planning, building design & details, energy usage and lighting, and learning Building Information Modeling (BIM) are just a few of the basics I am glad to have been trained on in college. On large green building projects a consultant may be on the project team; however, for small commercial interior projects, often this scope is performed as design build. In this case, the architectural team needs to know enough to begin the project process through design development, if not construction documents, until a contractor has been brought onto the project team.

Megan Ellen Little, CID, IIDA, LEED AP ID+C, interior project designer, Perkins + Will

Degree Option 1: Building Profession

The discussion on Option 1 will be organized in the context of the higher educational system's sequence in the United States, as follows:

Undergraduate/bachelor's degree (most often bachelor of arts, BA, or bachelor of science, BS, since most standard academic programs are based on the four-year plan)

Master's degree (most often master of arts, MA, or master of science, MS; either of these programs might be as much as three years in length)

PhD, or doctor of philosophy, which typically includes additional coursework and research and culminates in "comprehensive" examinations in one or more fields and then a written dissertation for the doctorate, and can typically take four years or more to complete

From undergraduate up to PhD, within all of the varying levels of college degrees, an increase in sustainable or environmental curriculum is on the rise. Christoph

University of the Pacific: The Lair (pub) (LEED NC Silver). Firm: Gensler. PHOTO: SHERMAN TAKATA

Reinhart, associate professor of architectural technology at Harvard's Graduate School of Design, noted that the school's decision to start offering a concentration in sustainable design was driven by both interest from students and changes in the field. "Over the past few years, there has been an increased interest and pressure to provide this knowledge in more depth, whereas before, maybe a class would have been sufficient," he says. "Now there's an expectation that more of these skills are being learned."[4]

UNDERGRADUATE/BACHELOR'S DEGREE

The following section outlines and evaluates each building role and how "green" plays a part in that particular discipline's education. When designing and constructing a building, every team member plays a different but equally vital role in creating optimum green aspects to every structure. The core team members typically involved in the design and construction of commercial green building projects include but, are not limited to: architect, interior designer, landscape architect, various engineers, and contractor. From a city or neighborhood planning perspective, the urban planner also plays a role. At some colleges, sustainability coursework is available across all disciplines and is well integrated into the curriculum. For example, Georgia Institute of Technology offers over 260 courses in sustainability across all colleges with a goal of each student taking at least one.[5] At other schools, you might need to dig a little deeper into course catalogs to find good green classes, or talk to professors about searching out the best eco-offerings in your chosen field of study. It is also important to keep in mind that for each of these specialized fields, a traditional degree can be supplemented with additional coursework, an integrated degree, or a dual degree.

SPECIFIC BUILDING PROGRAMS

The following is a typical listing of building-related majors and programs in which environmental education can be integrated to varying degrees. While degrees related to buildings are the common theme, there are two main types. First, there are programs related to the design and construction of buildings. Next, there are those degrees focused on buildings once they are operational, under the non-design and construction degree programs—focused on work such as leasing and maintaining buildings.

DESIGN AND CONSTRUCTION

- Architecture
- Building science (construction)
- Civil engineering
- Engineering (mechanical/electrical/plumbing)
- Interior design
- Landscape architecture
- Structural engineering
- Urban planning

NON-DESIGN AND CONSTRUCTION

- Real estate
- Facilities management

Any of the roles to be discussed could be filled by someone with a bachelor's or master's degree, and up to a PhD. Within each of the specific building programs, the following information will be relayed:

- What the profession does
- Related environmental classes
- Associated resources (in Appendix)

DESIGN & CONSTRUCTION ROLES

Architecture

Designing and supervising the construction of buildings is the role of the architect. Beyond the traditional architectural degree, green building design incorporates site selection, building orientation, selection of building materials to optimize energy/water efficiency, and selection of materials with low life-cycle impact. A sustainable architect will also facilitate the green goals of all of the other team members, so the green architect should also have a general knowledge of the potential strategies and technologies needed to achieve optimum environmental solutions for civil, landscape, mechanical, and plumbing issues, and other aspects of the building. Anyone wishing to pursue this path should look for class titles and descriptions in the course catalog that emphasize urban design, sustainable architectural design, and resource (energy/water) efficiency, and that explore the health, productivity, and quality of building environments.

Building Science or Construction Management

Degrees in building science or construction management prepare future contractors to one day create a building and manage the overall construction process, including the building site. The contractor uses the design as a guide on how to purchase materials, estimate costs, install systems, and construct the building. This role is critical to the reality of a building being green. Coursework to consider includes building envelope, environmental systems and science, sustainable site work, and environmental materials.

General Engineering

The various fields of engineering—structural, civil, mechanical, electrical, or plumbing specialties—all involve "systems thinking." Engineering applies a practical technical overlay to the design of buildings, systems, and processes. All of the following disciplines are green building professions that focus on different parts of the building or site.

New Zealand team members work to assemble their First Lighthouse at West Potomac Park. PHOTO: CAROL ANNA/ U.S. DEPARTMENT OF ENERGY SOLAR DECATHLON

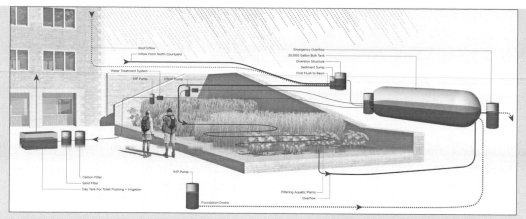

Yale University Kroon Hall School of Forestry and Environmental Sciences (LEED NC Platinum). Firm: Hopkins Architects and Centerbrook. IMAGE: © OLIN

Civil Engineering

Focus on site conditions, infrastructure (roads, access to water), potential hazards, and water issues in relation to buildings and structures (such as bridges, roads, and dams) is the expertise of the civil engineer. For example, with green buildings, they may coordinate how to clean up a contaminated brownfield site and propose solutions for stormwater management in terms of both the quantity and quality of water leaving a site—too much water can overwhelm local sewer systems, causing pollutants to drain into rivers and lakes and increasing soil erosion. Civil engineers factor all these issues into their building evaluations. Look for coursework that includes terms such as industrial ecology, environmental impact assessment, hazardous substance engineering, hydrology, and pollution reduction.

MEP Engineering

Three fields of engineering that are typically integrated and closely associated are commonly referred to as MEP engineering. This term combines mechanical, electrical, and plumbing engineering, all of which are concentrated on the major building systems. Post-college, professionals in each of these disciplines often work together in the same company, but will typically be assigned to different areas of the project, since each of their specialties has a specific focus. The following sections give more detail on each of these specialties:

Mechanical Engineering

The mechanical engineer is primarily responsible for the energy supply and distribution for buildings, which in large part powers the heating and cooling systems. Since buildings use huge amounts of energy, consuming nearly 50 percent of the energy in the United States, this field has a significant role to play in terms of environmental impact. With this path, there are a number of course options that would lead to an emphasis on sustainable design within the degree, including renewable energy (solar and wind), energy systems analysis and design, life-cycle science, carbon management process, and environmentally conscious manufacturing.

Electrical Engineering

The study of electricity and its various applications via circuits, wiring, and telecommunications design is the role of the electrical engineer. In some cases, this might include the electrical lighting for a building and its immediate site surroundings. Lighting is another large energy draw, accounting for up to 35 percent of energy usage in most commercial buildings.

This massive energy output needed to illuminate a space also heats up the building, creating increased needs for cooling systems—another energy draw. A sustainable eye to more efficient electrical solutions, then, has a great impact on the building itself as well as the overall environment. Coursework green options might include terms such as power electronics and controls, energy systems, high-performance sustainable design, and efficient eco-lighting.

Plumbing Engineering

Plumbing engineers design the connection of water systems and indoor water fixtures that the building inhabitants utilize, including sinks, faucets, and showerheads. This field is becoming increasingly important and therefore desirable, as global water resources dwindle and population increases. Classes to consider in this field could be in water efficiency topics, rainwater technology, and solar hot water heating.

Interior Design

Sculpting the shape of the interior of a building is the interior designer's role, for the spaces where people live, work, and play. Everyone who enters a building is impacted by the choices of an interior designer, from the lighting options to seating choices to flooring materials. Because of this, interior designers play a large part in safeguarding the interior air quality and evaluating materials and furniture, looking at such factors as where and how things are made, whether products off-gas, and the longevity and reuse potential of different items. Interior designers also often play a role in the tenant's selection of a base building, helping find locations in close proximity to public transportation and within a connected community. For this path, look for classes that emphasize ecology, sustainable design, material products and use, and energy-efficient lighting.

2101 L Street NW (LEED CI Platinum). Firm: RTKL.
PHOTO: ©RTKL.COM/ANNE CHAN

Landscape Architecture

Connecting a building to its natural surroundings is the role of the landscape architect. For a green specialist in this field, that would include specifying native trees and plant material that require little to no additional irrigation. Sustainable landscape architects might take other Earth-friendly factors into account. They plant shade trees to deflect heat gain on rooftops or sidewalks, helping to keep temperatures cooler, or they might specify porous or light-colored exterior hardscape materials such as walkway materials or planters, which could also help reduce heat gain and decrease water runoff. Landscape architects are also focused on the interaction between the site and how water interacts with the building, foliage, and surrounding waterways. Courses in this field that emphasize sustainability would include ideas such as applied landscape ecology, environmental analysis, xeriscaping, vegetated roofing, and site planning/preservation.

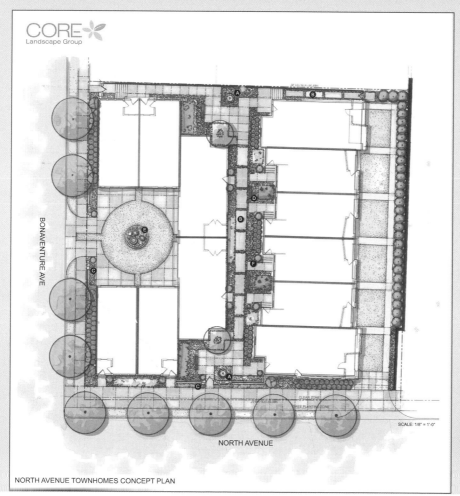

Illustrative site plan. FIRM AND IMAGE: CORE LANDSCAPE GROUP, INC.

NORTH AVENUE TOWNHOMES CONCEPT PLAN

Urban Planning

Urban planners create both short- and long-term plans for all types of communities (rural, suburban, and urban) and for the use of land. They provide a broad vision of how cities and neighborhoods may be organized and built, taking into account the infrastructure (roads, water, energy, transportation) in conjunction with the commercial and residential areas, in order to maximize interrelationships between all of the parts. Green urban planners may go one step further, considering the ecological impact of buildings and land use, for example, or helping with preservation of wetlands, advocating forest conservation, and addressing local pollution issues. Classes to consider are, for example, sustainable urban development and regional planning, community planning, and a combined course in sustainability, smart growth, and landscape architecture.

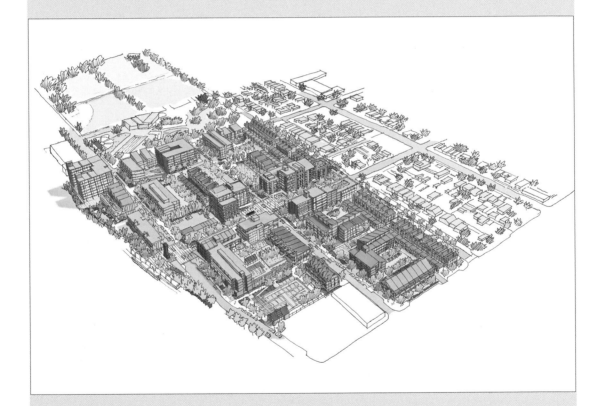

The vision for the Denver Housing Authority South Lincoln project emphasized economic development and public health connections with the built environment. South Lincoln Redevelopment Master Plan, Denver, Colorado. (Masterplan establishes a goal of LEED ND, NC and Green Communities rating of at least Silver for each component of development.) FIRM AND IMAGE: MITHUN

NON-DESIGN & CONSTRUCTION ROLES

Real Estate

The field of real estate is broader, with several subsets. Some of careers under the broader real estate umbrella include the following:

- Real estate developers (those who purchase land/buildings)
- Real estate brokers (those who facilitate the interactions between building owners and tenants, including leases)
- Real estate property management (those who manage properties, perhaps with multiple tenants)

There are a few paths of education for entry into the real estate field. Some popular degree options include: real estate, business, economics, finance, or marketing. Courses to consider would be sustainable real estate and lease management, environmental law, and sustainability and green leases.

Facility Manager

Operations, maintenance, and care of commercial buildings, from hospitals to hotels to convention centers, are the responsibility of the facility manager. According to the International Facility Management Association (IFMA), it is "a profession that encompasses multiple disciplines to ensure functionality of the built environment by integrating people, place, processes and technology."[6] Facility managers take care of all the building systems once the building is complete, from fire alarm systems to security access to waste management and car parking. Green courses include energy management and green maintenance.

How are facility managers or end users unique from the other traditional design and construction professionals (architect, contractor, etc.)?

❯ They deal with reality…the constant work of having to make the building work at its best no matter what the weather is like or what is going on in the building. Architects deal in "dreams" ("We'd love to have the building looking like 'this,' and hopefully this is how much energy it will consume.")…well, they have no idea how much it will *actually* consume until it's up and running

Barry Giles, LEED AP O+M, CEO, BuildingWise LLC

❯ A facility manager is unique because we maintain, monitor, and oversee the daily operations of the built environment that has been created. The architects and designers complete the project and then move on to another assignment.

Sheila M. Sheridan, IFMA Fellow, CFM, LEED AP O+M, president, Sheridan Associates

MASTER'S DEGREE

Many people seek master's degrees to distinguish themselves for career advancement, and to expand their knowledge base and, possibly, obtain a higher salary. Others seek master's degrees to change career fields. For example, perhaps you have earned a bachelor's degree in architecture, but have decided that you want to become a sustainability consultant: a master's degree in business sustainability would be eminently helpful. A master's degree will allow you to develop expertise in a new area and enter a new career.

Footprint Talent, an Atlanta-based corporate social responsibility recruitment firm, and WAP Sustainability, a sustainability consulting firm, conducted a survey titled "The State of The CSO (Chief Sustainability Officer): An Evolving Profile," for which they polled 254 CEOs, HR chiefs, chief operating officers, and CSOs to determine what exactly organizations want to see in a chief sustainability officer. Declaring that "the MBA is the gold standard for sustainability chiefs, with engineering, science and communications all coming in second," the report also noted that some areas could be combined as master's degrees to further exemplify a "green" focus, such as architecture and urban planning, urban planning and business sustainability, and architecture and engineering.[7]

MBA (MASTERS OF BUSINESS ADMINISTRATION)

Bainbridge Graduate Institute
www.bgi.edu/

Presidio Graduate School
www.presidioedu.org/

University of California Berkeley
http://berkeley.edu/

Note: This list is not all-inclusive and should be considered abbreviated.

PhD, OR DOCTOR OF PHILOSOPHY

Derived from the Greek meaning "love of wisdom," the PhD is just that: a degree that delves deeply into one subject area and lets students truly explore the intellectual and real-world ramifications of a particular project or idea. One of the higher levels of graduate education, the PhD requires diligence and a commitment to the academic pursuit. The requirements for this degree vary widely from discipline to discipline, but what does remain constant in all subject areas is a number of hours, years, coursework, and research as prescribed by each particular department and university. Typically, a doctorate concludes with a dissertation or thesis paper that is original academic work, presented before (and often evaluated by) a panel of peers and academic advisors/professors. This degree is helpful if a student wants to teach at the college level, pursue advanced research projects, or further environmental knowledge at a more specialized level in the green building field.

Why consider a PhD?

❭ To help affect real change—and to further explore how corporate mindsets switched from "didn't have a clue" to eco-innovators—Amodeo decided get a PhD in "Organization Development and Change" (a people-focused subset of management) at Benedictine University. In the course of her studies, she discovered a carpet company based in LaGrange, Georgia, called InterfaceFLOR, whose founder, Ray Anderson, had an "aha!" corporate moment. His epiphany came in 1994 after reading Paul Hawken's book, *Ecology of Commerce,* and he changed the course he set for the company to a green one. Amodeo decided to do her dissertation on this company's change process and to present her findings in both written and documentary film form.

Through interviews with long-time staff, who had seen the company both before and after Anderson's corporate thought shift, she found the work force had a new sense of purpose and a broader sense of corporate responsibility after the company became sustainable. Amodeo found that the organization had formalized its sustainable credo in a seven-step plan to achieve zero waste by 2020, and that it had stayed the green course even after running through a rough financial patch—to the eventual benefit of the bottom line. As a result, Amodeo was able to thoroughly investigate how and why businesses change their ways and become good green members of society. Taking the lessons she learned from her dissertation findings, she created a consulting firm, idgroup, which helps other companies make similar sustainable changes to their processes and culture.

Mona Amodeo, PhD, president and founder, idgroup Consulting & Creative

Sundae Splurge

LINDSAY BAKER, MS ARCH, LEED AP

PhD Student & Graduate Student Instructor, Department of Architecture

Center for the Built Environment, University of California, Berkeley

Please discuss your path on the "green brick road"—from nonprofits to your PhD. What influencers contributed to each of these milestones?

My "green brick road" really started in high school! I took an AP Environmental Studies course, where we learned about the basic concept of energy efficiency in buildings, and it really stuck with me. So I was very fortunate to find myself at the Southface Energy Institute the summer after I graduated from high school. Southface is a great model of a locally based nonprofit that has done a great job of staying attentive to local issues in Atlanta and the Southeast, while embracing the larger movement nationally.

I took that approach in summer internships throughout college as well. I worked for a city planning agency in Chattanooga, a very progressive city, and learned that I wasn't cut out for government agencies! I also worked for an architecture office, and learned that I probably didn't have the patience (or creativity!) to be an architect. But I'm glad that I tried those out first—because it's easy to see the greener grass in another person's situation once you're locked into a job after school.

So, by the time I finished college, I had a good understanding of the building industry and its growing sustainability movement. I applied for a job at USGBC, working with the LEED department, and it turned out to be a great fit for me, and for USGBC at that time. The wonderful thing about working in a place like USGBC is that you are exposed to so many amazing people working in the green building industry. Policy makers, architects, energy modelers, researchers, nonprofit advocates, product manufacturers—they are all in meetings with you.

I'll share just one more thing that I think is relevant for those pursuing a career in green building, which is the importance of collaboration in this field. If you like working alone, this might not be the field for you! Integrated design requires a high level of well-orchestrated collaboration, in which professionals must learn to speak a common language. Compromise is common, as are long meetings. Honestly, sometimes I think my greatest strengths in this work are just patience and the ability to help others communicate. Without those, my technical knowledge would be basically useless!

But, that said, I did leave USGBC to pursue a graduate degree, because I personally wanted to have more technical expertise in the area of building performance. I think the younger generation needs to be ramping up our capabilities as energy modelers, commissioning agents, energy auditors, HVAC engineers, architects, wastewater treatment system designers, city planners, controls designers, and building scientists. These fields all need young people, and they promise steady and increasing work in the coming decades.

USGBC Headquarters: Kitchen. Washington, DC. Completed 2009 (LEED CI Platinum). Firm: Envision Design, PLLC. PHOTO: ERIC LAIGNEL

Why did you choose the university and PhD program in which you are currently enrolled?

There are a handful of great programs around the country, but it is still a bit of a word-of-mouth system to find out about them, and what they specialize in. Especially given that more and more schools are starting new sustainable design programs every year. By the time I went back to school, I knew that I wanted to focus on post-occupancy evaluation as a method for better understanding our successes and failures in high-performance design. UC Berkeley has a long-standing tradition of that type of research, so it was a front-runner for me. Berkeley also has a great environment for interdisciplinary research, which is important in our field. Even though life-cycle analysis isn't my thing, for example, I love being on a campus where others are working on it, and we can keep in touch.

I also definitely would advise anyone thinking about a master's degree to look for people that you want to work with, who are doing similar work, who ask similar questions, who you get along with.

It was also really heartwarming to have support from a lot of people at USGBC during that time. When I got into Berkeley, Rick Fedrizzi happened to be out here for a meeting, and when I told him I would have the option of staying on for a PhD, he said, "Ooh, get a PhD!" He said it in this way that sounded like he was saying, "Ooh, let's splurge and get a sundae instead of a cone." I'm not sure that's the best metaphor for the difference between getting a master's degree and a PhD, but I do think it reflected the fact that PhDs are relatively uncommon in this industry.

Getting a PhD is usually a commitment to either lifelong scientific research or university-level teaching, both of which are great careers that are needed in our field right now. Teaching building science in architecture schools is especially needed, as the standards for architects continue to progress toward requiring more knowledge in this area. However, I decided to get a PhD for a more general reason; I want to bring a scientific approach to measuring the performance of buildings, to help the green building industry develop standard practices for assessing our success. My plan is to go back into the professional world, working on policies, codes, and changing practice.

A portion of your PhD dissertation discusses occupant behavior and its impacts on building performance. Why did you choose this topic? How much research has been done in the field of occupant behavior, and what do you forecast for the future in this field?

It's a newer interest, really, for the design profession, as we come to realize that it will be difficult to reach our energy targets without considering the aspects of building energy use that are controlled by occupants. I got excited about this field because it's been widely accepted that while we already have all the technology we need to radically reduce energy consumption in buildings, the problem is implementing these technologies. A big part of that is buy-in and participation of building occupants in our energy-saving schemes. It's a huge challenge to try and deal with the world of behavior change, but design is capable of great things, and ultimately we will likely need to change our behavior at least a little, if we want to keep this planet intact. My hope is for a future where people and buildings can interact actively and synergistically, in a way that optimizes energy consumption and well-being.

Degree Option 2: Specialized Environmental

Perhaps you have decided that a more "green" or environmentally focused degree is a better fit for you than a building-focused degree. When this is the case, there are a wide variety of specific environmental fields of study.

SPECIFIC ENVIRONMENTAL PROGRAMS

The following is a list of typical building-related majors and programs where environmental education is a key component:

Environmental design	Environmental engineering
Design and environmental analysis	Human ecology
Environmental architecture	Natural resource management
Environmental/ecological design	Sustainable design/development

Where are good places to find specific environmental programs?

❯ This course of study requires a high tolerance for ambiguity. Some will tell you if there isn't a Nobel award in it, it isn't a real field—but sustainability is the field that will determine whether humankind survives, so you'd best hope that universities can figure a way to make it an academic discipline. And increasingly, there are plenty of universities that focus on sustainability. Arizona State University gives a PhD in the field. I teach at Bainbridge Graduate Institute, which offers an MBA in sustainability. I'm also helping create a whole new MBA in sustainable management at Bard College in New York City.

These are great, but we need solutions at the speed of the Web. A group of us is trying to revolutionize how we approach education in sustainability. Today's students are going tens of thousands of dollars into debt to be educated in last century's worldview. To solve this, we're starting up the Madrone Project, which will provide students with short, curated, beautifully produced video micro-classes on sustainability. In the best-case scenario, you could aggregate these micro-classes to get a degree—and we're in conversations with several colleges that are interested in doing this—but even if not, you can download the content from world leaders in sustainability on your tablet and give yourself a world-class education. The goal is to take sustainability global and make it affordable.

L. Hunter Lovins, president and founder, Natural Capitalism Solutions

WEBSITE RESOURCES FOR GREEN DEGREE OPTIONS

Leading sites for a comprehensive listing of degrees in the green building realm:

www.enviroeducation.com/

www.builditgreen.org/degree-programs-semester-classes/

www.ulsf.org/resources_campus_sites.htm

http://intelicus.com/green-mba/

https://stars.aashe.org/institutions/

THREE APPROACHES

The following three colleges have well-established environmental programs, so they are given as examples here for the offerings and types of green degrees available. This is by no means a complete list, however; there are many other excellent programs available nationwide.

**Environmental Studies Undergraduate Degree—
Oberlin College, Oberlin, OH**

http://new.oberlin.edu/arts-and-sciences/departments/environment/

The Environmental Studies (ES) Program at Oberlin is an interdisciplinary major (although it can also be taken as a minor) that focuses on the interactions of human beings with nature and the environment. The program gives a solid foundation in natural sciences, the humanities, and social science to help students graduate with the tools and ideals necessary to solve sustainability issues within greater society.

**Minor in Sustainable Design Undergraduate Program—
University of California at Berkeley, Berkeley, CA**

http://laep.ced.berkeley.edu/programs/undergraduate/minors/sustainabledesign

Offered jointly by the Department of Architecture and the Department of Landscape Architecture and Environmental Planning, this undergraduate minor is open to students in all declared majors. The focus is on exploring how sustainable design decisions are made, from smaller scale (homes, buildings) to larger patterns of land use and urban planning. Though coursework focuses on architecture and landscape architecture, this program is interdisciplinary and includes classes from within diverse disciplines from electrical engineering to geology to sociology.

**Building Performance and Diagnostics MS, PhD—
Carnegie Mellon University, Pittsburgh, PA**

www.cmu.edu/architecture/academics/graduate/master.html

The Master's of Science in Building Performance and Diagnostics degree program is a two-year program for professionals in the building industry who want to be at the forefront of advanced building technologies and performance. The program ends with a hands-on project in which newly learned modeling, research, and analytic skills are used. Most that enter for this degree have had some training or professional work in the building field, whether as architects or managers or engineers.

Elevator lobby area at the Recording Industry Association of America, Washington, DC. Firm: Envision Design. PHOTO: ERIC LAIGNEL

MULTIDISCIPLINARY DEGREES

If after reviewing the two routes of a degree in a general building profession or a specialized environmental field, neither feels like the perfect fit, consider the multidisciplinary or interdisciplinary degree option whereby several degrees can be combined into one customized degree. A multidisciplinary degree has an integrated curriculum and is taught by multiple teachers from a variety of fields.

For example, Ball State University in Muncie, IN, has an Interdepartmental Educational Program that offers a cluster of academic minors in environmentally sustainable practices. This allows graduates to complement their major with an environmental minor in one of the following areas: Environmental

Context for Business, Environmental Contexts in Health Care, Environmental Policy, Sustainable Land Systems, and Technology and the Environment. This allows for a broader study of sustainability across the university as well as addressing the integrated nature of sustainability across disciplines.

CHOOSING A COLLEGE

You have determined that you want to become a green building professional, whether as an architect, an engineer, an urban planner, or any of the many other valuable career options. Now that you have decided upon your degree direction, it is time to choose a college. Think about the best fit from a "triple bottom line" (economic/environment/social) perspective—beyond the typical factors of reputation and location, since selecting a green institution can involve more detailed contemplation. As examples of other issues to weigh in your decision when choosing a good green school, you might consider a college's environmental commitment, number of green courses and degrees offered, and eco-volunteer opportunities.

To aid in your selection process, a number of well-regarded resources can help you evaluate schools in terms of their eco-friendly ideals. The following material represents the most respected ratings, reviews, and reports available from the industry. One consideration when consulting these resources is to evaluate if the colleges are members of one or more of the associations listed in the Appendix, and/or if a school occurs in the reviews. Beyond rankings and research, once the choices are narrowed down, nothing can replace a visit to the college.

COLLEGE: RATINGS FOR THE GREEN FACTOR

These are four of the best insider's resources for reviewing the "greenness" of the college under consideration:

- College Sustainability Report Card
- The Princeton Review
- Sierra Club Cool Schools
- STARS

All ratings are indicators of an institution on the green path, and look at the following key areas:

Administration

Climate change & energy

Food & recycling

Green building

Student involvement

Transportation

The two most similar reviews are the College Sustainability Report Card and the Princeton Review, as they are both evaluating approximately 300 institutions and are based on student surveys. In addition to the items on the key areas list, the College Sustainability Report Card evaluates endowment transparency, investment priorities, and shareholder engagement, and the Princeton Review looks at whether or not the campus has a sustainability officer.

Sierra Club's Cool School listing is a bit different in that it receives responses back from the colleges instead of the students. The STARS tool is a voluntary, self-reporting tool that provides ongoing continuous reporting. Review each of these ratings for potential schools and determine which attributes are most important based on personal priorities and other factors. Once the choices are narrowed down, the institutions can be cross-compared with each rating.

College Sustainability Report Card

www.greenreportcard.org

This resource claims to be the only independent evaluation of 300 of the largest endowments in North America. Presented in an easy-to-use format, the College Sustainability Report Card evaluates 300 schools on environmental criteria.

The Princeton Review's Guide to 311 Green Colleges

www.princetonreview.com/green.aspx

Developed in collaboration with the U.S. Green Building Council, this guide was first released in April 2010. This guide highlights everything from levels of campus sustainability to majors in green fields. Released annually as a report, it currently focuses on about 300 colleges based on a survey of their students' feedback. Survey questions are in ten topic areas, and results are compiled for a ranking.

"By many accounts, there are going to be a lot of job opportunities related to the environment and sustainability," says Robert Franek, senior vice president and publisher of "The Princeton Review." "For those who are interested in working in this growing sector, the 'Guide' highlights the schools that are doing an especially good job in preparing and placing the next generation of green professionals."[8]

Sierra Club Cool Schools

www.sierraclub.org/sierra/201009/coolschools/

The Cool Schools list is an annual top twenty green universities list based on eight qualification categories such as energy efficiency, academics, food, transportation, and waste management.

STARS—The Sustainability Tracking, Assessment & Rating System

https://stars.aashe.org/

Developed by the Association for the Advancement of Sustainability in Higher Education (AASHE) as a way for colleges and universities to gauge their own level of sustainability, STARS® is a handy way for prospective students to see how green a campus really is. Institutions submit reports to STARS, providing data on their levels of sustainability in different areas on their campuses, and then each college is ranked either bronze, silver, gold, or platinum, based on their leadership level as a green school. Currently, there are over 1,000 institutions participating in the STARS program.

Easy to reference, data for each school that participates in this program can be accessed online, to find out how and where each school meets the sustainability guidelines. For example, you can find out if a school has integrated sustainability into their curriculum, and if so, how and to what degree. There are detailed explanations of green classes, undergraduate and graduate programs, faculty involved in environmental research, and even extracurricular clubs and programs geared toward eco-literacy. Beyond coursework, colleges also report levels of greenness in terms of operations (energy efficiency, waste management, and even dining services), planning (affordability, human resources, and diversity), and innovation. It is a wonderful resource, and increasing numbers of colleges are choosing to participate and make their reports public since the program's inception in 2010.

COLLEGE GREEN BOOK RESOURCES

Beyond ratings, there have been a few books dedicated to the topic of green colleges. These books evaluate similar criteria to the ratings mentioned in the previous section, but books are often able to go into more depth and give a comprehensive overview for the purpose of making green school choices.

Ecological Design and Building Schools: Green Guide to Educational Opportunities in the United States and Canada, by Sandra Leibowitz Earley

www.newvillagepress.net/book/?GCOI=97660100671680

Making a Difference College Guide

www.green-colleges.com

College: Green Commitment and Campus

One of the common discussion points for college considerations, in both the ratings and the book resources given thus far, is the school's depth of commitment to environmental good. On the path to sustainability there are many "stops" along the way. Perhaps the school you are considering is not listed in any of the ratings or books offered. What other criteria could you consider? The institution may have commitments or campus initiatives or nothing at all—perhaps you could play a leadership role as an early adopter and help be a guide on the path.

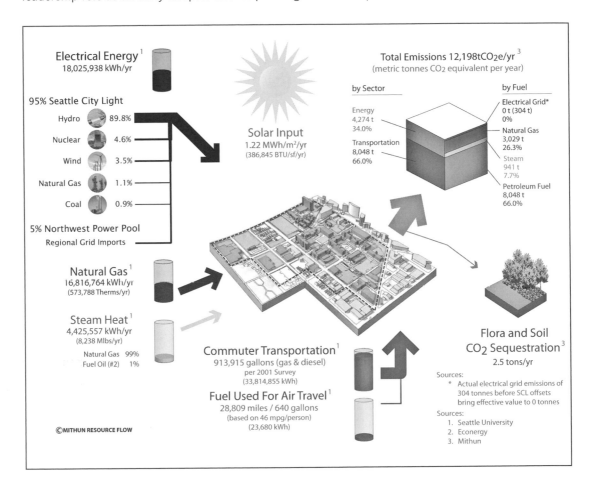

Electrical Energy [1]
18,025,938 kWh/yr

95% Seattle City Light

Hydro   89.8%
Nuclear   4.6%
Wind   3.5%
Natural Gas   1.1%
Coal   0.9%

5% Northwest Power Pool
Regional Grid Imports

Natural Gas [1]
16,816,764 kWh/yr
(573,788 Therms/yr)

Steam Heat [1]
4,425,557 kWh/yr
(8,238 Mlbs/yr)

Natural Gas   99%
Fuel Oil (#2)   1%

Solar Input
1.22 MWh/m²/yr
(386,845 BTU/sf/yr)

Commuter Transportation [1]
913,915 gallons (gas & diesel)
per 2001 Survey
(33,814,855 kWh)

Fuel Used For Air Travel [1]
28,809 miles / 640 gallons
(based on 46 mpg/person)
(23,680 kWh)

©MITHUN RESOURCE FLOW

Total Emissions 12,198tCO2e/yr [3]
(metric tonnes CO_2 equivalent per year)

by Sector

Energy
4,274 t
34.0%

Transportation
8,048 t
66.0%

by Fuel

Electrical Grid*
0 t (304 t)
0%

Natural Gas
3,029 t
26.3%

Steam
941 t
7.7%

Petroleum Fuel
8,048 t
66.0%

Flora and Soil
CO_2 Sequestration [3]
2.5 tons/yr

Sources:
*   Actual electrical grid emissions of
304 tonnes before SCL offsets
bring effective value to 0 tonnes

Sources:
1.   Seattle University
2.   Econergy
3.   Mithun

Seattle University's Sustainable Master Plan targets goals and strategies for energy, water ecological systems and human wellbeing that meet the University's goal of creating a model campus for sustainability. Seattle University, Seattle, Washington. FIRM AND IMAGE: MITHUN

GREEN COMMITMENT

Often when leadership comes from the top down, the entire team will focus on the leader's goals and vision. To this point, approximately 700 higher education institutions in all 50 states, representing about one-third of the total student population in colleges and universities, have committed to the American College & University Presidents' Climate Commitment.[9]

American College & University Presidents' Climate Commitment

www.presidentsclimatecommitment.org/

The American College & University Presidents' Climate Commitment is a plan in which institutions of higher learning pledge to a series of environmental goals to neutralize greenhouse gas emissions and accelerate the research and educational efforts of colleges and universities toward helping reverse the effects of climate change. The organization provides a framework of ideals and support, within which schools pledge such goals as taking immediate action to reduce greenhouse gas emissions on campus, including green courses and degrees in the general curriculum, creating a plan to become climate neutral, and perhaps most importantly, making their efforts and findings public. With these goals, it is anticipated that approximately 66 percent of participating schools will reach campus climate neutrality on or before the year 2050.[10]

National Council for Science and the Environment

www.ncseonline.org/program/Council-of-Environmental-Deans-%2526-Directors

GREEN CAMPUS

If you are interested in becoming a green building professional, you may want to gain your education surrounded by the inspiration of green buildings. This means learning will come not only from the classes but also from the classrooms and campus grounds. There are two key guides that support greening a campus. These guides can be utilized if the school is already engaged in green or just considering it.

Campus Green Builder

www.campusgreenbuilder.org/

USGBC Green Campus Campaign

www.usgbc.org/DisplayPage.aspx?CMSPageID=1904

Be Unique (EP)

MARC COSTA, LEED AP BD+C,CGBP

Environmental Technology Programs

Long Beach City College

What made you choose green building as a career (or volunteer)?

I had been working on the supply side of the building industry for four years by 2006 and had heard a little buzz about green building.

Then my uncle sent me a LEED v2 Reference Guide and told me bluntly that I would be a fool for not getting my LEED AP if I were to stay in the industry. At first I wasn't sold on the process and benefits that I was reading. After connecting the intent, process, and impact of the LEED rating system to principles of economic efficiency, the sustainability movement made sense on too many levels not to pursue further. Looking back at studying management science (a lot of economics, public policy, strategy, game theory, etc.) at University of California, San Diego, it was one of those times that paying attention in class paid off in the real world.

Soon after, a friend of a friend put me in touch with a senior estimator at a leading green construction company for an informal interview. I learned two things at that time: 1. I didn't know anything about construction or green building. 2. Be unique, stand out, and go above and beyond all expectations. It has seemed to be paying off so far.

Share a green building story.

Well, one of my "ah-ha!" moments came when I was taking a sustainability-training course that was specific to residential contractors. At the time, I wasn't exposed to many green building approaches or rating systems, besides what I already knew. Especially in California, we are really progressive when it comes to green building; however, Northern California is where a lot of organizations are head-quartered when it comes to nonprofits in our industry. It was an eye-opener for me to be exposed to the number of similar organizations that did not have a Southern California presence with similar, yet different approaches to sustainability across market sectors. The circles of influence across the green building community were apparently larger than most people starting out in the industry realize.

How have your professional and volunteer experiences coincided to benefit and enrich your career and personal life?

My first green internship was because of a USGBC committee involvement. From there my first green job came from the same committee. On the professional side of things, I think that being plugged into the USGBC community has allowed our programs at work to see success they would otherwise not have seen. When we need to forge partnerships for new programs, or get ideas for growing existing programs, there is rarely a time when there is not a person that comes to mind that we have met through USGBC. Working at LBCC in the Environmental Technology Programs under the Economic and Workforce Development Department, we deliver the Clean Energy Workforce Training Program—the nation's largest green jobs training program. We offer LEED Green Associate Training—so work and volunteering worlds have collided. We also host USGBC educational events on our campus that give our participants the opportunity to network and in most cases find jobs.

USGBC GREEN CAMPUS CAMPAIGN TOOLS

USGBC Green Campus Campaign resources and tools available for free download:

Roadmap to a Green Campus

www.centerforgreenschools.org/campus-roadmap.aspx

Hands On LEED: Guiding College Student Engagement

www.centerforgreenschools.org

GREEN COMPETITIONS

Competitions are a great forum for a short-term dip into the green building practice. They are also an opportunity for collaboration with like-minded individuals. Competitions also can create visibility, access to environmental organizations, and potentially awards! Several competitions are available from middle school up to higher education. One of the most widely publicized and respected national college competitions is the Solar Decathlon.

Among the most serious environmental issues the United States faces today, energy consumption is paramount. Residential home energy usage comprises approximately 21 percent of energy used in the U.S. annually.[11] The Solar Decathlon Competition is part of the U.S. Department of Energy's efforts to solve this mounting national issue. Begun in 2002 and held every other year from 2005 to 2011, the Decathlon invites student teams from twenty colleges across the country to design, build, and operate solar-powered sustainable dwellings that are affordable, energy-efficient, and aesthetically appealing.[12] The houses are then displayed and open to the public and hundreds of thousands of people wander in and out of them, giving great visibility to green building and to the talents of the student teams. Students learn how to work collaboratively and across disciplines, get hands-on experience of building sustainable houses, and learn invaluable real-world lessons in the evaluations of their completed designs.

GREEN STUDENT ORGANIZATIONS

From competitions to collaborations, students are coming together to advance the green building initiative. After all, when you are considering a grassroots effort for change, the most powerful group at any college or university is the students. When students come together for green good, the results can be impressive. As just one example, the student-led Connecticut College Renewable Energy Resource Club at Connecticut College held bake sales and a petition drive to lobby to join the Connecticut Energy Cooperative. As a result of their diligence, the group successfully convinced college administrators to purchase about 17 percent of the college's electricity through renewable resources—reducing the emissions of carbon dioxide by 2.3 million pounds each year.[13] For ideas on how to advocate for change, consult the nonprofit organization Second Nature's help-

The University of Maryland's entry, which placed first overall, in the U.S. Department of Energy Solar Decathlon 2011 in Washington, D.C.

The "Liquid Desiccant Waterfall" uses lithium chloride to dehumidify the first-place overall winner of the U.S. Department of Energy Solar Decathlon 2011, University of Maryland's WaterShed house in Washington, DC.

PHOTOS: STEFANO PALTERA/U.S. DEPARTMENT OF ENERGY SOLAR DECATHLON

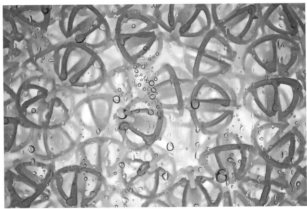

ful free online resource, Students' Guide to Collaboration on Campus, which provides solid ideas, tips, and encouragement.[14]

Other resources abound. In 2011, there were close to 50 U.S. Green Building Council Student Chapters. In addition to access to conferences and a network of like-minded students, the organization offers online toolkits for starting a green building student group on your campus, and helping your campuses become LEED certified. At St. Petersburg College, for example, there is a campus Office for Sustainability (Sustainable SPC) comprising four active Sustainability Clubs and a chapter of USGBC's Emerging Green Builders.[15]

These volunteer clubs are engaged in supporting Earth Day, Campus Clean-ups, Save a Shore events, and sustainability film and lecture series. The Office for Sustainability also supports the college's eco-curriculum, student activities, and focus on energy conservation/carbon reduction.

You can check with the admissions office of whatever college you are considering to see what groups are available there. But do not let absence of such groups be a final deciding factor in choosing a school—you can always start your own group once there!

FUNDING FOR COLLEGE

Once a green design path has been determined, how to pay for it? Scholarship and fellowship (merit-based scholarship) opportunities to support the student's desired course of study are available. The following websites offer a variety of scholarship, fellowship, and grant opportunities.

FELLOWSHIPS AND SCHOLARSHIPS

General

www.enviroeducation.com/financial-aid/
www.epa.gov/ogd/grants/information.htm
www.sustainablemba.org/

Fellowships

www.epa.gov/enviroed/students.html
www.centerforgreenschools.org/fellowship.aspx

Scholarships

www.enviroeducation.com/articles/scholarships/
www.collegescholarships.org/scholarships/engineering/environmental.htm

Post-College Educational Options

Perhaps after reading the previous section on higher education, you have decided that a specialized degree in green building is not for you. Or maybe you have already graduated from college, and now you are deciding that a green building career is the right one for you—but you have no time, nor desire, to complete another educational degree. Never fear, the opportunities for learning abound.

In fact, until recently, it was more common than not for sustainable professionals to practice in their fields without specialized environmental degrees. The author of this book and many of those interviewed in this book became green building professionals after completing their undergraduate degrees. If this path feels best, there are a number of educational options that will help you become a green building professional.

Training Programs

Training is defined here as gaining technical skills that specifically increase one's capability for performance. Education typically focuses on the history, philosophy, and principles of a particular subject—in other words, an academic exploration of a subject. Training, however, focuses on a specific skill set to be gained upon completion of the course of work—in other words, hands-on tools. The focus is usually on gaining additional knowledge or on the path of a career shift. When considering additional education versus training programs, time and cost are also often taken into account; in most cases, an educational degree will cost more and take more time than completion of training programs.

TIME AND RESULTS

Options for either a part-time or full-time training venture exist. It can range from one hour up to several weeks of total time. At the end of the training process, there should be a tangible certificate or credential to add to the resume of experience.

FORMAT AND FORUMS

When determining which training is the most appropriate, you will also consider whether online or live training programs best suit your needs and learning style. Whichever format you choose to follow, look to well-known education resources in the green building community. The training resources listed in this chapter are renowned programs that offer both online and live presentation options. Typically, the curriculum ranges from introductory to intermediate up to advanced. Also, most resources will offer specialized training on specific strategies and technologies such as energy-efficient lighting design or how to provide xeriscaping.

One example of a well-regarded training program is the Everblue program. Their training course Carbon Accounting & Reduction Manager focuses on how companies can best approach the issues of carbon management, regulations, and policies, as well as applicable resources and incentives in a variety of industries. Students are taught greenhouse gas accounting and reduction techniques, and come away from this course with a solid knowledge of the subject.[16]

HOW TO EVALUATE TRAINING PROGRAMS

ASK THESE QUESTIONS WHEN EVALUATING A TRAINING PROGRAM:

- In this training program/mentoring/internship, what are the specific learning objectives?
- Will there be milestones in the process where learning application can be "tested" and adjusted if needed for either party?
- Are references available from people who have completed this program and could be contacted?
- If this experience is successful for both parties, could it be listed as experience on a resume? Is there a certificate or acknowledgment of completion?
- Is the program certified by a reputable organization? For example, the North American Board of Certified Energy Practitioners (NABCEP) is a certifying agency that strives for industry standards and consumer confidence in the solar industry.[17]

GREEN TRAINING RESOURCES

EPA Institute
http://epainstitute.com/index.html

EPA Certification/Environmental Training/Environmental Compliance/Green Building Certification
http://environmentaltrainingonlineepa.org/index.html

Everblue
www.everblue.edu/

Green Building Initiative Training
www.thegbi.org/training/

Green Ideas Environmental Education
http://greenideaseducation.com/about_gie.html

Green Building Services (GBS)
www.greenbuildingservices.com/

RedVector
http://greenbuilding.redvector.com/

Leonardo Academy
www.leonardoacademy.org/

U.S. Green Building Council, E-Learning
www.usgbc.org/DisplayPage.aspx?CMSPageID=2332

HANDS-ON TRAINING PROGRAMS

One of the best ways to know with certainty which of the green building career paths is the right one is to simply get "in the trenches." In addition to more formal training programs that include coursework and academic rigor, there are also programs that, while still educational, are typically more focused on imparting a specific skill set. Boots on the Roof, for example, offers a plethora of training programs specific to the construction of green buildings, such as the Solar PV Bootcamp. Designed for general and electrical contractors, architects, and engineers, this course covers the fundamentals of PV theory and applications, system design and estimation, and hands-on installation of typical residential and commercial rooftop systems in six days of hands-on training.[18]

Another excellent resource, Yestermorrow Design/Build School, offers 150 courses and workshops each year, taught by top architects, designers, and builders in the sustainable field. This school in Warren, Vermont, offers everything from an intense three-week course for a certificate in green building and design (covering topics from prefab to biofuels to urban regeneration, and culminating in a hands-on project and presentation) to one-day workshops about topics from edible forest gardens to insulated concrete forms to solar design.[19]

Students work together on an interior renovation project at Yestermorrow Design/Build School, Waitsfield, VT, 2009.
PHOTO: BARRIE FISCHER

Continuing Education

Different from training, continuing education typically is lifelong adult education focused on short courses designed to bring professionals up to date. Even for accomplished green building professionals, there are always new technologies and strategies being developed and introduced to the industry that are helpful to learn. In order to stay current and on the cutting edge of information, it is a good idea to incorporate continuing education classes into your career. Beyond personal enrichment, some accreditations require continuing education to maintain the credential status. As just two examples of good resources for continuing education, Boston Architectural College has an excellent sustainable design program called The Sustainable Design Institute with a variety of classes to offer,[20] and BuildingGreen hosts a variety of online courses in green building on topics from LEED certification to which windows are most energy efficient.[21]

Perspectives from Educators

The following interviews are from a cross section of educators who teach in a variety of programs in architecture, interior design, landscape architecture, and building science. They each have academic as well as professional experience, and they provide the framework for how to approach a good environmental education, whether that education takes place within a traditional college classroom or not.

The Value of Culture

SHERI SCHUMACHER, LEED AP

School of Architecture

Auburn University

Auburn University Sustainability Initiative Office, student design build project. PHOTO: SHERI SCHUMACHER

Who, or what experience, has been a major influence in your career path?

Indigenous peoples and cultural experiences on a global scale have been a major influence in my career path. The study of other cultures, conducted through social, cultural, and historic lenses, has influenced my thinking about design and contributing to the built environment in a manner that is environmentally, socially, and ethically responsible.

This book focuses on a potential green building career pursuit. How does your curriculum integrate this topic now?

The School of Architecture at Auburn University integrates sustainability, environmental, and ecological issues into most of the existing studio and lecture courses offered within the professional degree curriculum rather than a separate course. This integration is achieved by incorporating LEED, Living Building Challenge, Biomimicry workshops, and other environmental criteria into the studio program requirements and lecture course content. We also include green building professionals in our lecture series, design studio critiques, and as collaborators for studio projects.

There is a significant shift in architectural education toward the integration of systems overall versus the segregation of building parts. For example, walls that heal themselves or walls that have the capacity to be translucent or transparent, eliminating the need for window units. This integrated systems approach encourages a progressive way of thinking that will require new tools, procedures, and technology for certification and measuring green building. The School of Architecture is also incorporating opportunities for students to "craft" their curriculum in accordance with their interests and bridge the discipline boundaries that have historically been limited in higher education.

How do you best prepare students for the "green" work force?

- Encourage the application of sustainable and restorative research to studio projects.
- Provide research, collaboration, and hands-on building opportunities that encourage multidisciplinary collaboration and sustainable building.
- Incorporate new scholarship, research, and practice in the coursework to better enable students to contribute to the further advancement of the discipline.

Intersection of Design and the Real World

LINDA SORRENTO, FASID, IIDA, LEED AP BD+C

Principal Sustainable Practice

Sorrento Consulting, LLC

How does teaching differ from practicing?

Actually, they're the same. It's not that distinct or separate, especially given today's emerging practice of green and quickly changing technologies and policies requiring constant testing and training.

The field of green building is broad, with many specialized professions. How would you recommend that someone new to the field narrow the options?

Explore the profession. Constantly evaluate yourself. Ask, would I be best on a team, working for a large or small firm, supporting the process or leading the vision? Do I like presenting or do I thrive behind the scenes? What's the specialty that fits my personality—corporate, retail, health care, schools, hospitality? And couple these with what's your sustainable legacy?

How do you best prepare students for the "green" workforce? What advice would you give an aspiring green building professional?

Start with a vision and get serious; read, read, read; connect with the experts; and volunteer your time for hands-on experience.

What does faculty say about selecting an educational program specifically geared to green building?

Don't isolate—integrate! Law schools, liberal arts, philosophy, social sciences– across disciplines are embracing the environmental movement—this helps bring the conversation, understanding, and integration of green building principles throughout the campus; and then, ultimately, to everyday life.

Hands-On Experience

BRIAN DUNBAR, LEED AP BD+C

Professor of Construction Management, Sustainable Building Program

Executive Director, Institute for the Built Environment

Colorado State University

Why and how did you decide on where to teach?

I teach at a land-grant institution that values applied research and service to help citizens of our state and nation. Our institute is able to consult on actual green building projects, and faculty gain research or service credit for their project work as well as gaining extremely valuable experiences to share in the classroom.

What degrees do you possess?

Bachelor of science in architecture and master of architecture.

This book focuses on a potential green building career pursuit. How does your curriculum integrate this topic?

Since 1999, we have taught an integrated Sustainable Design and Construction course at Maho Bay, U.S. Virgin Islands, for students in interior design, landscape architecture, engineering, construction management, and other disciplines. In 2001 we created our Sustainable Building graduate program, which has three courses in sustainable building topics, all of which emphasize the importance of integrated design. Furthermore, we have integrated green building into a number of under-graduate courses in construction management and interior design.

The field of green building is broad, with many specialized professions. How would you recommend that someone new to the field narrow the options?

An emerging young professional should participate in sustainable design charrettes, green building tours, and professional association events where various disciplines are gathered to work or learn together. As a young professional participates in these interdisciplinary events, observing the work and focus on all the disciplines and asking good questions will allow for a narrowing of interests.

How do you best prepare students for the "green" work force?

A student must first understand the concept of sustainability and its comprehensive, connected subtopics. Secondly, a student must gain exposure to and knowledge of green building, its processes, related disciplines, and prospects for future development.

What does faculty say about selecting an educational program specifically geared to green building?

A prospective student should analyze whether the program includes emphases in sustainability, communication skills, humanities, and sciences. I would discourage a student from selecting a "training" program for green building that is too narrowly focused on current job skills.

Epiphany on the Preserve

R. ALFRED (ALFIE) VICK, ASLA, LEED AP BD+C

Associate Professor, College of Environment & Design

University of Georgia

Why and how did you decide on which school to attend?

I decided to attend landscape architecture graduate school one autumn afternoon in Chicago when my mom and I were walking along a greenway path through a restored prairie at a park district nature preserve. My mom is a biology professor, and she was pointing out the different species of prairie plants and insects that were buzzing about. We crossed a small footbridge over a creek, and suddenly it dawned on me that this whole thing had been designed by someone—the prairie was restored from an old cornfield, the stream had been stabilized and planted with willows, the path had been thoughtfully laid out and constructed. At the same time, I thought of many of the other old cornfields that, even during my childhood, I watched get converted to sprawling subdivisions and manicured lawns. I knew then and there that I wanted to be the person to protect, restore, and create natural areas in the built environment. I researched graduate schools, narrowed it down by finding places that seemed to have strengths where my interests were, and eventually settled on UGA after visiting it in person.

Who, or what experience, has been a major influence in your career path?

First and foremost, my parents. In addition to the story I recalled before, exploring the outdoors with my mom, my dad was also a big influence. He is a landscape architect and, although it took me a while to decide that was the profession for me, trips to his studio when I was a child and visits to his built projects were major influences. In graduate school, a course with Darrel Morrison, FASLA, called The Plant Communities of the Southeast, solidified my belief that natural landscapes exhibit tremendous functionality and that there are incredible opportunities to protect and restore that functionality to landscapes that are in the context of the built environment. Professionally, I attended a conference back in 1996 or 1997 at which Paul Hawken, Amory Lovins, and Ray Anderson spoke. It was an incredible moment for me to realize that so many of my ideals and values were shared by these visionaries, and that they were making things happen and were successful. As a young professional in Atlanta, I was lucky to have the Southface Energy Institute in town. I began volunteering as often as I could and attended every event they had. There were many other young professionals like me, and we were able to share a lot of ideas and excitement with each other. I remember seeing the first draft of LEED 1.0, and thinking that this was going to be an incredible resource for the design professions.

This book focuses on a potential green building career pursuit. How does your curriculum integrate this topic now?

I teach a course called Issues and Practices in Sustainable Design that is focused solely on green building. I cover green building history and background concepts, go through the technical content of the LEED for New Construction Rating System, and introduce the full scope of green building, including: regional context and neighborhood design, residential construction, sustainable sites, operations and maintenance, economic issues, and the future of green building.

I also integrate green building concepts and strategies into every single course I teach. In my opinion, sustainability is not a distinct subject—it is an overriding imperative in design and construction that impacts every aspect of the curriculum.

What do you forecast for the future on this topic?

I forecast:

- Continuous improvement in our understanding of sustainability and our effectiveness in achieving it;
- Continued shift in the priorities in all students and faculty to hold sustainability as a core measure of a design's effectiveness, along with things like cost, constructability, aesthetics, and functionality;
- Shift in emphasis from sustainability to regenerative design;
- Expansion of the scale that is addressed in green building to look at whole cities and regions.

The field of green building is broad, with many specialized professions. How would you recommend that someone new to the field narrow the options?

Get involved with local green building or environmental organizations where you can talk to a variety of professionals and possibly find volunteer or internship opportunities. Attend free lectures at local universities and other meetings. Talk to people. Visit firms that you are intrigued by. Most importantly, try to identify what it is that you are most passionate about and figure out how to build a career around that.

How do you best prepare students for the "green" work force?

Be proficient in your particular discipline, and be knowledgeable and communicative in related disciplines. The best preparation is a combination of academic training, community involvement, and professional experience.

Kiowa County Schools: Gymnasium. The north wing houses the high school and gymnasiums. With sawtooth skylit roofs, the gymnasiums are placed north of the classroom and administration areas to avoid blocking sun and air access to these areas (LEED NC Platinum). Firm: BNIM. PHOTO: © ASSASSI

Connection Point

M. SHANE TOTTEN, AIA, IIDA, LEED AP BD+C

Professor, Interior Design, Savannah College of Art + Design

CEO of Offgrid Studio

What are your daily roles and responsibilities?

I am both a university professor and practicing architect. I teach in an interior design department where I specialize in design, building systems, sustainability, and theory. In my private practice I undertake residential and small commercial design where sustainability is inherent in our process and restorative design is our goal.

What degrees do you possess?

I possess a bachelor of environmental design, architecture and a master of architecture. I also have extensive graduate coursework in public administration and urban planning.

What do you forecast for the future on this topic?

I forecast green building will be more fully integrated into curricula as accessible design has become over the last twenty years since the passage of the ADA Act. Incorporating sustainability will "just be something we do" as opposed to a special topic. Where I think the conversation will expand most is in the realm of social justice, and how the built environment can treat people more equitably.

How do you best prepare students for the "green" work force?

Learn the basics and the essentials. The technologies are changing nearly as fast as the publications can write about them. But, if you learn the principles and essentials of sustainable design and green building, it's much easier to assimilate and use the ever-emerging technologies associated with the industry.

What advice would you give an aspiring green building professional?

Be proactive in pursuing your career. Don't wait to be assigned readings or case studies. Don't wait to reach out to professionals to discuss topics that interest you or visit projects or firms that engage you. The more you take responsibility for your own education and career strengths, the easier it is to convey that talent and knowledge to potential employers or admissions counselors.

Values + Career

LINDSAY BAKER, MS ARCH, LEED AP

PhD Student & Graduate Student Instructor, Department of Architecture

Center for the Built Environment, University of California, Berkeley

What is your undergraduate degree in, and from which school?

I completed a BA in environmental studies at Oberlin College in Ohio. I went to Oberlin because I had heard about the Adam Joseph Lewis Center for Environmental Studies, which was just being completed when I started at Oberlin in 2000. David Orr, a wonderful visionary and environmentalist, was the most exciting educator I could find at that time, because he was coming from the perspective of an environmentalist, talking about the potential he saw for the building industry to be a leader in the necessary global transformation to a more sustainable world. I was becoming a very dedicated environmentalist, but I also wanted to work on something positive and productive, and loved the creativity that the architectural world offered. So while I was at Oberlin, I studied ecological design and architectural history, worked during the summers at like-minded organizations, dabbled in city planning and more formal architectural studies, and just tried to be a sponge for all things related to sustainable design. Oberlin was a wonderful place to get a larger perspective on the societal, political, economic, and scientific issues at play in the world of sustainability.

You provide teaching and mentoring for students focused on green buildings—what do you find to be unique about instructing on this topic?

Teaching students about green buildings is a really rewarding experience, all around. Mostly, I teach college students who are pursuing degrees in architecture, and for many of them, sustainability is a core personal value, so teaching them helps them to connect their values to their career, which is always delightful to experience. At the same time, not everyone can stomach the quantitative nature of energy-related work in buildings. Sustainability can be measured—not always completely accurately, but unlike design, it is quantifiable in many ways. For architecture students, this is either exciting or confounding. However, I always try to emphasize that there are many facets of sustainable design that are less math-heavy than building science. But basic solar principles and heat transfer are universal skills that are core to what we all do, so I do strongly encourage anyone in the green building field to get comfortable with those areas.

What advice would you give an aspiring green building professional? What resources do you recommend?

I would definitely suggest exploring the field, learning what types of different jobs are out there, and trying some out as an intern, if you can. I would also strongly encourage specializing in one of the areas I've listed, along with any general education on LEED and green building principles you pursue. Going to conferences like Greenbuild will also help you to understand the emerging issues that the industry is dealing with, and is a great way to meet people who can help you find a job. I also tell my students to stay connected to their fellow architecture students and coworkers. It seems silly to say, but it's important to build these relationships now—you'll be the leaders of this industry in a few years, so it's important to get to know each other now!

In terms of resources, I encourage students to start acquiring basic skills and knowledge that are helpful in our field. Reading *Environmental Building News* is very helpful to understand the current issues we are facing, so that's smart. Also, for architects, learning some basic software programs like Ecotect and EQuest can help expose you to the types of work you may be called to do. Also, I encourage all students to get some real experience with construction projects, through volunteering with Habitat for Humanity or other organizations, so that they get a basic understanding of what building assemblies look like. That helps immensely.

Then, when it comes to finding jobs, I have a list of websites that I send students to that post jobs in this industry. As far as I'm concerned, there's no one website that posts every job you might want to apply for.

Tell me your favorite green building story.

I teach a course on the green building industry here at Berkeley, which is mostly a course for undergraduate and graduate students in architecture. One of the first exercises we do is that everyone gets into groups, and I ask them to describe their notion of the most sustainable building they can imagine. When I first thought of the exercise, I imagined that people might name high-profile green buildings like the California Academy of Sciences. Surprisingly, of the 120+ students that have gone through the course, almost all of them have gone way further. The top response? Igloos. It might seem funny, but they all point out the elegant simplicity and ultimate renewability of igloos, as a local and climate-responsive design solution. Other ideas have been adaptive reuse and remediation of highly urban sites into community centers, and other far-

Inside an igloo. Personnel who attend field survival training are taught how to build an igloo, dig a snow pit, and put up a tent—all forms of shelter that may be needed in emergencies. However, igloos are not commonly used in Antarctica.
PHOTO: KELLY SPEELMAN, NATIONAL SCIENCE FOUNDATION

reaching visionary schemes. It always reminds me that we don't have to be limited to thinking within the constraints of a rating system or by the way we build today, and that students are ready to take on the challenges of sustainability in a fundamental way. We have to help our young people keep these broad and visionary minds as they go into the workplace.

NOTES

1. "No Child Left Inside," www.cbf.org/Page. aspx?pid=947, accessed October 2, 2011.

2. David Orr, "Environmental Literacy: Education as If the Earth Mattered," the Twelfth Annual E. F. Schumacher Lectures, Great Barrington, MA, October 1992; Great Barrington, MA: E. F. Schumacher Society and David Orr, 1993.

3. U.S. Environmental Protection Agency, Environmental Education (EE), Basic Information about EE, www.epa.gov/enviroed/, accessed October 2, 2011.

4. Jillian Burman, "College students are flocking to sustainability degrees, careers," USA Today, August 3, 2009, www.usatoday.com/news/education/2009–08–02-sustainability-degrees_N.htm, accessed October 3, 2011.

5. Georgia Institute of Technology, Office of Environmental Stewardship, "Degrees with Sustainability Focus," www.stewardship.gatech.edu/educationsustainability.php, accessed October 3, 2011.

6. International Facility Management Association, "What is Facility Management? Definition of Facility Management," http://ifma.org/resources/what-is-fm/default.htm, accessed October 13, 2011.

7. Eryn Emerich of Footprint Talent and William Paddock of WAP Sustainability, "The State of The CSO (Chief Sustainability Officer): An Evolving Profile," Footprint LLC (blog), http://footprinttalent.wordpress.com/, accessed October 3, 2011.

8. Robert Franek, The Princeton Review, Press Release, "The Princeton Review & U.S. Green Building Council Release 'Guide to 286 Green Colleges,'" April 20, 2010, http://ir.princetonreview.com/releasedetail.cfm?ReleaseID=461285, accessed October 3, 2011.

9. American College & University Presidents' Climate Commitment, "Overview of the ACUPCC," http://www2.presidentsclimatecommitment.org/html/documents/ACUPCC_Overview_v1.0.pdf, accessed on October 3, 2011.

10. American College & University Presidents' Climate Commitment, 2009 Annual Report:, Climate Leadership for America: Education and Innovation for Prosperity.

11. U.S. Energy Information Administration, Use of Energy in the United States Explained, "Share of Energy Consumed by Major Sectors of the Economy, 2010," www.eia.gov/energyexplained/index.cfm?page=us_energy_use, accessed October 3, 2011.

12. U.S. Department of Energy Solar Decathalon, "About Solar Decathalon," www.solardecathlon.gov/about.html, accessed October 3, 2011.

13. Connecticut College, "CC joins energy Co-op, first college in nation to make commitment," May 18, 2001, http://aspen.conncoll.edu/camelweb/index.cfm?fuseaction=news&id=485, accessed October 3, 2011.

14. Second Nature: Education for Sustainability, "Students' Guide to Collaboration on Campus," 2001, www.secondnature.org/pdf/snwritings/factsheets/StudentCollab.pdf, accessed October 3, 2011.

15. St. Petersburg College, Office for Sustainability, http://sustainablespc.wordpress.com/category/st-petersburg-college/, accessed October 3, 2011.

16. Everblue Program, Carbon Accounting & Reduction Manager, www.everblue.edu/carbon-reduction-manager, accessed October 3, 2011.

17. North American Board of Certified Energy Practitioners, www.nabcep.org/, accessed October 3, 2011.

18. Boots on the Roof, www.bootsontheroof.com/, accessed October 3, 2011.

19. Yestermorrow Design/Build School, www.yestermorrow.org/, accessed October 3, 2011.

20. Boston Architectural College, The Sustainable Design Institute, www.the-bac.edu/education-programs/the-sustainable-design-institute, accessed October 3, 2011.

21. BuildingGreen, Inc., www.buildinggreen.com/live/, accessed October 3, 2011.

4 Experience of Green Building Professionals

A designer is an emerging synthesis of artist, inventor, mechanic, objective economist and evolutionary strategist.

—R. BUCKMINSTER FULLER *(American engineer, systems theorist, author, designer, inventor and futurist. Fuller popularized both the geodesic dome and the term "Spaceship Earth.")*

A VAST ARRAY OF GREEN BUILDING TYPES range in type and scale from the petite Blue Eyed Daisy bakeshop in Palmetto, Georgia, at approximately 1,000 square feet up to international giants such as EnCo's Energy Complex at close to 2 million square feet. From modest single-family homes to retail stores to corporate offices and airports, each place fulfills a different function and serves diverse groups of people. In the same way, there is an equally wide variety of design, construction, and maintenance team members that support the creation and the operations of these structures. Whether as an architect or engineer, contractor or facilities manager, all professionals in the building field have their own parts to play. But the one common thread that is shared by all of these different professionals is an underlying commitment to a healthy and productive space that could be called the green cause. It is this dedication to a sustainable future that also drives a job search for anyone seeking to enter the field of green building.

Early Adoption Becomes Mainstream

Being a green building professional is no longer seen as being a specialized segment of the job market; rather, sustainability is becoming part of common practice. Whereas the early adopters of sustainable technologies may have been viewed with some skepticism in the 1990s as either

Energy Complex, Bangkok, Thailand: Alternative Transportation Facility. Special facilities have been provided within the campus to encourage alternative modes of travel, in order to reduce emissions associated with transportation (LEED CS Platinum). Firm: Architect 49. Owner: Energy Complex Co., Ltd. PHOTO: 2011, ENERGY COMPLEX

superfluous or trendy, in the past few years, a general consensus has developed that energy conservation is imperative and that green is here to stay. Now, those who are pursuing Earth-friendly jobs will be considered the early majority—in other words, smart enough to adopt recent innovations and emerging technologies after seeing measurable successes, and before everyone else enters the sustainable marketplace. Advantages to being an early adopter include compliance before regulation and competitive market advantage. In other words, sustainable design and construction are quickly on their way to becoming pro forma and part of standard code—and those who jump on the green bandwagon now will quickly find themselves ahead of the game when their non-environmentally focused peers are forced to finally follow suit in a few years.

Indeed, those getting in on the green scene today will enjoy a strong competitive advantage over other job seekers, as well as the benefit of voluntarily establishing compliance with codes that will soon become state and federal regulation. A recent *New York Times* article discussed how career changers are seeing economic profit opportunities in green jobs as well. "Ivan Kerbel, director of career development for the Yale School of Management, a graduate-level business program, noted that environmental issues like reducing waste and carbon footprints were increasingly important to corporations of all kinds, something business students are recognizing. Even ultra-ambitious M.B.A. candidates with C-suite aspirations are integrating issues like sustainability into their education, he said." [1]

Many examples abound of how standards and codes are quickly becoming required—and how early adopters in the green building field will benefit. One such example is the Americans with Disabilities Act (ADA), passed in 1990.[2] Prior to 1990, architects, designers, and builders who took accessibility issues into account were seen as overachievers or unique to projects that were tailored for people with special needs. Then the ADA became law, requiring all retrofits and new buildings to accommodate those with disabilities. This impacts everything from the layout of restrooms to the width of doorframes. As with ADA, many of the environmental reference standards, codes, and rating systems are beginning to become common practice amongst design and construction professionals. The advantage to this type of widespread market penetration is the true goal of environmentally healthy buildings, communities, and the world at large. Therefore, any professionals in any field (especially the building field) would be wise to educate themselves in the language of green building—and those committed to sustainability will have a leg up on the job-seeking competition.

How to Get Green Experience

After you have completed your academic and educational training to become a green building professional—whether from a college with a specialized environmental degree, or post-college with a series of training programs and additional classes, or simply through a strong desire and personal mission to fulfill a professionally green path—there is a necessary first step when starting down the path to becoming a full-fledged green building professional: acquiring hands-on skills through volunteering, mentoring, or internship. Once experience is gained through either study or hands-on training, accreditation can be sought as recognition for this achievement.

> The difference between school and life? In school, you're taught a lesson and then given a test. In life, you're given a test that teaches you a lesson.
>
> —TOM BODETT (American author and radio host)

HANDS-ON EXPERIENCE

A wonderful way to develop real-world skills in the green building field is to gain some hands-on experience. It comes in many forms, from formal training programs that typically offer milestone skills testing and perhaps a certificate of completion once the training concludes, to mentoring programs with renowned leaders in the field, to more formal internships with a company or individual. The milestone skills testing could be considered similar to school test scores on individual tests, and the certificate of completion is based on the cumulative analysis of all the individual tests, final exam, attendance, and other criteria. When gaining hands-on experience there are varying degrees of formality to consider, from volunteering to a slightly more structured arrangement of mentoring, up to the more formal internship. In order to determine what kind of experiential program would best suit your needs, it is useful to request a series of informational interviews. The purpose of informational interviews is to gain firsthand knowledge from someone in the field and to begin building a network. These interviews can also provide forecasting into the changes that may occur in the industry, as well as where the new opportunities may be. The purpose of an informational interview is not to request a job, although it could eventually lead to one.

INFORMATIONAL INTERVIEW

How to find a potential informational interview candidate? Try one of the following methodologies:

- Tap into your existing network and inquire if they know anyone in the green building field.
- Contact your alumni association or other professional organizations.
- Target your dream job and contact someone who is currently doing it.

Prior to the informational interview:

- Research the person and his or her work both online and with referral contacts.
- Check local business and industry publications.
- Mention your findings in the interview so they know you did your research (plus, people love hearing about themselves!).
- Speak the green lingo: It is useful to know industry standard terms. Two good resources for learning how to talk the talk:

  http://green-building-dictionary.com/
  www.epa.gov/greenbuilding/

Show your passion and commitment to green causes during the interview. Mention how environmental initiatives have been integrated into your current or past roles. Briefly discuss how eco-initiatives are a part of your personal life in terms of a commitment to reducing climate change, to responsible energy and water use, and to resource efficiency.

In these interviews, ask questions such as these:

- Could you describe a typical workday?
- What do you see as the potential for growth in this field?
- What can I do now to help me find employment in this field?

EVALUATION AND FOLLOW-UP:

Create some criteria prior to the interview that are based on your goals and vision for your green building career. List what is important to you, and compare the responses given to your criteria.

Remember to follow up with a thank-you note as appropriate etiquette for the professional's valuable time.

VOLUNTEER—GET INVOLVED!

Dedicating your time as a volunteer might be appropriate if your career path is unclear and your goal is to glean a very general sense about a particular profession. For example, perhaps you are trying to decide between architecture and interior design. In this case, students or professionals could volunteer for the local Architectural Professional Association or Interior Design Professional Association (both listed as resources in the Appendix). Volunteering can also be a great way to network with like-minded individuals, and it can be short- or long-term, fitting into a variety of schedules and other commitments. Finally, volunteering can be a starting place for green credibility.

In contrast, mentoring or an internship would be appropriate if you have already decided on a specific career path. As with volunteering, the time spent may be unpaid, but it contributes toward resume building experience and tends to be more structured in nature.

Rebuilding Together Oakland. PHOTO: KAROLINA PORMANCZUK

How has your volunteer experience with various professional associations influenced your green career?

❯ Every professional success I have had, in one way or another, is directly attributable to my volunteer experiences with ASID and USGBC. I believe that passion and commitment lead to networking opportunities and relationships essential to business and personal success that can't be found any other way.

Penny Bonda, FASID, LEED AP ID+C, partner at Ecoimpact Consulting

VOLUNTEER RESOURCES

U.S. Green Building Council (USGBC)—Local Chapters
www.usgbc.org/DisplayPage.aspx?CMSPageID=1741

Greenbuild International Conference and Expo
www.greenbuildexpo.org/Volunteer/Volunteer.aspx

Habitat for Humanity—Green Build
www.habitat.org/youthprograms/greenbuild/

MENTORING

Someone experienced in a field transfers knowledge and lessons learned to someone new entering the field during the mentoring process. This relationship can be informal or formal. One of the more typical examples of mentoring would be "shadowing" someone throughout a typical day—in other words, simply observing his or her work process. Eventually, this form of mentoring may turn into an internship.

Mentoring offers the support of an experienced green building professional to teach a new professional the "ropes" of entering the field. A mentor can give the pros/cons of careers and an inside look at the job. The assistance of a mentor can often help a newcomer to navigate away from making beginners' mistakes, and to leapfrog ahead into important hands-on experience.

MENTORING RESOURCES

The Green Building Institute: Youth Environmental Coalition (Youth ECo)
www.greenbuildinginstitute.org/youtheco.html
National Council for Science and the Environment: EnvironMentors
www.ncseonline.org/program/environmentors

What lessons have you learned from the mentoring process?

> The Diversity Mentoring Program, which I worked on launching, is so new that we are now just getting to the point where we can start to learn some lessons from our mentoring program. One of the early lessons we have learned is that we need to be effective in matching expectations of mentor and mentee regarding the amount of time that will be committed and expected outcomes.

Mentees are clearly looking for direction in life and connection to networks for jobs, additional academic and intellectual experience to which they might not otherwise have had contact.

Carlton Brown, COO, Full Spectrum of New York

INTERNSHIPS

A more formal agreement than a mentorship is an internship where the intern gains practical work experience in an "on the job" format. Typically, internships are of short-term duration (generally less than six months) that may or may not develop into employment. An internship is similar to an apprenticeship. Interns can be paid, unpaid, or partially paid for their participation; however, the knowledge gained should be of great value. An interior design intern focused on green building may do product or furniture research for an interior designer, looking at issues such as recycled content, levels of emissions, and toxicity.

INTERNSHIP RESOURCES

Within the sustainablebusiness.com website there is a section called "Dream Green Jobs" where someone seeking an internship can find opportunities. Beyond this, a host of sites are available that offer green building internship opportunities:

www.ncseonline.org/program/Campus-to-Careers

www.sustainablebusiness.com/

www.greencollarblog.org/green-internships/

www.thesca.org/

Another option for a green building internship is to investigate local green building professionals and their networks—in other words, to reach out and inquire if they would be interested in an intern. This is a common practice, and sometimes if the work is available and the internship experience was mutually successful, the company may hire the intern for a full-time position.

How important do you think an internship is in the green building field? Responses from educators:

❯ Internships are critical for hands-on experience of working with a range of organizations to better tailor your education in terms of the courses selected within the curriculum of study. Internships or shadowing a professional for a day offer the opportunity to test a specialized profession for a short period of time in attempt to narrow the options.
Sheri Schumacher, LEED AP, School of Architecture, Auburn University

❯ I think an internship is a very important part of the educational experience. The perfect internship may be hard to come by, so it is important to be realistic about what can be gained from any internship, and that is experience. It may help you find the career path that is exactly what you have been looking for, or it may help you to focus your interest in a different direction. You may learn about how to run a business, or become an expert in the permitting process of a particular local government. No matter what it is, there is something valuable to be learned from the experience, so be open-minded.
R. Alfred Vick, ASLA, LEED AP BD+C, associate professor, College of Environment & Design, University of Georgia

❯ I would go so far as to say take an internship even if it isn't your first or second choice of opportunities. Most often, employers are willing to let you explore your passions within their internship programs. You never know what opportunities arise from the contacts you make.
M. Shane Totten, AIA, IIDA, LEED AP BD+C, professor of interior design, Savannah College of Art + Design/CEO, Offgrid Studio

Did you do an internship, and if so, how important do you think an internship is in the green building field? Responses from emerging professionals:

❯ I did my first internship with the Smart Home Project while I was in school at Duke. The internship involved working essentially as an owner's rep through the design of the Smart Home—what is now a sustainable, technologically advanced living laboratory dorm for ten students on Duke's campus. It was a great hands-on introduction to sustainability and the design process.

Will Senner, LEED AP BD+C, senior project manager, Skanska USA Building

❯ I had a mid-career internship working with a leading architecture and urban planning firm. It was incredibly valuable to experience this front edge of sustainability that was designing carbon-neutral cities and energy-positive buildings. It helped to frame the future of sustainability and created a desire to push my understanding of sustainability further within my career and within my current firm.

Katherine Darnstadt, AIA, LEED AP BD+C, CDT, NCARB, founder + principal architect, Latent Design

❯ I did not do a green internship. However, I surrounded myself with green building professionals. As a result, I was asked to chair the Emerging Green Builders of the United States Green Building Coalition North Florida Chapter. By staying involved and getting others involved, the momentum built and continues to build around the green building movement.

Brian C. Small, LEED AP BD+C, city planner, City of Jacksonville

❯ Yes, I am doing one right now. I am an intern with the City of Houston working on the Green Office Challenge with ICLEI personnel and the City's Director of Sustainability, Laura Spanjian. It has been a very valuable experience and I have a whole

year to go! Just being in the position to help effect change on a bigger scale and helping people be happier and healthier at work is a great feeling. We have tenants who are pushing building owners to start recycling programs, and vice versa. We have some real champions who are taking their efforts to the next level. We spend so much of our time at work, it should contribute to our health, not make it worse!

Heather Smith, City of Houston on the Green Office Challenge, VP of program development for veterans programs under the Bush Cares Project

❯ I did an internship at the Pentagon Renovation program Wedge 1, just prior to the September 11 attacks. It was incredibly valuable. I also interned for a summer in San Francisco with a design build firm called Charles Pankow Builders, which was also very valuable experience and gave me a great insight into the nitty-gritty construction details and coordination efforts required to put a building together. I also got to see what life was like for people who worked in this field: ten-hour days, starting bright and early, and typically working Saturdays as well. While this is good for some people, it wasn't exactly what I had in mind for myself.

Michael Pulaski, PhD, LEED AP BD+C, Thorton Tomasetti / Fore Solutions

❯ Yes, while at the University of Miami I interned for the City of Miami Office of Sustainability and within the Mayor's Office for the City of Lauderhill, which gave me some great practical experience and insight into what was happening at the local government level. It also helped teach me early the importance of effective communication when conveying green building ideas.

Mark Schrieber, LEED AP BD+C and Homes, project manager, The Spinnaker Group

Reception area at the Recording Industry Association of America, Washington, DC. Firm: Envision Design. PHOTO: ERIC LAIGNEL

ACCREDITATION

Third-party-verified accreditation or credentials are an important step in a green builder's career. For all building professionals, including architects, contractors, engineers, and interior designers, being licensed or registered in their field helps verify their sustainability knowledge and provides a stamp of approval on their skills from an objective outside source. Typically, the accreditation process involves a formal standardized test of subject matter knowledge and may involve continuing education criteria, as previously mentioned.

There are two main green building credentialing organizations, both of which offer different levels of accreditation based on factors such as knowledge and expertise. The Green Building Initiative (GBI) gives two levels: Assessor and Professional. The Green Building Certification Institute (GBCI), on the other hand, has a total of six credentialing options, from the most basic (LEED Green Associate) to a mid-career professional (LEED BD+C), all the way up to a seasoned expert (LEED Fellow). Details to consider with accreditations are the years of project experience, testing methodology, continuing education, and other requirements of each of the credentials for these two key green building professional organizations.

GREEN BUILDING CREDENTIAL PROVIDERS

Green Building Initiative (GBI)
www.thegbi.org/green-globes/personnel-certifications/

Green Building Certification Institute (GBCI)
www.gbci.org/main-nav/professional-credentials/credentials.aspx

> Do you think green building accreditation or green building credentials are important for professionals, and if so, why?

❯ Yes, I think that LEED accreditation and similar programs such as the Living Building Challenge are important for new green building professionals because they establish guidelines, tools, resources, standards, and credentials for professionals in a range of disciplines to work toward the goal of a restorative future.

Sheri Schumacher, LEED AP, School of Architecture, Auburn University

❯ If you're serious, get credentials. In the green building industry, especially because it's new, there's an opportunity to discredit you. "Walk the Talk" with bona fide, third-party approved credentials. The GBCI LEED accreditation credential demonstrates current knowledge of green building technologies and best practices, and it can be layered with degrees, professional credentials, and certificates.

Linda Sorrento, FASID, IIDA, LEED AP BD+C, principal sustainable practice, Sorrento Consulting, LLC

❯ While there isn't a substitute for actual green building project experience, I have found that the students who are motivated to study green building core concepts and the LEED systems, and work to attain a LEED credential such as the LEED green associate, are more likely to be considered for hire by professional firms and other organizations involved in green building work.

Brian Dunbar, LEED AP BD+C, professor of construction management, Sustainable Building Program, Colorado State University

❯ I absolutely think so and I encourage all of my students to become LEED green associates before finishing school. I have also helped to establish a LEED internship with our Office of University Architects and Office of Sustainability to give students the ongoing LEED project experience that makes them eligible for the LEED AP exam. These credentials are currently the most recognized and rigorous way to demonstrate one's expertise and professional interest related to green buildings. There is a lot of grumbling about the new credentialing maintenance program that has been introduced but I think that this is a positive step that helps to protect the value of the LEED AP credential.

R. Alfred Vick, ASLA, LEED AP BD+C, associate professor, College of Environment & Design, University of Georgia

❯ As more and more government jurisdictions move to incorporate aspects of green building into their codes and ordinances, I believe the market relevance of accreditation programs will reach a plateau. The difference will be if codes again settle to dictate the minimum performance and such rating systems strive to recognize optimal performance. Then, I believe, such accreditations will carry market relevance that can benefit practicing professionals.

M. Shane Totten, AIA, IIDA, LEED AP BD+C, professor of interior design, Savannah College of Art + Design/CEO, Offgrid Studio

SUSTAINABILITY FACILITY MANAGER PROFESSIONAL

Recently building managers and operator's professional association International Facility Manager Association (IFMA) created a credential Sustainability Facility Professional (SFP) as a specialized green route. For additional information on the accredited programs visit:

www.ifmafoundation.org/scholarships/degree.cfm.

www.ifmacredentials.org/sfp

The Green Job Search

As with any search directed toward a specific goal, a well-laid plan that includes appropriate resources and tools will typically yield the best results. In this case, the goal is to find a satisfying and enriching job within the green building field.

THE PLAN

Though the plan for how to best get a job should be customized to each person's needs, there are several factors that are universal for all successful job searches. Here are some issues to consider when starting out:

- Based on your current financial budget, what is your time frame for transitioning to this new career?
- What type of budget do you have for investing in the search?
- What is your personality—are you bookish, computer savvy, or a go-getting networker extraordinaire?

Next, find appropriate resources and tools to execute the plan you have created, keeping in mind your strengths. Do not forget that any plans should be fluid and adaptable; if one route does not work, be open to changing direction or pursuing multiple options simultaneously.

RESOURCES

Resources can take several forms, from books to online resources to people. This section compiles the most complete and current resources available for today's green job search.

Online Resources

Two of the most popular online resources are job boards or postings and social media sites, because they are "live time" and have constant updates. There are pros/cons to these online resources versus printed media (books, newspaper, articles). Pros? All the information is very current and also free.

Typical office and workstations at the International Interior Design Association, Chicago, IL (LEED CI Gold). Firm: Envision Design. PHOTO: ERIC LAIGNEL

Balance this with the potential cons—online resources are numerous and have questionable reliability. The following section outlines how to pick and choose to maximize efficiency and efficacy when searching online.

JOB BOARDS

This is where potential employers post opportunities, and job hunters can provide their resume. But the job boards are numerous, and they are often overloaded with overlapping layers of information. Many job boards claim to be the biggest, oldest, and best—further complicating how to determine which ones to consult. There are a few key ways to cut through the clutter:

Online Organizing Methods

1. Create a Google Reader Account with RSS Feeds

   For those who are not tech-savvy, this is a Web-based aggregator (similar to a search engine) that will sift the pertinent sources based on your criteria or key words. RSS stands for "Really Simple Syndication," and it is like the CliffsNotes of pertinent information, saving you the time and hassle of having to read through all of the details on every site yourself. With this resource, favorite green job boards can be indicated, and the quick, user-friendly format provides an easy way to look at all the newest job openings.

2. Use a Job Board Aggregator

   Job board aggregators can be used with key words such as "green jobs" or, even better, with additional details such as "green architect" or "green engineer." The more specific the search words are, the more refined the results of the aggregator will be. Criteria can also be based on desired location or salary goals.

3. Install a Ranking Toolbar

   A ranking toolbar is a monitoring service for Internet traffic, showing metrics and analytics of frequency of visits. This could be important when viewing green job boards because it could show those most frequently visited.

SOCIAL MEDIA SITES

These are online professional networks. One of the most popular social media sites is LinkedIn. The advantage of using a site like this is that it allows for invitations and connections to be made with key green building professionals. This site has a specific group called Green Jobs and Career Network Group, where one can apply for membership. If approved for membership to this group, the members have access to new job posts with the associated key contacts.

Industry Associations/Conferences/Publications

Often industry associations will post a potential position. These may be general sustainable associations or specific to the discipline. Some companies only advertise in this place, so check out their local and national conferences. The industry association may also have a pertinent newsletter or other publications. Their website may also have other job-posting areas.

GREEN JOB BOARD RESOURCES

GreenBiz
http://jobs.greenbiz.com/

Green Dream Jobs – From SustainableBusiness.com
www.sustainablebusiness.com/index.cfm/go/greendreamjobs.main/?CFID=4650251&CFTO
KEN=65919098

Green Jobs
www.greenjobs.com/

Green Jobs Network
www.greenjobs.net/

Green Job Spider: Green job search engine with thousands of jobs
www.greenjobspider.com/

Grist
http://jobs.grist.org/

Idealist
www.idealist.org/info/Careers

Justmeans
www.justmeans.com/alljobs

Net Impact
http://netimpact.org/do-good-work/job-board

Sustainable Business
www.sustainablebusiness.com

SustainLane
www.sustainlane.com/green-jobs

Tree Hugger
http://jobs.treehugger.com/

U.S. Green Building Council – Career Center
http://careercenter.usgbc.org/home/index.cfm?site_id=2643

Job Board Aggregators	Ranking Toolbars
Indeed www.indeed.com/	The Alexa Ranking Toolbar www.alexa.com/toolbar
Simply Hired www.simplyhired.com/	Compete www.compete.com

Green Coach

If you are unsure what kind of green building job might best suit you, you might consider hiring a green coach to counsel you in your search for the right professional match. Similar to a personal trainer, a green coach can help narrow your field of career choices. Perhaps you know you want to become more physically fit but you are unsure of which exercises and healthy eating habits are best, and you are overwhelmed with the myriad of options from which to choose. Green coaches are motivators and strategy partners whose goal it is to assess your professional skills and then assist in guiding you down the right career path. These specialized coaches can help you to narrow the job search by matching your personalized skill sets with your desired green building position. For example, a green coach could assist you by interviewing you to determine the best green job field and position for you. Perhaps a coach would determine that engineering would be a great field for you based on your goals and skills. Next, he or she would help you narrow that field even further to settle on a specific career, such as mechanical engineer with a specialty in energy analysis. Finally, the green coach would develop a map and tools to assist in accomplishing the goal.

Green Career Central: Interview with a Green Career Coach

CAROL MCCLELLAND, PhD

Founder and Executive Director, Green Career Central

Author of *Green Careers For Dummies*

Who is a good candidate for green coaching?

❯ We find there are two main types of green career candidates: those who need jobs immediately and those who typically have more experience and are transitioning their career in a green direction.

Please give details about the three phases of green coaching.

❯ We call our approach "Get Ready, Get Set, Go." Many job seekers want to jump straight to resume and searching, and when they do this they are skipping two essential phases of the process. We begin by helping people clarify the specific green industry and position that aligns with candidates' "best-fit career niche." Next, we design a customized action

plan and help them prepare for their new career in terms of education, building credibility in the field, and experience. Finally, we support the job search process. Each of these three levels includes coaching options and relevant resources.

Sometimes it is easy to get the impression that all green jobs are highly technical and scientific. Is that really true?

❯ In the early stages of an industry, the focus is on invention, which typically requires scientific and other technical expertise. However, when strategies and technologies are more established, the same team members as seen in any business setting are needed, including professionals in areas such as financial, human resources, operations, and administrative.

As a green coach, what do you see as the long- and short-term futures for green careers?

In the short term, the green jobs economy is expanding faster than the traditional economy based on job growth statistics. Unfortunately, growth has not met the expectation of many based on early forecasts. There are a number of reasons for this, including the state of the economy in general. Green careers are out there in a wide variety of industries, but availability varies by geographic region, state of the industry, expertise, and other candidate-specific aspects. The long-term prospects are strong as a number of emerging industry sectors take hold and as more companies incorporate environmental and sustainable elements into their business practices. The world has hit its peak oil supply and requires other energy solutions, so long-term decision making will at minimum be based on the three key factors of energy, environment, and financial aspects. All of these developments point to long-term green career opportunities.

Map of Industries and Sectors within the Green Economy, developed by Carol McClelland, PhD, of GreenCareerCentral. com. IMAGE: 2011 TRANSITION DYNAMICS ENTERPRISES, INC.

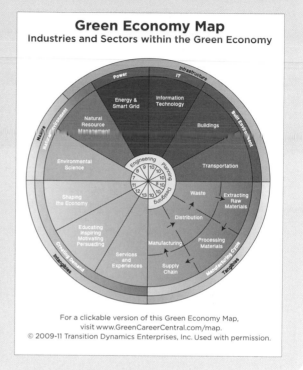

Green Economy Map
Industries and Sectors within the Green Economy

For a clickable version of this Green Economy Map, visit www.GreenCareerCentral.com/map.
© 2009-11 Transition Dynamics Enterprises, Inc. Used with permission.

Green Recruiters

Green recruiters bring a human element to online resources, and they are a great liaison in the green job search. They bring expertise to each step in the process. Consider working with green recruiters to be similar to hiring a personalized job matchmaker. In the early stages, green recruiters can provide a listing of excellent candidates with openings. Next, they can facilitate landing an interview. The best green recruiters can coach you on how to approach the interview and dialogue with the potential new position. Finally, if a green job is offered, they can assist in salary, benefits, and details of the negotiation. The green recruiter is a customized resource that personalizes the search. Many job openings will exclusively list their open positions with recruiters, in order to ensure this level of custom matching. Finding the best green recruiter involves research to ensure that those people with whom you are considering working are specialized in your career area; interview a minimum of three recruiters before making a decision. A few sample questions to ask to find the best recruiter for you might include the following:

- What is their green recruiting process?
- How will you both measure success during the process?
- Do you feel a personal connection or rapport with the recruiter?
- Can the recruiter share a list of references that you could contact?

THE GREEN EXECUTIVE RECRUITER DIRECTORY

The Green Executive Recruiter Directory
   http://greeneconomypost.com/store/green-executive-recruiter-directory

Green Jobs Network
   www.greenjobs.net/green-recruiters/

Footprint Talent: Interview with a Green Recruiter

ERYN EMERICH

Managing Director + Sustainability Officer

Footprint :: Sustainable Talent

How did you become a recruiter who specializes in the green realm? How did you increase your environmental knowledge along this path?

❯ To be honest, I sort of fell into it! I was a partner in another national executive search firm in Atlanta that happened to be doing a lot of work in the sustainability arena because of our clientele (which included companies like Interface). I then stepped out to start my own firm, specializing in placement of sustainability professionals and serving large corporate entities as well as NGOs and higher education organizations. Thus, my training in the ins-and-outs of what makes a great green/sustainability/environmental professional was somewhat trial-by-fire, and I came to learn quickly that (for better or worse) there is no real/one template for the perfect environmental resume.

I've always been a sponge for knowledge in this sector, and to this day, I read everything I can get my hands on in terms of periodicals, blogs I follow, and books on the matter. I also write a column for EnvironmentalLeader.com and speak frequently,

which gives me a great opportunity to synthesize all of my reading along with real-time market observations into a belief system and thought leadership on the matter.

What is unique about a green recruiter?

❯ "Green" recruiters—perhaps a problematic term because it's so general—should have a unique perspective on the marketplace for environmentally inclined professionals: who is hiring, and what kinds of organizations are growing and thus may have opportunity. However, there is some discourse and confusion as to what about that recruiter is green: Their business itself? The candidates they recruit? The organizations for which they recruit? All three (ideally)? It can be quite confusing, and thus important for candidates to dial down into those details when looking for a recruiter to work with.

How do I know which green recruiter is right for me?

❯ Not to get on a soapbox, but it must be said: Whether a recruiter is "green" or focusing on another specialty function or space, reputable recruiting firms ultimately work for the company or organization who has retained or engaged them to run the search for a VP of Sustainability, CSO, etc. It doesn't typically flow in the other direction

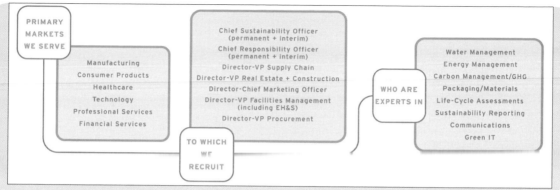

A description of Footprint Talent executive search and recruiting offerings. IMAGE: COPYRIGHT 2011 FOOTPRINT TALENT/MICHAEL PALERMO

(i.e., we don't market candidates to companies that have been retained by that organization). That said, I would thoroughly get to know a recruiter that you believe to be focused on your area or sub-area of "green expertise." It may seem like hairsplitting, but some firms only recruit for non-profits. Some do corporate sustainability recruiting but not all that much energy-focused recruiting (and you'd think that it could all be lumped in together). Some firms look at their sustainability practice as separate from "corporate social responsibility," and so on.

What are some good questions to ask—of any recruiter that you contact or that reaches out to you unsolicited?

❯ What is the nature of your agreement with your client? Are you working with them on an exclusive/contingent/retained/semi-retained basis?

What kinds of roles have you filled in the last one to three years? (To get a sense of their track record.) What level role (junior, mid-level, senior/executive)?

What is your geographic focus—local/regional/national/international?

What frequency of communication can I expect from your firm when we are in the midst of an interview process?

What if we are not actively engaged—will you stay in touch, or are you open to me staying in touch? (Note: This is often a point of contention between candidates and recruiters because candidates have an unrealistic expectation of how often that recruiter will be in touch. The volume of contact will typically be infrequent if the recruiter does not have an active search to explore with that candidate.)

What tools/resources do you recommend for those looking for green jobs?

❯ LinkedIn.com, Indeed.com, EnvironmentalLeader.com, and other similar e-zines; local USGBC chapters; and local Green Chamber chapters.

When someone doesn't have green job experience—what would be your recommendation for gaining some experience?

❯ You've got to get sustainability/green/environmental experience as a keyword on your resume somehow. I always recommend that candidates either join or start up their company's internal green team/green council. What an incredible way to "learn on the job" and get substantive experience. I've seen many candidates work themselves into a manager or director of sustainability role internally—that then positions them well for similar roles outside the organization! Also, if there is not an internal opportunity to volunteer for such an effort, look for opportunities to volunteer with organizations you support as a board member or otherwise, and do the same: Volunteer to be the "green chair," etc. Be bold!

What do you forecast for green jobs of the future?

❯ I've said this for two years now, but we have to "bob and weave" a bit, as this sector for green jobs changes incredibly rapidly. Case in point: While we are recruiting today for CSOs and their adjacent team members with sub-competencies in water, energy, carbon management, etc., I believe that we will come full circle in the next three to five years

and the sustainability function may well be grafted back into traditional functions (marketing, IT, finance). That means we've done our job: when sustainability is no longer seen as another silo in the organization, but is actually integrated alongside an organization's core operations!

If you could give one tip to someone pursuing a green building profession, what would it be?

❯ Obtain your LEED credential—still the only certification we see as truly credible in our space. It doesn't mean you have all the answers or are ready for a CSO role, but it may get you the interview or in the door.

TOOLS

Prior to, or in tandem with, an interview, one of the most important job search tools is the written representation of your personality and work experience to date.

Green Cover Letter and Resume

When writing a resume, keep in mind the following guidelines:

- List any and all green experience, even if it is only academic coursework or a weekend workshop.

- Include your personal commitment to being green, and elaborate with example(s) that demonstrate your passion for sustainability.

- Provide metrics—this could be in the form of experience and/or could be in terms of what you could provide this potential employer.

- Use their lingo. Cross-reference the job posting, and if it asks for a "green go-getter," use the same language when describing yourself. This shows attention to detail and their needs.

- If requested to send a hard-copy resume, think of the details that support your commitment. Consider how to demonstrate your commitment with the way you are presenting your resume— for example, use paper with recycled content that is also chlorine-free, think about using soy-based ink printing and an environmental stamp, etc.

Networking

Even if you are armed with the best resources and tools, the number one way to land a green (or any) job is most often through networking. Statistics show that more than 75 percent of jobs are acquired through this method.[3] Networking is about building relationships and, as with any good relationship, some of the key components are listening and giving. Even if the networking session does not result in job references or referrals, the byproduct of this activity may still be a wonderful list of contacts for the future. A few tips for successful networking:

- Evaluate your existing network and determine who would be appropriate to contact for the current job you are considering. Also consider those who are well connected, even if they don't completely align with your planned job path, as they may have tangential recommendations.

- Networking is typically in person in a casual setting. One of the most common and least expensive networking methods is to meet for a "cup of coffee." Other options include meeting for lunch or a networking activity such as a job fair or educational event. When meeting, first consider what you could do for this person, such as provide contacts or resources. Next, think about what this person could do for you. Remember, these people are spending valuable time to help you and provide you with feedback, contacts, resources, etc. Make sure to show that you appreciate their assistance.

- How you treat the networking meeting will form people's perception of how you would treat a job interview or other lead. Therefore, it is important to conduct the networking in a professional manner and follow up promptly with any promised resources or additional information and a thank-you note. Remember, details are important, so the thank-you note should be eco-friendly. Consider using recycled content, chlorine-free, sustainable forestry paper with soy-based inks. Keep a record of whom you have contacted, and when, as well as confirmation of follow-up. This tracking will show progress and help with scheduling follow-up meetings and/or calls. This record is also a good place to make notes on the details of the meeting, including relevant details about the person's green or personal interests and any recommendations they may have made.

- Who and how to network is important, but another aspect is where. The venue could be a planned social event where several people are in attendance or a smaller, more intimate one-on-one situation. There are pros and cons to either option. In general, the larger social events involve a higher number of contacts, if you rotate through the crowd in an efficient way, and a planned meeting with someone is a more focused conversation.

Here are a few places to consider for planned networking events:

GREEN JOB FAIRS

Structured events such as green job or career fairs bring together both those seeking green job candidates and those in the green job hunt. Often there will be a variety of companies with booths set up where the candidates can approach whomever they may be interested in meeting to ask questions. This gives both parties an opportunity to "check one another out" prior to the bigger commitment of a formal interview.

Green Educational and Social Events

Many green educational and social events are offered from several entities; one popular resource is professional associations. Often these are offered as free or low-cost events that allow both members and nonmembers access to green educational information; attendance at the seminar garners continuing educational credits that are often required annually for maintaining credentials. Often these events have a planned networking element that accompanies the educational session.

Green Conferences

Both locally and nationally, green conferences are historically good networking and educational forums. This can be an efficient way to connect with local leaders and hear current eco-education. Typically, these conferences will have educational sessions dispersed with networking opportunities, and they may also include a manufacturer's product show, job fair, or field trip to green buildings.

GENERAL—GREEN JOB RESOURCES

Green Jobs Network
  www.greenjobs.net/green-recruiters/

U. S. Bureau of Labor Statistics – Green Jobs Initiative
  www.bls.gov/green/home.htm#question_10

Job Fairs and Conferences

Green Collar Blog – Green Job Fair and Event Listing
  www.greencollarblog.org/green-job-fairs.html

Green Jobs Network – Green Job Fairs and Environmental Career Events
  www.greenjobs.net/green-job-fairs/

USGBC Greenbuild Conference & Expo—Green Job Fair (Annual)
  www.greenbuildexpo.org/education/Green-Jobs-Summit/Green-Job-Fair.aspx

Social Events

LinkedIn — Green Jobs and Career Network Group
  www.linkedin.com

Green Drinks
  www.greendrinks.org

USGBC Chapters' Educational and Social Events
  http://www.usgbc.org/Events/EventsConferenceCalendar.
  aspx?PageID=1853&CMSPageID=1722

Determining a Best Fit

Once you've prepared yourself for the job market, prepping your resume and filling your tool belt with all those tools that will best equip you for your chosen profession, the next step is to decide where you would most like to work. Think about all aspects of the companies or firms you are considering. Would you prefer a smaller or larger place? Do you like working on teams or independently? Are you driven by internal benchmarks and competition, or do you instead thrive on self-motivation and satisfaction in a job well done?

Beyond these basic explorations of your future job site, also consider the company's commitment to being green. It is extremely courageous to forge new paths within companies resistant to sustainability. As a new professional in the field, perhaps you will enter into an existing green infrastructure that will support your efforts at eco-design and construction, while providing you with opportunities to glean new skills, and expose you to leaders in the field from whom you can learn. At some point in the future if you should find yourself with years of experience, and as an avowed green mentor to others, perhaps it will be the time to start a green revolution within companies without a sustainable infrastructure.

So how to determine which companies will fit your ideal of great, green places to work? The following are some key facets of any corporation that would be good to consider when assessing all of your choices:

- Read the mission statement and values on the company's website or annual report. A few key things to look for include a clear statement of environmental goals endorsed by upper management; metrics for tracking purposes, including transparency in the reporting methodology; and well-rounded goals that include social and environmental aspects. Also, review the statements of successful green building companies such as Perkins + Will, to use them as benchmark models.[4]

- Often, statements mention the company's commitment to their footprint, including their supply chain and social community.

- Assess the number of high-level management positions (if any) that are dedicated to the green field. The focus and ideals of companies are often top-down, so it is helpful to have the people in charge setting good green agendas from the outset.

- Does the company's mission manifest itself in its people, places, and products? In other words, does staff receive sustainable job training seminars or workshops? Is their focus on being green translated into their dealings with clients (and who are their clients)? Are the offices eco-friendly and healthy places to work? If an manufacturing company, are the products engineered in an Earth-friendly manner, do they use sustainable techniques and technologies, and what kind of portfolio of work (and with whom) have they achieved?

- Does the company have a Corporate Social Responsibility report (CSR)? Is it third-party audited to ensure objective rating? This is similar to an annual report for corporations, but it focuses on the corporation's commitment to social and environmental responsibility.

Once you have taken all these factors into consideration, prepared yourself for the job market, and chosen the company for which you would like to work, then the next step is to search for employment.

Great River Energy Headquarters, Maple Grove, Minnesota (LEED NC Platinum). Firm: Perkins + Will. PHOTO: © LUCIE MARUSIN

1225 Connecticut Avenue. RTKL (LEED CS Platinum). Firm: RTKL. PHOTO: © PAUL WARCHOL

The Green Architect

The U.S. Bureau of Labor Occupational Outlook Handbook 2010–2011 edition provides statistics and information for those considering the architecture profession, and forecasts a 16 percent increase in architecture jobs between 2008 and 2018.[5] Regarding green architecture there is a special mention:

"There should be demand for architects with knowledge of 'green' design. Green design, also known as sustainable design, emphasizes the efficient use of resources such as energy and water, waste and pollution reduction, conservation, and environmentally friendly design, specifications, and materials. Rising energy costs and increased concern about the environment has led to many new buildings being built green."

Steward of Little Actions

GINA BOCRA, AIA, LEED AP BD+C, ID+C
Associate, Director of Sustainability
ENNEAD ARCHITECTS LLP

What was your path to becoming a distinguished green architect?

❯ I was influenced early by my parents, who both have a love of the outdoors. A lot of my childhood was spent in nature—exploring in the woods, fishing in ponds, and gardening in our backyard. I developed a sense of environmental stewardship early. Then, I was fortunate to study at Ball State University (BSU) for architecture school, where many of the professors had a commitment to passive solar design and the environment. Together, the two meshed to send me down this path from the beginning of my career.

How did you increase your environmental knowledge along this path?

❯ My interests began while I was in my third year of architecture school and were influenced by a joint EPA/AIA summit that was hosted by Ball State. The presenters made a lasting impression and made sense of our responsibility as architects. After completing a graduate degree at University of Virginia (UVA), I had the fortune to work for Burt Hill and closely with Harry Gordon, the former CEO. Harry was among the presenters at the "Building to Save the Earth" summit that had been hosted at BSU, where my passion was seeded. In addition to the constant encouragement I had at Burt Hill throughout my career, I was lucky to work with others who had also been at that summit—Bob Berkebile, Greg Franta, Pliny Fisk, and others. And, only a few years after I joined Burt Hill, I was lucky to become involved with USGBC in its early years, working on various committees with the development of LEED and other champions that have always added to my knowledge base.

If you could give one tip to someone pursuing the green architecture profession, what would it be?

❯ My tip would be to take as broad an approach as possible and to consider a multidisciplinary education. Though it is important to develop an expertise, it is equally important to understand how an integrated and multidisciplinary approach is necessary in nearly all sustainable design projects, at all scales. And study ecology and environmental sciences. We have to work with the hydrological cycle, the nitrogen cycle, the carbon cycle, chemistry, and physics—so you might as well get a good foundation in them!

Please give a few highlights of lessons learned on projects.

❯ Rather than talk about a project, I'll share a few lessons on how to approach sustainability in design. You must be able to speak different languages. One person may be motivated by a purely environmental benefit, because it is the right thing to do. But, most often, that's not the only factor that a client or owner considers. You need to be able to talk about the economic benefits and think into the future about the full costs and benefits of a strategy. You have to be able to talk about the operational and performance benefits of a strategy. How will it be able to impact the day to day functions for the user's mission? Measuring performance has to be both quantitative and qualitative. And you have to be able to let go of ideas sometimes that seem like they are beautiful solutions. Lots of little actions have brought us to where we are, and lots of little actions still count toward getting where we need to be.

Trusting Nature and Nurture

HEATHER M. MARQUARD, AIA, LEED AP BD+C, O+M, ID+C

Architect

The Paul Davis Partnership, LLP

What was your path to becoming a distinguished green architect?

❯ My path to becoming a green architect was as much nature as nurture. I was fascinated by architecture from an early age. When some girls were drooling over the new Barbie, I was drawing floor plans of houses for everyone else's Barbies to move into. I was also raised by a strong, intelligent woman who has tons of common sense. She learned as a child that everything has a purpose and nothing is to be wasted. We were re-users and recyclers long before it was de rigueur, due to moral and financial reasons. When I got into the work world, it was a no-brainer that we'd use products that tread lightly on the Earth. It wasn't until later I realized that may not have been the status quo in the field at the time.

When hiring a green architect, what are three important characteristics for which you look?

❯ In order to dig deep and be able to help their clients, they need to not only have the experience or knowledge about green design and the various systems they may need to use, but they should have the ability to work well with others and explain things clearly (and concisely!). Some of the more inspiring sustainable experts I've met have had a great sense of history and culture, too. They don't just "get" the concept or system; they understand inherently how it fits in, why it occurred in the past, and where it can go in the future given the current state of our world. Bottom line to all of these qualities is one major thing: truly listening with all of your senses and without jumping to conclusions.

Please give a few highlights of lessons learned on projects.

❯ One project I worked on very early on in my career was a huge corporate office complex on a sizable piece of land. All kinds of consultants and user groups and codes were involved just in the "regular" design. Then the president of the client firm announced it would be a green project. Some people in his company were excited, others worried, and others actively pushed against it. The bad: trying to work through the red tape that happens on projects and still keep our collective eye on the prize, which in our case wasn't just a great project, but a great green project that could pencil out saving money (energy, water) and make employees happier and healthier. Many days were spent just trying to get the job done, and sustainability would get pushed to the back seat. It was a slog sometimes just trying to hold the line on green. The ugly: some of the attitudes people came into the process with. What I learned was in the end everyone wants a project to be proud of, and even the most belligerent people can have fantastic sustainable ideas. Of course I also learned it's so much better to start a project by trying to break down the preconceived notions people bring to the table. The good? The project was completed and spurred more people and more projects onto a green path than I could have imagined. The effect on everyone who came in contact with that project was amazing! Sustainability has its own momentum— you just have to trust the process and keep trying.

Humble Communication

JIM NICOLOW, AIA, LEED BD+C

Director of Sustainability

Lord, Aeck & Sargent Architects

What was your path to becoming a distinguished green architect?

❯ Many architects decided they wanted to be architects at a young age and are very passionate about buildings. I came to the field less directly. I thought I would be a scientist and focused on science and math when I initially entered college. After taking (and enjoying) a drawing class, someone suggested that architecture was a field that blended science and art, so I applied to the architecture program. I also developed a strong environmental ethic in college, but initially saw environmentalism as part of my personal life and architecture as part of my professional life. Then I attended a lecture by Bob Berkebile about an epiphany he experienced when one of his buildings collapsed and he began to question his legacy as an architect. Bob's talk helped me see that there was a possibility of merging my personal environmental ethic with the professional practice of architecture. After graduating, I moved to Atlanta and had the good fortune to find a position with a firm that had a reputation for early green design. As the demand for green design grew, they soon put out a call for someone to become the "point person" for green design issues, and I was eventually selected. That role has continued to evolve during my fourteen years with the firm, and I now serve as the firm's first director of sustainability with responsibility for greening our projects across five studios and three offices.

When hiring a green architect, what are three important characteristics for which you look?

❯ Humility is a key characteristic. The clichéd egomaniac architect is not a good fit for the integrated design process required to create truly high-performance green buildings. It's a team effort and the best results are arrived at with a collaborative, integrated process. Strong communication skills are also a must. I never would have guessed how much talking, writing, and presenting are required to be successful in this field. Finally, a passion for green building is really important. By definition, you're trying to do something different than conventional practice. Change is difficult, so your heart has to be in it.

What do you forecast for green architecture of the future?

❯ I think there needs to be a change in the mindset from viewing green architecture as some new, high-tech thing to instead recognizing that much of it is simply returning to how we used to think about buildings. Buildings historically made use of naturally available resources and cycles. We used windows for daylight and ventilation, we used locally available natural materials, we harvested rainwater, etc. We need to learn how to do that again first and THEN talk about renewable energy and net-zero design. We have millions of square feet of existing inefficient buildings (and neighborhoods and cities) that we must figure out how to capture.

If you could give one tip to someone pursuing the green architecture profession, what would it be?

❯ Focus on technical skills. There are lots of great analysis tools that enable designers to make evidence-based design decisions in the pursuit of low-energy buildings, but only a limited number of people have these skills. They are in high demand.

Please give a few highlights of lessons learned on projects.

❯ Pay attention to the big picture with green architecture. Focus on the free and low-cost stuff first: proper orientation, good envelope, efficient programming. Projects inevitably evolve and change but if you get this stuff right in the beginning, it tends to stick.

Thornton Place is situated within a pedestrian-friendly, community-focused environment and a new "water quality" park, which cleans the neighborhood's stormwater drainage before it flows into Thornton Creek. Thornton Place, Seattle, Washington (LEED ND Registered). FIRM AND PHOTO: MITHUN

> *You are considered a "green architect"—how did you achieve this reputation? What advice would you give to others who want to follow in your footsteps?*

> My path to being a "sustainable designer" at HOK actually wasn't one I had planned or thought much about specializing in. As an early LEED-accredited professional, I simply started teaching others about the content and exam as it became more popular. There's no better way to learn content than by teaching it.

My advice to anyone who wants to become a sustainable architect or designer is to keep practicing and drop any insecurities about your efforts. Thinking about sustainable design as a goal and not a journey is dangerous. Always strive to be better and learn more than the day before, and at the end of the day, the outcomes will be rewarding.

John Cantrell, LEED AP BD+C, sustainable design manager, HOK

> For my entry essay to architectural graduate school I expressed an interest in someday having a firm that would focus on blending architecture with its site. Some fifteen years later, after working on both small- and large-scale projects, I explored the idea of an "unbound" site in a post-graduate program for urban design. This helped to focus my design process toward systems thinking—where small decisions relate to a much greater whole. Green is much greater than choosing a rapidly renewable material or siting well on an individual site, it is also cultivating a resilient physical environment—sustainable, prosperous, and meaningful—that encourages the best in how we can live.

Tonja Adair, AIA, NOMA, LEED AP, principal, Splice Design

> Pursue what attracts and inspires you; trust in your talent and passions. As a student, I learned the importance of widely varying perspectives and to approach every challenge within a broader context. Know your own essential values so that you can engage with both ardor and understanding. Things work well when you can be artful, technically savvy, and politically astute all at the same time. As a professional, I strive to encourage and honor all the heroes on every team, and to make everything (serious) fun. I am deeply grateful and hold in my heart the powerful message of other sustainability pioneers like Gail Lindsey and Greg Franta who remind me each day that sustainability is at its core about connection, abundance, joy, and love. These things might well be the most essential traits of a good green building professional.

James Weiner, AIA, LEED Fellow, president, Collaborative Project Consulting

> My advice would be to remain open to any and all opportunities. Try new things. Do not shy away from anything that piques your interest or gives you a sense of pride each day in everything that you do. Opportunity knocks; make sure you are willing to open the door and explore new ideas, even if they are considered industry trends. What is described as a trend may evolve into a movement and then one day become standards and codes that shape the way in which we design our built environment.

Melissa M. Solberg, LEED AP BD+C, principal, The Mantis Group

GREEN ARCHITECT RESOURCES

American Institute of Architects (AIA): Sustainability Resources
www.aia.org/practicing/groups/kc/AIA0077100

Navy Federal Credit Union (LEED NC Gold). Firm: ASD, Inc. CONTRACTOR AND PHOTO: GREENHUT CONSTRUCTION COMPANY

The Green Contractor or Construction Manager

Being green is of utmost importance these days for contractors. The largest and oldest professional association representing general contractors, the Associated General Contractors of America (AGC), lists five areas of specialized training on their website that indicate areas of recommended knowledge to help contractors stay current in their profession. One of these five areas is green construction, in which they offer a Green Construction Education Program.[6] In addition, according to the U.S. Bureau of Labor *Occupational Outlook Handbook 2010–2011 Edition,* rises in energy costs have driven demands for increased energy efficiency in building for both renovations and new construction.[7]

Key Commitments

GRANT J. STEPHENS III, LEED AP

Principal

DFS Construction Corporation

What was your path to becoming a distinguished green contractor?

❭ I have always had a keen interest in the environment, from the time I was a beach-going high schooler in San Diego. During the pursuit of my architectural design degree, and subsequently my master's in construction management, my awareness of the impact of construction and the approaches taken during design began to resonate. Specifically it was a single statistic regarding the sheer volume of construction waste headed to the landfills. With this, I focused my exit projects on panelized/reconfigurable structures which minimized waste and extended the life cycle of a structure. Simultaneously, I enrolled in every environmental law course I could take, as at that time there were no specific green courses and curriculum.

Then when I entered the industry as a full-time employee, I was presented with the opportunity to work on a LEED pilot project for commercial interiors. I had one primary mentor during this period and still today, Ken Wilson of Envision Design, who got me involved early and helped steer my awareness of opportunities, as well as the introduction to the USGBC itself.

When hiring a green contractor, what are three important characteristics for which you look?

❯ Experience in performing similar project types. An awareness of current trends and opportunities a client can gain through the green construction process, whether financial or environmental. Corporate commitment. The last I feel is really important. The company that takes the time to train their subcontractors, employees in all positions, and is vested from the most senior levels down creates an environment that is quicker to respond to the ever-changing landscape of the industry. All too often, contractors will have LEED or "green" specialists, which are great resources, but generally are too far removed from the day-to-day operations of a project and unable to monitor, react, and adjust differing conditions and situations that arise during the course of a project.

Please give a few highlights of lessons learned with your experience on projects.

❯ Many end users will only construct at best a handful of projects throughout the course of their career. It's necessary to orient them to the process, the impact of their decisions, and ultimately how to use their new space. This shows up in the new lighting levels, speaker phone use in open office plans, designated recycling areas, maintenance and care of green products with green cleaning materials, control of integrated systems, HVAC maintenance, and orientation to offset amenities.

Investment in the Future

SARA O'MARA, LEED AP BD+C

Director of LEED/Environmental Services

Green Advantage Certified

Choate Construction Company

What was your path to becoming a distinguished green contractor?

❯ My green path started in 2002 when LEED and the USGBC were just beginning to become more well known to the public and to the construction industry in the Southeast. The construction company that I work for has always been open-minded about new initiatives. I went to them when I heard about LEED and the USGBC, and they allowed me to assemble some scenarios that could be beneficial to the company as well as start me on a path of green construction. Charlotte, NC, was starting to create a local USGBC chapter, and I became part of the initial steering committee for this forming chapter. Shortly after passing the LEED exam, my company won a hard bid project and in conversations with the owner we deter-

Cranes, planes, construction vehicles, and sections of Solar Decathlon houses dot the landscape at West Potomac Park during the first day of assembly. PHOTO: CAROL ANNA/U.S. DEPARTMENT OF ENERGY SOLAR DECATHLON

mined that this would be a great project to pursue LEED; the Audubon Society was going to have an office in this building. We educated the owner on the LEED rating system, the benefits for him and his employees, and the return on investment that

he could gain in the process. He agreed it was a great fit for a LEED project, and thus this became the first LEED-certified project in Mecklenburg County.

When hiring a green contractor, what are three important characteristics for which you look?

> LEED experience: Accountability

Knowledge: A full understanding of the procedures and requirements established by the LEED Rating System and promoted by the USGBC

A true commitment: Dedication to sustainability and its impact on the community, not just chasing the LEED points necessary to reach a certification level

If you could give one tip to someone pursuing the green construction profession, what would it be?

> Be open-minded to new technologies and never stop questioning how things can be better. Curiosity and imagination are key to developing the best practices in the industry.

Please give a few highlights of lessons learned on projects.

> It's definitely more cost effective if LEED is identified prior or early on in the design phase of the project. If possible, try to determine the exact level of certification the owner desires so that the most appropriate building systems can be reviewed for energy efficiencies and true ROIs.

Another lesson—when possible, allow the employees to take part in the process, even comment on the design of the building. This increases the benefits of the healthier work environment, their dedication to the company and their jobs.

> **What was your path to becoming a green contractor? What advice would you give to others who want to follow in your footsteps?**

❯ I was introduced to the U.S. Green Building Council and LEED certification in 2000 when I worked for Holder Construction Company. Holder was an advocate for the LEED program, and I was fortunate enough to attend several training classes about LEED and sustainable construction. My interest really was sparked when I had the opportunity to work on a LEED Commercial Interiors project for Interface Carpets. The project was part of the Commercial Interiors Pilot Program and the project achieved Platinum certification.

I am also active in environmental organizations, especially my local U.S. Green Building Council Chapter (Northern Gulf Coast USGBC Chapter). I try to align myself with other like-minded design and construction professionals and maintain relationships with mentors and professionals I have met throughout my career—they are always my most valuable resource.

I would advise a young professional to get involved in environmental initiatives in their companies if they exist; if not, start one. I also would advise anyone young in their career to find a mentor; having someone you respect and can trust to help you make wise career choices is invaluable. More specifically, I would recommend that getting environmental certifications or accreditations prior to graduating college is a plus. I also highly recommend doing internships or co-ops while in college with a firm that promotes sustainable construction.

Kim Aderholdt, LEED AP BD+C, director, Pre-Construction Services/Business Development, Greenhut Construction Company

❯ My recommendation to anyone who is interested in pursuing a career in the green building industry

is to try to combine professional field experience with classroom learning from the very beginning. Look for a degree program that provides you with time in an office or on a construction site. If you are a professional looking to change careers, take professional classes, get appropriate accreditations and certifications, and look for employment with a firm that has a sustainable business philosophy. Don't ever stop learning, take any opportunity to attend training classes, conferences, and network with like-minded professionals.

Carl Seville, LEED for Homes and Green Rater, president, Seville Consulting, LLC, co-author of Green Building: Principles and Practices in Residential Construction

❯ Getting real-life experience is the most critical element of any career in my opinion. I think I gained the most insight having built my latest project, my own green home in Florida. It made me realize that we really need to simplify the process by an order of magnitude if we want greater adoption of green construction in the industry.

Paul Shahriari, LEED AP, CTO, SmartBIM

❯ Every business operates from a collection of individual thoughts and ideas focused around the company's goals and mission. Change in most companies is slow and calculated to ensure the change is worthwhile and enhances the services or product the company produces. Environmental policy is often market/consumer driven or created to address regulatory compliance. The best advice I have is to scale your passion around the business need, pushing for change and communicating the strategy in ways that address the business objectives and goals.

Beth Studley, LEED AP BD+C, vice president, Holder Construction

❯ My personal evolution from a good contractor to a "green contractor" began with the realization I was losing jobs, as well as client confidence, due to my resistance to changing my construction methods. I was uneducated about green building methods and therefore avoided them. Once it began to register that these technologies work and others were successfully implementing them, I decided to educate myself. Understanding the intrinsic relationships between a structure and its surrounding environment gave me confidence that green building techniques truly increase the value of the project by providing durable and healthy structures with reduced environmental impact.

Educate yourself about new technologies and accept that innovation is happening all around us; understand how new construction methods work so you are confident you can apply them successfully in your projects. I am confident sustainable building methods will begin to be mandated more often in the future, so be on the front end of this, educate yourself and blaze new trails.

Jeff Cannon, LEED AP, director, green|spaces

❯ Before you pick up a LEED Reference Guide, read Thomas Friedman, Janine Benyus, Paul Hawken, David Orr, Ann Taylor, Bill Mollison, John Todd, and as many others like them as you can. Maintain an informed perspective. Integrated design is great, as are buildings that produce more energy than they consume. Lastly, give back and pay it forward. I walk in the footsteps of people who have given generously of their time and talent. I am always willing to help anyone walking in mine.

Robert J. Kobet, AIA, LEED AP BD+C, president, The Kobet Collaborative

❯ For any contractors looking to offer green building services, get ready for a whole new perspective on building. Green building is better and it takes more than just compliance within a checklist that gets you a certification. It takes commitment and the training of your whole internal management team and your vendors and suppliers.

Matt Hoots, president, SawHorse, Inc. and CEO, The Hoots Group, Inc.

GREEN CONTRACTOR RESOURCES

The Associated General Contractors of America (AGC): www.agc.org/

AGC Recycling Toolkit: www.agc.org/cs/recycling_toolkit

National Association of the Remodeling Industry (NARI): www.nari.org

The Green Civil Engineer

Civil engineering is yet another quickly growing green profession. Federal estimates show a 20 percent projected growth rate from 2008 to 2018 for civil engineers with a sustainable focus. Some of the more green paths a civil engineer can take include remediation of environmentally hazardous sites, management of water resources, and stormwater management.[10]

Massachusetts Institute of Technology, Ray and Maria Stata Center. Firm: Frank Gehry. PHOTO: © OLIN

New Horizons for Infrastructure

STEVE BENZ, PE, LEED AP BD+C

Partner, Director of Green Infrastructure

OLIN, Philadelphia

What was your path to becoming a distinguished green infrastructure/civil engineering expert? Would you recommend the same path or resources to others? If not, what alternative(s) would you recommend?

❯ I have been practicing as a civil engineer for 32 years. During the first half of my career, I became involved with transportation and site development projects that changed the land itself, creating scars that needed to be healed. At that point in time (the early 1980s), environmental regulations pertain-

ing to the work I was doing were coming into the mainstream. Many engineers—myself included—created solutions that were acceptable to environmental regulators and we stuck with them because they worked. I specialize in water resources and stormwater management, and the more I understood about the subject the more I felt that we as practitioners perhaps didn't quite yet see the entire picture fully. While we were able to get our projects designed and permitted using technologies and solutions that were acceptable to our clients and regulators, I wanted to expand my knowledge and explore the subject in more detail.

I researched topics such as land and water interfaces, ecology, and the environment. It became clear to me that we had a lot more to learn as civil engineers doing land development work. The more I learned, the more I understood that the status quo of our then-current practice was not sustainable. And I had an epiphany—nature had already figured out the "right" way of dealing with how land and water intersect, and we engineers needed to understand how we should design our sites using natural systems. We just didn't know how to deal with the practicalities of this subject yet.

In the early 2000s, intrigued by the new initiatives in green design, I became one of the country's first civil engineer LEED-accredited professionals and was successful in reaching out to and joining the U.S. Green Building Council's Sustainable Sites Technical Advisory Group (TAG), where I spent seven years (retiring as the TAG's chair in 2010) helping to develop and define the field of sustainable site development.

I believe that a person entering the field of sustainable site engineering today has several advantages. First, the role of civil engineer in site sustainability is clear, but the need for civil engineering leadership is paramount. Secondly, the market for sustainable design services is maturing.

Please give a few highlights of lessons learned on the project of your choice.

❯ In 1999 I had the good fortune to be the civil engineer on the MIT Stata Center project. The building was being designed by Frank Gehry, and the site was designed by my now-partner, Laurie Olin. It was an amazing engagement, and the process we used during the design and construction stages could be labeled as "integrated design" by today's standards. By understanding the client's, the city's, and the designers' interest together, I was able to help balance their multiple goals and objectives for the project. In the end, our design was wide reaching and included many elements that solved a host of challenges. The city had an aggressive stormwater ordinance, and the client was keenly interested in demonstrating stewardship for the environment through this project. Furthermore, the design for the site included a vision for expression of water in the landscape. By balancing these objectives, we were able to create a highly functional landscape that enhances the quality of the social space on campus while cleansing runoff water. The system recycles 90 percent of the site water that would have been shed as runoff.

What characteristics do you look for when hiring a new "green" civil engineer?

❯ The prospective green civil engineer should have a solid technical background coupled with an interest in working in a collaborative environment with multiple disciplines to deliver innovative and high-quality projects capable of providing positive benefits to both the end user and the community at large. The applicant should be committed to seeking out educational opportunities to cultivate their interest and expertise in sustainable design and civil engineering as they grow within the profession.

Eric A. Kelley, PE, CHMM, LEED Green Associate, senior engineer, Environmental Partners Group, Inc.

> **If you could give a few tips to someone pursuing the green civil engineering profession, what would they be?**

❯ Someone interested in pursuing sustainable design and civil engineering could benefit by having a solid background in traditional civil engineering (water, wastewater, storm water, geotechnical, transportation, etc.), but they should also take advantage of opportunities to complement that background with exposure to construction management and law, certification systems for green design, and the various mechanical, electrical, architectural, and instrumentation systems that are presently installed in buildings.

Eric A. Kelley, PE,CHMM, LEED Green Associate, senior engineer, Environmental Partners Group, Inc.

❯ The easiest way may not be the best way. Many civil engineering solutions require careful analysis including the environmental impacts of proposed solutions. Just because a solution worked before does not make it appropriate in every case. Creative engineering solutions typically require more thought, although the implementation may cost the same or less.

David Freedman, PE, LEED AP BD+C, principal, Freedman Engineering Group

GREEN CIVIL ENGINEERING RESOURCES

American Society of Civil Engineers: www.asce.org/

1225 Connecticut Avenue (LEED CS Platinum). Firm: RTKL. PHOTO: ©PAUL WARCHOL

The Green MEP Engineer

The U.S. Bureau of Labor provides statistics and information for those considering the engineering profession. The analysis groups all engineering fields together from aerospace engineering, civil, mechanical, industrial to environmental engineers. In general terms, the engineering profession as a whole appears to be growing on par with other professions and has been rated a "good" outlook. As construction needs change, some types of engineers will have greater professional growth periods; civil engineers, for instance, are currently projected to have a better than average rate of growth as a group due to an increased need for road infrastructure, and environmental engineers are also projected to have a strong future in their field.[8]

Technology Artist

MALCOLM LEWIS, PE, LEED FELLOW

CEO

CTG Energetics

What was your path to becoming a distinguished green engineer and green building consultant?

❯ I've been doing MEP engineering and energy analysis for many years, so I was very intrigued when I first heard about green buildings in the early 1990s. I did a couple of green buildings in 1994 and I was hooked! My focus has always been on pushing the envelope and also to helping other professionals learn how to do it. Sadly, most engineers were slow to pick up on green building, but that made it easier for me to build a reputation for being green.

Would you recommend the same path or resources to others? What alternative would you recommend?

❯ Today there are all kinds of resources available for learning about green buildings. I would encourage people to look for what the unsolved problems are and the likely coming trends—net-zero energy/water/waste, zero-carbon buildings,

regenerative buildings and communities, and more. Then start contributing to the state of the art by solving a piece of one of those problems, and then doing it again. It is challenging, stimulating, fun, and rewarding!

What is the future of the energy field, and what do you see as cutting-edge strategies and technologies?

❯ The energy field is one of the most dynamic and rapidly changing sectors of our economy, and one which has massive potential for both economic growth and environmental benefits. There are huge opportunities in both the supply side (energy generation) and the demand side (energy utilization).

On the supply side, my personal belief is that the effective utilization of natural energies (incoming solar energy, climatic variations, biomass, etc.) has the potential to meet most of the energy needs of buildings. However, this will require a radical reshaping of the energy supply system to truly accommodate many sources of distributed power. It will also require thinking of the energy system on a community scale, rather than a building-by-building scale. There are certainly also major opportunities for combined cycle power systems that will radically increase the efficiency of energy conversion.

On the demand side, there are still major opportunities for reductions in the energy usage of buildings and communities. Lighting, HVAC, appliances, controls will all continue to climb the path of less energy and for the same or better performance. Smart building envelope components (photo-chromic glazing, glass that lets in light and produces electricity, dynamic shading devices) will be developed. Beyond the technologies, the biggest opportunity of all is for the increased knowledge and awareness of how to operate and maintain buildings for better performance. This will be facilitated by training and by interactive systems which "coach" the occupants in how to respond to changing the way the building is operated.

Please give a few highlights of lessons learned on projects.

❯ Some of those lessons include:

- Simple design solutions are better than highly complex technology-based solutions.
- Having all stakeholders involved from the beginning is essential to a successful project.
- Cross-disciplinary discussions will almost always produce "aha!" moments that will save money, improve performance, and teach something new to those involved.

Most laypeople are not aware of the possibilities for better indoor environments (daylight, fresh air, good acoustics, good temperature control, pollutant-free conditions), but when they get to experience them in a green building or community they immediately prefer them to previous environments to which they have been exposed.

Optimist Embracing the "and..."

JOHN MCFARLAND, PE, CCP, LEED AP BD+C
Director of Operations, Principal
Working Buildings

What was your path to becoming a distinguished green engineer/commissioning agent?

❯ I studied mechanical engineering in college. Eventually, I focused on energy systems, thermodynamics, heat transfer, and the like. After college, I worked as a design engineer in a design-build mechanical contracting company. I have always had a desire to make things more efficient (use less energy but accomplish the same

goal) and use renewable sources for energy. I got introduced to the concept of commissioning while working for the design-build contracting company. I give a lot of credit for my approach to commissioning to what I learned from the sheet-metal mechanics, plumbers, and pipe fitters with whom I worked. They taught me how systems get installed and what problems they often encountered.

How did you increase your environmental knowledge along this path?

❯ I read a lot. I think I've read every article in the ASHRAE Journal [American Society of Heating,

Refrigerating and Air-Conditioning Engineers publication] for the first ten years of my career. I've also read a few pertinent books, namely *Earth in the Balance* by Vice President Al Gore and *The Ecology of Commerce* by Paul Hawken. I took a LEED-training workshop taught by Gail Lindsey back in 2001. That got me started with LEED/sustainability consulting. Most of it came from on-the-job experience, learning the hard way what works and what doesn't. I started teaching some workshops on LEED, primarily targeted toward engineers. I learned a lot teaching.

When hiring a green engineer/commissioning agent, what are three important characteristics?

❯ 1. He/she must have a team-player mentality. I need to see that they have an innate desire to see others succeed and to help someone else be successful. That is the essence of commissioning to me.
2. She/he must be technically proficient and have a solid grasp of the fundamentals of

engineering. The solution to most problems lies in getting at the fundamentals of the process.
3. He/she must be a very good communicator, both written and verbal, and be able to relate with the entire gamut of those involved in the design and construction of buildings. There are times you have to communicate to a CFO and times you communicate to a field technician. Both are equally important to the success of the project.

What do you forecast for green energy of the future?

❯ I am a genuinely optimistic person. I think that we will move past our dependence on fossil fuels for energy and effectively utilize the free energy that is all around us. Certainly, now we need to focus on energy efficiency. But once we are producing all of our energy from renewable sources, we can be as energy inefficient as we want. That may be a radical statement, but I think we should

Ohlone College Newark Center for Health Sciences + Technology Geothermal Diagram; Newark, California (LEED CS Platinum). Firm: Perkins + Will, Inc. IMAGE: COURTESY OF PERKINS + WILL, INC.

embrace the possibility that we can have both a renewable energy infrastructure AND the comfort, health, and conveniences of a conditioned built environment. I don't think we have to sacrifice one for the other.

If you could give one tip to someone pursuing the green engineering/commissioning agent profession, what would it be?

❯ Listen. Listen to the sheet-metal mechanic on his ideas on how to solve an issue. Listen to the engineer as they explain why they designed something the way they did. You'll likely learn something you did not know and would not have thought of.

If someone were considering a profession of engineering or commissioning, what are the unique features of each?

❯ To me, engineering is about designing solutions. Commissioning is about ensuring those solutions achieve the desired goal. The engineer has a blank slate from which to work. The commissioning authority is a resource to help guide the solution. Engineers may be tasked with thinking outside the box, designing something that has never been designed before. Commissioning authorities may be tasked with determining why something is not working, eliminating the "noise," and finding the root cause of the problem.

> **If you could give a few tips to someone pursuing the green engineering profession, what would they be?**

❯ Tip 1: Continuous learning. After being immersed in the green world for more than eight years (built on top of twenty years of energy efficiency experience), I am thrilled to be able to learn valuable new things about the green world every day. I try to spend at least an hour every day researching something new that I do not yet understand.

Tip 2: Develop a large network. Since you do not know everything about green (yet), get to know as many people as possible in the green industry in your area. Many cities and towns have green networking groups (such as Green Drinks, or USGBC Chapters) that meet regularly. Professionals that know more than you in certain aspects of green can be vitally important resources for you. The most effective project team is one that includes people who bring expertise in various aspects of green.

Tip 3: Decide on a specialty. After you find out what green activities and businesses are in your local area, you should choose one aspect of the green world to focus on. Obviously, select a subject of which you are very knowledgeable. Not only do you need to choose a discipline or technology of interest, but you should also think about the type of support that you might wish to provide, such as design, finance, marketing, construction, and/or certification support. To be most successful, other businesses must see you as an expert who can help them achieve their green goals as painlessly as possible.

Jay Hall, PhD, LEED AP Homes, president, Jay Hall & Associates, Inc.

> Tip 1: Volunteer time in a cause in which you believe.

Tip 2: Publish in trade magazines/journals/newspapers and volunteer for presentations. You don't have to be an expert—you may simply gather various "expert" perspectives/events/technologies and offer your interpretation/commentary of what is out there. These two items get your name out and enable you to build networks.

Tip 3: Be practical; green needs to be appealing as a business model (make more profits, reduce costs, enhance share price, attract customers/clients, reduce utility costs, reduce taxes, improve worker productivity/retention/recruitment, meet corporate requirements, etc.).

Tip 4: Never stop learning. Take courses, read journals, etc.

John C. Adams, PE, LEED AP O+M, John C. Adams, PE & Associates, Georgia Institute of Technology (retired)

GREEN ENGINEER RESOURCES

American Council of Engineering Companies
http://acec.org

The American Society of Heating, Refrigeration and Air Conditioning Engineers
www.ashrae.org

The Green Interior Designer

Interior design is yet another industry forecasted to enjoy rapid growth of almost 20 percent between 2008 and 2018. Moreover, two areas within interior design, including indoor air quality and energy, are called out for specific mention as being important in the future. Indoor air quality and associated knowledge for designers will become ever more important as allergies and asthma continue to rise dramatically in the overall population. Those interior designers with expertise in energy-efficient solutions for lighting, equipment, appliances, and so forth, are also forecast to have a future advantage in the job market.[9]

Concourse of McCormick Convention Center, West Expansion (LEED NCCertified). Firm: tvsdesign. PHOTO: BRIAN GASSEL/tvsdesign

Visionary Humanitarian

KIRSTEN CHILDS, ASID, LEED AP

Director of Facilities Planning & Interior Design

Croxton Collaborative

What was your path to becoming a distinguished green interior designer?

❯ Having a good understanding of interior design and my part in the team as a baseline, my own path to sustainable design grew out of a desire to improve the working conditions for regular workers by enhancing the quality of their space. We didn't know much about green or sustainable design back in the mid-1980s, but common sense told me that windowless, interior-core offices, minimal amounts of outdoor (fresh) air, and decaying, overhead fluorescent lighting that flickered did not offer optimum or comfortable working conditions for the greater part of the work force.

My first rather simple efforts to better such conditions—opening up corridor ends to window views, prying a few executive offices off the window wall to allow more access to daylight and views for the workforce, adding clerestory windows or glass doors at perimeter walls, installing task/ambient lighting systems, and insisting on operable windows in new buildings and retrofits—significantly enriched the humanitarian character of these early projects. This work led to winning the new Headquarters Building for the Natural Resources Defense Council (NRDC) in 1986 in New York City—the first comprehensive sustainable project in the U.S.

How did you increase your environmental knowledge along this path?

❯ The term "sustainable design" had not yet been invented, and there were no mentors and no educa-tional resources available when I started to pursue what we called "environmentally informed design." NRDC was therefore a critically important client. Their desire to reduce energy consumption in buildings meshed exactly with my human well-being efforts to improve the quality of the indoor environment. Together with NRDC's support and encouragement, and with my office, Croxton Collaborative Architects, we developed the elementary criteria that became the foundational standard of the green building movement. It certainly was "on the job training"!

Please give a few highlights of lessons learned on projects.

❯ A key consideration is to get the fully integrated team together and on board with the green program in the beginning of the design process. Designers should note that the team includes the developer, the owner, the owner's point person, and the maintenance staff, as well as the professional group. Nothing undermines a project more quickly than a CEO or even (perhaps especially?) the senior maintenance engineer who thinks that the sustainable design endeavor is just a current fad. Such folk can do untold damage to the project goals, as well as its continuing performance, and must be convinced to become participants in the sustainable process as early as possible. It's worth the time and effort, every time. To do this, energy statistics can be used. These are easy to come by, and there are multiple bar charts of previous projects that demonstrate the costs of the base case versus savings achieved in the design case. Saving money is a powerful incentive!

Since the work of interior designers contributes hugely to the achievement of this strategy, another relevant example is to demonstrate the level of increased worker productivity that might be anticipated through green design. Though more challenging to quantify, the savings are significantly more striking than those achieved through energy conservation. A well-treated, comfortable work force is an organization's greatest asset—and this approach can enhance a company's bottom line like no other.

Healthy Passion

CLIFFORD TUTTLE, ASID, LEED AP ID+C, NEWH

Senior Vice President

ForrestPerkins

How did you initiate your environmental knowledge?

❯ ForrestPerkins became commissioned as the interior designers for the Nines in Portland, OR, a hotel project that was destined to be LEED Silver certified. As director of design for that project, I came to learn about green building practices and how they could translate to hotels. Unfortunately, there was little product available from which to draw, so the design team worked diligently to press manufacturers to develop products for a luxury hotel which resulted in a design that was environmentally responsible, economically feasible, and healthy for guests without compromising the luxury guest experience. During that process, I became a LEED-accredited professional, which furthered my knowledge about environmental design.

I had the pleasure of becoming more educated through my good friend and mentor, Penny Bonda, as well as through another dear friend, Lyndall De Marco. Being involved on ASID's Sustainable Design Council has afforded me the opportunity to learn and increase my knowledge by working with strong leaders in the movement.

With the evolution of NEWH Sustainable Hospitality, through its amazing sustainable directory, its leadership forums and educational programs, we have brought together hotel owners, developers, operating companies, architects, designers, and manufacturers to work together to increase awareness about the importance of sustainable design in the hospitality industry.

If you could give one tip to someone pursuing the green interiors profession, what would it be?

❯ Someone new to the green profession needs to understand that not all clients will necessarily want to pursue sustainable design solutions. The interior designer needs to provide choices to develop design strategies so that the client becomes educated and sees the value of sustainable solutions. If there are solutions that make sense to the client, then most likely those options will be implemented. Unfortunately, sustainable solutions that don't make sense to the client most likely won't make the cut. Understand that solutions for one client may not be the same solutions that are valuable to another.

Your work has been instrumental in integrating green into hospitality. What do you think have been the biggest hurdles in this sector?

❯ Discussions with several hotel brands and ownership companies resulted in a tremendous interest, as did market demand for environmentally friendly hotels.

I was appointed to the LEED Hospitality Adaptations Working Group in October of 2009. The LEED Hospitality Working Group consisted of owners, operators, developers, an architect, as well as me with an interior design background. The group was a holistic group encompassing luxury brands as well as independent boutique and limited service brands. One of the more interesting conversations I had in developing the LEED for Lodging standards centered on the fact that few people realize that everything in a hotel guest room is custom in nature. The new standard for case goods and upholstered seating rewards projects for low-emitting materials. The standard is achievable and measurable, without causing excessive costs due to third-party certification.

Why is it important to green the hospitality market sector?

❯ The hospitality industry is one of the largest employers worldwide.

A typical hotel uses 218 gallons of water per day per occupied room. Water-efficient plumbing fixtures are a cost-effective choice that can reduce water and sewer bills by 25 to 30 percent. We have found such fixtures from several manufacturers, readily available in the market, that convey luxury standards but don't have a cost premium.

Hotel energy costs can consume from 4 percent to 7 percent of a property's revenue, which for many properties is more than their profit margin. If hotels improved their energy performance by an average of 30 percent, the annual electricity bill savings would be nearly $1.5 billion. According to the Hospitality Research Group of PKF Consulting, a 10 percent reduction in energy costs is equivalent to increasing occupancy points by 1.04 and increasing average daily rate by 1.6 percent for a full-service hotel.

O'Melveny: Reception seating area (LEED CI Gold). Firm: Gensler.
PHOTO: DAVID JOSEPH

If you could give a few tips to someone pursuing the green interior design profession, what would they be?

❯ Educate yourself and apply your knowledge to your projects and work with your teams to brainstorm sustainable solutions. Be creative and surround yourself with mentors. Always remember that BEAUTY is the most important sustainable attribute. We are all inspired by the beauty in nature.

Rachelle Schoessler Lynn, FASID, CID, LEED AP BD+C, national ASID president-elect, Meyer, Scherer & Rockcastle, Ltd.

❯ Establish Credibility. Seek certification. Programs such as LEED and REGREEN Trained provide a baseline of knowledge and establish your authority as a green professional.

Read, Read, Read. Information is vital, knowledge is power. Read everything you can get your hands on—books, periodicals, reports, research, reference material. Stay abreast of new technology and innovative materials by subscribing to a variety of blogs that do much of the legwork for you.

Get Involved. Join professional associations such as ASID and USGBC. Actively participate in social gatherings, continuing education classes, and pro bono projects. Networking expands your contact list and is the best way to hear about emerging opportunities.

Lori J. Tugman, Allied Member ASID, LEED Green Associate, sustainable design coordinator, American Society of Interior Designers

❯ Seek to understand the intent and interrelationships of all sustainable systems involved in a building, not simply those specifically under the purview of interior design. Look beyond the immediate resources for implementing sustainable strategies. Respect and promote your professional expertise, recognizing the value you bring to the process.

Jennifer Barnes, IIDA, LEED AP ID+C, vice president, RTKL Associates Inc.

❯ Follow your passions and talents. Stay current with emerging protocols and technologies either through returning to school or continuing education.

Join organizations and committees, work hard, and network, network, network.

Penny Bonda, FASID, LEED AP ID+C, partner, Ecoimpact Consulting

GREEN INTERIOR DESIGN RESOURCES

American Society of Interior Designers (ASID): Sustainable Design
www.asid.org/designknowledge/sustain/

International Interior Design Association (IIDA): Sustainability Forum
www.iida.org/content.cfm/sustainable-design

REGREEN (ASID and USGBC), Green residential remodeling
www.regreenprogram.org/

Artist's rendering of Stroud Water Research Center. FIRM AND IMAGE: M2 ARCHITECTURE, MUSCOE MARTIN, AIA

The Green Landscape Architect

Entrepreneurs abound in the landscape architecture field. The U.S. Bureau of Labor Statistics states that an estimated 21 percent of the profession are self-employed. This number is almost three times what is seen in most other career fields. The landscape architect career path is anticipated to have a much faster than average growth in employment, with an anticipated 20 percent growth between 2008 and 2018. Landscape architects are important links between the building architecture and its impact on the surrounding natural environment. The role of traditional landscape architecture can expand to environmental site remediation, regional planning, and water resource management. Landscape design will contribute to this growth, both in terms of overall landscaping (for new and existing structures) and in terms of green advancements such as the construction and design of green roofs and innovative storm management systems.[11]

Land + scape = Practitioner + Educator

KELLEANN FOSTER, RLA, ASLA

Managing Partner, Visual Interactive Communications Group

Associate Professor, Penn State Department of Landscape Architecture

Author of *Becoming a Landscape Architect*

What was your path to becoming a landscape architecture expert? Would you recommend the same path or resources to others? If not, what alternative(s) would you recommend?

❯ I wanted to be either an architect or a forest ranger. Back before the Internet, a high school guidance counselor suggested that I might want to investigate a career as a landscape architect. I wrote away to the American Society of Landscape Architects and they sent information. I applied to two universities. For anyone who wants to be a landscape architect, you need to graduate from an accredited program—either with an undergraduate or graduate degree. The choice of school is important, as not all schools offer landscape architecture degrees. The American Society of Landscape Architects is still a good resource, as is the Landscape Architecture Foundation.

Your work is a blend of academic (department head of the Landscape Architecture Department at Penn State) and corporate (a managing partner in the firm Visual Interactive Communications Group). How do the two positions influence one another?

❯ The two positions are complementary. Much of the work my business partners and I complete for the VICgroup contributes toward the scholarship and creative activities I need to do as an academic professional. In my administrative roles for Penn State's Landscape Architecture Department, I must be able to represent all aspects of our profession. Since Penn State has two accredited degree programs (undergraduate and graduate), it is valuable that I maintain professional experience as a registered and practicing landscape architect.

In a best-case scenario, how does landscape architecture blend with regional planning and urban planning—and overlap with other areas such as architecture and civil engineering? How do all of these disciplines come together for a successful end goal?

❯ The problems that need to be addressed in our world today are too complex for any one person or profession to deal with alone. The most successful plans and designs are a collaboration of many professionals, with input for the public or local stakeholders. In my experience, success at the end requires all the disciplines to work together from the start—the ideas of all, if acknowledged and respected from the beginning, make for a stronger result.

What tools are you most excited about in the field of landscape architecture?

❯ Much of my work revolves around working with Jane and Joe Citizen to devise a vision for what they want their community to be in the future. Most nondesigners have trouble understanding a basic plan-view drawing or what text-based requirements (such as dimensions, road widths, and the like) will actually look like

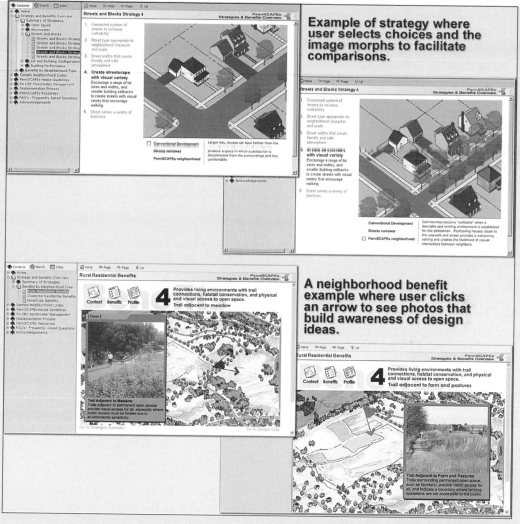

Example of strategy where user selects choices and the image morphs to facilitate comparisons.

A neighborhood benefit example where user clicks an arrow to see photos that build awareness of design ideas.

One of the most vexing problems in implementing smart growth is poorly conceived land use policies. Many places have outdated policies communicated in generic-place legalese. As a landscape architect, Kelleann Foster works with teams to create engaging tools designed to communicate options in a manner average citizens can understand. PennSCAPES' greatest value to this audience is helping them comprehend the complex, interrelated nature of land use and design issues, and inspire them to believe that smart growth development is truly possible in their communities.
IMAGE: COPYRIGHT PENN STATE DEPARTMENT OF LANDSCAPE ARCHITECTURE

once built. Three-dimensional animations, and even film shorts, are increasingly being deployed to assist in communicating design ideas. In our PennSCAPES project—an online smart growth awareness tool—we used a series of flash-based animations, in which the user controls the interaction, to engage people in learning about the design strategies.

Transparency Gives Illumination

JAMES PATCHETT, FASLA, LEED AP

Founder and President

Conservation Design Forum (CDF)

You have said that CDF has learned as much from its successes as its failures. Could you give an example of each?

❯ It is certainly rewarding to observe an integrated design solution that is perceived to be attractive, yet also performs at or beyond engineering and ecological expectations. For instance, water-based green infrastructure systems, if well designed, constructed, and maintained, often perform well beyond our original estimates of hydrological performance.

On the other hand, one of the most important lessons I learned as a professional was based on a series of failures. For a period of years in the 1980s I was substantially involved in the field of wetland mitigation design. My colleagues and I handled all phases of the wetland process, including wetland delineations, permitting, mitigation design, construction administration, and post-construction monitoring for regulatory compliance. No matter how disciplined we were about the details of design, ultimately, these created marshy habitats were dominated by weeds within the first two or three seasons following installation. Nearly all of the native species that were installed had disappeared.

In the late 1980s I met Dr. Gerould Wilhelm, a botanist and ecologist with the Morton Arboretum in Lisle, IL, who would later become one of my principal partners at CDF. Over lunch one day I shared my frustration concerning wetland restoration. Jerry, in turn, explained one

simple fact that changed my understanding of ecological systems and prompted my own professional epiphany. He stated that most of the native plants installed in these stormwater-influenced wetland habitats would never persist because I had "broken the botanical law." Simply put, he said, "plants grow in habitats to which they are adapted."

He went on to explain that, historically, the terrestrial ecosystems of North America, particularly in the tall grass prairie ecosystems of the upper Midwest, were very effective at receiving and absorbing rainfall where it fell. Very little water ran off the surface of the land. The historical patterns of hydrology throughout the region, and throughout most of the continent, were prevailingly dominated by groundwater hydrology coupled with contributions from direct precipitation. Most natural wetland and aquatic systems, including lakes, streams, and rivers, were predominantly formed and sustained by constant sources of groundwater discharge. Virtually all of our endemic terrestrial and aquatic species, both flora and fauna, are adapted to these patterns of infiltration, evaporation, transpiration, groundwater discharge, consistent hydrology, and stable water chemistry.

Conventional land development and water resource engineering practices, in contrast, are generally directed at the collection and conveyance of stormwater runoff through enclosed storm-sewer systems that generate concentrated points of discharge with an associated volume and velocity of flow that is extremely difficult to mitigate. The underlying goal is to remove water from where it falls as quickly and efficiently as the law will allow.

All of our education, creativity, and practical experiences are embedded in a doctrine of collection and conveyance, where water is treated as a waste product rather than a resource.

This approach is nearly always in violation of the historical laws of hydrology as governed by the watershed.

In typical urban and agricultural environments, aquatic systems including wetlands, lakes, streams, and rivers often experience rapid fluctuations in hydrological velocity and volume, generated almost completely in response to surface water runoff. The force of these combined stormwater flows is focused on a landscape, with its inherent soils, fauna, and flora that evolved with a completely different type of hydrology and water chemistry. The erosive power of this shift in hydrology is impressive. Drainage ditches are gouged into the landscape where no surface drainage existed before.

In short, there are no native plants that have a long-term, genetic history of growing in habitats constantly inundated with sediment-laden, polluted surface-water runoff. You might appreciate my frustration in that throughout my years of educational training and professional practice as a landscape architect, environmental planner, and hydrologist, I had never been exposed to this one most basic and important principle of hydrology. This basic understanding changed my entire professional focus. It is always our intent to strive, to the degree possible, for the integration of all types of land use, including ecological restoration, in a manner that restores stable, clean, groundwater-dominated hydrology at the site and regional level. The degree to which we succeed is essentially the extent to which we can restore health to remnant ecosystems, or recreate the conditions necessary to support biodiversity and systems stability.

If you could give a few tips to someone pursuing the green landscape architecture profession, what would they be?

❯ Train yourself as a renaissance thinker. Go out of your way to obtain a well-rounded education in the arts, social, environmental sciences, and engineering. Interestingly, one of the historically perceived weaknesses of the profession by some parties is associated with the notion that landscape architects are essentially "jacks of all trades and masters of none." In my opinion, this is the strength of the profession. I know of no other contemporary education in the applied fields of design that is so roundly trained in the arts, engineering, and science. With that said, once you have a well-rounded education, work over time to develop great depth in at least one area of your profession.

Secondly, you must learn to recognize what you know and to appreciate what you don't. No one person or profession possesses the full range of training, skills, and life experience to accomplish high-performance, sustainable design in a vacuum. It requires a multidisciplinary team of professionals that are experts in their respective fields working collaboratively in an integrated fashion throughout the planning and implementation process.

Jim Patchett, FASLA, LEED AP, founder and president, Conservation Design Forum

> *For those interested in entering the green landscape architecture profession, how would you recommend they acquire some entry-level experience?*

❯ A great way to gain experience is to attend local green industry social gatherings. It's a unique opportunity to meet and talk to a broad spectrum of leading green professionals in the area, such as developers, architects, bankers, and product representatives. An understanding of the local native plant material is also a useful skill to take into the professional field. Consider working at a local nursery while in school; you'll gain a knowledge of plants that are available and thrive in the region.

Nicholas Harrell, ASLA, CORE Landscape Group

Landscape + Art

STEPHANIE COBLE, RLA, ASLA 🅔🅟

Landscape Architect

HagerSmith Design PA

What made you choose green building as a career (or volunteer)?

❯ I've always had a love and respect for the natural world and for art. Even as a child it bothered me when family members would leave the water running too long or waste resources. As I grew up, I always felt that humankind was becoming unbalanced with the natural world and it bothered me. When I heard about a class called Ecological Revolutions at university, I signed up. Really, I've always felt like it was a calling.

Share a green building story.

❯ The Builders of Hope (BoH) Volunteer Day I helped to create has really impacted my life, as well as many others. It is an annual event that started two years ago, and continues to grow each year. I had an idea that our USGBC chapter should do a volunteer day to give our membership an opportunity to give back to the community in a way that would promote our mission, while getting some hands-on green construction experience. They are an amazing nonprofit affordable housing developer in the Triangle region with a triple-bottom-line approach. First, the group goes into a blighted neighborhood and buys land at a very affordable price. Next, homes slated for demolition and destined for the landfill are donated to the program. BoH rehabs these homes to be as energy efficient and green as possible, and then sells them as affordable housing to low-income individuals. As a result, green affordable homes are sold to an underserved population and neighborhoods are revitalized. Additionally, BoH also has a mentor program to teach at-risk youth and nonviolent ex-convicts green construction skills to help better their lives.

Instead of it just being a day of green construction work, we decided to broaden the experience by offering on-site green product installation demos, walking tours of the neighborhood and homes, affordable-green themed education classes, and a design charrette. Around 130 people attended, including Triangle USGBC members, like-minded organizations, municipal leaders, university students, and community residents. The event received a declaration from the mayor, and new members and volunteers for the chapter.

What advice would you give to a student who is considering the green building field?

❯ Learn as much as you can while you are in school. Take advantage of green classes offered, campus organizations such as the USGBC student groups, green internships, and be a part of the innovation happening at your school and within your local community. When you are in school you have a unique advantage that is difficult to find out in the working world. As a student you have cutting-edge technology, leaders in the industry, and resources reaching across many fields of study, at your disposal.

How have your professional and volunteer experiences coincided to benefit and enrich your career and personal life?

❯ In addition to the work I do with the Triangle USGBC, I also helped to form a Green Committee here at my firm, HagerSmith Design. I created an award-winning bimonthly lunch series that is free and open to the public, covers a spectrum of sustainability-themed topics, and draws developers, real estate agents, designers, construction administrators, municipal staff, engineers, and students. As a community service project, I got our firm to donate services for the schematic "green" renovation of two exterior spaces at an affordable apartment complex for seniors in downtown Raleigh. There

Renaissance Schaumburg Convention Center Hotel, Schaumburg, IL. Sculpture *Chronos* by John Portman in the water garden. Firm: John Portman & Associates. PHOTO: JAMES STEINKAMP

was an amazing community charrette process, which got a lot of folks engaged in the project. Our office has been contracted to do the work to carry out the next phases of finalizing a design, and developing construction documents. I'm serving as project manager, and we are now in the construction document phase.

> *What characteristics do you look for when hiring a green landscape architect?*

❯ I would look for someone who values preservation first, who has a broad understanding of natural systems, and who can subordinate site design to the preservation of ecosystem services and the linkages to human well-being.

Stephen Cook, ASLA, LEED AP O+M, division account manager, The Brickman Group, Ltd.

GREEN LANDSCAPE ARCHITECTURE RESOURCES

American Society of Landscape Architects (ASLA): www.asla.org

ASLA Sustainable Design: www.asla.org/sustainabledesign.aspx

Becoming a Landscape Architect: A Guide to Careers in Design, by Kelleann Foster: www.wiley.com/WileyCDA/WileyTitle/productCd-0470338458.html

The Green Urban Planner

Urban planning, by its very nature, is focused on the triple bottom line (economic/social/environmental), working on a community scale with multiple buildings. Federal estimates again show a quickly growing job market, with a projected 19 percent growth rate from 2008 to 2018. Some of the future jobs for urban planners are anticipated to be in stormwater management and interpreting environmental regulations.[12]

Ponce City Market, aerial view. Developer Firm: Jamestown Properties, Jamestown Development & Construction. IMAGE: 2011 GREENBERG FARROW

Urban Translator

TED BARDACKE, AICP

Senior Associate, Green Urbanism Program

Global Green USA

What is the difference between an urban planner and a green urban planner?

❯ Much of urban planning in the United States is about the administration of existing land use and zoning policy; you go to the local government counter for a plan review called "current planning" to observe your application of code and zoning ordinances. Green urban planning is not content with that model. It is a philosophical difference; the eco urban planner is not interested in just the administrative side of the work. The sustainable urban planner has more focus on the environmental "leg of the stool." They look at ecological systems with systems thinking, examining long-term eco-issues including climate change and energy/water usage. All things have a social and economic component; the green urban planner may just look through more of an environmental lens.

As a professor at UCLA in environmental design, what advice would you give students reading this book?

❯ 1. Planning can be "touchy feely"; if you are going to get involved, be prepared for this.
2. Green urban planners have to be able to quantify things; if you're afraid of numbers, you'll need to get over this. Decisions are made based on quantifying impacts/scenario options/potential outcomes.
3. You should have an innate curiosity about how things work. For example, how does a ventilation system in a building function or a wastewater treatment plant work? Being

able to have these types of discussions is key. Planners tend to be generalists; you'll get things done when you speak with specialists. Listen and ask the right questions in order to figure things out.

You are considered a "translator" between designers and the financial community. How do you bridge this conversation?

❯ 1. First, try to figure out the decision makers. What drives decision making in a variety of disciplines?
2. Next, as translator, try to give people the information that impacts decision making.
3. The architect may be concerned about these three items, the engineer about another two items, and the developer about five completely different items. My goal is to bring enough information to all parties so that they can arrive at a place with which we are all comfortable. The trick is to extract all of the information from the various parties. However, the client is not looking for only facilitation and analysis—they also want your advice. The client wants what you think, not just what you know.

How did you come to the field of urban planning?

❯ One of the ways I entered into the field was via my past work as a journalist. I contemplated all of those people I have interviewed over my career, and I asked myself this question, "Who was the most fun to interview?" The response was that often it was people in land use, development, and city planning. With this in mind, urban planning was a natural place to land. The message is to be open to that moment when you think, "Oh, I could do that…" and don't over-intellectualize it too much. Find inspiration in what others are doing. Look at what you think is interesting.

Often it seems students are contemplating "What are you good at?" or "What criteria are you looking for?" and this tends to become the career path via the online dating method (which may work for some people). However, it could be a more intuitive decision-making process.

Interdisciplinarily Conversant

TONY SEASE, PE, RA, LEED AP
Civitech, Inc.

You have a unique background/perspective with degrees in architecture and civil engineering. How do these two fields form your approach to urban planning?

❯ Each discipline fundamentally is about design and its role in shaping the built environment. While one is perceived to be more technical, and the other more artistic, each requires creativity, technical proficiency, and an understanding of the context in which design practitioners work. I do believe it is very helpful to have a design background, regardless of the specific discipline. More importantly, though, I believe that interdisciplinarity is key in viewing issues and challenges through multiple lenses. One of those lenses could easily and perhaps should be a non-design-oriented perspective, such as finance, law, or public policy.

As for recommended paths, I recommend the study of at least two disciplines, more than specialization in any one arena. Broadening one's perspective is essential to working with design teams, clients, regulatory entities, and the public through project initiation, design, approvals, implementation, and occupancy.

You/Civitech have collaborated with some of the most notable architects and planners in the field–Duane, McDonough, Arendt. Any interesting lessons learned from the process?

❯ One characteristic shared by those visionaries and other leaders in the field with whom I have worked is their ability to communicate with incredible passion and with great technical accuracy. They are students of culture and technology, and consume immense amounts of information to stay abreast of issues well beyond the field of green design. They are highly conversant across political, governmental, cultural, and economic contexts, each being a crucial arena in which to advocate for sustainability and resilience in the built environment.

What scares and excites you about the future with regards to green building concepts?

❯ Global urbanization in this century simultaneously affords and demands innovation, particularly with regards to water and energy. Isolated systems concepts which informed much of our planning and infrastructure over the past 100 to 150 years have to be completely transformed, and this transformation will require changes across many arenas, from how our educational systems are structured to policy arenas to financing. We need fewer requirements in many instances, to allow innovation as well as common sense, as the labyrinthine structures of regulation, institutionalized practices, etc., often conflict with basic best practices, whether they be time-honored vernacular approaches or cutting-edge innovation.

Fascinated Advocate

ERIN CHRISTENSEN, AIA, LEED AP

Associate Principal

MITHUN

If you could give a few tips to someone pursuing the green urban planning profession, what would they be?

❯ Be open to collaboration and sharpen your teamwork skills. Green planning relies on collaboration amongst disciplines and sectors and with the community. An integrated approach is critical to success, and it takes practice to lead this process effectively.

Lloyd Crossing introduces the concept of "predevelopment metrics," a methodology for measuring habitat, water, and energy use, and for planning an urban environment that mimics natural systems and reduces environmental impact over time. Lloyd Crossing Sustainability Master Plan, Portland, Oregon. FIRM AND IMAGE: MITHUN

━━ ━ ━ ━ ━ Wastewater
━━━━━━━━━ Reclaimed Water
━ ━ ━ ━ ━ ━ Rainwater Collection

Note: This concept plan is not intended
to represent specific planned or required
development proposals.

1. Vertical Axis Wind Turbines	7. Rainwater Storage (opt.)
2. Vegetated Roof	8. District Thermal Loop Connect to Building
3. Solar Shading	9. To Subsurface Irrigation at Landscape Areas
4. Cafe / Living Machine	10. District Thermal Loop Connect to Lloyd Center Tower
5. Solar Control at South Facade	11. Catalyst Project
6. PV or SHW Panels	

Keep up to date with the latest policies, technologies, research, and funding streams. They are always changing.

Seek experts and consultants that share your vision and are informed in sustainability. Build your team to ensure that equity, health, and economics/feasibility are being addressed.

Can you explain the newly recognized importance of connecting urban form to social infrastructure?

❭ Just as the physical makeup of our environment—such as access to parks, the width of the sidewalks, and our homes—affects our well being, the social infrastructure has an important influence in our lives. Policies such as inclusionary zoning, which promotes the construction of affordable housing, or how permitting requirements can affect the ability to have a farmers' market, are directly related to supporting a diverse and healthy community. In a practical application, a neighborhood redevelopment plan might address the allowed land uses and street widths as well as plans for a new community center or creation of a social services program. It is critical that sustainable planning addresses the physical, social, and equity components to support self-sufficient communities.

If someone wanted to investigate becoming a green urban planner, what kind of experience would you recommend?

❭ Get involved with your local planning commission or neighborhood groups to see firsthand the decision-making process and how community input plays a role. I would also suggest participating in USGBC and CNU events to learn more about principles of sustainable planning that encourage pedestrian-friendly, vibrant, and resource-smart communities. You can get involved as a citizen, advocate, volunteer, and potentially a professional. You will find that specific issues will be of more significance in each region, which is part of what makes it a fascinating field.

GREEN URBAN PLANNING RESOURCES

American Planning Association (APA): http://planning.org

Congress for the New Urbanism: www.cnu.org/

New Urbanism: www.newurbanism.org

Smart Growth: http://smartgrowth.org/

Urban Land Institute: www.uli.org/

Becoming an Urban Planner: A Guide to Careers in Planning and Urban Design, by Michael Bayer et al.: www.wiley.com/WileyCDA/WileyTitle/productCd-0470278633.html

> *If you could give a few key tips to someone pursuing the green urban planning profession, what would they be?*

❯ The successful green urban planner is someone who has knowledge and expertise in a number of different areas: land use and environmental planning, public health, social equity, urban design, air and water quality, transportation planning, real estate development (residential/commercial/mixed-use), and natural resource protection, to name a few. Take advantage of and make opportunities to explore all these issue areas.

Experience place. The best planners are those who use empirical evidence to inform their opinions. Exploring new places and observing how they function (or fail to function) will help planners better understand how to plan in the communities where they work.

Always ask why. Sprawl development continues today, in part, because people are afraid of change. Most communities don't want sprawl, but their plans and codes are outdated and their policies are followed without question. Don't accept the response of, "That is how it is always done." Be bold!

Jessica Cogan Millman, LEED AP ND, president, The Agora Group, LLC

❯ Planners need to immerse themselves in the issues and become informed about the science that underlies the concept of sustainability. It is easy to copy what others are doing and assume that a solution developed for another problem will apply to your situation as well. We need to research the issues and scrutinize the data to understand how best to address a problem.

Planners should look for opportunities to collaborate with professionals from other disciplines. Sustainability and green planning issues span the expertise of many professions, and developing green solutions often requires those collaborations.

Michael Bayer, AICP, Environmental Resources Management, co-author of Becoming an Urban Planner

The Green Real Estate Professional

Transactions such as owning, leasing, managing, buying, and selling buildings, as well as land, are the realm of green real estate professionals. They could own and manage a building with tenants or could be involved in the transaction as a broker for the tenant looking to rent space in an office building. Key drivers for the real estate market are the value of the property, building, and tenant incentives. While some of these drivers are concrete numbers, such as energy savings or increased rental rates, other less tangible measurements such as increased worker productivity have also been studied with positive results. The McGraw Hill Construction 2007 CRE SmartMarket Report interviewed 190 C-level (top level) executives about tenant demand, finding two central markers regarding real estate. The report's findings included the following:

- Sixty-seven percent see green building as a market differentiator.

- Eighty-two percent anticipate greening at least 18 percent of their real estate in a two-year span.[13]

In fact, RREEF Research stated that, "Green buildings continue to grow exponentially. The amount of green building area has been growing at about fifty percent compounded growth rate since 2000. About twenty-five times the growth rate for commercial real estate overall in the United States, which averages a bit under two percent annually."[14] This growth shows expansion amongst all real estate professionals for green-related positions.

While the offerings within real estate are broad, the following are a few key positions in this field:

- Broker: The intermediary between the buyer and the seller for all transactions.

- Facility manager: Manages a building.

- Researcher/consultant: Conducts analysis of the region, geography, market conditions, and trends to determine if a property is a worthwhile investment. These recommendations could be internal to the real estate company and/or external to their clients via consulting.

- Investors: This group of real estate professionals considers the research and recommendations provided, then determines where and when to invest.

Each of the green real estate professions looks at buildings through an environmental lens. Where the broker seeks out green building properties, the facility manager operates the building with green principles through purchasing and maintenance, and the researcher and investors include social and environmental considerations such as revitalizing neighborhoods in their portfolios.

Four Embarcadero Center, San Francisco, CA. Aerial view looking down into Justin Herman Plaza, circa 1985 (LEED EB Gold). Firm: John Portman & Associates. IMAGE COURTESY OF JOHN PORTMAN AND ASSOCIATES

Smart Payback

GREG O' BRIEN, LEED AP BD+C

Senior Vice President, Clean Energy

Grubb & Ellis

Can you explain your path to this point (education and experience)?

❯ I am a believer that a person should focus on a niche in a profession that they enjoy and in a subject matter that they have a concern for—some people call it a "passion." I had been in the office building leasing and development business, and in 2003 I read an article about the future of green office buildings. It was my first awareness of the terminology and I was intrigued and compelled to investigate. Less than three months later, I was one of the first commercial real estate brokers in Georgia (if not the U.S.) to achieve LEED AP accreditation.

How is the real estate community unique in the green building discussion?

❯ Commercial real estate has many perspectives, but the commonality is that each decision must have a "payback"—or a return on investment. Particularly in the recession, every dollar spent is scrutinized as to how it will either generate revenue or reduce expenses. The "do right" for the environment has been delegated to the back seat as investors and property owners are generally in a financial survival mode. But there are corporations/users/tenants that see environmental responsibility as an imperative—and will only choose real estate that meets those objectives. However, a common theme is that the next generation of buildings will be considerably different than the past generation.

Please give a few highlights of lessons learned on the green building project of your choice.

❯ Being involved in the Intellicenter office development program in 2004, I was surprised to see the importance of solar orientation on the future operating expenses (heating and cooling) of a building, as well as the ability to reduce the initial size of mechanical systems. Proper solar orientation of a building along an east-west axis is a hidden asset to existing buildings that have it—and a liability to buildings that don't.

I also learned that providing underfloor air distribution is in theory a great option to provide increased occupant comfort, but the actual installation and operation of such a system is challenging, especially in a multitenant building environment. But the learning curve is under way, and each project should improve on the previous one.

Additionally, I have been surprised at how inexpensive potable water is, given its critical importance to our overall lifestyle. To invest significant money upfront to reduce water consumption tends to have a long payback period because the actual cost of water (hence the savings) is small. Indeed, one of the biggest uses of electricity across our country is in moving and purifying water. There is a direct link to society in what is called the energy/water nexus, and reducing the need for one should reduce the need for the other.

What do you forecast as the future of green buildings/real estate?

❯ The majority of commercial real estate and the associated buildings will evolve toward neutral or positive environmental impact. The ones that don't will quickly be deemed functionally obsolete and they will significantly lose market value.

Investment real estate will seek certified energy-efficient and environmentally responsible properties as a way to reduce risk factors. Developers will be mandated to design and construct to green standards such as ASHRAE 189.1 and will need to offer high-tech amenities that appeal to Generation Xers and Millennials in the marketplace.

Users and tenants of various commercial real estate products will find more and more of their consumption patterns being documented and calculated into their effect on a carbon footprint. The next-generation work force will find it unacceptable to work for an organization or in a building that is not purposefully seeking to reduce it negative environmental impact.

Property managers are already being pushed to apply best practices that have been well documented by groups such as BOMA, IFMA, and the USGBC. Opportunities will abound for creative alternatives to conventional methodology, but the risk of technology not meeting expectations will be great. Renewable energy will be a steady contributor of electricity, but only as long as government subsidies make the business case attractive.

Brokers of commercial real estate will need to be aware of how legislation and market trends will impact the attractiveness of various alternatives. Life-cycle costing should come more into play rather than just deciding based on lowest first costs.

Overall, the trends supporting humankind's need for sustainability will heavily influence the future of commercial real estate and the professionals that make a living in this field.

Part of the Solution

BRIAN LEARY
President & CEO
Atlanta Beltline, Inc.

Please give a brief description of how your education and experience as architect/real estate developer with an overlay of sustainability came to fruition.

❯ I'm a city person. Always have been. There's an energy in great urban places that for any number of reasons couldn't be matched in the suburbs of Washington, DC, where I grew up. I knew that these urban places, their buildings, and the spaces in between had for centuries been where a mix of people, ideas, and commerce came together to accomplish great things. I wanted to be part of this and I fell in love with the notion that an idea could spring from my mind onto a napkin, then be designed and engineered and become part of the urban fabric mentioned above. The sustainable focus is really a function of what works best and what has worked for millennia. In nature, there is no waste. Nothing is superfluous or unnecessary. Cities in their earliest days were, by necessity, sustainable because they couldn't afford to not be. It is only through our "progress" over the past thousand years that we've been able to be as efficient at consuming as we are. This bothers me to the core, and I'd like to be part of a solution, not the problem.

Atlantic Station (one of the nation's largest brownfield developments) was your thesis project at Georgia Tech. Please explain the genesis of the concept and how it became a reality.

While my undergraduate studies were in architecture, my early experience working at a large corporate architecture firm left me anxious with a future career path that might take years to make a difference—so, in parallel, I also focused on the dual areas of land development and real estate. While pursuing a master's degree at Georgia Tech and working downtown at Central Atlanta Progress, I penned the first pages of my graduate

work, titled "Atlantic Station—A Place to Live, Work and Play," in 1995 as a vehicle to a career in real estate development. The thought of actually having the chance to redevelop the 138-acre Atlantic Steel Mill seemed like such a long shot, I wanted my master's work on Atlantic Station to show a prospective employer in the development world that I was capable of underwriting a deal, envisioning a development plan, and laying out a path to success for a complex project. With the very helpful, and much-appreciated, advice from the loan executives at Central Atlanta Progress, I was able to refine the concept and pitch the idea to the people who had the money, experience,

Atlantic Station Movie in Central Park (Several buildings in the project have achieved LEED Certification and the project is designed with smart growth and new urbanism principles). PHOTO: ATLANTIC STATION

and relationships to make it happen. To make the long story short, it was first Charlie Brown and then Jim Jacoby who I briefed on my ideas and who, in turn, hired me to help lead the redevelopment.

What advice or tips would you give to others who want to follow in your footsteps?

❯ No matter where you are in your journey— whether it be in higher learning or early in your career—start thinking about where you want to be and start using your current opportunities to take the steps toward your goal. When I was in graduate school, I benefited from professors who were willing to work with me to accomplish the assignments they demanded for their syllabus while being flexible enough so that the coursework could directly support my research and the writing of the Atlantic Station thesis.

Please explain where the concept of the Atlanta Beltline originated, and what the current vision is for it in the future.

❯ The Atlanta Beltline originated from a thesis by a graduate student from Georgia Tech named Ryan Gravel in 1999. The thesis proposed reclaiming a 22-mile ring of mostly abandoned and underused rail corridor, and transforming it into a new public transit system combined with economic development and connectivity strategies. Gravel's thesis sat on a shelf for a few years after graduation before it inspired a grassroots movement to build the most ambitious public works project in the city's history. With the involvement of several key partners and constituencies, including the Trust for Public Land and the PATH Foundation, the vision grew to include 33 miles of multi-use trails, 1,300 acres of new parks and green space, thousands of units of affordable housing, public art, and historic preservation.

If you could give a few tips to someone pursuing the green real estate profession, what would they be?

❯ Start building your personal network very early on in your career. Seek out mentors who can help you understand your current responsibilities but who can also advise you throughout your career. Associations also offer education opportunities specific to your industry/profession.

Pay attention to corporate reporting. Over the last few years, Global Reporting Initiative has focused on building the reporting community in North America. Last year, GRI added a supplemental reporting system specific to real estate and construction. As the potential for governmental regulation increases, more and more companies will begin using reporting systems such as GRI.

Don't focus solely on the real estate aspect of your job. Look closely at the dependencies and effects of the industry. You have to be cognizant of the communities around any property and the effects of the property on those communities. Social responsibility requires that during planning for a building, you involve the local community at the design stage to make sure the development integrates into the city well.

Troy Adkins, director, Membership & Marketing, CoreNet

❯ Real estate developers are bottom-line oriented. If a good-credit tenant is not renting a major portion of your project, it is impossible to get a building financed. Thus, everything works back to a rent number. If the green initiatives do not help reduce the rent, the good-credit tenant will most likely go to a building with cheaper rent.

However, if I can offer space to tenants at the same rent or less than everybody else and say that my building is green in some way, it makes it much more desirable to tenants. It is like everything else in life—the buyer wants all of the features on the car but doesn't want to pay any more for them.

Gary Fowler, LEED AP, architect, Gateway Development Services

GREEN REAL ESTATE RESOURCES

CoreNet Global: www.corenetglobal.org/

Commercial Real Estate Development Association (NAIOP): http://naiop.org

National Association of Realtors: www.realtor.org

National Association of Real Estate Investment Trusts (NAREIT): www.reit.com

The Green Facility Manager or Owner

Buildings function similarly to living organisms in that they need to be fueled, maintained, and directed. The lifespan of a building is often tied to the care taken of it. Often tenants reside in the buildings, and the operation of the building directly impacts their satisfaction and well-being in the space. The orchestrator of this important process is the facility manager, who may or may not be the owner of the building. Green facility managers reach beyond the building and typically also care for the grounds, manage housekeeping, monitor energy/water efficiency, and take care of all material purchases from paper towels to furniture. Special efforts by the facility manager to operate the facility in a green manner may include:

- Integrated pest management (protocol, low impact pesticides)
- Green cleaning process and products
- Sustainable purchasing programs
- Solid waste and recycling programs

Light Shelf at Bright Generations (LEED NC Gold). Firm: Heery International. PHOTO: DAN GRILLET

Human Motivation

GEORGE DENISE SR., CFM, FMA, RPA, LEED AP BD+C

Global Account Manager

Corporate Investor & Occupier Services

Cushman & Wakefield (On Behalf of Adobe Systems Incorporated)

Your core educational background is psychology and sociology with graduate work in law. Later you were the general manager for a 600,000-square-foot campus in Silicon Valley, CA. Currently, you are the global account manager, Cushman & Wakefield for Adobe Systems, responsible for one million square feet of certified LEED-EB Platinum space. How did you find your environmental knowledge along this path?

❯ I grew up in the Russian River Valley in Sonoma County, CA, one of the more beautiful spots on Earth, so that probably helped to form a basic love for the natural environment and the outdoors. Earning conservation and nature merit badges in the Boy Scouts probably helped, too. During my senior year in college, I took a part-time job with the Sierra Club at their headquarters in downtown San Francisco.

I thought I might become an environmentalist, so I decided that a law degree might be the way to go. About this time, however, I also decided to buy a house, then discovered I didn't earn enough to qualify for a loan. Working full time for the Sierra Club early mornings and late afternoons, going to school full time during the day, and renovating a 100-year-old apartment building at night and on weekends proved a tad much, even for me! Something had to give. Of the three, I realized I liked law school the least, so I dropped out at the end of my first year.

Two years later, I completed the restoration of the Victorian, traded it for a larger one, and my fate was sealed. I loved real estate, especially the improvement process. I also found I loved the concept of green buildings and maximizing operating efficiency. A short time later, I left the Sierra Club after seven years to pursue a career in real estate.

My first job in real estate was working as regional manager overseeing a portfolio of smaller, mostly low-income apartment buildings. I then continued in residential management for eleven more years as regional vice president and senior vice president, before being talked by a friend into going to work for Cushman & Wakefield as a commercial property manager. From the beginning, energy management was and is one of my areas of specialization. Altogether, I have managed 16,000 apartment units, six million square feet of commercial office space, and a smattering of industrial and retail buildings.

Would you recommend the same path to others?

❯ Yes. A successful property manager must be able to wear many hats: bookkeeper, accountant, analyst, advertising rep, marketing manager, salesman, handyman, public relations officer, security specialist, maintenance manager, counselor, psychologist, coach, counselor, supervisor, interior decorator, legal clerk, customer services representative, energy manager, and more. Accordingly, a varied background is ideal, but an obsessive attention to detail combined with a love of spreadsheets is critical!

With your focus on existing buildings, how is facility management unique among other building-related fields with regards to sustainability?

❯ Facility managers control the ongoing operations of the buildings they manage. The role of the facility manager is to provide a neat, clean, safe, healthy, productive, sustainable, and uninterrupted workplace at the lowest cost possible. The largest single expense for most buildings is energy, which typically comprises 30 percent or more of the operating expense. And the easiest expense to reduce is energy. Perhaps because energy has been so cheap for so long, it just fell off the radar. However, the facility manager's job is to operate the building efficiently, improve the level of service, and reduce operating costs. Interestingly enough, that is synonymous with operating a building sustainably.

What are three important characteristics you look for when hiring a new facilities manager?

❯ In their resume, along with all of the other things, I look for references to "LEED," "green buildings," "sustainability," "energy management," and "conservation." In person, I watch them as I describe how we manage our buildings. If they get excited, if they get a spark in their eye, if they start interrupting me to tell me their own experiences as I tell them our story, then I know they are right for the job. And personality—always personality. MBAs don't manage; people do. I recently hired a manager without a degree over a candidate with an undergraduate degree in engineering, and an MBA. They were equally experienced. But the one without the degree had so much more personality and personal energy. I knew she would be able to rally her team and motivate them. Human motivation is a very large part of the job of management.

What do you forecast for green facility management of the future as it relates to energy usage in particular?

❯ Buildings are increasingly being designed and built more efficiently, and with the help of tools like ENERGY STAR and LEED, buildings are increasingly being managed more efficiently. Quite frankly, competition and peer pressure are the primary drivers, followed by cost savings and code compliance. Lighting and load management are leading the way. We upgraded our garage lighting from high-pressure sodium to 32-watt fluorescent seven years ago; we just upgraded again, this time to 25-watt fluorescent with high-efficiency ballasts. We changed our linear fluorescent lamps inside the building from 32-watt to 28-watt lamps six years ago. Now we are changing them to 25 watt. We converted all of our incandescent lamps to compact fluorescent lamps in 2001. Now we are changing many of our CFLs to LED. Lighting, as a percentage of our total demand, has gone from close to 30 percent, just a few years ago, to 8 percent today. Building engineers are conditioned to respond to work orders, so we developed predictability into our system and designed the software to alarm and to generate its own work orders through our CMMS (computerized maintenance management system) when operations fall outside of normal operating parameters.

How would you recommend someone gain experience in the green building facility realm if they are just starting out?

❯ Obtain a relevant degree: business, accounting, engineering, design, architecture, etc. Obtain your LEED-Green Associate credential. Look for internships while you are still in college—preferably paid internships, but unpaid if necessary. Attend USGBC chapter meetings, BOMA meetings, IFMA meetings. Identify the key players of the companies who are operating green facilities. Talk to them. Share your enthusiasm. Ask them about their projects. We currently employ four summer interns, plus one full-time employee who was an intern the past two summers. Two of the interns will stay on this coming school year, working ten hours per week. One of the interns will continue working full time until she starts graduate school.

Please give a few highlights of lessons learned on the Adobe project.

❭ It's not enough to do a good job, you have to communicate it effectively. Good works mean nothing if the right people don't know you did them, or don't understand what it is you did, or why it is of value to them.

A certain percentage of the population will find something wrong with any visible change you make. Be prepared to defend any changes you have made with facts.

Establish systems, controls, governance through the use of periodic inspections, preventative maintenance work orders, and periodic reports. Don't expect what you don't inspect!

Substantive Surfer

DAN ACKERSTEIN LEED AP O+M
Principal
Ackerstein Sustainability

You have a graduate degree in corporate environmental strategy from the Nicholas School of the Environment at Duke University and a degree in political science from Tufts University. How did you increase your environmental knowledge along this path? Any recommendations for those currently on the education track?

❭ Academically, I was fortunate to be exposed to some really interesting thinkers and ideas while I was at Tufts. I did work in the Urban and Environmental Policy program, which was very innovative and gave students a lot of room to pursue their own interests within the field. After graduation, I worked outside the field but spent a lot of time reading and researching on my own to try and understand where things were going

and how I might be useful to the environmental movement. Once I was at Duke, it was a struggle to maintain my chosen academic path rather than a more conventional route, but I eventually found a faculty mentor who understood what I was interested in. At every step, I found internships and conversations with young professionals in the field invaluable; people who are five or ten years out of school recall this phase very clearly and can often be really helpful.

With your focus on existing buildings, how is facility management unique among other building-related fields with regards to sustainability?

❭ Honestly, facility management is singularly unglamorous relative to other fields. Design, architecture, even engineering, are substantially sexier areas of the field. When people get excited about sustainable buildings, they aren't usually getting excited about HVAC set points and cleaning policies. But I think a clear understanding of the dif-

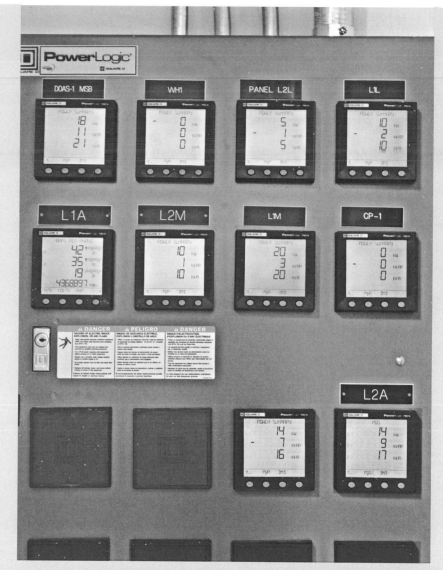

The Square D high density metering cabinet that collects and displays detailed information (voltages, currents, KW, etc) on each of the ten electrical panels that we have submetered so that we know where and how much energy we are using in the building (LEED NC Platinum). Firm: Richard Wittschiebe Hand. OWNER AND PHOTO: ASHRAE

ference between sexy and substantive is what sets facility management apart with regards to sustainability. Operation is where this struggle will be won or lost—the rest of it is important but rarely determines the outcome.

When hiring a new green facility manager, what are three important characteristics for which you look?

❯ Competence as a facility manager first and foremost. For green facility managers to be effective, they have to be an excellent facility manager above all.

Even the greenest facility manager can't survive endless occupant complaints or repeated roach infestations.

Personal commitment to sustainability goals. Credentials and CE hours aren't enough; you are seeking someone who has a personal connection to, and commitment to, the environment. They should be conversant about sustainability from the perspective of "what are the problems we are trying to solve" rather than only "what things can our building do." The former is the driver; the latter is simply the implementer.

Making sustainability work requires communication skills that will smooth the road. The facility manager will constantly be explaining things to occupants and to the building staff as well as to other stakeholders. Good communication skills are critical. At the same time, open-mindedness about new ideas is essential. This field is too young and immature for any of us to believe we've figured it out.

Unbleached and Savvy Owner

CICI COFFEE

Founder & CEO

Natural Body Spa & Shop

What was your path to becoming a green business owner?

❯ I have always said we were a brown business owner or unbleached since 1989. Our sustainability path started as a function of being underfinanced. We were forced to be resourceful and purchased used fixtures. We acquired glass and shelving units from a closed department store and antiques from a closed flower shop. We papered over the ceiling to cover holes instead of putting up new drywall. We loved the way our store looked and were forever inspired to stay resourceful. Decades later we are still recovering from replacing soiled carpet. So, life experiences continue to awaken us as to possibilities for improvement—I love InterfaceFLOR modular systems for carpet now.

With your experience on the Natural Body Spa Brookhaven location (First LEED-CI Platinum in the Southeast) your role was both owner and contractor. It is a unique situation to have both of these perspectives—could you speak to both roles?

❯ Yes, having control of when subcontractors were paid attached to submitting reports really helped with controls. Each team had to take responsibility for their documentation and recycling their construction waste. As leader of collecting these items and the signature on the payments, I seemed to achieve great results.

If you could give one tip to someone pursuing the green facility management profession, what would it be?

❯ I think the most important thing that person could do right now is to identify a specialty within the field that excites them, and pursue genuine expertise in that area. Right now sustainability has a lot of generalists (like myself) and an emerging core of specialists. Those specialists will be the ones moving the industry forward. There will always be a place for generalists, but it's easier to become one later than to try to forge a path without that one skill set that sets you apart in the marketplace.

Dan Ackerstein, LEED AP O+M, principal, Ackerstein Sustainability

❯ Read everything about green buildings you can get your hands on. Go where other green people go. Speak intelligently, but listen carefully. You have two ears and one mouth, so listen about twice as much as you speak. But do speak, and speak enthusiastically; enthusiasm sells, and it is contagious.

George Denise Sr., CFM, FMA, RPA, LEED AP BD+C, global account manager, Corporate Investor & Occupier Services, Cushman & Wakefield (on behalf of Adobe Systems Incorporated)

GREEN FACILITY MANAGEMENT AND OWNER RESOURCES

Building Owners and Managers Association International (BOMA): www.boma.org/

Independent Institute for Property and Facility Management Education (BOMI International): www.bomi.org/

International Facility Management Association (IFMA): www.ifma.org/

If not us, who? If not now, when?

DUKE ENERGY CENTER

Charlotte, North Carolina

tvsdesign

Vision + Challenge

Owned and operated by Wells Fargo, the principles that guided the Duke Energy Center's energy and environmental awareness are rooted in a corporate initiative to reduce greenhouse gas by a significant degree. After a lecture in the summer of 2005 where the question was asked, "If not now, when? If not us, who?" Wells Fargo adopted a method of social, ecological, and economic accounting called the triple bottom line (TBL). Designed as a break from "business as usual," TBL recognized the overlapping interests between buildings and the environment and used that middle ground to address environmental concerns while improving their bottom line at the same time.

Sustainability was not part of the DEC conversation at the very beginning of the project, but rapidly became a factor in all decisions made and many of the questions asked. According to Susie Spivey-Tilson, director of sustainable design at tvsdesign, "It is so important to start early in the design process considering access to daylight, solar exposure, insulation levels, lighting systems, building management philosophies, among so many other factors. It is very easy to miss an opportunity to include an element of sustainability if we don't consider it from the start." As a sustainability consultant, Susie worked to facilitate a dialogue between all DEC design team members to establish common goals, avoid redundancy, and produce a successful project that performs both environmentally and economically. Like putting together a puzzle, she looked at the different aspects of the project to find synergies. Studies were conducted to evaluate the benefit of utilizing an interior, mechanized sun-shading device with automatic illumination dimmers. While incurring a great cost to the project, the benefit aligned with the triple bottom line (TBL) goals of the project and was ultimately installed.

DEC is part of the larger Wells Fargo–developed Levine Center for the Arts with four other cultural

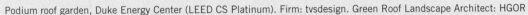

Podium roof garden, Duke Energy Center (LEED CS Platinum). Firm: tvsdesign. Green Roof Landscape Architect: HGOR

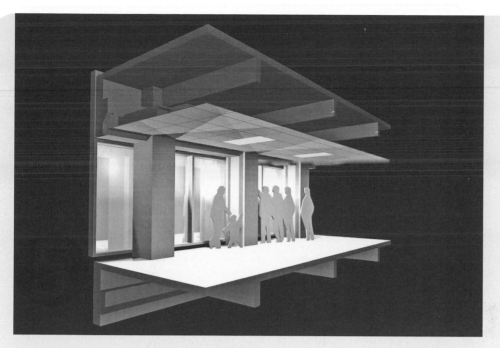

Aerial of original daylighting study for Duke Energy Center (LEED CS Platinum). tvsdesign/DAVID BROWN

Demand-side water diagrams for Duke Energy Center (LEED CS Platinum). tvsdesign/DAVID BROWN

arts buildings and future residential condominiums, and the design team was therefore able to consolidate building programs and support systems to minimize their environmental impact. Two cultural arts buildings share an auditorium, maximizing public open space on the site. One central parking garage services all the buildings. DEC reclaims 100 percent of the stormwater runoff on its site, 100 percent of the condensate, and reclaims and treats 25 million gallons of contaminated groundwater. DEC is thus able to water not only the campus's own green spaces and roofs, but the public green space across the street as well, and provide the make-up water for the HVAC systems.

Strategy + Solutions

RESOURCE EFFICIENCY

A result of hard work, team collaboration, and a collective desire to create a long-lasting environmentally sensitive building, DEC saves 30 million gallons of water a year and five million kilowatt hours of energy a year, making it 85 percent and 22 percent more efficient, respectively, than a building of comparable size and function. Notably, in a bold move by the owner with hesitation from the developer, all tenants are required, as term of their lease, to earn LEED for Commercial Interiors certification, which includes a minimum 15 percent lighting power density reduction, minimum 50 percent construction waste diversion, and meeting low-emitting materials credits.

SUCCESS

As the second-tallest building in Charlotte, North Carolina, and the largest building by area (1.5m sq ft), the Duke Energy Center (DEC) is not only a beacon of industry and commerce for the second-largest banking capital in North America, but also a shining example of environmental stewardship and ecological sensitivity. It is the first and tallest office building to receive LEED CS v2.0 Platinum certification and was named the "Smartest Building in America" in a national contest sponsored by Siemens. It is also the first LEED CS building to require all tenants to pursue LEED certification for commercial interiors.

Experience + Resources = Results

A well-planned green career quest will integrate two critical components: experience and well-utilized resources. With the experience gained from mentoring, volunteering, and accreditation, any interested job seeker (no matter what your educational or career background may be) will have an immediate leg up on the competition. Add to this mix a blend of personal contacts and well-connected people, including coaches, recruiters, and members of professional associations, then stir into the pot such useful ingredients as job search sites, fairs, and networking opportunities. Finish off with a dash of motivation and green dedication—and you have the perfect recipe for success in your sustainable job search!

NOTES

1. Austin Considine. "Green Jobs Attract Graduates," the *New York Times* June 24, 2011, www.nytimes.com/2011/06/26/fashion/new-wave-of-graduates-prefers-environmentally-friendly-jobs.html?_r=2&ref=fashion, accessed October 3, 2011.

2. Americans with Disabilities Act of 1990, *As Amended,* www.ada.gov/pubs/ada.htm, accessed October 3, 2011.

3. Tory Johnson, CEO, Women for Hire, "Professional Networking," http://womenforhire.com/advice/professional_networking_tips/, accessed October 3, 2011.

4. Perkins + Will, Perkins + Will *Sustainable Leadership Plan 2011: Broader Goals,* www.perkinswill.com/publications/perkins%2Bwill-sustainable-leadership-plan-2011.html, accessed October 3, 2011.

5. Bureau of Labor Statistics, U.S. Department of Labor, *Occupational Outlook Handbook, 2010–2011 Edition, Architects, Except Landscape and Naval,* www.bls.gov/oco/ocos038.htm, accessed October 3, 2011.

6. The Associated General Contractors of America, "Training & Education," www.agc.org/cs/career_development, accessed October 3, 2011.

7. Bureau of Labor Statistics, U.S. Department of Labor, *Occupational Outlook Handbook, 2010–2011 Edition, Construction Trade and Related Workers,* www.bls.gov/oco/oco1009.htm, accessed October 3, 2011.

8. Bureau of Labor Statistics, U.S. *Department of Labor, Occupational Outlook Handbook, 2010–2011 Edition, Engineers,* www.bls.gov/oco/ocos027.htm, accessed October 3, 2011.

9. Bureau of Labor Statistics, U.S. Department of Labor, *Occupational Outlook Handbook, 2010–2011 Edition, Interior Designers,* www.bls.gov/oco/ocos293.htm, accessed October 3, 2011.

10. Bureau of Labor Statistics, U.S. Department of Labor, *Occupational Outlook Handbook, 2010–2011 Edition, Engineers, www.bls.gov/oco/ocos027.htm,* accessed October 3, 2011.

11. Bureau of Labor Statistics, U.S. Department of Labor, *Occupational Outlook Handbook, 2010–2011 Edition, Landscape Architects,* www.bls.gov/oco/ocos039.htm, accessed October 3, 2011.

12. Bureau of Labor Statistics, U.S. Department of Labor, *Occupational Outlook Handbook, 2010–2011 Edition, Urban and Regional Planners,* www.bls.gov/oco/ocos057.htm, accessed October 3, 2011.

13. McGraw Hill Construction Research and Analytics Group, study conducted for Siemens, *The Greening of Corporate America SmartMarket Report,* McGraw Hill Construction, 2007, http://analyticsstore.construction.com/, accessed October 3, 2011.

14. Andrew J. Nelson, vice president, RREEF Research, "The Greening of U.S. Investment Real Estate: Market Fundamentals, Prospects and Opportunities," *RREEF Research* Number 57, November 2007, www.rreef.com/home/research_5548.jsp, accessed October 3, 2011.

5 Sustainability and Green Building Consultants

Be faithful to that which exists nowhere but in yourself—and thus make yourself indispensable.

—ANDRÉ GIDE *(French writer awarded Nobel Peace Prize in literature in 1947. Writings include topics of freedom, empowerment, and the repudiation of communism.)*

A Sprouting New Sector

Twenty years ago, it would have been a challenge to find a job title containing the word "sustainability" among the ranks of any company, big or small. Environmental awareness was gestating slowly. Some building professionals realized its importance and adapted a green mindset, but those people were, for the most part, few and far between, and the idea of taking green mainstream was still a far-off notion. Certainly, it would have been a rare occurrence to have someone whose job was dedicated to keeping a company's footprint small, or helping navigate the various ways and means of LEED certification through the design and construction process. Now, those jobs are becoming a well-integrated matter of course, intrinsic to corporate infrastructures and building teams.

Indeed, a multitude of green building jobs are today increasingly becoming essential throughout the design and construction process. From green building consultants—independent team members who help target, model, and focus a building from design through construction in terms of sustainable elements—to small business operators within the energy field, such as solar power installers and sustainability systems developers, there is a cornucopia of sustainability professionals whose jobs are new within the last couple of decades—and who are already becoming indispensable.

Green roof garden. Gardens have been included on the rooftops to help reduce urban heat island effect and provide natural heat insulation. Energy Complex, Bangkok, Thailand (LEED CS Platinum). Firm: Architect 49. Owner: Energy Complex Co., Ltd. PHOTO: 2011, ENERGY COMPLEX

The numbers support this rise in importance of green consultants. In terms of the USGBC, its LEED-related economic outlay has been forecast to generate an additional $12.5 billion in gross domestic product (GDP) and provide $10.7 billion in labor earnings between 2009 and 2013.[1] Additional increases in job growth in smaller sectors is also in evidence, such as a projection by the Solar Energies Industry Association of an increase from 35,000 jobs in the solar energy sector as of 2007 to over 110,000 in 2016.[2] Even major corporations, once seen as relatively resistant to green concerns, are now quickly incorporating eco-concerns into their missions and spaces.

THE RACE TO STAY CURRENT

In ever-changing job markets, with new studies and technologies being introduced at breakneck speeds, it is often a challenge for professionals to strive to stay current in their particular fields. This is true in any profession: A family practice doctor, for example, would be expected to attend conferences and be informed on the latest in general medicine; it would hardly be possible to also be up-to-date on breakthrough new techniques in neurosurgery, for example, or osteopathic medicine. The same is true in the building fields. With architects, engineers, and contractors flooded with new codes, information, and practices within their own fields, it would be an extraordinary feat to also keep up to date with the newest and best happenings in green building.

Moreover, while the field of green building is growing in leaps and bounds every year, so too are the knowledge basics needed to meet high levels of professional performance. As a fast-emerging job sector, green building often sees this happening faster than in other job fields. Sometimes this manifests as updates to preexisting requirements. This is often true in the case of LEED updates. The next version of the LEED rating system (under development in 2012) is projected to change by as much as 30 percent over the LEED 2009 version, addressing a new category, credits, and prerequisites. For someone new to the field or used to the older versions of LEED, the LEED *Reference Guide* issued by the USGBC could feel like new rules.[3] While the

USGBC has a good rationale for the updates, such as continuous improvement and increasing scope and stringency as the market and technologies become available, in the end, LEED is a voluntary system.[4] Other times, mandatory codes are introduced and adopted by local government to be incorporated into everyday practice by building professionals, such as the International Green Construction Code (IgCC), revised in 2012 incorporating ANSI/ASHRAE/IES/USGBC Standard 189.1 as a path that can be customized for local governments and a green option for projects pursuing LEED or not.

In addition to voluntary rating systems and compulsory codes such as LEED and IgCC frequently being updated even as they are implemented, requirements are also becoming more commonplace. The state of California, for example, introduced a lengthy set of green building requirements as of the start of 2011. Called CALGreen, the new codes impose mandatory conditions on all new construction—residential and nonresidential—that address everything from metrics for lowering the amount of light pollution and wastewater reduction during design and construction to allocating parking places for energy-efficient vehicles and areas for recycling after the building is complete.[6] Other states are looking to follow; Florida has already mandated increasing energy efficiency in buildings by up to 50 percent as part of the 2019 state building code, and local jurisdictions are discussing adoption of the IgCC for mandatory regulation, as just one other example.[7]

With regulations ever changing, and taking into account a building's life span—from design inception to construction to maintenance to even possibly deconstruction—green building specialists can be involved in the process of making every aspect as eco-conscious as possible. Green building consultants can help center architectural blueprints and technology around green solutions, and assist with navigation through the intricate nature of LEED and other green rating systems, as well as green building codes. Each and every specialist has his or her own part to play in the process of greening our buildings, and all of these professionals ensure that the green building field stays abreast of the most current technological and regulatory changes affecting the built environment.

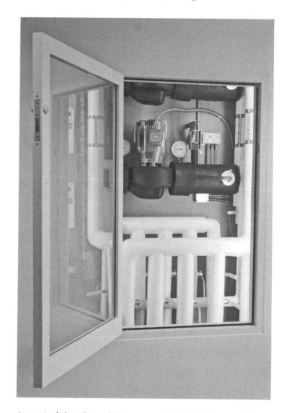

As part of the "living lab" concept, the building uses three separate HVAC systems. Shown is the piping manifold of the second-level system that is conditioned using twelve 2-stage, 27-EER variable-speed ground source heat pumps, including a geothermal field of twelve 400-foot-deep wells and a closed-loop piping system (LEED NC Platinum) Firm: Richard Wittschiebe Hand. OWNER AND PHOTO: ACURAS

RANGE OF ROLES

All of these additional codes and requirements necessitate savvy understanding of the green building market and energy needs—something a sustainability specialist is best equipped to do. Green consultants range in professional scope of focus from broad to quite narrow. At the broadest end of the focus range is a sustainability consultant, whose role may include, but not be limited to, work on or with buildings. In the middle of the spectrum are green building consultants, who target buildings and their surrounding sites in their work, but who have a diverse set of skills and tasks within that role. Then, there are the myriad of key specialists—such as a brownfield remediation expert or a daylighting consultant—all of whom help support the GBC in their sustainability efforts. We will look at these specialists who have a narrow focus that targets a single or few green strategies or technologies of which they have a deep knowledge and understanding in the next chapter.

SUSTAINABILITY CONSULTANTS

Sustainability consultants are big-picture people, hired to infuse companies with green thinking and a sustainable mindset. They are often contracted as corporate advisors for businesses that wish to strategically incorporate green throughout their whole company or only in key sectors. Often the choice to incorporate more sustainability into a company is driven by market demand, or it could be an internal grassroots effort. Either way, typically a company's internal team does not have the capacity or knowledge to expand into the green realm by themselves, so they turn to a sustainability consultant to help them target green goals, and then to provide the road maps and the support system with which to achieve these goals. At times, the sustainability consultant is also asked to implement the overall vision. Though sustainability consultants may provide energy consulting or green building ideas as part of their overall services, their focus is more often strategic in nature—unlike green building consultants, whose primary approach centers on buildings.

Services

These are examples of typical services that sustainability consultants would provide:

Assessments

- Provide gap analysis (a status report that looks at where a company is and where it wants to be) of current company with recommended action steps.
- Assess energy sources and use, review the supply chain, and look at operation audits.
- Research/analysis, such as benchmarking of competition or trends in the market.
- Finance for green strategies.
- Innovate environmental initiatives.

Plans

- Provide sustainability plans/assessments/reporting.
- Strategize for green change management/employee engagement.

Reports

- Recommendations for internal and external communication
- Training/presentation to internal staff on sustainability goals
- Advising internal chief sustainability officers (CSOs)

> ### How would you define a sustainability consultant?

❭ Being a sustainability consultant means doing three things well. It means acting as an *expert guide*, helping clients to interpret emerging environmental, social and economic trends (e.g., climate change, the rise of megacities) as well as their long-term implications for business. Secondly, it means serving as an *agent for change* by giving clients the tools needed to drive their company—and industry—toward a more sustainable future from within their organization. Finally, it means working as a *bridge builder*, ensuring that clients are engaging effectively with key stakeholder groups—be they employees, customers, communities, and so on—creating trust and adding long-term value to their business.

Kyle Whitaker, manager, SustainAbility

❭ A sustainability consultant assists organizations in becoming more sustainable in their business (both products and services) and operations.

Sustainability consultants can vary from generalists to technical specialists and assist in both environmental and social aspects of a business.

Ms. K. J. McCorry, CEO, eco-officiency, LLC

> ### This book focuses primarily on the green building field. There can be a "cross-over" between sustainability consultants and green building consultants. What would you say are the key differences?

❭ The similarities and differences between sustainability consultants and green building consultants depend in large part on where one is working along the sustainability value chain. SustainAbility is a *strategy consultancy* and *think tank* working to inspire transformative business leadership along the sustainability agenda. Therefore, the difference between our work at the strategic level and the work that green building consultants do at the implementation level can be considerable. Our business emphasizes soft skills (e.g., relationship management, communication, and critical thinking) whereas green building consultants may require more technical skills. Moreover, the research that our think tank produces is an integral part of our business model. Whereas green building consultants may invest heavily in certification and other technical programs, the institutional knowledge that we amass through research initiatives is critical to our positioning in the marketplace.

Kyle Whitaker, manager, SustainAbility

This book focuses primarily on the green building field. There can be a "cross-over" between sustainability consultants and green building consultants. What would you say are the key differences? (Continued)

❯ Green building consultants can also be considered sustainability consultants. Sustainability as a term covers a broad range of sustainability topics and areas, one of which includes green building. I consider green building a more "technical" specialty within the sustainability-consulting field that requires certain certifications, such as LEED, and experience in the construction industry.

Ms. K. J. McCorry, CEO, eco-officiency, LLC

SUSTAINABILITY CONSULTANT RESOURCES

The International Society of Sustainability Professionals
www.sustainabilityprofessionals.org

Center for Sustainable Organizations
www.sustainableorganizations.org/

Context-Based Sustainability workshop
www.sustainableorganizations.org/context-based-sustainability.html

Corporate Sustainability Management: The Art and Science of Managing Non-Financial Performance, by Mark W. McElroy and J. M. L. van Engelen
www.sustainableorganizations.org/corporate-sustainability-management.html

GREEN BUILDING CONSULTANTS

Ranging from global facilitators (much like architects) to niche specialists, the role of green building consultants (GBCs) can expand or contract depending on the green needs. The lens with which the green building consultant views the building project takes in all of the pertinent environmental issue areas such as site, water, energy, materials, and air quality. GBCs provide the appropriate service based on the client's needs, offering education, facilitation, or implementation of their green goals.

Typically, GBCs focus on the holistic environmental design, construction, and operations of buildings from a triple-bottom-line perspective—in other words, decision making while taking into account all possible economic, environmental, and social implications. "Buildings" could mean a singular building and its surrounding project site or it could mean a neighborhood consisting of several buildings—or on an even larger scale, it could imply a company's national or global building portfolio.

Net Zero court building: Courtyard elevation and water wall garden (Prototype designed to meet Net Zero standards). FIRM AND IMAGE: HOK

When to Engage Green Building Consultants?

Ideally, green building consultants are brought to the table as early in the process as possible, when an owner is at the onset of considering doing a green building project. This enables the green building consultant to:

- Facilitate the vision/goal-setting with the owner in terms of the environmental aspects of the building.

- Help with site selection based on environmental issues such as regional resources (water, renewable energy, etc.), urban infrastructure, and site conditions.

- Determine if it would make more sense to utilize an existing building or to build new.

- Assist in optimum team selection with specialized expertise based on project goals.

- Recommend building orientation to best capitalize on natural resources such as maximizing daylighting.

- Sometimes, the GBC is not brought to the table until later in the process, such as during design or even construction. Even in these cases, however, green attributes can still be incorporated, though it is good to keep in mind that postponing engagement of a GBC usually results in diminishing green opportunities. Waiting until the later phases of design to introduce sustainable elements often means having to change building drawings and specifications, which negatively impacts both schedule and project costs. Delaying work with a green building consultant until construction is under way can prove more costly and time consuming for all parties in terms of soft cost fees and hard construction costs for materials and delays.

The Team Role of a Green Building Consultant

A good analogy for the green building consultant's role on a project team is that of an architect. Architects are trained to design and detail buildings. Renaissance professionals, they have a broad knowledge of many different areas, with a solid but general understanding of everything from site needs to building systems to interiors (including such subspecialties as fire protection and lighting). Architects are not usually specialists, however, and for that reason, they hire a team of professionals, each of whom has a deep focus in a specific area. In assembling the dream team, architects will take into account the client's goals, specific project type (corporate, civic, retail, hospitality, etc.), the type of specialty consultants needed, where the project and the consultants are located, fees, political connections, and any number of other factors. In this same way, green building consultants are also renaissance professionals who either assemble the best possible team based on similar factors or have an in-house staff that specializes in key areas. For comparison, the types of specialty consultants an architect and a green building consultant might hire may look like this:

Architect	Green Building Consultant
Structural engineer	Energy modeling expert
Civil engineer	Daylighting specialist
Mechanical engineer	Commissioning agent
Interior designer	IAQ testing agency
Landscape architect	Green power provider
Lighting consultant	Carbon inventory firm

Sometimes, too, the architect is the point person for the whole project, and the green building consultant is one of the specialists on the team. Other times, the green building consultant works independently to form a team for a client. In other words, there are no hard and fast rules about how and when green building consultants might be part of a team—or might form his or her own team. These lists are only representative examples and can vary from project to project. The first step in determining the best green team for a project is to learn about the client and the client's goals.

What Do Green Building Consultants Do?

Projects can utilize green building rating systems such as Green Globes and LEED. These systems serve as a guide for the planning, design, and construction process, offering a variety of initiatives whereby building professionals can better quantify a structure's environmental benefits and confirm, through an audit or by monitoring data after completion, that it is actually operating as intended. While each of these systems has differences in terms of points, ratings, specific terminology, fees, and so forth, their shared commonality is that they all center the structure around key environmental issues—and it is on these issues that GBCs spend most of their time. Acting as the centralized facilitator for each project in terms of sustainability, GBCs will ask the right questions, engage the best team members, gauge critical project milestones, and, in general, consider the best green building strategies for getting the job done well.

Key Environmental Issues

For each of the key environmental issues, there is a host of green strategies and technology options that green building consultants evaluate as part of their professional role. This section shows some sample ways GBCs might approach a variety of key issues, the strategies they might use, and team members and optimum timing they might employ.

Site Issues

- *Strategy:* Brownfield or other sites in need of remediation are often concerns that GBCs must address. Brownfields are blighted areas with environmental hazards, such as fuel tanks from an abandoned gas station or remnants of an old manufacturing plant, and they require remediation before construction can begin. Although they are not premium sites, there is great environmental benefit to reusing a previously developed site, and to repairing a damaged brownfield area—rather than building new on an untouched site. However, selecting a brownfield site necessitates consideration of other factors, such as remediation costs, surrounding urban infrastructure, nearby community, and a host of other factors, to determine whether the brownfield site is indeed the best place for a particular project.

- *Key team members to engage:* Owner, civil engineer, urban planner, architect, real estate advisor.

- *Timing:* Site selection happens during pre-schematics (the earliest phase of the building process).

Water

- *Strategy:* Rainwater harvesting for irrigation is a key way in which green building consultants often address water catchment. This strategy involves creating a cistern or holding tank to capture rainfall that can then be pumped into irrigation tanks and be used to water landscape, thereby reducing the use of municipal water and the associated energy use needed to treat that water.

- *Key team members to engage:* Owner, architect, civil engineer, landscape architect, contractor, facility manager.

- *Timing:* Planning for irrigation systems would occur during the schematics or design development phase, when all external and internal energy and water systems are considered.

Energy

- *Strategy:* Harvesting daylight reduces the need for electrical (artificial) lighting. Electrical lighting not only uses fossil-fuel-sourced energy, but it also contributes to heat gain, forcing the cooling systems to expend more energy. In this daylighting strategy, the building orientation, window openings, and regional and site conditions (shading, etc.) are considered in determining how to balance the maximum amount of daylight into a building with the amount of accompanying heat gain. Coordinating light shelves, light tubes, skylights, shading devices, controls, furniture heights, and interior wall materials enhances the penetration of daylight into the space.

Great River Energy Headquarters, Maple Grove, Minnesota (LEED NC Platinum). Firm: Perkins + Will, Inc. IMAGE: COURTESY OF PERKINS+WILL, INC.

- *Key team members to engage:* Owner, architect, mechanical engineer, electrical engineer, interior designer, lighting consultant, energy modeling expert, daylighting specialist, furniture manufacturer.

- *Timing:* Considerations of lighting, along with other energy systems such as heating, cooling, equipment, appliances, and plug loads, take place during the schematic or design development phase.

Materials

- *Strategy:* Having a strong and well-considered recycling strategy during construction and after a structure is built requires knowledge of what materials need to be diverted during construction, as well as the ability to conduct a thorough waste

Habitat for Humanity: Grinding waste material for use in soil. PHOTO: DAN GRILLET

audit once construction is complete. Once materials and use are assessed, the GBC (or other green specialist) helps create an internal system that details where recycled materials will be stored, the staff members responsible for the system, and haulers to pick up the recycling. Key components often include details such as good signage for users and company-wide education about how to use the new recycling system.

■ *Key team members to engage:* Owner, base building owner who may be a real estate professional, architect, interior designer, contractor, subcontractor, installer, facility manager, and recycling provider.

■ *Timing:* Ideally, for construction waste, this would all happen in the pre-schematics phase, but building recycling systems can be incorporated at any point in the overall process, even after a building is fully occupied and operational.

Air

■ *Strategy:* Incorporating low-emitting interior building materials such as insulation, paint, carpet, composite woods, adhesives, sealants, stains, etc., creates healthier air quality for both the installers and the occupants of the space.

■ *Key team members to engage:* Architect, mechanical, electrical, plumbing engineers, interior designer, fireproofing specialist, acoustical specialist, product manufacturers, contractor, subcontractors, and installers.

■ *Timing:* The best time for specifying materials is during design development, when construction documents are being detailed, describing what the team members are recommending for all necessary materials and methods of installation.

Cooper Carry, Atlanta, GA: Office (LEED CI Platinum). Firm: Cooper Carry. PHOTO: GABRIEL BENZUR PHOTOGRAPHY

While the GBC's main focus is on strategic implementation of all of these important environmental issues, dissemination of this knowledge comes in many forms.

Educate/Facilitate/Implement

GBCs can provide a variety of levels of service and can have areas of focus that are both broad and deeply ensconced in sustainable concerns. In addition to consulting throughout the design and construction of a building project, GBCs are also well versed in other parts of green building initiatives, including:

- Education in the form of training or presentations on green building
- Facilitation of strategic planning
- Facilitation of sustainable processes
- Facilitation of green building rating systems
- Implementation of sustainable or green building goals

These different roles of a GBC are detailed in the following sections:

EDUCATION

Green building consultants often provide educational services through training or facilitation programs aimed at a wide variety of audiences. A few examples of these services might include accreditation credential training, rating system workshops, and building product manufacturer presentations.

FACILITATION OF STRATEGIC PLANNING

GBCs can provide green strategic planning across a range of scales, from working with urban planners on a city or neighborhood scale to assisting corporations with long-term planning. In order to most accurately assess client needs, a GBC first looks at where the client currently is on the green continuum—and where they want to go. The FairRidge Group provides a model that shows the five levels in which a GBC might determine a company's level of sustainability:

1. *Business as Usual:* The company has some awareness of sustainability concerns but is not currently doing anything to address them.
2. *Ad Hoc Response:* The company is starting to respond to questionnaires from customers and/or NGOs but does not have a formal sustainability function.
3. *Plan and Pilot:* The company has created a sustainability department, which has started to plan and pilot some eco-efficiency projects.
4. *Operationalize:* The company's lines of business have taken ownership of sustainability initiatives, and have started to leverage sustainability to extend their products and services portfolio.

5. *Transform:* The company has a system-wide sustainability mandate that is fully integrated into all aspects of the business; the resulting transformation creates clear competitive differentiation.[8]

Ideally, the GBC uses this model to quickly assess where a company is, regarding its level of green maturity. Often, in this situation, a GBC might also help set visionary goals and a gap analysis for the company, as well as make recommendations on how to meet goals and the tools with which to do so. The following are some of the initial questions a GBC may ask to determine the direction for sustainable strategic planning:

- What is your company's sustainable vision and/or leadership statement?
- Why are you interested in green strategic planning, and is this interest generated from competitor benchmarking? Client requests? Good corporate stewardship?
- Do you have corporate leadership for environmental initiatives?
- What environmental regulations do you need to meet in order to do your business?

Once the GBC receives responses back to these questions, she or he will determine the best next steps, which might include everything from writing a sustainable business plan (including a green vision statement, long-term goals, competitor analysis, internal staff organization chart, competitor and financial analysis reports, and a metrics evaluation) to recommendations for pulling together a sustainable advisory group to provide future green direction for the company.

FACILITATION OF PROCESS

"Integrated design" is fundamental to successful green building, and many GBCs have a good working knowledge of how to incorporate integrated design into the green building process. For example, a GBC may facilitate a green building integrated design charrette or train others on how to provide one.

Michael Bayer at St. Croix Integrated Team Charette. PHOTO: ZANDY HILLIS-STARR, NATIONAL PARK SERVICE

FACILITATION OF RATING SYSTEMS

Frameworks or guides that have developed benchmark metrics around environmental issues are the foundation of rating systems. In layman's terms, they are similar to the Olympic Games—your building is competing, is scored with points, and at the end is awarded a "medal" or level of certification for its good green building practices. Facilitating these systems puts the GBC in the position of a "knowledgeable guide," or coach of sorts. The GBC should be able to provide education, technical guidance, insight on resources, strategies, and technologies to meet the green goals.

■ Audits for existing buildings (energy, water, systems, etc.), including a gap analysis benchmark. Typically this involves recommendations for improvement and should include return on investment (ROI) details so the client understands what the initial investment is, compared with long-term savings.

■ Facilitation of sustainable or green development. This type of service may be appropriate for clients who do not want to commit to a certification system with definitive metrics. In this case, often the client is just testing out the idea of going green, or funding is not in place to support larger multifaceted efforts.

■ Facilitation of certification systems (BREEAM, Green Globes, LEED, etc.). Facilitation of certification rating systems often can require a GBC's expertise, because this layers an additional component onto the existing design, construction, and operation of a building; furthermore, the rating systems are often evolving, and a GBC is able to keep abreast of ever-shifting nuances in codes and ratings. Sometimes, the architect, engineer, or contractor on the core project team possesses the necessary green expertise, and hiring a separate GBC is unwarranted. However, when stakes are higher, such as funding that is tied to the achievement of a certification or higher levels of certification, a GBC might be hired to better ensure success. The work of facilitating certification systems involves envisioning the client's desired green goal, then utilizing the most appropriate system as a framework on the project. The GBC guides the project team through the process with education and quality control checkpoints. Typically, the GBC will also be the key contact with the certifying body and report back to the project team.

IMPLEMENTATION

Once a company or client's sustainable vision is set, the GBC can facilitate implementation of the next phase, or the vision may be handed over to a company's internal team. Implementation may involve several different areas, but this stage typically has very specific and measurable responsibilities, actions, and deliverables, including the following:

■ Goals/actions/long-term actions

■ Point of contact responsible for strategies

■ Education

■ Internal/external communication

■ Quality control milestones

HOW GREEN BUILDING CONSULTANTS WORK

GBCs can work with clients on these services In a wide range of ways. In some cases, the client may need full facilitation with a "soup to nuts" approach, and the GBC can provide straightforward recommendations and assist in implementation. In other cases, there may be internal environmental contacts that can provide some support to the GBC, allowing for a reduced scope of work. One of the ideal scenarios is that of a client approaching the project from a "learning experience" perspective, hoping to glean knowledge and ideas from the GBC so that the client may become skilled in green building and internalize the role. For example, a large national financial institution approached H2 Ecodesign, the author's firm, with a desire to improve their sustainable knowledge within the company. Soon after the initial meeting, the bank entered into the USGBC's LEED pilot program with their entire building portfolio, which encompassed a large number of buildings and tenant spaces across the United States. In this case, the GBC was a teacher and mentor throughout the process, helping establish a sustainable prototype and setting up a three-pronged system of education, quality control, and documentation that was then integrated into the company's internal design and construction process. Using this learned knowledge as a guide, the bank was able to hire an internal team member to manage this ongoing process as the company adds buildings to its portfolio in the future.

External Green Building Consultants

When the green building consultant is external to the client's team—as was the case in the bank example just described—some of the advantages are:

- In-depth green knowledge based on area of expertise
- Staff, education, process, and tools investments that are green specific
- Ability to provide assistance for short-term needs without the overhead expenses of a staff employee
- Advantage of external perspective, which may offer a broader view of the market
- Ease of engagement without having to go through the bureaucracy of human resources departments
- Third-party or more neutral expertise, which has the benefit of less conflict of interest

Internal Green Building Consultants

Some companies prefer to internalize their green building consulting needs with a little outside help here and there. Some of the reasons that it might be preferable for companies to keep green services in-house include the following:

- Ability to control management and cost of the work
- Creating an additional profit center

- Potential to better integrate the work, using internal systems
- Long-term investment in environmental strategies across multiple business aspects
- Marketing of internal expertise
- Training of internal team
- Diversification of multiple offerings

The following interview provides an excellent example of how one design firm was able to internalize its green building services and create a functioning business unit.

Green Design Pioneer

BRIAN M. MALARKEY, FAIA, LEED AP

Executive Vice President, Director of Kirksey EcoServices

Kirksey | Architecture

What has been your path to your current role?

❭ In the late 1990s, our firm formed a green committee and joined the U.S. Green Building Council. A few of us attended one of their early conferences in 2000 in Tucson, Arizona. There were 450 people there, and what we saw was amazing. Individuals and businesses with passion and expertise in sustainable design were doing well by doing good. Their businesses were flourishing and clients were seeking them out for their green building skills. We immediately returned to Houston and founded a local chapter of the U.S. Green Building Council and convinced our first client to pursue LEED certification for their project. As our skills and expertise improved, I founded Kirksey EcoServices, a group of dedicated individuals performing green building research, LEED documentation services, daylight and energy modeling, and green building

training. Our reputation has allowed us to expand into green building consulting for other firms, and now a good portion of our work is "out of house." Critical to this journey was my firm's willingness to let me explore and ultimately create a stand-alone team focused on sustainability. I continuously assessed the market, looked at trends, and shared the data illustrating that green building was not a fad, but a market shift.

How do you feel design firms are adapting for the future of offering sustainable design consulting services?

❭ Many design firms form dedicated groups that focus on sustainable design such as Kirksey; however, most concentrate on work within their own offices. There are opportunities, both in house or out, to offer sustainable design services to clients once certain skills are learned, such as energy modeling and daylight simulation. Many firms have chosen to make these services part of their typical design offerings, but I believe there are opportunities to capitalize on those skills once you can illustrate their benefit as a decision-making method and return on investment tool.

Solar and vegetated roof study for the George R. Brown Convention Center, Houston, Texas (LEED EB Silver). Firm: Kirksey Architecture. PHOTO: 2008 KIRKSEY

How do you forecast the role for green building consultants and specialists on your teams in the future?

❯ There will always be a need for green building consultants to perform LEED documentation and keep up with the latest tools such as energy modeling and daylight simulation; however, more and more design firms are bringing energy and daylight simulation tools in-house. After using these tools for many years, Kirksey has come to realize that they need to be employed immediately upon starting a project to truly leverage their effectiveness. They have to be used as design tools, and not documentation tools. In fact, having valuable information about energy performance has helped galvanize our relationships with our clients, reestablishing the value that designers have in the building process.

How have green building consultants helped your work?

❯ Our company was thrust into the sustainability world with a very tight construction timeline. Luckily, we engaged a qualified GBC that guided us through the LEED process. I know that without the leadership and guidance of the GBC, our project would not have achieved Silver certification.

Kevin L. Matherly, LEED AP, vice president, Project Management, Partners Development

❯ Exposure to green building consultants has broadened my knowledge base with regard to green building issues. The consultants have also brought a passion to green building which has inspired me to become involved with several organizations at the local and national levels and eventually become the director of sustainable design for my company. I feel what I have learned the most from green consultants is that you have to be committed and not take no for an answer—you just have to find a way to get it done.

Donald K. Green, NCARB, AIA, LEED AP BD+C, associate/ managing architect, THW Design

Perspectives from Green Building Consultants

The Human Element

REBECCA L. FLORA, AICP, LEED AP BD+C, ND

President, RLF Collaborative, LLC

Sustainable Communities Practice Leader, Ecology and Environment, Inc.

What is your primary role and responsibility as a green building consultant on a project team? As a green building consultant, what do you bring to the project process?

❯ I have recently transitioned from working in the nonprofit realm as an "unpaid" consultant, working as a salaried staff person for community benefit, to the for-profit world, where billable hours are critical to survival. Despite this shift, my role remains the same, that of a facilitator, source of technical knowledge, connector, and often an advisor, with the primary objective of teaching others how to integrate green building concepts in all aspects of their work.

Do you anticipate green building consulting to be a long-term practice, or do you think it will eventually be incorporated into other existing team members' roles (architect, engineer, etc.)? If eventually integrated, how long do you estimate this to take? What do you anticipate your "new role" will be in the future?

❯ I do not see the need for a green building or sustainability champion disappearing. As world priorities change, there will always be the need for individuals and firms to maintain the values of green building practices. I believe we have gone through cycles of sustainability over the centuries, and various cultures have embraced nature better than others. While the title may change and there may be less need in some areas where this becomes common practice, there will always be a continued need for innovation and evolution of our practice; otherwise, there will be a new status quo that may be better than what we see now, but there will always be room for improvement.

What is the future of the green building consulting field, and what do you see as cutting edge?

❯ I am currently working the human element—how do we impact societal transformation? I think that the market and community leaders are ready to move beyond the building to the people inside and the broader scale of communities. Additionally, questions of life-cycle analysis and impacts are also starting to get more attention.

Conversation Creator

GUNNAR HUBBARD, LEED AP BD+C, ID+C
Principal
Thornton Tomasetti | Fore Solutions

How did you get started in green building consulting—please describe your education and prior work experience. Who or what was a major influence on your career choice?

❯ My parents built an off-the-grid, log home with semi-passive solar, a composting toilet, and gravity-fed water. I was twelve years old when we started and seventeen by the time we got the roof on—the log-by-log building process is slow! I went on to the University of Vermont to get an environmental studies degree, with a self-designed major in environmental architecture. I then worked for a couple of years for architects and design/builders in Vermont, after which I went to the University of Oregon for a master's in architecture. I was very active in many green-related building initiatives, but I decided not to pursue a traditional architecture job, and instead worked at the Union of Concerned Scientists running a national renewable energy education effort. I was asked to apply as the director of the Yestermorrow Design/Build

School, I got the job, and I ran the school for three years. While there, I connected with the green champions at the time and invited them to teach at the school. I was invited to work on the greening of the White House, and then got hired by the Rocky Mountain Institute as a research scholar in green development. I consulted around the U.S. and some internationally and got the consulting buzz down. I was at RMI for two years, involved in projects such as 4 Times Square, and then I decided to get my architecture license and headed to San Francisco. After a short stint with Sim Van der Ryn, I started an architecture practice with a University of Oregon colleague Ned White (who was licensed) and worked toward becoming an architect, doing some consulting along the way. We shared an office with Lynn Simon, and after four years there, my East Coast homing buzzer went off and I headed east to Maine with my wife, where I balanced both architecture and consulting, and then kicked into full consulting mode with the growth of LEED.

What is your primary role and responsibility as a green building consultant on a project team?

❯ I am the team leader, educator, and herder of cats. Ultimately, the green building process is a shift from the traditional process, so it involves front-loading efforts, educating, and asking the right questions of the design team and owner to ensure the highest-performing green building possible with the budget and timeline provided. As the green building consultant, we not only facilitate the process, we also are a team of green experts that offer and implement eco-solutions.

Most people consider green building consulting to be a relatively new field—do you see it as a long-term consulting practice, or do you think it will eventually be incorporated into other existing team members' roles (architect, engineer, etc.)? If eventually integrated into other disciplines, how long do you estimate this to take? What do you anticipate your "new role" will be in the future?

❯ I think that over time more and more team members will see the value of green building, but that

will only be the basics. I think there is still a lot of work to be done with firms. Architects are getting it quicker than engineers, and then as we look at our global economy and work internationally, there is lots of work still to be done. I am not sure if it would be a new role, but I think securing the role of sustainability innovator on a design team is a fun way to think about what I can do now and in the future—with the intent to achieve buildings and communities that produce more energy than they use, create minimum waste, clean the air, clean the water, and mimic nature.

There are currently more building professionals than ever before in the field. What effects on quality and fees have you seen with this shift?

❯ I see a lot of people trying to add this service for "less," and the reality is that many just put their

Museum of the Built Environment.
FIRM AND IMAGE: FXFOWLE

focus on LEED certification and not on integrated design. So, while we may lose some jobs to the lower-fee consultants, we are finding clients come back to us the next time, or we just hear stories of frustrated clients. The reality, though, is that some clients just want the certification and don't know what they don't know, so they do not understand that they could get more. The differentiator is the ability to get beyond the soft-cost focus and impress upon consultants about the impacts on the design team, contractor, and ultimately the owners' operating budget and employee satisfaction.

What is the future of the green building consulting field—what do you see as cutting edge?

❯ It's the ability to affect the process—which will result in a better product. From a process perspective, it's about creating project teams that are truly integrative and that ask the right questions, such as "Is this functional? What systems best support this design?"

For the design and construction of buildings, cutting edge is about making buildings that produce more energy than they use, that clean the water, clean the air, and add to the well-being of a community. In short, buildings that are regenerative and net-zero energy.

What traits/qualifications/characteristics/ background do you look for when hiring a new green building consultant?

❯ Passion and the ability to communicate. Also, a willingness to learn and be humble, paired with a go-getter history. Time in the trenches—as well as the right kind of trench.

Responsive Evolution

LAUREN YARMUTH, LEED AP BD+C

Principal

YR&G Consulting

How did you get started in green building consulting? Who or what was a major influence on your career choice?

❯ I studied architecture and while I was in school was introduced to Bill Browning at Rocky Mountain Institute (RMI). Hearing about his work turned me on to green concepts and I focused my schoolwork on that theme, got internships in the field, and eventually (with determination) went to work at RMI myself.

What is your primary role and responsibility as a green building consultant on a project team? As a green building consultant, what do you bring to the project process?

❯ I manage a team of people (my firm) who do everything from energy and daylight and cost modeling, to LEED consulting, design assistance, corporate policy, marketing, and operations support. As consultants we try to be the "green lens" on a project, serving as a resource and guide to the team in nearly all aspects associated with sustainability. I also teach sustainability-related concepts to clients and at various universities.

Most people consider green building consulting to be a relatively new field—do you see it as a long-term consulting practice, or do you think it will eventually be incorporated into other existing team members' roles (architect, engineer, etc.)? If eventually integrated into other disciplines, how long do you estimate this to take? What do you anticipate your "new role" will be in the future?

❯ I think that the field will continue to evolve. Yes, elements of our current services like LEED consulting and energy modeling may be incorporated into other industries, but by then other elements of sustainability/green building will emerge in stronger force like, perhaps, related to community services, integrated agriculture, green investments, education, etc.

What is the future of the green building consulting field, and what do you see as cutting edge?

❯ "Living" or regenerative buildings, community-based economies, building integrated agriculture.

What do you think are the biggest rewards and the biggest frustrations in the green building consulting field?

❯ Rewards: Collaboratively arriving at exceptional and meaningful solutions, and seeing people and projects transformed as a result.

Frustrations: Many projects/project teams are closed minded, rushed, and have resources allocated in a traditional manner that does not accommodate real opportunities for optimization and excellence.

Lauren Yarmuth, LEED AP BD+C, principal, YR&G Consulting

❯ Rewards: Seeing the "aha!" moment when the people begin to make the connections between how we treat the environment directly impacts our social and economic health.

Frustrations: when people are it just for the money or the publicity.

Rebecca L. Flora, LEED AP BD+C, president, RLF Collaborative, LLC, sustainable communities practice leader, Ecology and Environment, Inc.

❯ The biggest rewards are seeing the great results of a project well done: a happy client, a proud design team, a passionate contractor, and if there are some lessons learned, figuring out how to use them to effect change on the next project.

After months of work arriving at the best integrated design solution, some outside source or new client rep is brought on—such as a value engineer—who makes recommendations that steer a project the wrong way for the wrong reasons, even if the team has the counter-facts of performance. So the lesson learned is to make sure all the players are at the table from the beginning, including the client.

Gunnar Hubbard, LEED AP BD+C, ID+C, principal, Thornton Tomasetti | Fore Solutions

Green Lanterns

From Starbucks to small residential homes, corporations and projects are started to incorporate green as a fundamental and well-integrated aspect of the overall big picture. As a result, sustainability and green building consultant jobs are being created to meet these new needs, resulting in a wealth of highly trained professionals who are able to deeply delve into green issues and lead others to more sustainable solutions. From sustainable consultants who go beyond buildings to green building consultants whose knowledge spans the breadth of the building industry in solar energy, water management, and material selection, there is a wide variety of types of sustainable jobs in this area. Indeed, for the green job seeker, opportunities in this market seem nothing but positive and on a rapid rise. Choosing an internal or external green consultant to chart your eco-path can make all the difference in creating the optimum environmental project. Just as a lantern provides light in an otherwise dark night, so too can a sustainability or green building consultant provide a beacon of leadership.

NOTES

1. Booz Allen Hamilton for the U.S. Green Building Council, *Green Jobs Study,* Executive Summary, page ii, 2009.

2. Anya Kamenetz, "Ten Best Green Jobs for the Next Decade," *Fast Company,* January 14, 2009, www.fastcompany.com/articles/2009/01/best-green-jobs.html, accessed October 3, 2011.

3. Tristan Roberts, "Your Guide to the New Draft of LEED" BuildingGreen.com, www.buildinggreen.com/auth/article.cfm/2010/11/8/Your-Guide-to-the-New-Draft-of-LEED-2012-public-comment-USGBC/, accessed October 3, 2011.

4. U.S. Green Building Council, "LEED 2012 Development: FAQ," www.usgbc.org/ShowFile.aspx?DocumentID=9826, accessed October 3, 2011.

5. International Green Construction Code, www.iccsafe.org/cs/IGCC/Pages/default.aspx, accessed October 3, 2011.

6. The State of California CALGreen, http://www.hcd.ca.gov/CALGreen.html, accessed October 3, 2011.

7. Christopher Cheatham, "Florida Supports Green Building Code," *Green Building Law Update,* The Law Office of Christopher Cheatham, LLP, June 9, 2011, www.greenbuildinglawupdate.com/2011/06/articles/codes-and-regulations/florida-supports-green-building-code/?utm_source=feedburner&utm_medium=feed&utm_campaign=Feed%3A+GreenBuildingLawUpdate+%28Green+Building+Law+Update%29, accessed October 3, 2011.

8. FairRidge Group, "Sustainability Management Infrastructure: What It Is and Why You Should Care," June 25, 2009, www.triplepundit.com/2009/06/sustainability-management-infrastructure-what-it-is-and-why-you-should-care/, accessed October 3, 2011.

6 Green Building Process and Tools

If the only tool you have is a hammer, you tend to see every problem as a nail.

—ABRAHAM MASLOW *(American professor of psychology with focus on the positive qualities in people. Known for development of Maslow's Hierarchy of Needs.)*

EVERY PROFESSION HAS ITS OWN SET of processes and tools that help get a job done. Doctors have medical kits and books, artists have paints and canvas, and tailors have scissors and thread. The same is true of the building profession, which has its own uniquely stocked toolbox with key elements of the trade. In order to create a good, green building, it is ideal to have two key elements in place: a practiced, proven process for designing, constructing, and operating a building utilizing an experienced team, and second, a toolbox full of the best-practices tools needed to do the job. Though the actual tools and procedures might vary, all green building professionals, from architects to contractors to facility managers, look to the same key elements in their toolbox when striving to find the optimum approach through which to complete their own role in the green building process.

Process

A successful building process involves a series of common elements that includes a quality control plan to ensure that the entire team is on the right track, a set of lessons learned on previous projects that might be brought to bear on the current scheme. The green layer should be threaded seamlessly within the building site and indeed throughout the entire construction process.

2101 L Street NW (LEED CI Platinum). Firm: RTKL. PHOTO:
© PAUL WARCHOL

As basic quality control is overlaid on the process, a green plan emerges with a committed quantitative project goal in place. Setting measurable milestones to success also provides markers to ensure that the process is going as planned, with the opportunity to make changes along the way if improvements are needed and to confirm that the best tools are being used for the job. Since any process is only as good as its implementation, it is imperative that effective, efficient project managers are carefully supervising the overall process, as well as maintaining and overseeing it on a daily basis. One key distinction with a green process is the ability to be flexible and organic in the methodology, similar to nature's ability to adapt as better solutions are introduced.

Team members from the U.S. Department of Energy Solar Decathlon 2011 gather for their first morning meeting on the solar village construction site in West Potomac Park. PHOTO: CAROL ANNA/U.S. DEPARTMENT OF ENERGY SOLAR DECATHLON

> *You have created "process development" for a variety of different green building systems. Would you say that there are some common elements or keys to success for a good process?*

❯ Process development is all about comprehensiveness. If a process does not accomplish its task in its specific application and all associated incarnations, then it is not a very good process. The best processes result from a combination of research and experience. Research is key because oftentimes a similar process has been developed previously and experience is necessary so that the process is tailored appropriately based on its application.

Gregg Liddick, LEED AP BD+C, manager, GDL Sustainability Consulting

GUIDE: INTEGRATED DESIGN

The Institute for Market Transformation to Sustainability & American National Standards Institute created a formal process for integrated design called the Integrative Process Standard© for Design and Construction of Sustainable Buildings and Communities. This standard defines the intent of an integrative process as one in which the purpose is to "effectively manage and optimize synergies between the complex set of technical and living systems associated with design and construction in order to effectively pursue sustainable practices.... To achieve cost effective and increasingly more effective environmental performance, it is necessary to shift from conventional linear design and delivery processes to design and construction practices that focus on interrelated systems integration."[1]

In an article titled "Everyone is Practicing Integrative Design...at least that's what they say," by Barbra Batshalom and Kevin Settlemyre, the authors have developed a list of telltale signs that mark a "dis-integrated" process, some of which include:

■ The absence of mutual agreement of the project's end goals and a misunderstanding of fundamental project aims during the early design phase.

■ Lack of communication between specialties and professionals resulting in a sense of intrigue around how specific data have been resolved or how problems have been treated (such as with an architect not being clearly told how an electrical engineer arrived at a design conclusion).

■ Meetings are inefficient and seem uncollaborative in nature.[2]

In contrast, there are specific aspects of an integrative process that will help ensure project success, basic minimum requirements to achieve an environmentally and cost-effective integrated project as outlined by the Integrative Design Process Standard for Design and Construction of Sustainable Buildings and Communities. Certainly, it is possible to achieve a high-performance project without these elements; however, the large majority of project teams will stumble in their efforts to achieve high-level goals if any of these aspects are not addressed:

■ The client (the main financial decision maker) needs to be involved in the design decision-making process so that he/she is aware of how decisions are made and will not mistakenly disrupt established and integrated decisions.

- The right design team should be in place; there should be no "experts" to take charge, only co-learners who will work as part of a team.

- The stakeholders and design team should be mutually aligned around the purpose and values that are the driving reason behind the project and its greening effort; the ideal of making money or simply wanting to construct a building are rarely, if ever, the primary purpose of the project.

- Key systems and patterns—such as habitat, water, energy, and materials—should be identified and in place.

- Find solutions and synergies between building and natural systems during the pre-design process, using evaluation tools to assess needs and goals when green solutions can still be easily added without the additional cost or difficulties of adding in sustainability later in the process.

- There should be a strong commitment by team members to specific measurable goals for key systems.

- There should be a clear map of the integration process.

- There should be complete follow-through during the construction process.

- After completion of the project, there should be a commission in which the building is assessed to ensure it performs the way it was designed to perform—just because it is built does not mean it works.

- Maintenance and monitoring must continue after building completion since entropy happens and consistent feedback is essential to sustained high performance.[3]

What is the Integrative Process (IP) about, and why is it important for the industry?

› Integrative Process (IP) for the first time integrates the professionals in the design and construction process so that they act as a team in required workshops at the pre-design and other key stages. As a result, IP reduces risk according to Fireman's Fund's IP Risk Reduction Statement, and reduces construction and operating costs based on the experience of the Navy and Liberty Mutual by substantially reducing change orders. IP also increases cash flow for commercial buildings and economic value for homes as indicated in the consensus Green Building Underwriting Standard.

Mike Italiano, president & CEO, The Institute for Market Transformation to Sustainability, founder, U.S. Green Building Council, director, Sustainable Furnishings Council, CEO, Capital Markets Partnership

Master Integrator

BILL REED AIA, LEED AP, HON. FIGP

President, Regenesis

Chairman, Integrative Design Collaborative

Co-author of Wiley book, *The Integrative Design Guide to Green Building*

When did you first learn of integrative design, and how did you know it would be transformative?

❯ I first learned of the integrated approach browsing the stacks as an undergrad in the early 1970s and finding a small book by William Caudill of Caudill, Rowlett, and Scott (CRS). He was promoting the benefits of the process of designing the Texas School District projects using a series of design workshops or weeklong design sessions. I remember his definition of a successful workshop process as one where, at the end, no one could point to any one person as the designer. The team and the client became fully integrated in the process.

It was after a trip to Europe in the mid-1980s where it all came together. As I reviewed my trip photographs, I realized that every building pictured was pre-industrial. As a contemporary architect it seemed odd that this was the case. The common aspect of every building was that one person—a master builder—had built it. If one person could create such long-lasting and beautiful structures, why aren't we doing this today? It was immediately apparent that the age of specialization was not going to be done away with—so how might we create a process to have everyone meet around the table to, in effect, become a composite master builder? This seemed so right to me, yet it wasn't until the greater complexity and unexplored issues of green design came on the scene

in the 1990s that integrating the participants in the design and building process became essential.

It took a few years of experiments to realize one couldn't afford to bring "everyone" around the table at every meeting; an integrative design process required a much more focused management of the what, when, and whom of the process.

By the way, originally the LEED AP Innovation Credit was conceived to be a way to indicate a designer's use of integrative design to achieve higher performance.

How is the process unique compared with traditional building design?

❯ Most architects feel that they are integrators by the nature of having to embrace many different consultants and the expertise they bring to the project. While they may be incorporating these ideas, they are typically not very effective at inviting the consultants to co-create or co-design the project. A truly effective integrative process is one where everyone is invited to be a co-designer and move the project beyond the usual assumptions, expectations, and performance levels. This process is one that embraces an exploration of what we don't know. In doing so, new ideas with new potential emerge. If a design team is simply gathered together in a workshop to align themselves around an architect's or client's ideas—there will be much lost in terms of creative potential.

What are a few key elements or key outcomes of good integrative design?

❯ Engage in a discovery process that should happen BEFORE any thought of building or project form is considered.

Address both mechanical and living systems: discover (i.e., research and analyze) all systems—energy, water, habitat, human habitat, and materials—to at least the boundary of the largest manageable watershed.

Align the project team around the deep purpose of the project; no one builds a building just for kicks. This will allow creativity to flourish.

Design the design process. Schedule all workshops, interactions, required research, and analysis. That way everyone has a road map of the scope of issues.

It is useful to hold what we call a part A and B process. Consultants are paid (or not) to do initial simple studies and meet in a workshop to discuss the potential of the project in terms of design and performance opportunities.

Work toward ever-increasing potential—iterate, iterate, iterate ideas. Do not set performance goals early in the project; these thresholds can limit creative thinking. After all, we haven't come close to reaching a sustainable condition.

Continue to iterate about building performance and the potential to improve it and people's engagement with it and the watershed/community. Forever.

Tell us a story about a successful integrative project or lessons learned.

❯ Regarding the discovery of the aforementioned "deep purpose" of a project, we derived the following approach from the management guru, Charles Deming: The purpose of any important issue should be understood to a level of Five Whys. We asked these five questions at the beginning of an international corporate headquarters project. Here is a paraphrased account of the discussion that occurred with the executive vice president of the company:

Why do you need this building? (Bear with us, we know this seems obvious.)

We need more space.

Why do you need more space?

To house our growing work force.

Why do you need to house the work force?

To achieve a higher level of effective communication and esprit de corps.

Why will they interact better if you build the design concept that's already up there on the wall?

After thirty seconds of silence, the EVP slapped his hand on the table, opined with an expletive, and exclaimed that we had just saved him $30 million.

Obviously curious, we asked him how. He explained that having just been asked to reflect on how his work force would interact as a result of the design concept, he realized that a full quarter of the company's staff got no benefit at all from the building. The information technology (IT) and call center department members wore headphones all day long and communicated with each other either over the phone or electronically. They only got together face-to-face for a staff meeting once a week, and they would likely much rather avoid the commute and work from home. After coming to this realization, the owner got very excited about building a building that was 25 percent smaller, which equated to a 150,000-square-foot reduction. This is not a bad way to begin a discussion about environmental building—these questions had just opened the possibility for seriously reducing the environmental impacts of this building, not to mention saving the client a huge amount of money. Here, the approach to sustainability started with building less. (Paraphrased from *The Integrative Design Guide to Green*

Building, by 7Group, Bill Reed, et al., John Wiley & Sons, 2009.)

The lesson learned from this occurred two weeks later. We were immediately hired to help with the integration process for the design. However, the experience the VP had with us had not been experienced with the entire real estate and facilities team. When the VP told them what he had learned from our meeting, they told him that the project was already too far down the schedule to reconsider. What they were really saying is they had no will to work for something more important. Of course, the VP could have redirected the project. However, the lessons learned were: We were brought in too late; the right participants and leaders were not present (not integrated) into the discussion; and the company started designing the building before they really understood the potential of the issues.

We were politely thanked for our effort and told that it was too late for our services. Another mistake—as it is never too late to think creatively and discover some level of synergy.

Future versions of LEED incorporate a new element to all rating systems called "Integrative Process" where it guides teams to collaborate early in the process about energy and water systems related to cost analysis.

Cooper Carry, Atlanta, GA: Innovation Room (LEED CI Platinum). Firm: Cooper Carry. PHOTO: GABRIEL BENZUR PHOTOGRAPHY

INTEGRATIVE PROCESS RESOURCES

American Institute of Architects (AIA): *Integrated Project Delivery: A Guide*
www.aia.org/contractdocs/AIAS077630

American National Standards Institute (ANSI)
Whole Systems Integrative Process (WSIP) Guide for Sustainable Buildings and Communities
http://webstore.ansi.org/FindStandards.aspx?Action=displaydept&DeptID=3144

Market Transformation to Sustainability (MTS) & American National Standards Institute
"Integrative Process Standard© for Design and Construction of Sustainable Buildings and Communities"
http://mts.sustainableproducts.com/IP/IP%20Standard%20-%20BALLOT%20Version.pdf

BetterBricks—Integrated Design Process & Tools
www.betterbricks.com/design-construction/tools/integrated-design-process-tools

Whole Building Design Guide
www.wbdg.org/wbdg_approach.php

The Toolbox

Once a comprehensive and integrative process is in place, it is time to bring out the tools that can help support and maintain the overall plan. Toolboxes were created to house many different tools with a variety of options, strengths, and weaknesses. In addition, most toolboxes are also portable so that if a tool needs adjustment, another option is readily available. Furthermore, toolboxes are filled with tools that fit the needs of a particular profession or project. Such is the case in the green building profession, where tools and toolboxes come in a variety of options, sizes, and shapes.

As one example, green construction tools come in a range of formats, from construction plans, Excel spreadsheets, and photographs all the way down to the basic hammer and nail. A few other best practice tools might include the following:

■ A support tool, or area in the construction trailer that houses the key green resources.

■ A reminder prompt tool that lists green goals as an agenda item for weekly construction meetings.

■ A spreadsheet tool that tracks the certified wood, low-emitting, and regional materials on the project.

■ A spreadsheet tool that monitors the amount of construction waste diverted from landfill.

- Photographs that show where there may be air quality issues or where water is infiltrating, possibly leading to mold issues in the future. Photographs are also a great way to show reuse of existing materials—perhaps steel studs are repurposed from an existing building, but once covered with gypsum wallboard, they would be impossible to see unless captured in process via a photograph.

- On-site equipment might include an air quality testing device that reports amount of emissions, a daylighting-monitoring device that measures the amount of daylight in a space, or commissioning testing devices for the building's energy systems.

SELECTING THE BEST TOOL FOR THE JOB

A common screw can be released with a butter knife or a screwdriver. The question is, what is the best tool for the job? Rarely is there a one-size-fits-all solution—otherwise, all construction could be done with a hammer. Instead, selecting the best tool for the job depends on each unique situation.

In order to discern the best tool for any job, it is important to first evaluate which tool would work, and then the best tool for a particular desired final outcome. Some of the questions to ask in evaluation of green tools may be:

Which tool would work?

- What is the final goal?
- Are there existing restraints or parameters in the project?
- Is the tool credible based on specific criteria?
- Is the tool certified by a third-party provider (neutral source)?
- How will the client perceive this tool?
- If this is a new tool, does it have a proven track record?

Which is the best tool for the desired final outcome?

- Is there a required format for the output, based on either a green rating system or client requirements? What is the best format for archiving?
- How frequently does the tool need to be updated or revised?
- How familiar is the project team with the tool?
- Will experts need to be engaged to assist in using the tool?

As one can imagine, even with responses to all of these questions, it may or may not be clear which tool is best to use. Beyond an initial evaluation, there are rapid shifts in tools and products due to ever-changing and constantly updated technology. What may have been the right tool two months ago may not be the same today. Often, these new technologies and strategies can inform and even reshape the integrated process. In turn, the process can also give feedback, creating revisions to tools, which is why it is important to be flexible to adaptations when necessary.

Even when you are able to evaluate and compare all available tools that are up to date with the latest technologies, help still may be needed to determine which tool is best. This help could come in several different forms:

- Websites will often evaluate tools and give pros and cons of each.
- Journals or white papers can provide tool rankings and matrices of offerings.
- Recommendations can be obtained from professionals who have experience with the tools in question.
- The project team can seek expert assistance in evaluation of tool options.
- The team can collaborate with specific tool experts.

TRANSPARENCY

While a number of process and tool combinations can be produce good results, the best and most reliable are verified using two key elements: neutrality and specific performance metrics. A common example of neutral verification using specific numbers is the tallying of votes in a high-profile contest such as the Academy Awards or *American Idol;* typically, a neutral third-party accounting firm such as PricewaterhouseCoopers will check the final numbers and provide the winning results in a sealed envelope. In the green building context, neutrality would be accomplished through use of a transparent process or tool followed by the ability to measure success in terms of natural capital savings in resources (such as water/energy/materials) or financial capital (return on investment dollars) all to be reviewed by common rules and judges.

Academic Center at Georgia Gwinnett College, Lawrenceville, GA. In areas that receive sunlight for most of the day, a frit has been applied to the third surface of the inner lite of the glass to further reduce the amount of solar energy transmission. Firm: John Portman & Associates. PHOTO: MICHAEL PORTMAN

Rules and Judges

In order to create an even playing field, as in the case of almost all contests and games, there are both rules and judges.

STANDARDS

In the world of green building, the rules are the "standards," and the judges are the "certifications or certifying bodies."

Who Makes the Rules and How

Two of the main "rule makers" for green building processes, standards, certifications, and tools have historically been:

- American National Standard Institute (ANSI)[4]
- International Organization for Standardization (ISO)[5]

Both of these organizations are widely accepted by the international community as trusted sources because the rules they create are consensus-based, open, and made with regard to due process. The scope of ANSI and ISO standards is very broad, from organizational processes in the field of agriculture to large products in shipbuilding down to small products (appliances), so building construction is just one sector in the overall scheme of things. Organizations will sometimes use only part of an ISO or ANSI process rather than the whole, since the process can be slow and cumbersome to complete. Other new trusted standards developers are emerging, such as UL Environment (ULE), a subsidiary of Underwriters Laboratories Inc. These organizations (ISO, ANSI, and ULE), however, are not the only "lawmakers"; at times, the regulatory or standards organization may be an environmental group, or standards might even be developed by the industry itself. In fact, at times the industry will develop standards and self-certify—although there is an inherent conflict of interest in this scenario.

Why are standards important?

❯ Standards that are developed through a consensus-based process that is voluntary and promotes openness and a lack of dominance are credible solutions to environmental, performance, and material testing.

The standards development process ensures balanced input from industry representatives, public health/regulatory officials, users/consumer representatives, and other relevant interest groups.

The American National Standards Institute (ANSI) accredits standards developers to develop ANSI standards. ANSI procedures require public review periods for all proposed standards and revisions. This promotes openness in the standard development to ensure a comprehensive approach within the standard.

Mindy Costello, RS, sustainability standards specialist, National Center for Sustainability Standards, NSF International

❯ Standards that are developed through a consensus-based process that is voluntary and promotes openness and a lack of dominance are credible solutions to environmental, performance, and material testing.

The standards development process ensures balanced input from industry representatives, public health/regulatory officials, users/consumer representatives, and other relevant interest groups.

The American National Standards Institute (ANSI) accredits standards developers to develop ANSI standards. ANSI procedures require public review periods for all proposed standards and revisions. This promotes openness in the standard development to ensure a comprehensive approach within the standard.

Mindy Costello, RS, sustainability standards specialist, National Center for Sustainability Standards, NSF International

❭ Consensus standards are required for use by federal agencies pursuant to the Technology Transfer Act and are favored by the Leadership Standards Campaign. Also, consensus standards achieve the needed buy-in by all key groups so that they are implemented by the market and have regulated the building industry since the 1800s.

Mike Italiano, president & CEO, The Institute for Market Transformation to Sustainability, founder, U.S. Green Building Council, Director, Sustainable Furnishings Council, CEO, Capital Markets Partnership

STANDARDS RESOURCES

American National Standard Institute (ANSI): www.ansi.org

International Organization for Standardization (ISO): www.iso.org –

Underwriters Laboratories Inc. — UL Environment: www.ulenvironment.com

THIRD PARTY

Third is the Winner

There are three separate levels of certification. First party means that a project or company has judged itself. Second-party certification typically means that someone in the "family" or industry judged project or company, with some inherent partiality. The most objective judge, therefore, is entirely separate from the company or project, and is therefore the third-party certifier or "judge." To provide an additional layer of credibility and neutrality, ANSI accredits third-party certifying bodies. In addition, ISO developed a standard "ISO Guide 65: 1996" that specifically outlines and defines the terms of the different levels (first, second, and third party) of certification, mentioning impartial reviews without any financial obligation, and transparent standards, process, and associated documentation as being necessary parts of third-party review.[6] As with anything, the winner is only as good as the "rules" by which it is being judged—so savvy green building professionals should pay attention to the standards.

Critical Plug-In

LINDA BROWN

Executive Vice President

Scientific Certification Systems

Scientific Certification Systems (SCS) third-party certifies everything from agriculture to building materials to carbon. Does this breadth of certification reveal the interconnected nature of all things?

❯ Our breadth of certification reveals that all human activities—including the manufacture and use of products, the delivery of services, and the organization and operation of systems—have impacts on human health and the environment. These impacts are often interconnected. The more transparent these impacts are, whether adverse or beneficial, the more informed decisions we can all make every step of the way.

For instance, marine life is imperiled by a host of problems stemming from human activities, such as overfishing, temperature and chemical changes associated with greenhouse gases, excess nutrient runoff, and garbage dumping. No one solution will solve this problem, and everyone shares responsibility. Oceans may be the farthest thing from the mind of an architect, designer, or facility manager or operator, but they all have constructive roles to play in saving the oceans by designing more energy-efficient buildings, exploring avenues to reduce commute miles and increase transportation options, minimizing waste disposal, and encouraging food vendors to sell only fish from responsibly managed fisheries.

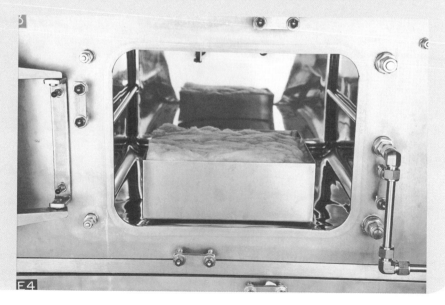

Samples of products or other materials, such as insulation, are evaluated in Air Quality Science's (AQS) small chambers. PHOTO: RON BLUNT PHOTOGRAPHY FOR AQS SERVICES

> ### What does "third-party certification" mean to you, and is it important?

> Third-party certification provides the purchaser confidence that the product was produced to a defined standard. Consumers can be confident that the product is produced to the same high standard, every time. Additionally, a process that meets such standards can be audited to ensure ongoing conformance to a standard or certification.

Diane O'Sullivan, global director of marketing, INVISTA

> Before I founded el: Environmental Language, I was a commercial interior designer. As a specifier of green products, I considered items with third-party certification to be the only credible option.

Once I started my own company, I shifted my perspective. I was now manufacturing eco-chic furniture and quickly learned about the expense involved in earning and maintaining a certification.

Third-party certification is a critical tool that holds manufacturers accountable for their environmental claims and maintains integrity in the sustainable design industry. It is the best strategy for avoiding greenwash and allows specifiers to quickly understand the environmental contribution of their selections.

Jill Salisbury, founder and chief designer, el: Environmental Language, LLC, senior designer/associate, Torchia Associates

> The importance is in the credibility and confidence that the result brings when a third party certifies the outcome. Without the third party, it becomes a result that statistics shows is not well trusted. Consumers and specifiers have been frustrated with misleading information over the past decade and are looking for a means of trusting the information or source. That's one of the reasons why I like UL so much—we are "Stewards of Trust."

It's so much more than a means of communicating a brand, though. I hear countless stories from people coming up to me and talking about the value that UL as a third party brings. It is a value that often seems to be overlooked by many who feel they should just be trusted. Even today, at an international conference where I was a presenter, I listened to a friend of mine who is with a leading manufacturer vent frustration at the costs of certifications from a global perspective. Yet, in the end, if specifiers are looking for a reason to be confident in a manufacturer's claims, the third-party certification still ends up being far cheaper than marketing campaigns to try to explain why all of the background information, calculations, achievements, and performance measures are credible.

Paul Firth, manager, UL Environment

> Third-party certification is essential. It provides specifiers the ability to make more informed decisions about materials and products and receive assurance that what manufacturers are representing about their products has been audited and verified by a credible organization. The certification process must be transparent and conducted by parties that do not have a financial interest in the outcome.

As a manufacturer we have an obligation to provide third-party certification of the claims we are making about our environmental programs and product attributes to specifiers. I believe this is the most effective way to prevent the further escalation of "greenwash" and ultimately lead to more meaningful research and development efforts and advancements by industry.

Ross Leonard, LEED AP, director of marketing, Tandus Flooring

THIRD-PARTY RESOURCES

Certifying Bodies (Third Party)

Scientific Certification Systems: www.scscertified.com/

UL Environment: www.ulenvironment.com/

Standards (Third Party)

NSF National Center for Sustainability Standards Founded by NSF International:
www.nsf.org/business/sustainability_ncss/index.asp?program=SustainabilityNcs

Determining the Numbers

Since green building certification systems cover a wide range of environmental issues, the approach for meeting the necessary criteria varies with each topic. Essentially, there are two main approaches for compliance: prescriptive compliance and performance compliance.

Prescriptive compliance is typically the more straightforward of the two, as it simply spells out required guidelines. For example, the current version of LEED stipulates that paints and coatings must not exceed the VOC (volatile organic compound) limits in the South Coast Air Quality Management District (SCAQMD) Rule #1113.[7] If paints meet this requirement, they are deemed acceptable.

Performance compliance outlines a performance level to be met but gives more creative license to the project team members in how that benchmark is to be achieved. As one such example, LEED might require that a building's interior plumbing fixtures must meet the most current versions of the Energy Policy Act (EPAct)[8] and the Uniform Plumbing Code (UPC).[9] The plumbing engineer could then comply with the performance requirements through any number of strategies and technologies, such as using a combination of different types of low-flow fixtures and dual-flush or waterless toilets. Green building rating systems such as Green Globes and LEED both contain both prescriptive and performance compliance initiatives within their basic language.

What is being found over time, however, is that one of the most important factors in determining true sustainability is a different type of performance—the long-term performance over the life of a product or building.

PERFORMANCE

Performance is a weighty topic and is intrinsically linked to the products and systems that create the building itself. Every building professional wants the building to perform, whether they are installing windows or a piece of furniture. Though research, development, design, and construction are an integral part of creating those products, some team members do not really think about—or don't know to care—how a product came to be. Instead, from the user's experience, it is how products and systems perform long term that really matters.

Green product selection is multifaceted, and analyzing the environmental performance of products requires careful contemplation. In order to make the process easier, many entities of varying transparency and credibility have formed to give project team members (architects, interior designers, and engineers) product certifications indicating their level of greenness. The key is to know which certifications to trust. Here are some qualities that can help guide the search for sustainable products based on best practices:

- Neutral, third-party standards
- Certification
- Attribute claims
- Life Cycle Analysis (LCA)
- Environmental Product Declarations (EPDs)

Assessment of buildings is similar to that of products; it is good to design and construct green buildings with the help of a neutral, third-party system, as it creates a strong foundation for the building's long-term operations and subsequent performance over its lifetime.

For green buildings in particular, here are some specific best practices to better ensure high performance:

- Data collection and tracking
- Compilation of milestone reports of the data
- Engagement of third-party reviewers to audit building performance data
- Installation of monitoring equipment
- Hiring third-party professionals, such as a commissioning agent, to verify energy and water systems
- Training operations staff on handling fine-tuning equipment
- Comparing performance to code thresholds
- Benchmarking performance with similar projects

Part of the Green Globes process is to provide an on-site assessment to assess installed performance.[10] LEED also signified the importance of collecting data with a requirement in 2009 for all registered projects to agree to provide five years of energy data.[11] In future versions of LEED, a greater emphasis will be dedicated to performance that awards additional credits for water and energy metering, as well as commissioning.[12] Beyond tracking requirements, the USGBC has also joined the Global Reporting Initiative (GRI) that promotes transparent building market performance metrics.[13] "Building performance metrics and reporting are crucial to our movement," said Scot Horst, senior vice president for LEED, in a press release. "Data collection and reporting allow us to optimize the performance of our buildings in a transparent and teachable way."[14]

USGBC Headquarters: Lobby, Washington, DC. Completed 2009 (LEED CI Platinum). Firm: Envision Design, PLLC. PHOTO: ERIC LAIGNEL

Why are performance metrics important in green building?

❯ Buildings are complex and so is building performance. Performance metrics provide indicators that assist in understanding the performance of buildings so that refining designs and/or the performance of buildings doesn't have to be a trial and error process, which typically occurs today. Evaluation of performance metrics allows teams to compare to a benchmark and gauge where they are as the design progresses. In addition, it brings new and very relevant information to the "design decision-making table" that increases the likelihood that sustainable strategies are evaluated objectively and effectively.

In addition, keep in mind that analysis (simulation) is an integrative process. If a project team is required to compare to performance metrics throughout the design process (new and retrofit), an emphasis should be placed on quantifying performance. In this way, the team starts to view simulation and cycles of analysis as a key part of an integrative design process. They consider what types of analysis (solar shading, daylighting, airflow, energy, etc.) would be useful to develop at different design stages and step away from the typical approach of simulation as a diagnostic tool once the design is complete and when it can have little impact.

Kevin Settlemyre, LEED AP, BD+C, ID+C, president, Sustainable IQ

METRICS/PERFORMANCE RESOURCES

National Institute of Standards and Technology (NIST)–Metrics and Tools for Sustainable Buildings Project: www.nist.gov/el/economics/metrics_for_sustainable_bldg.cfm

Building Ratings Bring It All Together

So far in this chapter, the discussion of criteria to look for in good green building practice includes:

- Process (including integrative process)
- Tools
- Standards
- Third-party certification
- Performance

Green building ratings bring all of these qualities together in a package that creates a framework for green building professionals, beginning with the first steps of putting together a green design process through the construction phase and into post-construction when quantification of eco-aspects and performance becomes important. As discussed in Chapter 5, a green building professional is often the leader or facilitator of all green building rating systems for a project, overseeing implementation of eco-strategies and technologies, as well as engaging with environmental specialists to provide deeper technical expertise for specific initiatives. For the rest of Chapter 6, we will take a look at green building certifications and their ability to give a metric or framework to our success with environmental issues and the built environment.

GREEN BUILDING CERTIFICATIONS

Globally, there are hundreds of different green building certification systems and organizations. Although many of those certifications evaluate only certain aspects of a building or may focus only on residential structures, the discussion here will narrow the field to the main global commercial systems currently in use, indicating the primary geographic region for each type of certification:

- BREEAM (Building Research Establishment's Environmental Assessment Method). Primarily UK-based, this is the foundation for several other green rating systems.[15]
- CASBEE (Comprehensive Assessment System for Built Environment Efficiency). Mostly in Japan.[16]
- Green Globes. This began in Canada and now includes the U.S. market.[17]

- LEED (Leadership in Energy and Environmental Design). Currently in the U.S. and in 120 other countries.[18]

- Mohurd Three Star. Primarily in China.[19]

- Green Star. In Australia, New Zealand, and South Africa.[20]

It is important to note, however, that there is a delicate balancing act that must be considered between setting an international standard and taking into account critical environmental issues that are specific to certain regions—such as climatic conditions or local environmental regulations (or lack thereof). For international clients whose building portfolios may span several countries (or continents), benchmarking tools that provide comparative analysis of their buildings are very useful. Indeed, though each of these systems may have a slightly different approach to sustainability and set slightly different requirements, the overarching commonality that they all share is a level of consistency and transparency in their evaluations of whole buildings.

In the U.S., the two most significant green rating systems are the following:

- Green Building Initiative (GBI)'s Green Globes Building Rating System/Certification

- U.S. Green Building Council's Leadership in Energy and Environmental Design (LEED) Green Building Certification System

Following is a discussion on each of these certification systems, along with ideas of how a green building professional might evaluate which one best suits a particular project.

Green Globes

HISTORY

The Green Building Initiative (GBI) is a nonprofit and the licensor of Green Globes in the United States. Green Globes was originally available to the public starting in 2005 and was created to help bring green homes to the mainstream. The framework is based on the BREEAM green building rating system. In 2010, ANSI created a standard called ANSI-GBI 01-2010 Standard Green Building Assessment Protocol for Commercial Buildings, which was based on the Green Globes system.[21]

DEVELOPMENT/CYCLE

The Green Globes program is life-cycle based and developed by technical experts. Green Globes system is updated annually—another important point for the green building professional to note, so as to keep abreast of new changes.

SYSTEMS

Today, Green Globes can be used for assessment of many commercial buildings, using any of these three rating systems:

Green Globes New Construction (NC)

Green Globes Continual Improvement of Existing Buildings (CIEB)

Green Globes Continual Improvement of Existing Buildings Healthcare (CIEBHC)

CATEGORIES/LEVELS/SCALE

Green Globes offers a 1,000-point scale in multiple categories:

- Energy
- Indoor environment
- Site
- Water
- Resources
- Emissions
- Project/environmental management

Of these categories, energy makes up the highest percentage at approximately 37 percent of the overall system. There is not a minimum percentage that must be achieved in each category, so some categories can be eliminated depending on the project goals and restraints.

If a minimum of 35 percent of total points is achieved using either the new or existing building system, the project is then eligible for an award of between one and four globes.

35–54 percent = One Globe

55–69 percent = Two Globes

70–84 percent = Three Globes

85–100 percent = Four Globes

PROCESS

The steps in the Green Globes process involve:

- Subscription and login
- Request a quote
- Order and complete third-party stage 1 assessment, at which point the project will receive a predicted rating
- Order a third-party assessment and Green Globes certification
- Schedule and complete third-party assessment in two phases that track with building phases:

    Stage 1: During the design, working drawings, and energy analysis, the third-party assessor gives feedback on status.

    Stage 2: After construction is final, an onsite audit is performed.

- Certification

The user interface for the project team is an interactive Web-based tool that provides automatic feedback once building data is entered by the project team.

PERSONNEL CERTIFICATION

Two Green Globe personnel certifications are available:

- The Green Globes Professional (GGP) guides project teams through the Green Globes process.
- The Green Globes Assessor (GGA) audits the completed building on-site.

COST FOR BUILDING CERTIFICATION

As of 2011, the costs for one new construction building (depending on square footage, which ranges from less than 50,000 to over 500,000 square feet) are generally between $3,000 and $20,000 for members' fees,

Team members of the University of Maryland work on the landscaping of their house with Muhlenbergia in the foreground at the U.S. Department of Energy Solar Decathlon in Washington, D.C., Tuesday, Sept. 20, 2011. All of the landscaping at their house is indigenous to the state of Maryland. PHOTO: STEFANO PALTERA / U.S. DEPARTMENT OF ENERGY SOLAR DECATHLON

with a certain number of discounts for campus or portfolio scenarios, as well as some additional charges under $5,000 for third-party site assessments. The costs noted here don't include any potential hard-cost construction premiums or soft-cost professional fees. There is an annual per-building license fee for use of the online tool and a third-party assessment fee; the GBI website claims that most projects can be certified for $10,000.

MARKET PENETRATION

As of 2011, there are approximately 200 commercial buildings that have received Green Globes certification, either for new construction or work on existing buildings. Examples of buildings that have been awarded Green Globes include:

Walter Cronkite School of Journalism, Arizona State University (Phoenix, AZ) — Two Globes Award

Bristol-Myers Squibb Research & Development Facility (Wallingford, Connecticut) — Two Globes Award

Portland Veterans Affairs (VA) Medical Center (Portland, OR) — Three Globes Award

Whole Foods Market (Dedham, MA) — Three Globes Award

MeadWestvaco Corporation's (MWV) Headquarters (Richmond, VA) — Four Globes Award

Green Globes Interview

SHARENE REKOW

VP Marketing/Sales/Membership

Green Building Initiative

There are many different tools and metrics for use in the green building field. You have expressed a preference for Green Globes as your metric of choice; why do you feel that this system is better than others?

❯ Green Globes offers efficiency and ease of use— some see it as the "TurboTax" of green building rating systems. It offers an interactive online tool that ties the input data to the score tabulation. This is a great feature because it gives automatic feedback to the project team on the available initiatives or points. Also, on an existing building, from a scheduling perspective, if someone has already gathered their existing energy and water bills and has a proficient team to input the data, it could take as little as one week to input. So not only is it efficient from a documentation standpoint, but it is also about 30 percent the soft cost of LEED for certification. Once the building project is completed, a qualified Green Globes Assessor visits the site to audit the green building to make sure that the assessment strengths align with the on-site visit.

What would you say to those who question Green Globes versus LEED?

❯ Both can coexist. Our goal is not to surpass LEED, but rather Green Globes can be the alternative to LEED for the 85 percent of the market that is not utilizing any green building rating system and may not be able to use LEED due to cost or required prerequisites. We often see projects that

are "built to LEED" but actually certify through Green Globes for cost and accessibility to the on-line system. Ideally, projects would begin using Green Globes early in the design process, but if that doesn't occur, projects can retroactively certify once the building is complete.

What are the biggest initiatives Green Building Initiative/Green Globes are working on for the future?

❯ Green Globes is expanding to new markets in the U.S. Healthcare is the newest rendition of Green Globes based on the work and certification that we have done with the Veterans Affairs. We modified the current Continual Improvement of Existing Buildings tool to encompass healthcare. Currently, over 200 veterans' (VA) healthcare facilities are utilizing Green Globes.

In September 2006, a paper was released called "Green Building Rating Systems: A comparison of the LEED and Green Globes Systems in the US." The paper indicates a few strengths of GBI such as LCA focus, energy importance, and flexibility for the user. Were there any major changes that GBI initiated based on the findings of this report? If so, what were they?

❯ That was a good report; to continue building credibility in the marketplace, the official Green Globes ANSI standard was published in 2010. On the strengths mentioned, LCA or Life Cycle Analysis is used within the Green Globes new construction model. The Green Building Initiative provides a free online tool, the "eco-calculator," for assistance in determining the "greenness" of certain materials in relation to each other. The LCA tool currently resides on the GBI website;

a water calculator will be incorporated into the ANSI standard when that standard is committed to an online tool.

Two of the current struggles for all green building rating systems are reliable metrics to prove high-performance building during operations and an increased risk of liability for nonperforming buildings. How does Green Globes address these critical issues?

❭ In terms of metrics, Green Globes uses ENERGY STAR, a proven industry benchmark, and requires improving energy efficiency measures beyond the criteria by a minimum of 10 percent.

From a performance perspective, the inclusion of a Green Globes assessor who does on-site audits better ensures that the design, construction, and operations processes will result in high-performing buildings.

How do you describe the key differences between the Green Globes personnel certification versus the LEED AP designation?

❭ There are two key types of Green Globes personnel certifications: a Green Globes Assessor (GGA) and a Green Globes Professional (GGP). A brief synopsis for the difference between these certifications is as follows:

Green Globes Assessors need a minimum of ten years of experience in architecture, engineering, energy specializations, facility management, or ENERGY STAR expertise. There is training associated with this certification on how to write reports of site audits, as well as the ability to sit down with a team and facilitate green goals. At the end of the process, the Green Globes Assessor writes a report for the owner, giving feedback. These professionals can specialize in new construction or existing buildings.

Green Globes Professionals are required to have a minimum of five years of experience in the building industry or three years of extensive experience in sustainability. The training and education program is an online system. The test for this certification also resides online. There is no limit to the number of times the test can be attempted. One key feature of the test is that it is not based on memorization but rather on an understanding of building codes and the Green Globes program. We want people who can go out on the job site well informed once they complete the program and pass the test.

What is the best way for someone to get involved with GBI and their initiatives? Is there an avenue to volunteer?

❭ The GBI is a member-driven organization. Companies can join to show their commitment to a green nonprofit dedicated to sustainability. Or nonprofits can choose to become an industry affiliate and find more information at this site: www.thegbi.org/join/affiliates.asp.

Leadership in Energy and Environmental Design (LEED)

HISTORY

The U.S. Green Building Council (USGBC) is a nonprofit centered on its Leadership in Energy and Environmental Design (LEED) rating system. The framework was based on the BREEAM green building rating system, and it became available to the public starting in 1998. In 2000, the Green

Building Certification Institute (GBCI) was developed as an independent third party to focus on building certification and professional credentials within the overall LEED framework. This allowed the USGBC to be focused on the continuous improvement of the LEED rating system and the associated educational programs, resources, research, and outreach, while GBCI takes on the role of third-party evaluator.

DEVELOPMENT/CYCLE

LEED is developed through an open-consensus-based process via volunteer committees that are required to have a diverse industry makeup. The committees are balanced with Technical Advisory Groups (TAGs), as well as Market Advisory and Implementation Committees, that each offer specialized environmental expertise.

The LEED system is updated every two years—another important point for the green building professional to note, so that they make sure to keep abreast of new changes.

SYSTEMS

LEED is able to address any commercial building or space within any one of the following five main sections with customized rating systems based on project type or market sector:

Green Building Design and Construction

> LEED for New Construction
>
> LEED for Core and Shell
>
> LEED for Schools
>
> LEED for Retail: New Construction and Major Renovations
>
> LEED for Healthcare

Green Interior Design and Construction

> LEED for Commercial Interiors
>
> LEED for Retail: Commercial Interiors

Green Building Operations and Maintenance

> LEED for Existing Buildings: Operations & Maintenance

Green Neighborhood Development

> LEED for Neighborhood Development

Green Home Design and Construction

> LEED for Homes

CATEGORIES/LEVELS/SCALE

As of today, LEED offers a system with 100 base points and ten bonus points within multiple categories that include:

- Sustainable sites
- Water efficiency
- Energy and atmosphere
- Materials and resources
- Indoor environmental quality
- Innovation and design process
- Regional priority
- Locations and linkages (LEED for Homes)

In future versions of LEED, it is anticipated a new category will be included for location and transportation. The points are then given weight or points based on their environmental impact within each category.

There are also global requirements that must be achieved, called Minimum Program Requirements (MPRs), such as a minimum square footage or minimum occupancy rates. Then, within each category, there are other prerequisites that must be achieved in order

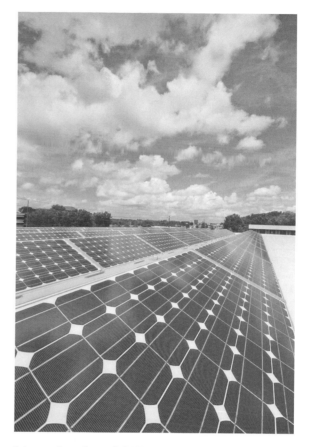

Solar panels on the roof of ASHRAE (LEED NC Platinum). Firm: Richard Wittschiebe Hand. PHOTO: DAN GRILLET

to achieve a LEED rating. Typically, the prerequisites are standard best practices for the industry; the optional credits within each category are selected based on the environmental goals and constraints of the project.

If the MPRs, prerequisites in each category, and minimum number of points are achieved, then the project is eligible for one of the following LEED certification awards:

40 points = Certified Level

50 points = Silver Level

60 points = Gold Level

80 points = Platinum Level

PROCESS

The LEED process involves two main options that allow choices for document submission based on timing within the design and construction phases, which can be seen as follows in the overall process:

- Register the project
- Submit application either
  - Split between the design and construction phase
  - In a combined submittal for both the design and construction phase once the building is complete
- Application Reviewed
- Certified

The user interface for the project team is a Web-based tool that provides a framework for building data to be input by the project team.

PERSONNEL CERTIFICATIONS

The GBCI provides credentialing for over 172,000 LEED-credentialed professionals. Several certifications are available relative to LEED:

- LEED Accredited Professional without specialty — This is the original accreditation, but it is no longer available to new participants.
- Green Associate — Assumes basic green knowledge for a professional.
- LEED AP with Specialty (ID+C/BD+C/O+M/Homes/ND) — For someone participating actively in green building with a specific technical skill.
- LEED Fellow — Fellows are the most prestigious and distinguished credential in the program.

COST FOR BUILDING CERTIFICATION

As of 2011, the GBCI LEED fees for a new building (depending on the square footage, which ranges from less than 50,000 to over 500,000 square feet) are generally between $3,000 and $22,500 for USGBC members, with different rates for campus or building portfolios. These costs are only given as examples relative to Green Globes, and they do not include any potential hard-cost construction premiums or soft-cost professional fees.

MARKET PENETRATION

As of 2011, market penetration for the LEED rating system is significant:

- 8 billion square feet in all 50 states and 120 countries
- 45,000 projects currently participating in system

- 16,000 member companies
- 78 local affiliates

Currently, LEED has unique rating systems for 21 different countries, providing global consistency that includes regional customization of the system to address local environmental issues. Some of the building project owners that have been awarded certification in the LEED system include:

Enco Energy Complex (Bangkok, Thailand) — Platinum Level

ARIA Convention Center & Showroom (Las Vegas, NV) — Gold Level

Empire State Building (New York, NY) — Gold Level

Nationals Park Stadium (Washington, DC) — Silver Level

U.S. Census Bureau Headquarters (Suitland, MD) — Silver Level

Leadership in Energy and Environmental Design (LEED) Interview

ASHLEY KATZ

Media Manager

USGBC

This book's audience is those considering transitioning into the green building career field. There will be multiple tools/metrics (such as LEED) for those entering the field to utilize. What would you say is the key reason to utilize LEED over other options?

❯ LEED has been around for more than 13 years and has established itself as the internationally recognized mark of excellence for the buildings that are redefining the way we think about the places where we live, work, learn, shop, dine, heal, worship, play, and anything else we may do in the course of a day.

LEED has been the catalyst for a fundamental shift in how we design, build, operate, and maintain buildings, as well as, communities while also literally creating a whole new vocabulary. It has become the nationally accepted benchmark because it provides a

concise framework for best practices in high-performance green building design and operations that can be applied to every building type during every day of its life. Additionally, LEED follows a rigorous and consensus-based development process. Thousands of technical committee members weigh in, public comments are accepted, and the final results are fully and publicly balloted and voted upon. The hallmark of LEED is that it's continuously aiming to raise the bar. On a regular update and development cycle, LEED was created to transform the marketplace, challenge the leaders of the building industry, and help us define and make an impact on sustainable design, construction, maintenance, and operations.

What do you say to those who question any other rating system (BREEAM/Green Globes) vs. LEED?

❯ It all depends on what is right for you. LEED is third-party verified, backed by a nonprofit and member-based organization and one of the most, if not the most, rigorous programs available to date. We are certifying 1.4 million square feet of building space per day, which adds up to nearly 1.5 billion square feet of project space participating in the LEED program. And these projects are all over the world—the U.S. and Canada but also in China, India, Europe, and South America.

How do you simplify an explanation of a project team/building going through the LEED process?

❯ It really is about integrated design. If the entire project team is on the same page from the beginning, you eliminate any errors or having to backtrack. And backtracking adds time and cost. It is also useful to have a LEED AP on the project team, someone who has been credentialed and is able to guide the project from start to finish—documentation through to certification.

What are the biggest concepts in USGBC's next version of LEED?

❯ The next version of LEED just finished its public comment periods in which we collected thousands of constructive comments and recommendations on the proposed drafts, which place heightened emphasis on an integrative process and building performance. USGBC has also integrated feedback received from project teams who have been pilot testing draft credits in the LEED pilot credit library.

The credits in the next proposed LEED rating systems have been allocated points based on a weightings process similar to the process used for 2009, but based on impact categories developed by USGBC specifically for use in LEED. These impact categories more directly align with outcomes sought by LEED with USGBC's market transformation goals. The weightings/point allocation process informed many changes in the rating system, including organizational changes proposed for the Indoor Environmental Quality (IEQ) and Materials and Resources (MR) credit categories.

The organizational revisions proposed for the IEQ section provide a more refined focus on air quality, lighting, and acoustics, in addition to improved incentives for testing and verification. The organizational revisions proposed for the MR credit category reflect a strong desire to encourage life-cycle-based thinking through manufacturing and product selection practices. USGBC is tackling issues related to responsible sourcing of raw materials and human health impacts associated with building products.

A notable change to the next version of LEED for Neighborhood Development draft includes a split into two rating systems: LEED for Neighborhood Development Plan and LEED for Neighborhood Development, aiming to provide a certification for entitled plans in addition to completed projects. Also, LEED for Existing Buildings: Operations & Maintenance users will recognize a concerted effort to streamline the process of recertification in the operations and maintenance rating systems.

Based on the pilot credits and the future version of LEED, some very big changes are happening such as:

Increased prerequisites

Life Cycle Analysis (LCA)

Integrative Process

Performance Focus

Two of the current struggles for all green building rating systems are: reliable metrics to prove high-performance building during operations; and increased risk of liability for nonperforming buildings. How does LEED address these critical issues?

❯ Performance has always been a critical goal of the LEED rating systems. With every version of LEED, as the industry rises to meet the bar set by LEED's marketplace transformation, performance requirements and credits evolve along with the rest of the rating system components. As you mention later, LEED-certified buildings are designed to perform, based on a set of prescriptive criteria. However, occupant and facility management behavior are also critical components of building performance. LEED helps projects design and construct a building to be high-performing, but it's an ongoing commitment by the owner and occupants that will deliver that performance. For that ongoing commitment, USGBC has implemented three distinct yet parallel mechanisms that track the ongoing performance of our LEED certified projects:

Building Performance Partnership (BPP)

The Measurement and Verification LEED credit

One Minimum Program Requirement, which was introduced for LEED 2009 projects, requires whole building sharing of data for water and energy usage data.

BPP is comprehensive data collection and analysis infrastructure to capture feedback from all LEED-certified projects, both commercial and residential. Participation is voluntary and helps building owners manage their project's water and energy use and provide benchmarking to see if it is operating as it was intended. Participants in the program receive annual performance reports and online data interfaces to aid in their building performance goals, and the data collected by USGBC informs future updates to the LEED rating systems.

The Measurement and Verification credit is a credit awarded to projects for developing and implementing a measurement and verification plan to evaluate building and/or energy system performance. Instituting an M&V plan sets LEED projects up to successfully track ongoing performance; USGBC recognizes this by offering a bonus point to projects that achieve the credit and commit to sharing energy and water data to USGBC through ENERGY STAR.

The previously mentioned MPR requires projects to commit to sharing all energy and water usage data for at least five years after certification, either by sharing data through ENERGY STAR's Portfolio Manager Tool, or another approved format; or by committing to apply for LEED for Existing Buildings: Operations & Maintenance certification.

In terms of certification, projects are required to focus on five LEED credit areas that include energy use, site selection, materials & resources, water efficiency, and indoor environmental quality. LEED is a whole building approach that uses a system of prerequisites and points that are interrelated among the credit categories. In the newest version of LEED, the credits are weighted, which means points are allocated between credits based on the potential environmental impacts and human health benefits with respect to a set of impact categories. Impact categories are quantified by a combination of approaches such as energy modeling, life-cycle assessment, and transportation analysis. So while a credit may not be in the energy category within LEED, it most likely would have an impact on energy use due to these factors outlined here and the overlap in credit intents.

How does USGBC/LEED decide which market sectors it will give variations to (health care, retail, hospitality, etc.)? Why is it important to customize the system?

❯ Certain building types have such unique uses, so modifying the rating system with a specific space type in mind can make compliance easier. As an example, healthcare facilities are heavily regulated, but we were able to use compliance with healthcare-specific standards to verify compliance with LEED. This means that healthcare facilities are able to attain certification without additional work to comply with LEED reference standards that they wouldn't normally use. Modifying the rating system with a specific space type in mind also allowed us to take into consideration some of the unique needs of the users of that building, such as the need for access to nature for both patients and staff. Other important considerations included infection control and the fact that hospitals are intense energy users that operate on a 24/7 schedule. The changes in operating schedule resulted in a change in the way we calculate number of occupants (or FTEs) that meant LEED made more sense for those facilities. The other key factor in modifying the rating system for specific space types is that it gives us the flexibility so that the rating system includes the necessary requirements to make sure that space type meets the requirements for LEED certification.

What do you say to someone who doesn't see the value and says, "LEED—a lot of online documentation and at a high cost premium"?

❯ The easiest thing to say to this is: With LEED you know it's green. And it's not just the building owner saying it, it's a third party that has tested, measured, and verified that the building is green. It's time buildings were transparent in how they were built—just like food labels. If you want organic food, you look for that organic certification mark on the package. If you want to know what's inside the package,

you read the list of ingredients and see exactly what you are getting. LEED is the same—it tells everyone what has gone into your building so you know what you are getting. LEED is well documented providing immediate and measurable results.

What is the best way for someone to get involved with USGBC/LEED initiatives? Is there an avenue to volunteer? What are some unique features?

❯ Certainly if your company is not a USGBC member, joining the Council is an easy step: www.usgbc.org/join.

Once you are a member there are a number of avenues that open up for participation ranging to Chapter involvement, participation on a number of committees and the Board, as well as, extensive networking plus, business development opportunities and reduced pricing for conferences, events, education, and other green building resources.

When you envision the distant future of LEED (10 years +), what do you see?

❯ We envision buildings that give back, rather than only take away. Right now with LEED we are able to reduce the building's footprint, but it's still taking away from the environment. If we are able to evolve LEED in a way that it is actually about regeneration, imagine what we could do for the planet.

How to Choose—Green Globes or LEED?

In the end, deciding which green building rating system is "right" or "best" for a particular project will depend on several factors that may include:

- Client goals
- Environmental goals
- Financial factors and incentives
- Marketing needs
- Need for compliance with legislation

As a general rule of thumb, Green Globes may be the system to use if:

- There are budget constraints for certification fees.
- There are schedule/lead time constraints for feedback on green rating status.
- It is important to include on-site assessment/verification.

In turn, LEED may be the system to use if:

- There is a need for a rating system that is customized for a certain building type such as retail, hospitality, or neighborhood community.
- The project has a General Services Administration (GSA) or other government entity requirement.
- The client wants the building to have high brand recognition in the international market.

Neither system is perfect, as both would likely admit; however, both LEED and Green Globes are helping to create buildings that are significantly more sustainable, as well as encouraging public recognition of the importance of such buildings—which are positive steps forward by any measure.

GREEN BUILDING RATING SYSTEM RESOURCES

Green Building Initiative: Green Globes Building Rating/Certification: www.thegbi.org/

U.S. Green Building Council: Leadership in Energy and Environmental Design (LEED)
    www.usgbc.org/

Understanding Green Building Guidelines, by Traci Rose Rider
    http://books.wwnorton.com/books/detail.aspx?ID=9914

BuildingGreen LEED User: www.leeduser.com

Great River Energy Headquarters;, Maple Grove, Minnesota (LEED NC Platinum). Firm: Perkins + Will. PHOTO: ©LUCIE MARUSIN

> **What are the key determining factors for which green rating system is best for the building (e.g. BREEAM, Green Globes, LEED)?**

❯ Nearly all projects come to PageSoutherlandPage with the requirement for an energy-efficient design. Most of the clients who indicate this desire will also require the design to use the LEED rating system as a benchmarking tool in design. The requirement to "design to LEED Silver" is prevalent in projects where the pursuit of formal certification is not required by either corporate or government criteria. In this case, we will create and follow a LEED checklist and provide estimates on the feasibility of credit achievement at design milestones (should the project later decide to pursue formal certification).

We will often provide a LEED feasibility study during pre-design (or early schematic design) to determine the feasibility of achieving certification given the developing project requirements and design elements. For example, if project criteria on site development or energy and water efficiency are part of the owner's project requirements, then formal certification is very often pursued. The strongest determining factors in certification stem either from local, state, or federal requirements, or from corporate design criteria. We've seen projects opt for formal certification because it was a requirement of project funding, to then find out that this opens up multiple discussions on design and construction which would have never occurred otherwise. These designs have been strongly enhanced by the decision to pursue certification.

We practice BREEAM consulting on projects based in Europe only. The primary advantage of LEED over other rating systems is in its increased rigor and accountability. It asks the design team to tap a broader range of experts than design firms typically might. For example, site ecologists contribute toward design on BREEAM projects of all scales. Non-BREEAM or conventionally designed projects may consult with an ecologist on only the largest project sites. And there is more attention given to enhancing a site's ecology than in other rating systems. Credit thresholds on water and energy are also more stringent. Finally, BREEAM Assessors are project team members who work directly with the team and the BREEAM AP helping to foster an integrated project development. The assessor also performs site visits and verifies the built conditions are in compliance, which is not a component of the LEED rating system. The disadvantage of BREEAM is that the requirement to provide documentation on all pursued credits at both design and construction stages creates a larger paper trail and more documentation work.

We also provide Green Globes consulting for selected projects. Specifically, the Veterans Administration is a strong proponent of Green Globes and very often chooses this rating system in lieu of LEED. Green Globes is very similar to LEED in content, but very different in process. The Green Globes process purposefully and directly follows the project delivery stages (from pre-design through post-occupancy), which helps the team to stage the work and to make decisions earlier.

Joanna Yaghooti, AIA, LEED AP, BREEAM AP, PageSoutherlandPage

Living Buildings

The International Living Future Institute has a rigorous system called the Living Building Challenge. This is not a contest, but more a rating similar to Green Globes and LEED; however, it requires data after 12 months of occupancy. The technical requirements are unique in that they have goals of net-zero energy and water. It gives credit for biophilia-based design that is inspired by nature's principles. The Living Building Challenge also has a "red list" of chemicals that are discouraged. In addition, the system awards for consideration of a thoughtful aesthetic such as beauty.

www.livingbuildingchallenge.org

Alpha to the Omega

OMEGA CENTER FOR SUSTAINABLE LIVING (RHINEBECK, NEW YORK)

BNIM

Vision + Challenge

Founded in 1977, the Omega Institute is the nation's largest holistic learning center. Its mission: "To look everywhere for the most effective strategies and inspiring traditions that might help people bring more meaning and vitality into their lives." In 2006 it embarked on a mission to develop a new and highly sustainable wastewater filtration facility for its 195-acre campus, which is located within one of the most important watersheds in the world, the 13,400-square-mile Hudson River watershed basin.

The primary goal for this project was to overhaul the organization's current wastewater disposal system by using alternative methods of treatment. As part of a larger effort to educate the center's visitors, staff, and local community on innovative wastewater strategies, it decided to showcase the system in a building that houses both the primary treatment cells and a classroom/laboratory. In addition to using the treated water for garden irrigation and in a grey-water recovery system, it uses the system and building as a teaching tool in its educational program designed around the ecological impact of its system. These classes are offered to campus visitors, area schoolchildren, university students, and other local communities.

The Omega Center For Sustainable Living is a very purposeful building and site. It is designed to clean water, educate users about the process, and return the clean water to the native systems. Eco Machine technologies were selected to clean water utilizing natural systems, including the earth, plants, and sunlight. The entire building and water process utilizes site-harvested renewable energy, achieving a net-zero energy system. This required the facility to be free of waste (volume, material, energy), organized and carefully tuned to harvest solar energy for passive heating and lighting, utilizing the entire mass for thermal comfort and embodying simplicity and elegance befitting its noble purpose. Creating an interior environment pleasant and comfortable for people and fertile for the water-cleaning plants to flourish was critical. The result is a careful balance of passive (daylight, passive solar heating, natural ventilation) and mechanical (geothermal, fans, electric lighting) comfort systems. For example, the building section demonstrates the purposefulness of the design. The plants growing in the interior lagoons required very precise solar energy levels on both the south and north exposures of the aquatic plants—the building section, windows, and skylights were carefully designed as an integrated system meeting those needs with a memorable human experience.

Strategy + Solutions

COMMUNITY MEETS WATER

Water is a critical issue for the region. The Omega Campus is located adjacent to Long Lake, which is part of a tributary system of the Hudson River. Each is facing challenges caused by human activities. The issues of the Hudson are well documented, and numerous actions are under way to improve the river and its systems. Given the proximity to the population base surrounding New York City, the Hudson is one of the most important bodies of fresh water on the planet. The neighbors surrounding Long Lake, including Omega prior to the OCSL, are causing degradation of the lake—from agricultural runoff, landscaping chemicals, septic systems, and urban water issues.

Omega envisioned the project as a means of thinking globally and acting locally. This began with deciding to clean up and build on the former dump to ensure that leaching or other threats to the aquifer ceased. The innovative natural systems approach of reclaiming water and returning it clean to the native water systems represents a direct approach of reducing the water footprint of every individual who visits the campus, of improving the aquifer and Long Lake locally, and

having similar impacts on regional and global water supplies beyond.

METRICS

Nutrients removed from sewage before returning to nature: 100 percent

Biological organisms prevented from entering native water system: 100 percent

Water supply is provided directly from the groundwater via wells on campus. Prior to construction, water was drawn from the wells, used for multiple human activities, then piped to a septic/leach field system. The new Eco Machine now returns a higher quality of water back to the Earth, using natural systems that see our waste as food. Aerated lagoons, one component of the system, are on display for all to see, carrying gray water through the reclamation process. At the end, the water may be utilized to support the needs of the building.

For potable water uses, well water is still drawn from the earth. For toilet flushing, rainwater is collected from the building's roof. Low-flow plumbing fixtures have been installed to minimize water consumption, including waterless urinals in the men's restroom. For all other water use on campus, black and gray water is sent to the Eco Machine lagoons and constructed wetlands for purification. By the end of this cycle that uses natural systems, cleaner water is reintroduced to the groundwater and lake.

LAND

The campus lies within the lower Hudson River Valley, one of the world's most populous areas. The site was formerly a gravel parking lot and the remnants of a dump from a previous use. It was nearly entirely free of healthy biodiversity above the ground or within. The new landscape is quite the opposite. Automobiles and waste have been replaced with deep-rooted native plants, a healthy

Omega Center for Sustainable Living. Daylighting, natural ventilation, and views are achieved in 94% of all spaces through a system of operable, fixed, and solar tracking fenestration. Operable windows are provided in each occupied space for both the health and enjoyment of guests, in addition to being part of the passive heating and cooling strategy for the building. Eco Machine® plants remove CO_2 and other gases while producing oxygen—indoors and outdoors (LEED NC Platinum and Living Building Challenge). Firm: BNIM. PHOTO: ©ASSASSI

water system, birds, insects, and other species. The site is pesticide and toxin free.

The landscape design is regenerative of native site ecology, didactic in form, and holistic in function, and above all, it provides beautiful inspiring landscapes within the ecological and cultural context of the campus. There are four constructed wetland cells that terrace down the southern slope adjacent to the building. Part of the wastewater recycling/treatment process, water passes through the gravel beds within these wetlands and is gradually released into subsurface areas north of the building. The overall effect is colorful and gardenlike. The diverse palette of perennial plants provides habitat for a variety of birds and beneficial insects as part of the overall landscape system.

ENERGY

Located along an east-west axis, the building is oriented for optimal control of daylighting and heat gain. Furthermore, the building form and section largely evolve from the practical need to serve the plants doing the work of the wastewater treatment in the Eco Machine. Recognizing that the plants would reach a light saturation point at around 30,000 lux, a design goal was made to flatten the amount of light falling on the plants' surfaces during the summer months to this level, in order to minimize the heat taken on by the space. (Conversely, during colder months, the amount of light would be maximized in order to warm the space.) Solar tracking skylights were installed to aid in this effort. Early research revealed that traditional greenhouse design, while maximizing sunlight for the plants, would defy the desire to maintain a comfortable environment for workers and visitors to the facility.

Sunshades along the southern face will bounce sunlight onto the ceiling of the greenhouse, allowing for an even distribution of light, and shade the lower portion of glass during the summer months,

Omega Center for Sustainable Living: Eco Machine. Eco Machine technologies were selected to clean water utilizing natural systems including the earth, plants, and sunlight. The Eco Machine now returns a higher quality of water back to the earth using natural systems that see our waste as food (LEED NC Platinum and Living Building Challenge). Firm: BNIM. PHOTO: © ASSASSI

Roof materials include a combination of vegetation and recycled metal, which help to cool interior spaces, mitigating the "heat island" effect.

Achieving net-zero energy required a design that eliminated waste and maximized the use of renewable energy resources. The building is purposely compact, organized to harvest daylight, passive heating, and cooling breezes to reduce energy needs. The insulated thermal mass of the building and the thermal mass of the water (55°F) passing through the treatment cycle are instrumental in reducing demands upon mechanical systems. During summer months the cool laboratory water has both a cooling and drying effect on the hot humid air entering the building.

Efficient geothermal wells and heat pumps are utilized to provide heat for all spaces. Cooling is only provided for the classroom.

Sunlight is the primary lighting source. The shape of the building is designed to harvest sunlight, utilizing windows, skylights, and shading devices to produce appropriate, comfortable lighting without adversely affecting air temperatures. Electric lighting systems are extremely efficient and controlled to be utilized only when conditions mandate supplementing daylight.

Photovoltaic panels generate more energy than the building utilizes annually. The excess energy is sold to the local utility. During evenings and certain winter periods, energy is provided by the electric utility.

MATERIALS

The architectural expression of materials is one of simplicity and transparency and is heavily influenced by the colors and textures of the region. No effort is made to mask the underlying nature of a material, but rather to express the unique beauty of each. This honest approach also reduces the overall embodied energy of the building and minimizes the potential off-gassing from various construction materials.

The facility is a perfect showcase for salvaged materials and demonstrates how easily any building can take advantage of material reuse. Reclaimed materials used on the project include dimensional lumber, plywood, interior doors, beech wood paneling, and toilet partitions (materials came from warehouses, schools, office buildings, and other projects). All installed wood is either from an FSC-certified forest or a reclaimed source, including the plywood roof and wall sheathing which was utilized in the 2009 Presidential Inaugural Stage. In addition, materials were sourced to avoid those on the Red Materials List from the Living Building Challenge Guidelines.

During construction, 99 percent of metal, cardboard, rigid foam, and wood scraps were recycled. One hundred percent of food waste was composted, and 100 percent of glass, paper, and plastic packaging waste was recycled.

As a practical and pedagogical measure, the overall strategy toward material selection for The Omega Center for Sustainable Living is to reduce or eliminate all interior finishes wherever possible. The "naked" building reveals its material nature and construction in honest dialogue with its occupants. This approach reduces the overall embodied energy of the building as well as minimizes the potential off-gassing from various construction materials. Where finish is required, it is evaluated for longevity, environmental impact, and impact on indoor air quality.

LIGHT + AIR

Daylighting, natural ventilation, and views are achieved in 94 percent of the spaces through a system of operable, fixed, and solar tracking fenestration. Operable windows are provided in each occupied space for both the health and enjoyment of guests, in addition to being part of the passive heating and cooling strategy for the building. Laboratory plants remove CO2 and other gases while producing oxygen—indoors and outdoors. Clerestory windows ventilate the lobby, mechanical room, and restrooms. Solar radiation heats the upper volume of air, and then natural buoyancy induces stack ventilation, which causes the air to push its way out of the open windows and pull in fresh, cooler air from lower windows in these spaces. Operable windows integrated into the south facade also allow for natural ventilation to assist in pushing hot air out of the building by channeling prevailing breezes that have been cooled while moving over the wetlands.

Building and site are integrated as a single system. The landscape produces a microclimate of clean air and beauty beneficial to the occupants. Water from the building feeds the plants and other living systems of the landscape. The two are visually connected by the transparency of each indoor space.

Lessons Learned

The pioneering nature of this project has left the team with many lessons learned from the design and construction process. Many of the lessons are a result of pursuing the Living Building Challenge and many others a product of the nature of the facility. A new lesson for this project was the complexity of ensuring that building components are free of the Living Building Challenge Red List of materials.

Process + Operations

The design approach was an intuitive, scientific and experiential process. Concepts we conceived intuitively and were then modeled using scientific tools to measure comfort, energy, daylighting and other metrics to achieve the desired experience. The team collaborated and relied upon the findings of the modelling to develop an integrated high-performance design for the building and site. One example was

Omega Center for Sustainable Living: Entry. The Omega Center for Sustainable Living is a very purposeful building and site. It is designed to clean water, educate users about the process, and return the clean water to the native systems. The entire building and water process utilizes site-harvested renewable energy, achieving a net-zero energy system (LEED NC Platinum and Living Building Challenge). Firm: BNIM. PHOTO: © ASSASSI

using the water as a tempering element to improve comfort and reduce mechanical system capacity.

The Omega Center was one of the first projects to adopt the Living Building Challenge as a certification process. There is a rigorous one-year period of performance evaluation that began in May 2009. During that time, operations were carefully monitored and evaluated by the Living Building Challenge. This monitoring established that the building was performing as designed, or better in some cases. The net-zero Omega Center for Sustainable Living is the first project in the world to achieve both 'Living' Status in Living Building Challenge and LEED Platinum.

Nature Nexus

All of these processes and tools are in the green building professional's toolbox. Once the primary concepts are understood, such as standards, third party audits, and integrative thinking, any green professional should have a good foundation of knowledge in her or his toolkit that may be applied to most environmental decision making. Then, armed with these processes and tools the green building professional can achieve the goal of being the champion of the green building process and can create healthy, productive, and even regenerative spaces.

NOTES

1. The Institute for Market Transformation to Sustainability (MTS), "Integrative Process Standard© for Design and Construction of Sustainable Buildings and Communities," Draft ANSI Consensus Standard Guide 2.0 – Ballot Version, February 22, 2011, Copyright 2005–2011, http://mts.sustainableproducts.com/IP/IP%20Standard%20-%20BALLOT%20Version.pdf, accessed October 14, 2011.

2. Barbra Batshalom and Kevin Settlemyre, "Everyone is Practicing Integrative Design...at least that's what they say," Integrative Process Standard© for Design and Construction of Sustainable Buildings and Communities, February 22, 2011. http://mts.sustainableproducts.com/IP/IP%20Standard%20-%20BALLOT%20Version.pdf, accessed October 14, 2011.

3. Ibid.

4. American National Standards Institute, "About ANSI Overview," www.ansi.org/about_ansi/overview/overview.aspx?menuid=1, accessed October 14, 2011.

5. International Organization for Standardization, www.iso.org/iso/about/discover-iso_isos-name.htm, accessed October 14, 2011.

6. International Organization for Standardization, "ISO/IEC General Requirements for Bodies Operating Product Certification Systems Guide 65: 1996," www.iso.org/iso/iso_catalogue/catalogue_tc/catalogue_detail.htm?csnumber=26796, accessed October 14, 2011.

7. http://www.aqmd.gov/rules/reg/reg11/r1113.pdf

8. The Energy Policy Act of 1992 (EPAct 1992) amended the National Energy Conservation Policy Act (NECPA), Library of Congress, H.R.776 section 152 and amended section 153, http://thomas.loc.gov/cgi-bin/query/z?c102:H.R.776.ENR:#, accessed October 14, 2011.

9. The International Association of Plumbing and Mechanical Officials, Uniform Plumbing Code (UPC) 2006, www.iapmo.org/Pages/2006UniformCodes.aspx, accessed October 14, 2011.

10. Green Globes, "Green Globes Rating/Certification," http://www.thegbi.org/green-globes/ratings-and-certifications.asp, accessed October 14, 2011.

11. U.S. Green Building Council (USGBC), "LEED 2009 Minimum Program Requirements,"

www.usgbc.org/DisplayPage.aspx?CMSPageID=2102, accessed October 14, 2011.

12. U.S. Green Building Council (USGBC), "LEED 2012 Draft Performance (after second public comment closed)," www.usgbc.org/DisplayPage.aspx?CMSPageID=2316, accessed October 14, 2011.

13. Global Reporting Initiative (GBI), https://www.globalreporting.org/information/about-gri/what-is-GRI/Pages/default.aspx, accessed February 15, 2012.

14. Scot Horst, Press Release: "USGBC Joins Global Reporting Initiative as an Organizational Stakeholder," August 15, 2011, www.usgbc.org/Docs/News/GRI_USGBC.pdf, accessed October 14, 2011.

15. Building Research Establishment's Environmental Assessment Method (BREEAM), www.breeam.org/, accessed October 14, 2011.

16. Comprehensive Assessment System for Built Environment Efficiency (CASBEE), www.ibec.or.jp/CASBEE/english/index.htm, accessed October 14, 2011.

17. Green Globes, www.greenglobes.com/, accessed October 14, 2011.

18. U.S. Green Building Council, "What LEED Is," www.usgbc.org/DisplayPage.aspx?CMSPageID=1988, accessed October 14, 2011.

19. Kevin Mo, "China Launches National Green Building Label Campaign," http://switchboard.nrdc.org/blogs/kmo/china_launches_nation al_green.html, accessed October 14, 2011.

20. Green Star, www.gbca.org.au/green-star/, accessed October 14, 2011.

21. American National Standards Institute, "ANSI-GBI 01-2010: Green Building Assessment Protocol for Commercial Buildings," www.thegbi.org/commercial/standards/form-ansi-new.asp?d=01-200XP, accessed October 14, 2011. 22. U.S. Environmental Protection Agency (EPA), "Tools for the Reduction and Assessment of Chemical and Other Environmental Impacts (TRACI)," www.epa.gov/nrmrl/std/sab/traci/, accessed October 14, 2011.

7 Green Building Impact Areas, People, and Tools

The person who knows one thing and does it better than anyone else, even if it only be the art of raising lentils, receives the crown he merits. If he raises all his energy to that end, he is a benefactor of mankind and its rewarded as such.

—OG MANDINO *(an American author who wrote*
The Greatest Salesman in the World*)*

Common Ecos

Ecos means "home" in Greek. Common environmental impacts on planet earth (home to us all) can be organized into key environmental areas that the vast majority of green building rating systems organize their third-party performance rating systems around.

Site/Location

Water

Energy

Materials

Indoor air quality

Within each of these categories, process, specific performance criteria, and tools all assist in helping green building professionals as well as specialists in each of these areas to quantify resource savings and health impacts.

SPECIALISTS

All building professionals—architects, engineers, contractors—can be considered a green building professional if they incorporate sustainability into their overall job focus and enhance their knowledge with green ideals and techniques. Sustainability and green building consultants take sustainability a step further by centering their jobs and expertise entirely on integrating the environmental with companies and buildings. Just as, in the medical profession, there are general practitioners who address everyday concerns and overall issues and then there are specialists such as dermatologists and heart surgeons who target more specific needs, the same is true in sustainability. Combining concentrated levels of knowledge, targeted areas of focus, and strong experience within a particular subject, green building specialists tend to dive deeper and more narrowly into their fields—which can provide additional efficiency, accuracy, and value to any building project.

One tool in particular overlaps general green building professionals as well as specialists, BIM or Building Information Modeling. This global tool holds all of the pertinent building data in one place and can be used in tandem with other tools such as energy modeling.

TOOLS

Building Information Modeling (BIM)

The buildingSMART alliance defines BIM as "a digital representation of physical and functional characteristics of a facility. As such it serves as a shared knowledge resource for information about a facility forming a reliable basis for decisions during its life cycle from inception onward."[9] If BIM is implemented, nearly every piece of information that an owner needs to know about a facility throughout its life can be made available electronically. One key aspect of BIM is that it makes energy modeling easier and faster, providing the chance for multiple iterations of a project and the ability to make minor tweaks in the architecture that may result in significant energy savings.

A relatively new term has been coined in the industry: "green BIM." "Green and BIM have been the two most dynamic trends in our industry," says Steve Jones, who leads McGraw-Hill Construction's BIM initiatives. "Although they have been growing independently, it was inevitable that they would converge because the analysis and simulation capabilities of modeling are such a natural fit with the objectives of green building."[10] In 2010, McGraw-Hill released a report that outlined five key green BIM trends for the building industry:

Software integration

Integrated output from different building systems

Greater use of integrated design

Modeling standards

Increasing use of BIM for small green retrofit projects

Using BIM for building performance and verification[11]

Indeed, BIM's integrated approach and sustainable leanings enable it to be effective within a range of building professions. The Whole Building Design Guide (WBDG) mentions over 25 building professionals to whom BIM provides valuable data. For example:

Owners receive a global summary of the property/building(s).

Realtors are able to access information on the property/building to support sales.

Mortgage bankers are given key demographic data to help with loans and financial details.

Contractors use results as a repository for construction bids and for purchasing materials.

Energy/LEED uses BIM as a way to make it easier to model multiple iterations for analysis.

First responders use BIM as a way to reduce loss of life and property.[12]

"Can-Do" Attitude

EDDY KRYGIEL, AIA, LEED AP

Architect

HNTB Architecture

BIM

Co-author of Wiley book, Green BIM: Successful Sustainable Design with Building Information Modeling

---

You are one of the leading experts on green BIM and Revit Architecture. How did this come about?

❯ The short answer? A desire of not wanting to cover the Earth with bad buildings (either aesthetically or environmentally), mixed with a high comfort level with change. Some like the tried and true way. I like to think that if I did something once, I can make it better or greener the next time around. Take that and mix it with a bit of luck working with some real industry thought leaders where "green" wasn't a color or a client request, but just how things were done. Once it becomes part of your lifestyle, the day-to-day design decisions become a lot more intuitive.

What are the pros/cons of green BIM/Revit? How does BIM best support integrated design?

❯ Don't look at BIM or Revit as software—look at them rather as tools. There are a lot of tools in your design toolbox to be used at different stages of design, construction, and O&M. These take some of the error out of communication with team members either within your firm or with consultants or with owners. A BIM model is more than just a picture—it's an information-rich virtual model of the building. This gives you an entirely new way to communicate design intent, ideas, and information with all project stakeholders with significantly less worry about misinterpretation. But as is the case with integrated design, you have to be willing to share the model with your larger team. Firms who don't give copies of their models are really missing a big part of what BIM can help a project achieve.

Please give a few highlights of lessons learned on the project of your choice.

❯ I was involved in the rebuilding of Greensburg, a small town in Kansas that was destroyed by an F5 tornado. They decided to rebuild sustainably everything from the houses to the schools to City Hall, on which I was fortunate enough to work. We were able to really leverage the whole toolbox from water conservation to taking the town off the utility grid and helping to make sure the buildings were strong enough to withstand another act of nature, should that happen again. It's less about trying to wait for opportunities for major impacts and more about daily little ones. They tell me the same thing about exercise.

Beyond the Surface

BRAD CLARK

Architecture

BNIM

How would you describe green BIM?

❯ "Green BIM" describes a process or way of thinking about building design that implies the use of an integrated "set" of building geometry and metadata and building information. The integrated nature of this data allows a building design team to simulate real-world scenarios and predict outcomes, thus informing better and more sustainable design.

You are a member of BIM Experts and BIM for Owners. What are some of the more intriguing dialogues that are generated in these groups?

❯ I am most interested in the discussions probing the value that BIM offers to building owners, both in the short-term design and construction phase, and the long term of occupying and maintaining a building. I see the use of BIM growing greatly in this latter area over the next ten years.

See Building Information Modeling (BIM) Resources on page 264 along with Energy Modeling Resources.

Site/Location

Several typical building professions focus on the building site or location, including urban planner, civil engineer, landscape architect, and general contractor. Work could include a civil engineer planning for storm water in coordination with a landscape architect, together designing bioswales—vegetated areas that are a natural means of water filtration. The contractor would then complement the design with the best-practices erosion and sedimentation control of storm water during construction via fiber roll (straw in a round porous sleeve) or straw bales. Those that focus on site specialty include:

Arborist

Green or vegetated roof specialist

Indeed, there are many types of site specialists, all of whom play an important part in greening a building site. We will look at two site specific issues that may require specialists: Heat Island Effect regards what is on top of the soil with building elements such as roofs and paving, and Brownfield Remediation investigates within the soil of damaged sites.

Cultural Accelerator

CHRISTINE (CHRIS) PAUL

Principal

Golder Associates, Inc.

Remediation is the practice of reversing environmental damage, typically damage that's occurred at a building site. Have you seen shifts in the remediation market in recent years? If so, how?

❯ The remediation market has become more mature. In general, people are becoming better stewards of the environment, which helps to reduce the number of new sites that require soil or groundwater remediation. Those sites that remain are mainly legacy sites, such as old, disused manufacturing plants, or sites that are being considered for reuse.

The remediation market itself is becoming more commodity-driven, although there continue to be new developments in technologies and analytical techniques, and understanding risk assessment, all of which raise the bar for the Golder team to innovate and showcase our excellence in those areas.

HEAT ISLAND EFFECT

Heat island effect is created where there is a temperature difference between developed areas versus undeveloped areas—sometimes as much as 6 to 8 degrees.[1] This is an issue because it impacts the natural environment, altering weather patterns and water temperatures. For a quick analogy, consider a black car in the hot summer sun versus a white car in the same conditions. The black car has a higher heat gain. Transfer this analogy to a building by considering two horizontal planes common to all building sites: the ground and the roof. Depending on the regional climate, in order to reduce the heat island effect, project teams design light-colored, reflective paving and roof materials to ensure that the surfaces stay cooler than dark roofs and pavers. In predominately warmer climate, light colored materials would reduce the heat gain and associated cooling needs.

BROWNFIELD REMEDIATION

Remediation is the practice of rehabilitating existing blighted sites that contain or are perceived to contain hazardous materials. Remediation could target an old steel mill site with contaminated soil, where a remediation expert might determine how best to remove the soil, or remediation could occur on a site that previously housed a gas station with underground tanks that need to be encapsulated. The process of remediation allows reuse of an existing site, avoiding the need to develop greenfield sites (undeveloped land that is often still in its natural state), and thereby healing and greening a polluted area.

Riverwood 100, Atlanta, GA. View down from one of the balconies (LEED EB Certified). Firm: John Portman & Associates. PHOTO: MICHAEL PORTMAN

How do you explain cool surfaces (roof/paving) to someone who may be unfamiliar with the concepts?

❯ Summer urban heat islands result from solar heating of dark, dry, urban surfaces. Sunlight is absorbed by dark pavements and roofs, which in turn warm the air. (Air itself absorbs very little sunlight, but it can be heated as it flows over warm surfaces.)

The goal with cool surfaces is to cool cities in the summer. One approach is to reduce absorption of sunlight by buildings and pavements. The simplest way to reduce solar absorption is to replace dark surfaces that strongly absorb sunlight, such as black or gray roofs, with light-colored surfaces that strongly reflect sunlight, such as white roofs.

Interestingly, slightly less than half of sunlight is visible to the human eye. Light-colored surfaces stay coolest because they strongly reflect both visible and invisible sunlight. However, when dark surfaces are needed for aesthetics or to reduce brightness, one can use special "cool-colored" materials that stay moderately cool by reflecting only the invisible component of sunlight.

Haley Gilbert, principal research associate, Heat Island Group, Environmental Energy Technologies Division, Lawrence Berkeley National Laboratory

Creative Rewards

DAVID WINSLOW, GZA

Vice President

Geoenvironmental, Inc.

How would you explain what you do? What does a "typical" workday look like?

❯ I commonly tell people that I evaluate and clean up contaminated soil and groundwater associated with our industrial past. Typically, I oversee investigations to characterize the hydrogeology and the extent of contamination at a former industrial site. Following characterization, we design and implement measures to address the contamination to protect both human health and the environment. Over the past few years, we have added another component to this work called green remediation. We try to design our investigations and remediations using green principles, so as to minimize energy use and reduce greenhouse gas emissions.

How does your work interface with the following players on a project team: urban planner, civil engineer, architect, landscape architect, green building consultants, and others?

❯ We work hand in hand with other members of the project team. For instance, we would work with civil engineers to balance stormwater management issues versus limiting infiltration over contaminated areas. We have also worked with civil engineers to incorporate stormwater retention basins into groundwater remediation programs. We work with architects in the design of building features that will help protect occupants from exposure to residual contaminants that may

be managed in place at a brownfield development site. We work with green building consultants to incorporate environmental remediation into the LEED process. We also help with indoor air quality issues as part of the LEED process. Soil and groundwater contamination and remediation may have impacts on the foundation design and earthwork during construction. For example, waterproofing materials need to be checked for compatibility with contaminants of concern. We also help balance soil reuse on projects by identifying what materials can be reused on site, where, and if any additional engineered controls (e.g., capping marginally contaminated soils with asphalt, concrete, or two feet of clean fill) need to be incorporated in the reuse.

If you could give one tip to someone pursuing the green site remediation profession, what would it be?

❯ Since this is a new field, there are many opportunities. I would encourage new scientists and engineers to take initiative and be proactive. The more seasoned engineers and scientists may not be thinking about green remediation. You can open their eyes to the program and suggest common everyday practices to make a project green. For example, on one project in which I was involved, the junior engineers all volunteered to carpool to the site, and they rented a small economy car rather than a large truck or SUV. This was then incorporated into our green remediation program as a standard operating procedure (SOP). Be creative, think green, and present your ideas to senior design engineers.

Maximize Net Eco-Benefit

JEFF PAUL

Principal

Golder Associates, Inc.

Why is green remediation important to the public and developers?

❯ Green remediation is important to the public as we have finite resources in the world and should not hurt people and the environment in one location just to clean up another. For the developers it

could be just good publicity, but to some I know, it is a way of life. They have wanted to improve land and structures, and now also realize they can do so while increasing the net environmental benefit and will do so even if it costs some of their profits.

What advice would you give to someone pursuing the green site remediation profession?

Obtain a master's or PhD in a low-energy site remediation subject or a field that can be applied to low-energy site remediation.

GENERAL SITE RESOURCES

Environmental Protection Agency: Heat Island Effect
www.epa.gov/heatisland/mitigation/coolroofs.htm

Lawrence Berkeley National Laboratory, Heat Island Group
http://heatisland.lbl.gov/

The Sustainable Sites Initiative
www.sustainablesites.org/

U.S. EPA, Brownfields and Land Revitalization
www.epa.gov/brownfields/

Water

Many types of water specialization careers exist, both inside and outside of buildings. Interior water specialists, such as plumbing engineers, might design areas such as a gym, kitchen, break room, or restrooms to use low-flow sinks, showers, and toilets, along with other water-efficient fixtures. Plumbing engineers might also consider reusing water (either gray or black water) for activities such as dishwashing and clothes washing. Exterior water specialists, on the other hand, such as civil engineers and landscape architects, will consider the water use and management around a building and site, looking at factors such as stormwater management, hardscapes, and landscaping.

Other water specialists who could be called in by the GBC to assist on a project might include:

Ecologist

Irrigation consultant

Ocean expert

Rainwater-harvesting consultant

Wetland expert

Xeriscape expert

For example, one aspect of water savings is via plumbing fixtures.

Indoor plumbing fixtures can contribute to significant water savings in buildings. Also, 15 percent of building energy use is attributed to water heating.[2] As a way to help preserve water in the U.S. and to give people an easy way to identify water-conserving products, homes, and services, the EPA created

WaterSense Label

WaterSense. All products and homes that bear a WaterSense label are certified to meet the EPA's standards (certifying that all WaterSense goods are 20 percent more efficient than the terms set out in the Energy Policy Act of 1992), both in terms of water efficiency and performance; testing is also part of the certification process, and all WaterSense fixtures are third-party certified by independent laboratories.[3]

This program is helpful for consumers and green building professionals alike who want to integrate water efficiency into their projects; it is the only such program of its type in the country. Currently, a whole array of products are certified with the WaterSense label, including residential toilets, faucets/faucet accessories, urinals, and showerheads, and in the near future, weather-based irrigation controllers. There is also a Water Budget Tool that allows landscapers and others designing outdoor spaces to create eco-landscapes that take regional water needs into account.[4]

Regardless of whether the water is used inside or outside the building, one of the key principles of water usage is a clear realization and understanding of the interconnected and cyclical nature of this precious resource.

One Water

JASON LEDERER, CPESC, LEED AP
Senior Water Resource Scientist
BSC Group

What was your path to becoming a distinguished senior water resource scientist, and how does it relate to green buildings? Would you recommend the same path or resources to others? If not, what alternative(s) would you recommend?

❯ My background as a geologist taught me how to look at the world through a wide-angle lens. Being able to think in terms of millions and billions of years and continents, oceans, and planets has helped me to understand scales of magnitude from the micro to the planetary. As a species, we are completely dependent on natural systems for our daily existence—air, water, energy—and they are all interrelated. The planet is effectively a closed system with no inputs or outputs other than radiant heat energy. Throughout my career, I gravitated toward the field of water resource management and quickly recognized that a clean and ample water supply was directly influenced by how we treat our watersheds. Additionally, having done my graduate education in the Midwest, I observed firsthand just how vulnerable we are as a society to flooding and large-scale erosion.

In order to understand how a project will contribute to or detract from the natural environment, it is critical to understand how our planet "works," with all its complex feedbacks and cycles. Site selection, site development, stormwater management, water efficiencies, and other aspects of project design, construction, and maintenance are directly related to a site's geology and the natural processes inherent to our planet.

Often, projects are implemented at the site scale, but it is critical to recognize that the impacts on a site reverberate over a much larger area. Green building principles take these broader-scale impacts into account by working to identify opportunities to limit and reduce water consumption and wastewater and effectively deal with stormwater output, carbon emissions, and energy efficiency.

How would you explain what you do? What does a "typical" workday look like?

❯ My typical days are quite varied. Right now, I am doing a lot of environmental permitting work. During the design process, it is important to consider the regulatory implications a project will have. Are you near a stream, wetland, or other sensitive area that is jurisdictional to a local, state, or federal environmental agency? These are important things to consider before going too far with a design that might end up not being permissible.

Other things I am working on include: helping a state transportation agency develop an erosion and sediment control field guide and plan for infrastructure (new and redevelopment) projects of various scales, environmental monitoring, etc. I perform assessments on streams, develop sustainable stormwater management design approaches, and manage a diversity of projects with interdisciplinary design teams that may include landscape architects, engineers, other scientists, and contractors.

How does your work interface with the following players on a project team—urban planner, civil engineer, architect, landscape architect, and others?

❯ Before even beginning to think of site design, it is imperative to first inventory and analyze

The High Point parks provide stormwater management, view corridors, and recreation within a connected, vibrant public realm. High Point Community Parks, Seattle, Washington (Built Green, Three Star Rating). FIRM AND PHOTO: MITHUN

the site's relative landscape components. Things like soils, water resources, vegetative cover, slope angles, and aspects are all critical components for influencing a design and construction approach. I am often involved on the front end of projects in this manner. However, I have also become increasingly involved in developing stormwater management approaches on projects and working directly with engineers and landscape architects to develop design approaches that mimic a natural hydrologic approach, provide for adequate drainage, complement or improve ecological structure and function, and are aesthetically pleasing to the extent practical.

Though a scientist, I am also typically a part of the design team helping with everything from broad planning approaches to technical details associated with water resource management on a site. This may include stormwater management, rainwater harvesting, erosion and sediment control (both during and post-construction), and ecological restoration.

Telling the Story

LAUREN E. GRAHAM LEED AP
Graduate Student

What made you choose green building as a career (or volunteer)?

❯ After finishing college, I was focused on pursuing a career in water resources management. Working and volunteering in the green building field presented an opportunity to enter the sustainability field without having a background in architecture or engineering. I was interested in the design aspect of green building, and the way that natural resources are extracted to create the built environment. I worked as a project manager/green building consultant and volunteered with the USGBC.

What advice would you give to a student who is considering the green building field?

❯ I would tell the student not to worry if they aren't majoring in architectural design, engineering, or construction management. There is a lot of room for people with nontraditional social sciences to contribute in the green building field and to create a lasting career for themselves. They should also think about what they are trying to accomplish by entering the field. Are you aiming for a short-term, "first job out of college" position to transition into something else, or do you see yourself really making a career in the field? Consider pursuing certifications or accreditations that will help to boost your skill set and distinguish you from other job seekers. Either way, consider how you are going to "tell the story" of your passion for sustainability.

What scary green factoid keeps you up at night? Any solutions?

❯ An open fire hydrant at full pressure pumps approximately 1,000 gallons of water per minute. That's enough to fill an Olympic-sized swimming pool in about eleven hours. The Great Pacific Garbage Patch is pretty scary too—it's a collection of small and microscopic pieces of plastic debris that have been worn down over time and are swirling in the ocean at a current mass estimated to be twice the size of Texas.

WATER RESOURCES

California Department of Water Resources
www.water.ca.gov/urbanwatermanagement/

Environmental Protection Agency: WaterSense
www.epa.gov/watersense/

The Alliance for Water Efficiency
www.allianceforwaterefficiency.org/

H₂O Performance

DAVID SHERIDAN, PhD, LEED AP BD+C

Owner

Aqua Cura

Please give a brief background on your education and experience.

❯ I have a BS in civil engineering, a MS in environmental pollution control, and a PhD in environmental engineering. In addition, I have 25 years in consulting engineering for municipal water and wastewater management systems. My focus is on guiding project design and construction teams in applying LEED to the process, helping them to see that early attention to high-performance, sustainable outcomes will allow them to produce a LEED-certified building at reasonable cost. I provide technical input to projects in the areas of water efficiency and energy efficiency.

What types of performance metrics and standards do you feel help conserve water the most in the green building realm?

❯ It is crucial to know how much water the building systems are using. Designing the plumbing system to be amenable to monitoring and installing submeters to allow building operators to see how much water is used by different portions of the system does not have to be costly. Submetering gives the operations staff useful information on system performance and potential water-wasting systems.

The use of a water body: The pond is another important element included in the landscape area. The design concept is to cool down the temperature of air introduced into the buildings. Energy Complex, Bangkok, Thailand. (LEED CS Platinum). Firm: Architect 49. Owner: Energy Complex Co., Ltd. PHOTO: 2011, ENERGY COMPLEX

Excellent performance metrics are being developed for water-using fixtures, equipment, and appliances. WaterSense, the EPA program, provides valuable information on performance as well as water use. Manufacturers are getting on board, providing useful information to guide the design team in fixture, equipment, and appliance selection.

Energy

Efficient use of energy is one of the biggest environmental concerns today due to its extraction, creation, pollution, nonrenewable sources, emissions, global warming, and other potential impacts. All of the nonrenewable energy sources such as oil, coal, natural gas, and nuclear have environmental ramifications from degradation to the site where they are extracted to harm of surrounding natural habitat and emissions that contribute to greenhouse gases.

Buildings expend approximately 39 percent of the energy and 74 percent of the annual U.S. production of electricity, according to the U.S. Department of Energy.[5] The majority of energy in the United States is fossil fuel, a limited resource that also creates emissions. Therefore, energy goals in green building are focused on simply reducing amounts of energy needed and transitioning to cleaner or renewable energy whenever possible.

Due to the significance of energy issues, it is weighted heavily in many of the green building rating systems. For example, in LEED the energy and atmosphere category represents the highest weight in 2009, with 35 potential points out of a total of 110 points available. With this emphasis on energy and buildings, this section will explore in greater depth green energy professional opportunities as compared to the other categories.

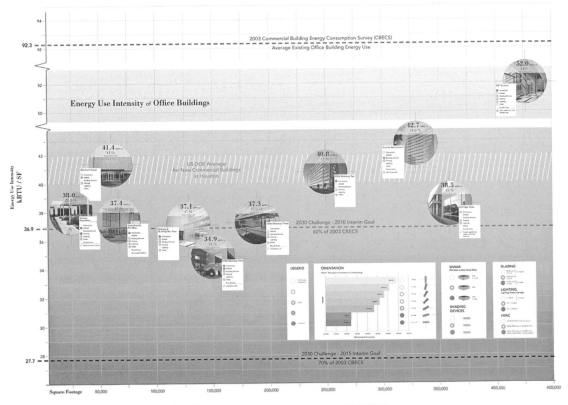

Energy performance metrics for Kirksey projects. FIRM AND IMAGE: 2009 KIRKSEY

Why is energy so important?

❭ Since global warming (climate change) is the critical issue, and since it is caused by the use of energy, sustainability is a 90 percent issue of energy.

People who make products and materials are very interested in promoting what they sell as green. Thus, we hear of sustainability in every aspect of building. It is not just "greenwash" that is a problem, but also focusing on issues and areas that will not make much difference.

Consequently, if we do not solve the big energy issues, nothing else will be of much consequence.

Thus, I believe that we need green professionals who will have the knowledge, skills, and recognition of the need to dramatically reduce the consumption of energy. It is especially important to understand solar-responsive design, because that is where the greatest energy savings are possible.

Norbert M. Lechner, LEED AP, architect and prof. emeritus, Auburn University, author of Heating, Cooling, Lighting: Design Methods for Architects

Native Meets West

MARCUS SHEFFER, LEED AP BD+C, LEED Fellow

President

Energy Opportunities, Inc./a 7group Company

What was your path to becoming an energy and green building specialist?

❭ While I am often confused for an engineer, I have no formal training in the subject. My formal training is in ecology and environmental studies, and I have always approached my entire career (and life for that matter) from that perspective. I read Amory Lovins's *Soft Energy Paths* in college, and I was inspired to work in the field of energy efficiency and renewables. The way we produce and consume energy has far bigger impacts on the environment than any other human interface (except perhaps the field of agriculture, which is also a passionate interest of mine) so this seemed like a worthy endeavor. As luck would have it, I had an internship at a regional energy center funded by the state and walked into a full-time job upon graduation. I spent twelve years working for the PA Energy Office doing public outreach work (workshops, energy audits, and providing information to interested citizens in the pre-Internet days). In 1993, I formed my company, Energy Opportunities, Inc., to help nonprofit organizations reduce their energy use (I still run a local program with that focus). In the mid-1990s I had the good fortune to work on a project which was one of the first twelve LEED buildings certified under the pilot. I worked on a number of green building projects following that first one and the relationships on those projects became the seeds from which 7group was formed. A series of videos documented some of those projects and put several 7group partners on the national scene at USGBC, where we have served in various roles as consultants and volunteers. Most notably, one of the original 7group partners, Scot Horst, is now the Senior VP for LEED at USGBC.

When hiring a green energy and green building specialist, what are three important characteristics?

❯ Open-mindedness, willingness to challenge conventional thinking, and strong environmental ethics. Good math skills help, but are not required since it is not numbers that ultimately change the human heart.

If you could give one tip to someone pursuing the green energy profession, what would it be?

❯ Don't think like an engineer—there is a whole other side to your brain!

Energy specialists focus on increased energy efficiency for the green building and renewable energy sources. Because of the depth and breadth of this focus area, there are numerous different kinds of energy specialists, some of which include:

Building automation specialists

Daylighting specialists

Energy modeling experts

Lighting consultants

NEW VS. VINTAGE

While building orientation and exterior products contribute to energy efficiency, often some of the biggest contributions are from energy systems such as heating, cooling, and lighting. The energy

Great River Energy Headquarters, Maple Grove, Minnesota (LEED NC Platinum). Firm: Perkins + Will. PHOTO: © LUCIE MARUSIN

usage in new buildings is different from that of existing buildings, since systems in new construction can be designed to be energy efficient from the very outset. Existing buildings, on the other hand, were often built at a time when energy codes were more or less stringent, which could result in dated, inefficient systems that may become even less energy friendly as they age, or with other factors at play. In the energy category we will organize the issues, specialists, and tools into new and existing buildings.

ENERGY FOR NEW CONSTRUCTION

There are a few key processes and tools that green building professionals use to help evaluate the performance and output of energy systems for new construction. Two of the most popular energy processes and tools that often require specialists are:

Energy modeling

Daylighting design and modeling

Energy Modeling

Experts in modeling energy use computer software to simulate a proposed building's energy usage over the course of a year, using parameters such as site orientation, exterior façade materials, insulation, roof, window apertures, insulating and reflecting properties, and energy sources and systems to evaluate and modify a building's design during the planning stage of construction. Modeling programs let experts adjust parts of the building's design to increase energy efficiency and see the trade-offs of their decisions (such as access to daylighting or life cycle systems costs)—and also to compare the proposed designs with minimum green regulations and to evaluate potential energy savings. Energy modeling experts are staff members at mechanical, electrical, and plumbing (MEP) engineering firms and commissioning agent firms, as well as independent experts who work on their own.

Could you please explain energy modeling?

❭ Energy modeling is a complex process that produces a simple result: how much energy a building is expected to consume and the associated peak demand for energy over a certain amount of time (i.e., one hour, one month, one year, etc.). An energy model takes into account the interactive effects of a number of variables, including lighting, HVAC equipment, plug loads (e.g., computers, elevators), and service-water heating.

The results are very useful when determining the expected operation of a building and how a building's consumption and demand loads compare to buildings of a similar usage type and size. Energy models are also useful for determining where efforts should be focused with regard to energy efficiency measures.

Gregg Liddick | LEED AP BD+C, manager, GDL
Sustainability Consulting

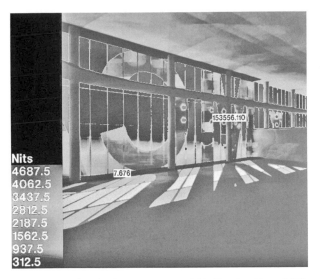

Glare Study 1 for the Downtown YMCA, Houston, Texas (LEED NC Gold). FIRM AND IMAGE: 2009 KIRKSEY

Glare Study 2 for the Downtown YMCA, Houston, Texas (LEED NC Gold). FIRM AND IMAGE: 2009 KIRKSEY

Downtown YMCA, Houston, Texas (LEED NC Gold). FIRM: KIRKSEY. PHOTO: 2010 JOE AKER

Downtown YMCA, Houston, Texas (LEED NC Gold). Firm: Kirksey. PHOTO: 2010 JOE AKER

PROCESS

Energy modeling is an excellent example of where an integrated approach can be most fruitful in optimizing energy efficiency. The ideal scenario is one in which the team begins energy modeling early in the design process, and the architect and mechanical engineer (or energy modeler) are some of the key players to be part of the early planning process. At the very start of the project, modeling could include big concepts such as the number of stories and size of a building's footprint. Then the team could consider site selection, site orientation, glazing location, type and size, and electrical lighting. In the later phases, a good model will have progressed to include two different versions for comparison's sake: the minimal code-compliant case and the maximized energy-efficient case. Throughout all phases of the project, life-cycle costing should be taken into account. Life-cycle costing or whole-life costs show the total cost of ownership.[6] For example, the initial cost of a more energy-efficient HVAC system may be higher, but when considered over the life cycle of the building, the total cost might prove to be a better value based on projections of long term energy bill savings.

Ohlone College Newark Center for Health Sciences + Technology enthalpy wheel, Newark, California (LEED NC Platinum). Firm: Perkins+Will, Inc. PHOTO: COURTESY OF PERKINS+WILL, INC.

Some of the types of information that are entered into an energy model might include:

Location: Weather, orientation

Exterior: Roof, glazing, insulation

Interior: Lighting, HVAC, plug loads (or the power supplied to wall outlets)

Systems: HVAC, hot water, specialty systems

Schedule: Lighting, HVAC, and occupancy

Often, faulty assumptions are made when people enter information, causing inaccuracies in the energy modeling program. One of the key mistakes is larger than necessary estimates of size and system capacity, resulting in HVAC and other systems sized larger than needed and increasing financial and environmental cost impacts within the model. For these reasons, it is important that the project team review the input data to confirm accurate assumptions.

Purposeful Process

MICHAEL J. HOLTZ, FAIA, NCARB, LEED AP

Founder and Principal

LightLouver LLC

As an energy expert and architect, what would you say are the key best practices/processes to achieving maximum energy efficiency?

❯ Bill Caudill, FAIA, founder and president of Caudill Rowlett Scott, had a saying: "You get great architecture through great designers!" I extended Bill's saying, with his approval, by saying, "You get great architecture through great designers working within a great design process!" Bill and I both recognized the importance of the design team working collaboratively within an innovative design process. Bill was a strong believer in bringing all parties—owner's team, occupants, design team, construction team, and other stakeholders—together to collectively define the design challenges, design opportunities, and alternative design solutions, and to collectively develop and agree to a design direction. Bill called these intense working meetings "squatter" sessions that would last from a few days to a few weeks.   A key aspect of a squatter session is a clear definition and consensus on design goals and a commitment to find a design solution that achieves these goals. Clearly defined, and owner and design team accepted, sustainable design goals are the first step to achieving these goals and will drive innovative thinking to develop solutions that meet all design goals within the project constraints—program, site, schedule, and budget.

A second key best practice is to have an advocate for achieving the agreed-to energy and environmental design goals. This advocate or advocate team could be within the architectural design team, the construction team, the owner's team, or a specialty consultant, such as a sustainable design consultant.

Which energy/daylight modeling tools and/or resources do you find most useful, and why?

❯ The most important factor in selecting energy or daylight modeling tools is the characteristics of the design solution to be evaluated. Modeling tools cannot generate innovative and appropriate alternative design solutions. They are only useful in evaluating the performance of the alternative design solutions against a set of specific design criteria.

The challenge is to accurately model the proposed design solution at a level of detail appropriate to the stage of design. The level of detail in the model can be different, and likely will be different, during the schematic design phase than at the design development phase or the construction documents phase. Thus, the modeling tool may be different, or the level of detail expressed in the modeling tool may be different. A wide variety of energy and daylight modeling tools are available to the design community. A good source of information on these tools is the U.S. Department of Energy website: http://apps1.eere.energy.gov/buildings/tools_directory/subjects_sub.cfm.

I personally prefer detailed modeling tools that can explicitly model the unique features and characteristics of alternative design solutions but can also be used early in the design process at a lower level of design detail. For daylight modeling tools, the Radiance software is one of the best in the world. For energy modeling, a number of tools exist, such as IES Virtual Environment, TRNSYS, EnergyPlus, and IDA/ICE. As important as the modeling tool is the person using the tool, as energy and daylight modeling is still as much an art as it is an exact science.

Please provide a few tips that are important to ensuring energy and/or daylight modeling success.

❯ Energy and daylight modeling are typically undertaken to inform design decisions. Thus, prior to initiating any modeling efforts, the energy or daylighting analyst should meet with the design team to review design objectives and environmental design criteria and to review the alternative design solutions that will be evaluated. The analyst must have a clear understanding of the proposed design alternatives that the design team is considering and any concerns or issues the design team has regarding these design alternatives.

Another way of stating this is to ask, "What is the purpose of the modeling?" For example, if the purpose is to calculate the projected energy savings of the proposed design, then a reference building (i.e., a minimally code-compliant building) may need to be developed and modeled so that a comparison in energy performance can be made between the proposed design and the reference design. Also, modeling can be done to refine a design solution—such as optimizing the window glazing properties, evaluat-

ing various insulation levels, assessing the impact of various HVAC systems, and so on. These "parametric sensitivity studies" are very instructive and help the design team fine-tune the proposed design solution.

With your background in energy and environmental research and design consulting, what criteria would you recommend sustainable building professionals use to assess which tools will be best?

❯ Many factors influence the appropriateness of the modeling tools that a sustainable building professional should consider when selecting a design or analysis tool to use, including the following:

■ Specific strategy or strategies to be evaluated

■ Specific phase of design in which the tool will be used

■ Level of knowledge of the user in the specific strategy to be evaluated

■ Level of modeling detail required to answer the question(s) that designer wants answered

■ Complexity of the user input and ability of the tool user to know or obtain this input

■ Integration with other design documentation tools, such as CAD or BIM

■ Cost of the tool

■ Clarity and usefulness of the tool output

TOOLS

Energy modeling tools (software) range in terms of capabilities, level of work, and areas of focus. Some tools require a large amount of input data, taking several hours to enter into the system. There are generally two key types of energy modeling tools.

The first type of energy modeling tools is for screening and economic assessment tools, both typically used for budgeting purposes. Screening programs include FRESA and FEDS; economic assessment tools include Building Life Cycle Cost (BLCC) and Quick BLCCT.[7]

The next category of energy modeling tools is used by architectural and engineering teams throughout the entire design process. These tools can be used for new construction, as well as for retrofits of existing buildings. The tools are created and owned by a variety of entities, from private companies to manufacturers of HVAC equipment, utility companies, or the government. Each tool has pros and cons and limitations. Building professionals are expected to understand key aspects of the energy modeling tools available and be able to recommend which program is best for the project at hand. Popular architecture and engineering design tools include ENERGY-10, Building Design Advisor, and Energy Scheming; some of the major HVAC load/size tools include TRACE, DOE-2, BLAST, VisualDOE, and EnergyPlus. In fact, ENERGY-10 can provide quick feedback to the design team early in the process while there are still many unknown factors.[8]

No matter which particular energy modeling software tool is used, however, they are all just predictors of estimated annual energy use, and cannot precisely project exact energy usage for the completed building. Plus, factors outside the control of the program—such as construction delays, drastic weather changes, and fluctuations in occupancy or maintenance schedules—impact the actual energy systems and cannot be forecast in advance by energy modeling programs.

> ## Please provide three tips or tools that are key to optimizing energy modeling success.

❯ Tip 1. Experience matters. Knowing enough about what aspects need to be carefully scrutinized versus what can be quickly approximated is important to being timely and cost effective in getting real and valuable results. An example would be very accurately modeling windows but not spending too much effort on exterior cladding.

Tip 2. Try to create a basic method that you use consistently, such as always starting a model from the front elevation and then always moving clockwise around to each façade.

Tip 3. You don't have to be an expert in all aspects of building performance to gain valuable insight from energy modeling. For example, an architect that was less experienced with HVAC could select standard default equipment and still use the model to optimize just the building envelope.

Mike Barcik, LEED AP BD+C, director of technical services, Southface Energy Institute

❯ For tools, probably the most popular and powerful energy simulation software available is eQUEST (www.doe2.com). This is a front-end software package that uses the DOE-2 energy simulation "engine" developed by the U.S. Department of Energy. eQUEST is free and available to the world.

There are also energy modeling blogs and list-servs available where users share ideas, solve problems, and stay up to date with new developments. The conversations are often interesting and informative.

An energy modeler would benefit immensely from gaining a basic understanding of HVAC physics, terminology, system types, and the various equipment configurations.

Jeff G. Ross-Bain, PE, LEED AP BD+C, BEMP, principal, Ross-Bain Green Building

ENERGY MODELING AND BUILDING INTEGRATED MODELING (BIM) RESOURCES

American Council for an Energy-Efficient Economy:
www.aceee.org/topics/building-modeling-and-simulation

American Society of Heating, Refrigerating and Air-Conditioning Engineers:
www.ashrae.org/

Bentley
www.bentley.com/en-US/Promo/High+Performance+Building+Design/

buildingSMART Alliance
www.buildingsmartalliance.org/index.php/projects/

Digital Alchemy
www.digitalalchemypro.com/

Environmental Building News, "Building Information Modeling and Green Design"
www.buildinggreen.com/auth/article.cfm/2007/5/1/Building-Information-Modeling
-and-Green-Design/

International Building Performance Simulation Association (IBPSA): www.ibpsa.org/

National Institute of Building Sciences (NIST)—Whole Building Design Guide (WBDG):
Energy Analysis Tools: www.wbdg.org/resources/energyanalysis.php

U.S. Energy Information Administration (US EIA) Commercial Buildings Energy Consumption
Survey (CBECS): www.eia.gov/emeu/cbecs/

Whole Building Design Guide: BIM Libraries
www.wbdg.org/bim/bim_libraries.php?l=d

Energy Integrator + IT Pioneer

**KEVIN SETTLEMYRE, LEED AP, BD+C, ID+C,
President, Sustainable IQ**

The Intersection of green building and information technology is interesting. How do you see these two career paths becoming more integrated?

❯ As project teams, owners, and building operators get more sophisticated about how we not only design, but monitor, hone, and automate building performance throughout the life cycle of buildings, the two areas will continue on an integration path and beyond. It might not seem like it, but we are only at the tip of the iceberg in terms of "leveraging information":

> During design to do different types of simulation analysis
>
> During initial operations to calibrate an energy model so it can be used to inform building operation decisions

> During operations to use actual performance data to influence how the building controls influence performance in real time

Building information modeling (BIM) to building energy modeling (BEM) still holds its challenges in terms of how building geometry flows between tools, much less so, how more interesting information can flow with the model or back to the model. The U.S. Department of Energy has seen this gap and they have initiated an interoperability project to develop a platform of tools that will enhance translation of BIM to BEM. This is a key piece of the puzzle, but it is only a piece.

There are numerous types of simulation other than energy that can leverage information from a central model to develop analyses that will not only allow teams to look at different types of performance of the design but performance over time as well. Currently, there are tool development efforts occurring in pockets all along the building design and life cycle, but glue to bring it all together is still in its infancy.

Daylighting Design

Daylighting design harnesses the sun's light inside a building to reduce the need for artificial lighting, and it is typically one of the roles of a lighting consultant, project engineer, or green building consultant. Daylighting analysis can be integrated into building information modeling (BIM) as a part of the overall energy analysis. Indeed, the energy savings from reduced electric lighting through the use of daylighting strategies can directly reduce building cooling energy usage by an additional 10 to 20 percent.[13] Creating good daylighting involves a combination of practices, from inclusion of high efficiency windows and skylights to incorporation of smart light controls that can read the level of sunlight and adjust the electrical lighting and shading devices accordingly. A well integrated design will also include regional climactic conditions, site orientation to optimize daylight and heat gain, and it will take into account interior and exterior building products such as exterior sunshades, window glazing types, and the reflectivity of interior paint colors.

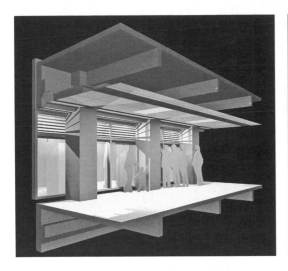

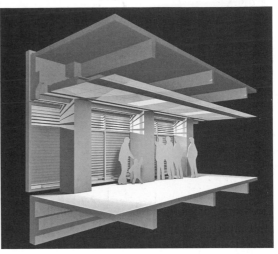

Daylighting study for Duke Energy Center (LEED CS Platinum). IMAGE: tvsdesign/DAVID BROWN

Daylighting study for Duke Energy Center (LEED CS Platinum). IMAGE: tvsdesign/DAVID BROWN

How would you describe the principles of daylighting?

❯ Daylighting is the purposeful use of sunlight to meet the illumination requirements of an architectural space. The key words in this definition are "purposeful" and "illumination requirements." *Purposeful* implies a specific intent to collect and distribute sunlight for an architectural lighting purpose. *Illumination requirements* indicate the quantitative and qualitative lighting design criteria that must be met by the daylighting design solution. Together, these words express the design challenges architects face when using sunlight as a primary light source inside their buildings. The specific design challenges architects face and must solve include elements such as glare and poor daylight distribution.

To create an effective daylighting/electric lighting design solution that addresses these design challenges, the building elements/components must be properly designed and integrated such as shading daylight aperture and distribution.

Michael J. Holtz, FAIA, NCARB, LEED AP, founder and principal, LightLouver LLC

Academic Center at Georgia Gwinnett College, Lawrenceville, GA: Skylight. Architects: John Portman & Associates. IMAGE COURTESY OF JOHN PORTMAN AND ASSOCIATES

Connecting Architecture with Nature

JILL DALGLISH, LEED AP BD+C
President
Dalglish Daylighting

How did you become a daylighting consultant?

❯ First of all, I completed an architectural engineering degree. Many great daylighting consultants also start out with an architectural degree. As an undergraduate, I was lucky enough to work as an intern for a daylighting consulting pioneer, Steven Ternoey, AIA, and this was where I fell in love with the profession. I then worked for many years as a lighting and power engineer, then for an architecture firm, and then as an energy modeler. I saw that there was a need for expertise in daylighting and I now own my own firm and co-teach a course in daylighting to graduate students in architecture.

How would you define daylighting design?

❯ There are many answers to this question. Some say it is creating a building and lighting design "where daylight is the main form of lighting," or "the electric lights are off and the occupants are happy." Most of the time I explain daylighting design as "consulting on the best way to bring natural light into a building and do it energy efficiently."

I consult on building orientation, window size and selection, sunshade design, daylight redirecting devices, skylights, room finishes, and electric lighting and lighting controls. I examine the impact of all of these things on the heating and cooling in a building, the electric lighting use, and the occupants' thermal comfort, visual comfort, and visual performance. Daylighting design is different from electric lighting design in that daylight is a dynamic source that changes every hour of every day and every day of the year. In daylighting, glare is the biggest concern, whereas in electric lighting, darkness is the biggest concern—so there is a bit of tension in resolving both of these concerns.

How does the integrated design process help daylighting design?

❯ The integrated design process (IDP) is the best way to cover the initial costs associated with a daylighting design. Ideally, a good daylighting design reduces the building's electric loads in both lighting and cooling and also reduces heating load. The initial cost savings comes from being able to downsize mechanical systems accordingly. In a properly executed integrated design process, the mechanical engineer is involved in information exchanges with the architect, owner, daylighting designer, and electrical lighting designer so that they are confident that a downsize of their mechanical system is possible. Ideally, IDP contracts are also set up with these parties so that they all agree to be separately, wholly, and equally responsible for the outcome of the whole project.

What are your "go-to" software tools and resources for daylight modeling—and why?

❯ I use Google SketchUp separately and in conjunction with AGI32 right now, although I am excited to try the new ElumTools.

I also use sun path diagrams, an illuminance meter, and a luminance meter. The sun path diagrams help me to plan out fixed sunshade devices, and the meters help me explain to others what the numbers in the simulations mean in real life.

Could you speak to evaluating lighting levels in existing buildings—what are good tools and processes?

❯ In my opinion, the human eye is the best tool for evaluating lighting levels. If an occupant has a glare problem, that is something that needs to be corrected. If an occupant says that there isn't enough light, this is also something that needs to be corrected, but it may not mean that more light is needed.

DAYLIGHTING RESOURCES

The Illuminating Engineering Society of North America (IESNA):
   www.iesna.org/

Software

Lighting Analysts, Inc.

AGi32:
   www.agi32.com/

Lambda Research

TracePro
   http://lambdares.com/lighting/

Radiance:
   http://radsite.lbl.gov/radiance/HOME.html

U.S. DOE: Energy Efficiency & Renewable Energy – Building Energy Software Tools Directory:
   http://apps1.eere.energy.gov/buildings/tools_directory/subjects.cfm/pagename=subjects/
   pagename_menu=materials_components/pagename_submenu=lighting_systems

Whole Building Design Guide: Daylighting
   www.wbdg.org/resources/daylighting.php

ENERGY FOR EXISTING BUILDINGS

There are a few key processes and tools that green building professionals use to evaluate actual energy usage in existing buildings. Three of the most popular energy processes and tools that often require specialists for existing buildings are:

Energy audits

ENERGY STAR

Building automation systems (BAS)

Energy Audits

Typically performed by MEP engineers or commissioning agents (or independent energy audit experts), energy audits survey an existing building's energy systems to confirm that they are performing at optimum efficiency—and if not, the experts provide recommendations to shore up existing systems. Energy audits are often performed based on the U.S. Environmental Protection Agency's (EPA's) ENERGY STAR program, which issues specific energy criteria and requirements specific to energy use of buildings.[14] Once the space achieves a minimum threshold in ENERGY STAR, the building is awarded an industry-recognized EPA ENERGY STAR score. ASHRAE is another resource, offering levels of energy audits:

Level 1: A basic building walk-through and assessment of utility bills

Level 2: A more detailed assessment of building energy usage categorized by energy consumption with a cost/benefit analysis of options

Level 3: One step beyond Level 2, in which the cost effectiveness of options is explored[15]

What are energy audits?

❯ The connotation of the word "audit" is generally not positive; however, an energy audit can produce some very useful results. A comprehensive energy audit accomplishes two main tasks: (1) It analyzes the energy consumption of a building, broken down by energy end use (e.g., lighting, interior fans, space cooling, plug loads, etc.) and compares it to buildings of a similar usage type and size, and (2) It suggests potential energy efficiency measures along with their expected savings (both energy and cost) and the return on investment. After an energy audit has been completed, the recipient should have an idea of how the building operates, even without ever having set foot in the building.

Gregg Liddick, LEED AP BD+C, manager, GDL Sustainability Consulting

What tools do you use in the energy audit process, and why?

❯ Tools such as tape measure, calculator, "mini" computer / tablet computer or audit forms, four-in-one screwdriver, volt meter (ideally with probe thermometer) and CB radio (if large building) are just some of the tools needed to assist you in gathering important site data. For example, if the building engineer is not available when you are on-site, or if maintenance personnel have recently changed, you may not have someone to tell you what types of light bulbs are being used. You will have to remove covers and manually inspect some lighting fixtures.

Jessica Rose, LEED Green Associate, chief navigator, Incite Sustainability

What are three tips to a successful process or some best practices in energy audits?

❯ PREPARATION & PLANNING: It is very, very important to gather and study building drawings, utility data, and a thorough occupant survey *before* conducting the site inspection. The material review will allow you to identify possible issues before you get to the site. That way, outside of general equipment inspections and counts, your site time can be focused on finding the *cause* of inefficiencies or dysfunctions.

What are three tips to a successful process or some best practices in energy audits? (Continued)

In general, a very accurate and thorough building audit should be approached. Specific details/examples:

UTILITY DATA: Always retrieve, compile, and analyze 12 to 24 months of utility bills *before* conducting the on-site audit

BUILDING DRAWINGS: Studying building drawings in advance allows the auditor two advantages: First, you will be more familiar with the general layout and location of important inspection areas such as mechanical rooms. Second, you will be able to identify any changes in building use or equipment from the original design.

BUILDING ENVELOPE: When on-site, be sure to do a thorough building envelope inspection.

Pay particular attention to stains on the building, building joints, any standing water near the building, ventilation outlets, etc.

Often, analysts/auditors become so focused on the obvious energy-consuming processes that they forget to analyze the "box" that all of this equipment lives in. Remember, this is a BUILDING audit. The building is a system, and energy is just one of the "foods" that the system needs. Balanced air flow, low moisture, and positive pressure are other important ingredients that make up a healthy building. So, for example, seeing mold growth on a building exterior may be a clue to bigger moisture issues within the building seal.

Jessica Rose, LEED Green Associate, chief navigator, Incite Sustainability

ENERGY AUDIT RESOURCE

ASHRAE Energy Audit
http://ashrae.org/

ENERGY STAR

The popular ENERGY STAR label not only applies to your computer and dishwasher, but is also relevant in terms of buildings or whole building portfolios. In 2010, over 6,000 buildings were ENERGY STAR–certified, which is up 60 percent from the previous year.[16] As defined by the U.S. Environmental Protection Agency (EPA), the organization that runs the program, "To qualify for the ENERGY STAR, a building or manufacturing plant must earn a seventy-five or higher on EPA's 1–100 energy performance scale, indicating that the facility performs better than at least seventy-five percent of similar buildings nationwide. The ENERGY STAR energy performance scale accounts for differences in operating conditions, regional weather data, and other important considerations."[17]

The EPA offers a free tool called "Portfolio Manager" in which energy and water information can be entered to quickly assess how a building (or an entire portfolio) is performing on the ENERGY STAR 100-point scale. The score should be verified by either a registered architect or licensed engineer.[18] Another useful free tool is the "Target Finder," which allows designers and owners to predict energy usage in a building's design phase.[19]

ENERGY STAR RESOURCE

www.energystar.gov/index.cfm?c=business.bus_index

> ### How do you find that ASHRAE walk-through audits and ENERGY STAR ratings provide value to the process?

❯ Understanding how the base building performs is paramount in addressing any inefficiencies in your overall building's performance. Following ASHRAE 90.1 2007 and ASHRAE 62.1, along with tracking your building in ENERGY STAR Portfolio Manager, are just a few processes and tools that are available for building owners today.

Elaine Aye, IIDA, LEED AP BD+C, O+M, ID+C, principal, Green Building Services

Building Automation Systems

A building automation system (BAS) is a computer-based system that fine-tunes the building for energy-efficient goals and occupant comfort. A BAS system can control HVAC, lighting, water, and other building systems. It accomplishes this via three mechanisms: sensors, controlled devices, and controllers. The facility manager and operations staff input the optimum setpoints for each, and the BAS system monitors the mechanisms for achievement or alarms if outside the predetermined boundaries. The BAS also overlays trend data and schedules of building operation hours.

Energy Audits, Energy Star, and Building Automation Systems are all process and tools the MEP Engineers and Commissioning Agents use in their review of energy efficiency in an existing building."

Monitoring and control station for variable refrigerant flow (VRF) system that services the first floor (LEED NC Platinum). Firm: Richard Wittschiebe Hand. Owner and PHOTO: ASHRAE

How do building automation systems (BAS) help with green design? What general resources would you recommend?

❭ Building automation systems (BAS) are a very good tool for building system operators to control, monitor, and improve building HVAC system operation. The systems provide the capability to automatically or manually adjust system-operating temperatures and operational schedules and to provide direct visual feedback on the resulting system performance. Operational data, monitoring, and trending can not only improve system efficiency by optimizing these parameters, they can be customized to the desired comfort of the occupant. In addition to HVAC system operation, BAS systems can integrate other systems such as lighting control. Operators with modern BAS systems are no longer limited to an on-site work station, as these systems are now Web accessible from remote locations—which is a further benefit for multiple system operation and troubleshooting from virtually any remote location.

A well-installed and programmed system will be a benefit to building system operation for the life of the project.

Steven J. Brewer, PE, LEED AP, partner, Barrett Woodyard & Associates

❭ Building automation systems range from simple programmable thermostats and light switch occupancy sensors to complete building management systems. Common HVAC applications include occupancy schedules, temperature setbacks, space temperature limits, equipment staging strategies, and monitoring equipment performance. In electrical systems, a BAS can be used for zoned lighting systems with occupancy sensors and daylight controls, power-quality monitoring, metering, and demand-limiting strategies. In domestic water systems, a BAS can reduce water heating energy use and monitor water usage. Additional strategies being implemented include smart elevator technology to optimize cab run time and waits.

As technology becomes more mainstream and costs decrease, other applications are certain to develop that will make buildings even more green. A Web-based type building automation system with pictorial graphics and the ability to utilize pull-down menus or a tree-type hierarchy seems to be easy and intuitive.

Jim Paulino, LEED AP BD+C, mechanical engineer, HESM

COMMISSIONING THE BRIDGE

Third-party evaluations and services that determine if and how the building's energy systems are indeed performing as they were intended and designed encompass the scope of the commissioning agent.

Though the majority of commissioning takes place once the building is completed, commissioning is ideally performed during all phases of a building's life so it creates a theoretical bridge from the new building to the existing building. It is a consistent third party expertise confirming the owner's goals are implemented. Projects that are pursuing green ratings such as LEED certification require a basic level of commissioning from the outset. Some of the criteria necessitate that the commissioning agent be engaged early in the process to review the owner's project requirements and monitor the development of the design drawings and specifications. Later in the

Great River Energy
Headquarters, Maple
Grove, Minnesota
(LEED NC Platinum).
Firm: Perkins + Will.
PHOTO: © LUCIE
MARUSIN

construction process, the commissioning agent will confirm that the HVAC, lighting, and other energy systems are being installed as per the owner's goals, as well as check that all systems once installed are functioning correctly.

"Organizations that have researched commissioning claim that owners can achieve savings in operations of $4 over the first five years of occupancy as a direct result of every $1 invested in commissioning—an excellent return on investment,"[20] per the WBDG, a program of the National Institute of Building Sciences. Many building types such as government, hospital, and university campuses invest in commissioning because they reap long-term benefits as a result. If something is designed or installed incorrectly, the commissioning agent can "catch" these mistakes and rectify them before serious issues or financial impacts arise. Commissioning agents often also engage in training the on-site facility management team for ongoing internal monitoring of systems.

After a building is completed and construction is finished, there are other kinds of commissioning that focus on existing structures. Two of the most popular such types are retrocommissioning and monitoring-based commissioning.

Goal Guardian

ROBERT (JACK) MEREDITH, PE, LEED AP BD+C
Founder and President
HGBC Healthy Green Building Consultants, Ltd.

What are your daily roles and responsibilities?

❯ The principal role I play in the green building industry is one of LEED commissioning authority,

which essentially means quality control (QC). This QC role is very broad and runs from the earliest stages of a project through design and construction and into operation of the building.

The mandate of the LEED commissioning authority is to ensure the building owner gets a building that performs as the owner intends. One of my main roles is to ensure that the design and construction team understand what the owner is expecting.

What are the most important skills/attributes a commissioning authority needs in order to be successful?

❯ A LEED commissioning authority (LCA) should have a strong technical background in architectural engineering with experience in both design and operation of buildings and building systems. LCAs should be good communicators and able to facilitate discussion in large groups that may be contentious and confrontational. They must enjoy planning, reviewing the work of others, and reporting in a detailed and professional manner. They must also enjoy attention to detail and be doggedly determined to resolve puzzling results and situations, and they must be able to work under pressure in an aggressive atmosphere. Buildings must be ready for occupancy as scheduled regardless of these "minor" issues.

NEXT-GENERATION ENERGY

Net-Zero Energy Building (NZEB)

The next generation of buildings takes energy efficiency one step further. Beyond energy savings; these new cutting-edge projects produce as much energy as they use over the course of a year, making them "net-zero" in terms of energy use. To get to this point, these buildings most often use best-practice energy-efficient strategies in combination with a renewable energy source produced either on- or off-site. Though these buildings are still connected to the electrical grid (in case the renewable energy supply is unavailable), NZEBs are ultimately a necessary step towards energy independence.[21]

Affordability Contest juror, Ric Licata, FAIA, collects data at Team New Jersey's house on the final day of assembly at the U.S. Department of Energy Solar Decathlon in Washington, D.C. PHOTO: STEFANO PALTERA/U.S. DEPARTMENT OF ENERGY SOLAR DECATHLON

Heading this initiative is the Net-Zero Energy Commercial Building Initiative, part of a larger effort by the U.S. Department of Energy created to meet the Energy Independence and Security Act of 2007, which is working "to achieve marketable net-zero buildings by 2025."[22] The commercial building market typically follows the federal government's lead. Federal Executive Order 13514 has mandated that all new federal construction entering planning in 2020 or thereafter be designed to meet zero-net-energy goals by 2030. In addition, the Executive Order mandates that a minimum of 15 percent of existing buildings (over 5,000 gross square feet) meet the Guiding Principles for Federal Leadership in High Performance and Sustainable Buildings by 2015, with movement each year toward 100 percent compliance.[23]

Replicate Seed

NET ZERO COURT

ST. LOUIS, MISSOURI

HOK

Vision + Challenge

An integrated design team led by HOK and energy and daylighting consultant The Weidt Group undertook a ten-month virtual design charrette to create a market-rate, zero-emissions design for a class A commercial office building in St. Louis.

Solutions + Strategy

ENERGY

Creating iterative virtual building models and measuring performance at every step of the design re-

sulted in a solution that achieved 73 percent energy use reduction through efficiency measures, with the balance satisfied by renewable energy sources.

The program was organized into two 4-story, 300-foot-long office bars oriented east-west and joined by two links that enclose a 60-foot-wide landscaped courtyard. The north and south facades optimize vision and daylight glazing with insulated opaque areas to leverage natural light while maintaining a high-performance envelope. The east and west facades are essentially solid, blocking glare at

Net Zero Court Building: Plan of garden for HOK's Net Zero Emissions Office Building (Prototype designed to meet Net Zero standards). FIRM AND IMAGE: HOK

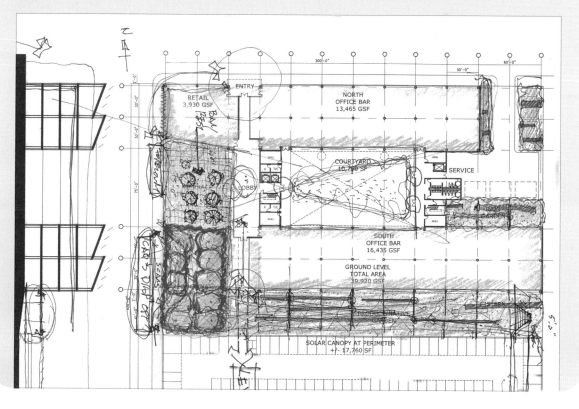

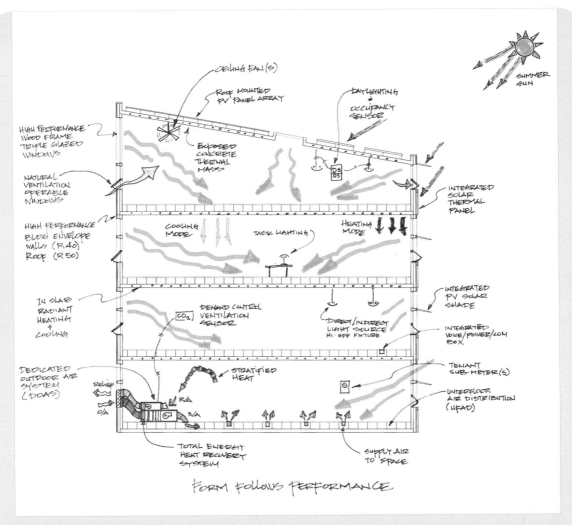

Net Zero Court Building: Form Follows Performance (Prototype designed to meet Net Zero standards). FIRM AND IMAGE: HOK

low sun angles and adding to the average R-value of the building skin.

On southern facades, evacuated solar thermal tube panels provide both a unique aesthetic and a heat source for the building. The roof is sloped at 10 degrees south and incorporates solar PV and solar thermal panels over an R-30 insulated roof. The design solution features extensive use of natural light. Features including the massing, orientation, floor-to-floor height, window sizes, quality of glass and landscaping are optimized to ensure that the building can be illuminated without electricity during daylight hours.

Because architectural solutions greatly reduced HVAC loads, the team was able to design an in-slab radiant heating and cooling system that is integrated with an underfloor air distribution (UFAD) system. As the radiant heating and cooling system provides temperature control for the space, air-handling systems are

Net Zero Court Building: Net Zero Court Building arrangement with south-sloping roof (Prototype designed to meet Net Zero standards). FIRM AND IMAGE: HOK

Net Zero Court Building: Water wall garden in courtyard (Prototype designed to meet Net Zero standards). FIRM AND IMAGE: HOK

primarily providing only ventilation and thus can be greatly downsized.

The integrated design of Net Zero Court reduced carbon emissions by 76 percent through energy-efficiency strategies, with only minor additional first costs compared to a conventional office building. To provide the remaining clean energy required to reach zero carbon emissions, the team identified on-site renewable energy systems that include approximately 51,800 square feet of rooftop and wall-mounted photovoltaic panels and 15,000 square feet of solar thermal tubes on the southern building facades and roof.

Payback

The payback for the investment required to reach carbon neutrality compared to a LEED-certified baseline building would be twelve years if the rise in the cost of fuel outpaced general inflation by 4 percent a year. But the payback would be less than ten years today in the many other areas of the country where electricity is more expensive.

The project created a design prototype and replicable process for creating affordable zero-carbon-emissions buildings in regions across the world.

Carbon Neutral

Carbon-neutral buildings do not use any fossil fuels but instead incorporate renewable sources (solar, wind, etc.); greenhouse gases (GHG) are therefore not produced as an emission, as they are in standard buildings that use coal, petroleum, natural gas, and other fossil fuels as energy sources. Energy in carbon-neutral buildings can be produced on- or off-site. Ideally, a building could be both net-zero and carbon-neutral if it utilized renewable energy as its sole energy source.[24]

Architecture 2030

In 2002, architect Ed Mazria developed the 2030 Challenge as part of his nonprofit Architecture 2030 organization.[25] A response to the building sector's negative impact on climate change, the 2030 Challenge is a voluntary pledge for building professionals to meet the following goals as outlined by the organization:

- All new buildings, developments, and major renovations shall be designed to meet a fossil fuel, GHG-emitting, energy consumption performance standard of 60% below the regional (or country) average for that building type.

- At a minimum, an equal amount of existing building area shall be renovated annually to meet a fossil fuel, GHG-emitting, energy consumption performance standard of 60% of the regional (or country) average for that building type.

- The fossil fuel reduction standard for all new buildings and major renovations shall be increased to:
    - 70% in 2015
    - 80% in 2020
    - 90% in 2025
    - Carbon-neutral in 2030 (using no fossil fuel GHG emitting energy to operate).

    These targets may be accomplished by implementing innovative sustainable design strategies, generating on-site renewable power and/or purchasing (20 percent maximum) renewable energy.[26]

The 2030 Challenge has met with resounding support, and many large entities have signed the pledge, including the American Institute of Architects (AIA), the U.S. Conference of Mayors, the U.S. Green Building Council (USGBC), and several large architecture firms, such as Cannon Design, HOK, Perkins+Will, and SmithGroup. The 2030 Challenge has even signed on a number of states, as well as inspired several sustainable federal mandates.[27]

Tool Creator

KEVIN SETTLEMYRE, LEED AP, BD+C, ID+C,
President
Sustainable IQ

How can modeling and other tools assist in the move towards net-zero and carbon-neutral buildings?

❯ It is one thing to say a team is working towards a carbon-neutral building; it is another thing to do it. Carbon-neutral design is a worthy high bar, and achieving the goal relies on creativity from a number of members of the project team. The tools can assist the integrative process by allowing project teams to "quantify the influence" of their design ideas at earlier stages and in much shorter time frames. One of the scenarios for which we are developing these tools is to see how users can interact with and develop simulations within a workshop setting to explore big design moves while also accounting for the impact of HVAC-system-type decisions. These tools can enable more innovative designs by providing performance data when the project team wants it and needs it to make decisions. We are working to reduce the mystery of carbon-neutral design.

What are your thoughts on the future of energy design in green building, especially in relation to net-zero, carbon-neutral designs and Architecture 2030?

❯ With the increased emphasis on green building from entities such as the USGBC, ASHRAE, and federal and state governments, it is not unlikely that many of the architectural, mechanical, electrical, and plumbing components of general building construction in the near future will approach efficiency levels that simply cannot be improved upon. As one example: It will always take energy to generate photons, and thus it is not reasonable to expect future lighting levels to be accomplished with zero-energy input. Although on-site renewable energy and purchasing of RECs [renewable energy credits] are ways to offset such energy consumption, to a certain degree they do not solve the problem so much as they mask the reason the energy consumption is occurring in the first place. In my opinion, the next successful wave of energy design in green building will result from a shift in how the corporate world views the aesthetic and function of the buildings they occupy. The thermodynamic laws will only allow a chiller to be so efficient, and thus to reduce HVAC energy consumption to meet some of the stringent requirements of Architecture 2030 it may take sacrifices in perceived comfort, possibly to the point where they would violate the current ventilation and thermal comfort standards. But no one said it would be easy.

James Hansen, PE, LEED AP, senior associate, GHT Limited

What are your thoughts on the future of energy design in green building, especially in relation to net-zero, carbon-neutral designs and Architecture 2030? (Continued)

❯ Net-zero is entirely technologically feasible for many buildings being built today. We have one that has been performing at zero for seven years and several that are currently in the design phase. There are some building types that are more challenging to become net-zero than others due to land configurations and zoning. However, the greatest barrier is in the cost of renewable energy since all buildings will need some external assistance during some hours or modes of operation.

David A. Eijadi, FAIA, LEED AP BD+C, The Weidt Group

❯ I think there has been a lot of emphasis on reducing energy consumption up to this point in time—and that will continue. Going forward, I see expansion into on-site energy generation to provide the necessary offsets for carbon neutrality and net-zero energy buildings. The technology and pricing of solar voltaic and micro-turbine power generation will bring these technologies to even more green buildings. Look for new methods of power distribution including direct current systems that reduce AC to DC conversion losses.

Patrick A. Kunze, P.E., LEED AP, principal, GHT Limited

❯ The past ten years have shown us that building net-zero and low-energy buildings is readily achievable. The challenge now, as we see it, is to use integrated design to create low-energy buildings that embody elegance, inspire visitors and occupants, and maximize economy. The German "Passivhaus™" system has shown that in residential and other skin-dominated building types, the building heating and cooling systems can be almost eliminated. Following this technique can result in a minimum life-cycle cost for skin-dominated buildings. Extending this type of ultra-low energy thinking to all building types is the next step in meeting aggressive building performance targets such as the 2030 Challenge.

Galen Staengl, PE, LEED BD+C, principal, Staengl Engineering

NEXT-GENERATION ENERGY RESOURCES

ASHRAE Vision 2020: www.ashrae.org/aboutus/page/248

Architecture 2030: www.architecture2030.org/

Carbon*Free:* www.carbonfund.org/

U.S. Department of Energy: Zero Energy Buildings: http://zeb.buildinggreen.com/

Energy Sources and Infrastructure

Next generation energy buildings focus on where the energy comes from and hold a vision of maximum energy efficiency, on or off-site renewable energy or even creation of energy back to the power grid. A whole host of green professionals who focus on the how energy is created and the associated infrastructure to supply it to buildings such as:

Biomass/biogas experts

Carbon accounting / footprint specialists

Geothermal experts

Green power specialists

Hydro power experts

Solar power or photovoltaic cell experts

Wind power experts

One burgeoning field of energy distribution overlaps with modern information technology in the nexus called the "smart grid."

Could you describe the Smart Grid and Electricity 2.0 and what you forecast for the future in this regard?

❯ Electricity is clearly the lifeblood of the world's economy, and the "electrification" of our country was rightfully chosen as the top "Engineering Achievement of the 20th Century" by the National Academy of Engineering. The initial objectives of the electric grid, which started in the early 1900s, were to provide readily available and inexpensive electricity across our country—and this was accomplished in fifty-plus years. But due to a number of interrelated reasons, very little innovation has been included by electric utilities as cheap, commoditized electricity was provided via monopolies to passive buyers. Unlike the telecommunications and information technology industries, electric utilities have invested little to spur innovation and embrace alternative forms and uses for electricity.

In its basic form, the "smart grid" is the integration of 21st century digital communications onto the 20th century electric power system

network. With new challenges related to capacity, reliability, environmental responsibility, climate change and the need to reduce dependence on foreign oil (e.g., electric cars), the electric network needs to have modern technology imbedded throughout the system. This will enable the wave of innovation that will allow Electricity 2.0, Smart Grid Edition to achieve its goals and support the sustainable (clean energy) economic growth of our country—and the rest of the world.

Greg O' Brien, LEED AP BD+C, Senior Vice President, Clean Energy, Grubb & Ellis

❯ Consumers will see many positive changes in their relationship with electricity as a result of Smart Grid solutions. The Smart Grid offers consumers the opportunity to become prosumers—producing and intelligently consuming electricity.

Could you describe the Smart Grid and Electricity 2.0 and what you forecast for the future in this regard? (Continued)

The Smart Grid doesn't create energy efficiency, but these technologies, applications, and services are important tactics to reduce overall consumption of electricity. Combined together, the Smart Grid and energy efficiency measures reduce overall consumption of energy, reduce CO_2 emissions, and improve our energy security.

Christine Hertzog, managing director, Smart Grid Library, author of third edition of the Smart Grid Dictionary

Definitions used with permission from the *Smart Grid Dictionary*.

As discussed, energy is often cited as a major contributor to greenhouse gas emissions and climate change. One method of "offsetting" these emission impacts is via carbon offsets.

Carbon Offsets

Carbon offsets are the practice of trading or balancing carbon released as a greenhouse gas emission by making an equal purchase of carbon "credit" to make up the difference.

Carbon Offset Interview

MARK LACROIX LEED AP

EVP of Business Development (US)

The CarbonNeutral Company

What has been your path to your current position at The CarbonNeutral Company?

❯ Looking back, I now realize how incredibly fortunate I was to work for an organization in which the very first person to really "get it" when it came to sustainability was the founder and chairman! Ray's message to the organization was simple; as he said, "Join me on the journey up Mount Sustainability." I did, and my life was changed forever, thanks to Ray.

I became a self-educated sustainability professional, devouring every book I could find on the topic. As an enthusiastic and outspoken sustainability convert, I quickly positioned myself as a subject matter expert within the company, sitting on the Interface Global Sustainability Council and eventually taking on the role of EVP of Global Sustainability for InterfaceFABRIC. In that role, I had overall responsibility for moving the division forward on each of Interface's Seven Fronts of Sustainability.

After five years in sustainability leadership with Interface, which included work in climate and renewable energy, an opportunity arose to specialize in climate that eventually led to The CarbonNeutral Company.

How would you describe "carbon offsets"?

❯ Carbon offsets are purchasable credits for reductions in greenhouse gas emissions made at another location. Carbon offsets are issued by projects that depend on this carbon finance to reduce, remove, or avoid greenhouse gas emissions.

They come from a variety of technologies, including renewable energy, energy efficiency, methane capture, and forestry.

Carbon offsets are quantified and sold in metric tons of carbon dioxide equivalent (CO_2e). Buying one ton of carbon offsets means there will be one less ton of carbon dioxide in the atmosphere than there would otherwise have been. For example, this could be a project to swap coal-fired power stations with solar panels or hydro power. Carbon offsetting is often the fastest way to achieve the deepest reductions within businesses, and it also often delivers important co-benefits such as supporting biodiversity and sustainable development through increasing employment opportunities, community development programs, and training and education.

Importantly, investments in quality offsets fund real and permanent emissions reductions within the context of the global economy—as far as climate change is concerned, where reductions take place is of no consequence. The reality is that a large percentage of products used in industrialized countries are derived from global supply chains with embodied emissions that are quite global in nature.

What are some "best practices" to look for in terms of good carbon footprint/management?

❯ For carbon offsets to be credible they must meet essential quality criteria that are rigorously applied by external standards bodies. They include proof that the offsets are additional (meaning the reduction in emissions would not have occurred without the carbon finance), that they will be retired from the carbon market so they cannot be double-counted, and that the project they come from addresses issues such as permanence (it delivers the reductions it stated) and leakage (the emission reduction

in one area doesn't cause an increase in emissions somewhere else).

In order to ensure the quality and integrity of carbon offsets, a robust program of standards, verification processes, and registries has been put in place. High-quality offsets are validated by the Voluntary Carbon Standard (VCS), Gold Standard, Climate Action Registry (CAR), Green e Climate, and Clean Development Mechanism (CDM). Each of these standards has specific requirements to ensure the emissions reductions they generate are real, measurable, permanent, and additional. The International Carbon Reduction and Offset Alliance (ICROA) independently verifies each of these to ensure that standards remain rigorous.

What are good tools for a green building professional to use in the carbon industry?

❯ As with most business processes, the old adage "what gets measured gets managed" certainly applies to carbon management. Green building professionals must consider embodied carbon (the carbon emissions that are represented in the materials and processes used to construct the building) and demand carbon (the emissions resulting from ongoing operations).

Recently, a number of tools to measure the embodied carbon intensity of materials have been developed. Most notably, BSI developed the Publicly Available Specification (PAS) 2050, and the World Resources Institute and the World Business Council for Sustainable Development jointly issued the Product Accounting and Reporting Standard. In the absence of quality data, green building professionals should consider the following:

Energy efficiency (demand)

Appropriate durability

Distance from site

Low-carbon alternates

Recycled content

Reused materials

For most traditional buildings, demand emissions eventually outstrip embodied emissions. Green building professionals interested in minimizing the

life-cycle emissions of their projects should start by optimizing:

Location

Footprint

Orientation

Envelope

Systems

CARBON RESOURCES

Carbon Free: www.carbonfund.org/

Carbon Calculator: www.epa.gov/cleanenergy/energy-and-you/how-clean.html

Carbon Footprint Calculators: www.carbonneutral.com/carbon-calculators/

Greenhouse Gas Protocol: www.ghgprotocol.org

GENERAL ENERGY RESOURCES

American Society of Heating, Refrigerating and Air-Conditioning Engineers: www.ashrae.org

Center for Resource Solutions, Green-e Program: www.green-e.org

U.S. Department of Energy
Energy Efficiency & Renewable Energy: Commercial Building Initiative Partnerships, Research, Resources: www1.eere.energy.gov/buildings/commercial_initiative/

U.S. Department of Energy
Energy Efficiency & Renewable Energy: Energy Education and Workforce Development Clean Energy Jobs: www1.eere.energy.gov/education/clean_energy_jobs.html

U.S. Department of Energy
Office of Energy Efficiency and Renewable Energy: Building Technologies Program: www.eere.energy.gov/buildings

U.S. EPA ENERGY STAR: www.energystar.gov/index.cfm?c=business.bus_index

New Buildings Institute: www.newbuildings.org

Materials

Buildings are constructed of many different materials, both inside and out, including paving, roof, doors, windows, exterior walls, interior walls, flooring, ceiling, paint, carpet, hard surface flooring, wall trim, furniture, and millwork. How these materials are harvested, manufactured, transported, packaged, installed, evaluated in terms of performance once they are installed, and disposed of or recycled once the end of their useful life is reached, are all important factors to evaluate. It is indeed a complex matrix of items to consider. The variety of materials specialists can include:

Bar area at the Mohawk Chicago Showroom, Chicago, IL (LEED CI Gold). Firm: Envision Design. PHOTO: ERIC LAIGNEL

Environmental product declarations (EPD) experts

Air quality emissions testers

Greenhouse gas protocol specialists

Life-cycle analysis (LCA) specialists

Refinishing/resource reuse specialists

Third-party certifiers

Toxicity specialists

Waste diversion/recycling experts

These experts support the process of material selection at key milestones.

Thus far, we have looked at each category unique to its specific characteristics related to the built environment:

Surface of surrounding sites

Cycle of water inside and out

Energy in new and existing

The last two categories, materials and indoor air quality, will be explored during the phases of a building's life from design to construction to operations.

MATERIALS IN DESIGN

Green building project team members—architects, interior designers, contractors—should all review the green aspects of building products as only one aspect of many variables to consider. Some of the most important attributes to examine are:

- Life safety
- Function/performance
- Durability
- Cost
- Lead time
- Maintenance

These factors should be weighed in equilibrium with the green criteria because if the product fails due to one of these issues, it could be replaced with something that is not environmentally friendly.

During the design phase of a building green professionals are considering:

- Selecting green building materials
- Avoiding greenwashing marketing tactics
- Evaluating certifications of building materials
- Reducing / reusing / recycling materials
- Focusing on health and reducing toxicity of products
- Understanding and applying life cycle analysis of building materials

Due to increased public perception of the benefits of going green, there have been relative increases in the number of products on the market that claim to be green, despite the fact that many of these are not sustainable at all (or very much) and are instead part of an overall trend called "greenwashing," in which manufacturers make overblown or inaccurate claims about their products' green qualities.[28]

An upside to greenwashing is that it has triggered a market reaction to create standards and other criteria that check the veracity of sustainable claims. These standards come in a few forms: multiple product certifications, labels, standards, and a myriad of what is often confusing and conflicting information when applied to the building industry. The following is a discussion of some of those standards and how they are best used in green building decision-making.

> **Do you have a few material selection tools that you recommend, or criteria to look for when specifying?**

❯ When I made the decision to immerse myself in green design, I had the ultimate convenience of working next door to McDonough Braungart Design Chemistry (MBDC). When I couldn't dig up an answer in my *World of Chemistry* college textbook, I could pop into MBDC and ask some of the science gurus working there whether I should avoid a certain chemical or not. Those days of working next door to MBDC are long gone and there are many green building material certifications and labels from which to choose now.

My first go-to resource for material research and reviews is BuildingGreen's GreenSpec and Green Product resources. BuildingGreen is an independent company that has been around for twenty years—a pioneer in the green building market.

Pharos is a relatively new green material database that is focused on transparency, material composition data, and life cycle of materials. I am watching this one and very intrigued by its depth.

EcoScorecard is a growing database of manufacturers that have compiled and submitted their data to this service for ease of locating green products. It is a handy resource for finding many architectural and interiors-related products.

There are many other third-party certifications that I hold in high regard, but these are specific to a certain material attributes—e.g., GREENGUARD for indoor environmental quality and GoodWeave for child-labor-free handmade rugs. BuildingGreen produced a wonderful white paper on certifications, *Green Building Product Certifications: Getting What You Need.* For those just getting started in green building, this should be at their right hand at all times. For those of us that have been in the green building field for a while, it's a great desktop reference.

Sharlyn Underwood, ASID, LEED AP BD+C, green building consultant, writer, and Virginia Chapter of ASID administrator

❯ For the purposes of dealing with or understanding certifications, scope is still important. The scope of a project provides an understanding of what the standard or certification actually covers. If you don't know what it covers, you might specify something that doesn't make sense, which is very frustrating for manufacturers. Life-cycle considerations are also always important, as you want the certification to protect against trade-offs and address the relevant aspects from cradle to grave. There aren't too many that still neglect a life-cycle focus. However, it is very clear that they all go about it in very different ways, which is still problematic to a certain degree.

A new one I would add more about is the coverage of human health aspects, which seems to be covered in a "list" type manner for the most part. This is not the most desirable means of accounting for human health concerns, but it does appear in many certification systems, as it is easier than taking a more risk-based or even hazard-based assessment.

I still like the idea of looking at transparency. However, I'm not seeing too many certifications that are requiring disclosure of results. This is mostly dependent on the industry and its comfort level with disclosing that information. If the industry isn't willing, then as a certifier, requiring disclosure doesn't help because it will lead to a lack of clients. With the rise of EPDs, transparency is starting to take on a new face.

Paul Firth, manager, UL Environment

How can we rid ourselves of greenwashing?

❯ Greenwashing is here to stay. We aren't going to ever rid ourselves of it. Perhaps we should try spending less time pointing it out and celebrate it instead. Maybe it's a metric of success. Brands and product leaders that are the archetypes of responsible manufacturing will always be recognized as such, provided they have some decent marketing people. But celebrating greenwashing could be quite fun. Paul and I have long discussed setting up a website for doing just that, but we can't get it off the ground due to our day jobs. Greenwashing is like Canal Street knocks-offs—it's unfair and dirty, but it ultimately represents only a small part of the larger world of environmental communications.

There's an absolute gem that I feature in my presentations about greenwashing. I feature an unnamed company that was responding to being de-listed by a major facilities group for a lack of environmental product disclosure and corporate environmental actions. Their response was to develop an environmental brand for their corporate actions that had the unfortunate alignment with an organization that the FBI listed as a domestic terrorist (Earth First). They launched a full-color, happy, talk-filled brochure to the A&D community that went over like a lead balloon.

So let's instead focus and celebrate the good. Herman Miller does a stellar job of communicating their actions, and associated metrics to boot! Interface, Tandus, Mohawk, and Shaw in flooring also do it well. And multiple consumer brands have environmental communications under control. So let's haul the greenwashers out like the bad late-night infomercials that they are and give them an award for their excellence in BS. That way, we'll have some sense of satisfaction in recognition and perhaps cause the bad actors to correct themselves.

Martin Flaherty, senior vice president, Communications, SmartBIM

MATERIAL CERTIFICATIONS

All of the following entities are third-party certifiers of multiple types of building products, from adhesives to recycled content in gypsum wallboard.

Forest Stewardship Council (FSC) (only forest products)

National Science Foundation (NSF)

Scientific Certification Systems (SCS)

UL Environment (ULE)

While there are distinguishing nuances, each of these parties has a good reputation for transparency and standards criteria. This list is only an abbreviated one, and is not representative of all of the certifying bodies for material attributes.

Certifications

You will typically find one of the following scenarios when looking at the breadth of material certifications:

■ A single standard with multiple levels of performance requirements

■ Multiple standards based on the specific type of product (carpet, paint, etc.)—all under one certification

■ Trade association or industry related certification that can be managed by an independent third party

Regardless of methodology, third-party certification is important for impartiality, so the following list of certifications represent several to consider:

■ EcoLogo/Environmental Choice

■ Environmentally Preferred Products (EPP)

■ SmaRT Consensus Sustainable Product Standards

■ Cradle to Cradle (C2C) Certified^{CM} Program

Trusted certifications can validate when green building products meet good green goals such as containing recycled content, eliminating toxins and consider the entire life cycle of the material.

You developed both GREENGUARD (third-party certifying) and Air Quality Sciences (testing)—can you speak to the differences/similarities between them and the importance of these two entities?

❯ Air Quality Sciences, Inc. (AQS) is a scientific testing and consulting firm dedicated to studying indoor air pollution and products that are used to construct, furnish, and operate our buildings. AQS has the largest environmental chamber test laboratory in the world used to measure chemical and particle emissions from products.

The GREENGUARD Environmental Institute is a nonprofit third-party organization that establishes standards for the IAQ acceptability of products and buildings and provides a certification process for manufacturers and building owners to ensure their products and buildings meet these standards. Together, they work toward finding solutions for safer products.

Dr. Marilyn Black, Founder, GREENGUARD Environmental Institute

ENTRY POINT—REDUCE/REUSE/RECYCLE

The entry point of understanding green materials for most is to reduce, reuse, and recycle as we recall that the "recycling triangle" taught to young schoolchildren shows first to reduce, then to reuse, and finally to recycle.[29] While recycling is more easily understood, it is actually the last step in the material use triangle. If the product cannot be reduced or reused the alternative is to use recycled parts.

From a wider perspective, take the first step "to reduce" and consider that buildings are created out of materials or products, and their impact on the environment is significant in numerous ways. The first question to ask when approaching any building project in terms of material use is: Do we need this building? Could we reduce the amount of square footage or particular set of rooms? For smaller scale, do we need this building product or material? Sometimes this is a challenging question to ask because the nature of the building professionals is to, well, build. But, as with good art or a song, often it is the quiet of the white or negative space that makes the painting or the music sing.

If the answer to these questions is indeed an emphatic decision to build, then it is the role of the green building professional to see if it is possible to reuse existing space or materials as part of the design and construction process. Reusing a material in its original function or in a new role reduces many environmental impacts, including the extraction of the raw material, the manufacturing, energy, and water usage, transportation, installation, and operations/end-of-life issues. A door used as a tabletop is one example of a material serving a new purpose. Plus, vintage expresses a new kind of cool.

One minor caution is to confirm that the reuse does not create unnecessary eco-impacts by its very repurposing. In other words, if reusing the door means that it must first be refinished with toxic varnish or remanufactured using harmful practices or high energy usage, then shipped overseas or trucked across the country—then that door might not be the best example of a repurposed green product after all.

If we can't reduce or reuse, we finally consider recycling. With regards to recycled content, there is an international standard, ISO 14021-1999, that regulates environmental labels and declarations.[30] Recycled content can be a commonly misunderstood ingredient in materials, as there are various types. In order to support the design and construction community there is a federal code that mandates "Guides for the Use of Environmental Marketing Claims."[31]

Recycled content:

Materials typically contain recycled content in two formats—pre-consumer or post-consumer. Pre-Consumer Recycled Content—This is material purchased from another manufacturer's waste stream. A good example is a manufacturer A that needs sawdust and purchases it from manufacturer B. However, if does not include waste that could be reutilized as scrap from the manufacturing process. Another similar term for this type of recycled content is Post-Industrial.

Post-Consumer Recycled Content — Say you have an aluminum soda can, and you just drank the last drop. If you recycle the can, it goes back into the aluminum-recycling stream and returns as something else aluminum, such as a car part or trim piece.

The Green Building Professional should also consider the entire life cycle of materials, including their packaging during transport and end of life use(s)—reuse, recycle, composting potential, or, as a last-resort, landfill. One example of alternative packaging with furniture is to wrap pieces in blankets rather than in plastic when shipping or moving. The blankets can then be reused for multiple projects. Note here that environmental performance and durability performance are intrinsically linked because typically "throw-away" or even recyclable products are less green. Ideally, the goal is a long-use "performance" product or one that creates no waste.

TOXICITY

Toxicity is rarely addressed in certification of green building materials, and indeed, levels of potential toxicity to humans in various materials are not regulated in the U.S. in most cases. Yet toxic substances are found in many common building materials such as sealants, fire retardants, and other finishes, and the longer that building professionals such as installers and contractors—as well as building occupants—are exposed to toxic materials, the more harmful the potential side effects.[32] In addition, toxic materials can burn in an unexpected fire and produce additional or new toxins. Of special concern in regards to toxic materials are people with sensitive immune systems, such as children, the elderly, and those who may have an ailment, so health-care facilities are particularly focused on this area of green building materials.

> **What do you forecast for upcoming trends with interior materials?**

❯ There's a growing awareness of the hazards found both in consumer products and building materials. PVC, mercury, halogenated flame retardants, phthalates, chlorinated plastics, and urea formaldehyde pose serious health concerns that designers should become aware of and become learned in searching for safe alternatives. A growing number of tools are being introduced: red lists, precautionary lists, and new LEED credits that deal with chemical avoidance in buildings.

The new Health Product Declaration helps to clarify exactly what is in a product, while Pharos uses that information to build a chemical and product scoring system. It will be incumbent upon designers and specifiers to encourage the development and use of these safety tools.

Penny Bonda, FASID, LEED AP ID+C, partner, Ecoimpact Consulting, author of **Sustainable Commercial Interiors**

Knowledge in Transparency

BILL WALSH

Executive Director

Healthy Building Network

How would you describe Pharos as a green building tool?

❯ The Pharos Project, at its core, is a campaign for transparency in the building materials market. It is a tool for users to locate the best materials to meet their current needs and enduring values, a tool to help cut through the prolific greenwashing, a space where users can discuss what makes a product truly green, and, most importantly, a platform from which to show manufacturers what constitutes a market in support of the best environmental, health, and social equity practices.

The main parts of the Pharos online tool are the Building Product Library (BPL) and the Chemical and Material Library (CML), both of which are available by subscription. Each product in the BPL is scored on several environmental and health impact categories. Detailed product profiles include chemical and material ingredients, which are linked to their respective entries in the CML. The CML sources health hazard information from over 25 authoritative national and international bodies and includes over 10,000 chemicals and materials.

How does the science behind Pharos analysis of products work?

❯ A description of our framework is available here: www.pharosproject.net/framework/index/, and detailed scoring protocols are available in the frame-

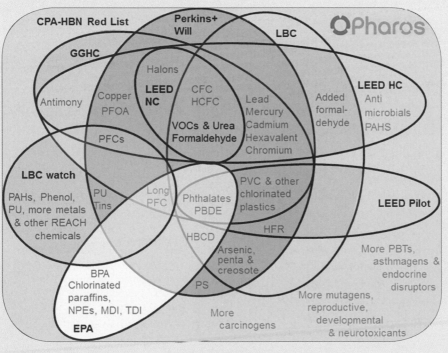

Chemicals of concern identified by a range of green building programs. IMAGE: 2011 HEALTHY BUILDING NETWORK

work section of the website. Pharos currently scores products in five impact areas: Volatile Organic Compounds (VOCs), User Toxics, Manufacturing and Community Toxics, Renewable Materials Use, and Renewable Energy.

How does Pharos compare with Life Cycle Assessment?

❯ Pharos does not compete with existing third-party product certifications but rather helps you understand how to make best use of them in product selection. Different certifications address different aspects of the health and environmental impact of products. Pharos helps bring it all together to give a comprehensive view. The Pharos framework scores different certifications by the rigor of their standards and the independence of the certifying processes, and it provides comparisons between the systems. Pharos step-by-step scoring descriptions lay out how different certifications impact a product's scores.

LCA tools hold significant promise for providing insight into some impacts of products, such as energy use and climate change, but practitioners have struggled to find robust ways to address human health in LCA tools. Pharos addresses the human health impact of both the material contents of the product and the chemicals used upstream in manufacture, using a robust framework based upon hazard assessment protocols also used by the GreenScreen™ for Safer Chemicals and the EPA's Design for the Environment program. The assessment is more transparent than any other certification system available today with all data and scoring protocols fully disclosed. The Chemical and Material Library in Pharos provides manufacturers and end users alike with tools to assess and compare the hazards of chemical choices outside of the Pharos Product Library as well. Pharos also assesses the certifications for the sourcing of renewable materials, such as sustainably harvested wood, that LCA does not address.

Leading Alternatives

PAULA VAUGHAN, LEED AP BD+C

Co-Director, Sustainable Design Initiative

Perkins+Will (P+W)

Please describe the P+W Precautionary List. Why did P+W decide to do this?

❯ The Precautionary List was developed based on our belief that products that are harmful to humans, animals, and the environment should not be used in our projects, and to that end, we seek to inform our clients, consultants, and industry of

available alternatives so as to permit them to make informed decisions. Rather than use products that contain these substances, we will seek out alternatives, in keeping with the precautionary principle, in an effort to be responsive to reported health effects and thereby to protect our health and the health of future generations. The database was primarily developed out of our New York office and its focus on healthy environments for health-care projects. Over the years, we have seen the importance of not holding it as an industry advantage, but making it freely available to anyone interested in the health impacts of building materials.

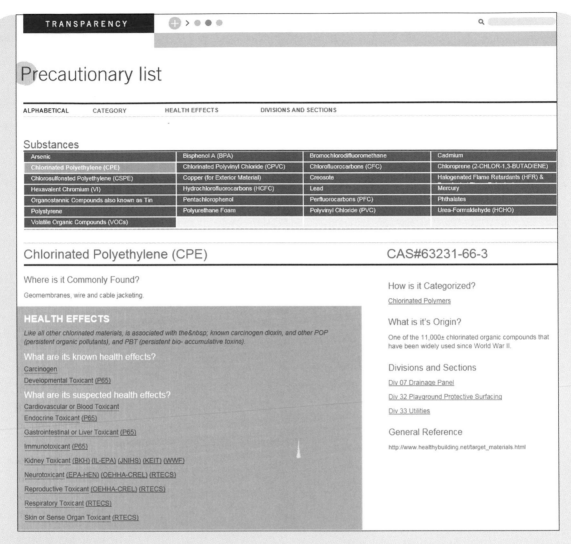

Perkins+Will Precautionary List website. IMAGE: COURTESY OF PERKINS+WILL, INC.

Since creating the Precautionary List, what have been your most interesting discoveries?

❯ That many manufacturers don't know what is in their own products. It's not that they're necessarily trying to be deceptive, but in many cases, they just never asked. Having our industry ask for more transparency in product disclosures so that we can make informed decisions will certainly result in healthier buildings.

Any particular lessons learned in the Precautionary List process that you'd like to share?

❯ The choices we make when we select and specify building materials for our projects can have a di-

TRANSPARENCY

"When an activity raises threats of harm to human health or the environment, precautionary measures should be taken even if some cause and effect relationships are not fully established scientifically."

The Wingspread Conference on **the Precautionary Principle** was convened by the Science and Environmental Health Network, 1998.

What can I find?

THE PRECAUTIONARY LIST

Substances compiled here have been classified by regulatory entities as being harmful to the health of humans and/or the environment. An evolving list that is updated as new data comes to light, this tool encourages the user to employ the precautionary principle while uncovering building products that may contain these substances and identifying potential alternative products.

ASTHMA TRIGGER + ASTHMAGENS IN THE BUILT ENVIRONMENT

Substances on this list have been identified as Asthmagens found in our built environment. This list brings awareness on the causes of the disease and helps users make informed decisions on design and construction with respect to building products. This list was compiled from third-party, government and academic sources.

FLAME RETARDANTS

This list catalogues flame retardants found in the built environment from organic to inorganic, brominated to halogenated as well as those that are naturally occurring. A comprehensive list providing in-depth knowledge of flame retardants, this tool helps users understand not only where flame retardants are found in the built environment, but also their subsequent health effects.

WHITE PAPERS

A growing number of resources on material health can be found at this link, ranging from Perkins+Will white papers on Fly Ash and Asthma, to video interviews of Robin Guenther and Peter Busby.

Perkins+Will Precautionary List website. IMAGE: COURTESY OF PERKINS+WILL, INC.

rect effect on the people who build, occupy, and maintain those projects. In places like schools and hospitals, where occupants may be younger or more vulnerable, the impact is heightened. As building design professionals, we have a responsibility for knowing what substances are in the products we use and what the health implications of those substances are.

TOXICITY RESOURCES

ECC Corporation (ECCC) Hazardous-Substance-Free Mark: www.ecccorp.org/

Pharos Project: http://pharosproject.net/

Perkins+Will Precautionary List: http://transparency.perkinswill.com/

NEXT-GENERATION MATERIALS

The many good green material guidelines, certifications and third-party verification, as well as attributes such as reduce, reuse, recycle, toxicity alternatives have been discussed to this point in the book. The future generation of material selection lies is increasing transparency and life-cycle understanding. At this intersection, signs point towards holistic tools such as Environmental Product Declarations (EPDs) and Life Cycle Assessments (LCA) including audit and verification by a third party.

Environmental Product Declarations (EPDs)

The Green Standard is a nonprofit that provides ISO-compliant Environmental Product Declaration (EPD) programs to manufacturers.

> **To meet ISO requirements, an EPD must meet three criteria:**
> 1. Use product category rules for the relevant product type
> 2. Be based on a product Life Cycle Assessment (LCA)
> 3. Provide an EPD Report certified and signed by an outside expert

In short, an EPD is a single source for finding scientifically robust and transparent product performance information about a product's environmental performance, verified by a qualified third party.[33]

LCA

Life cycle thinking is the most comprehensive way to evaluate buildings and products because it looks at all aspects from "cradle to cradle."[34] The name "life cycle" gives a clue to understanding it as the "cycle of life." Think of how a building is constructed in terms of material production and use:

■ Extraction of raw materials

■ Assembly or manufacture of materials

■ Packaging and transportation of materials to the building site

■ Installation of materials on site

■ Operations of building and use of materials

■ Maintenance of materials

■ Repair or replacement of materials

■ End of life

This continuous cycle demonstrates the full span of the lives of both products and buildings, from creation to demolition, and life-cycle thinking indicates impacts of each step in the process—material extraction, energy/water usage, as well as human health impacts.

History of LCA/Concept Development

In the late 1960s, an internationally recognized Life Cycle Assessment or (LCA) was developed and continues to be refined.[35]

In 2002, architect William McDonough of McDonough Braungart Design Chemistry (MBDC) developed a key concept outlined in the book *Cradle to Cradle: Remaking the Way We Make Things,* which he co-wrote with German ecological chemist Dr. Michael Braungart.[36] The concept of the book is about making the process of building or creating building materials cyclical, whereby waste (end of life) = (or becomes) food (resources for the next life), versus the traditional linear model in which process ends only in waste or in a landfill. With an enlightened life-cycle process, there is no waste—material either continues to recycle through the industrial world, or it composts back to the biological world. The life-cycle process can be applied to any simple building product or assembly products, as well as an entire building.

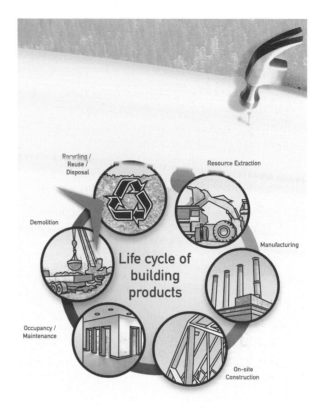

Diagram of the Life Cycle Assessment process for building products. IMAGE REPRINTED COURTESY OF THE ATHENA SUSTAINABLE MATERIALS INSTITUTE.

Challenges

Some of the challenges with LCA are assumptions in the data, inconsistent calculation methods, and finding a way to easily convey the findings to the mass consumer market. Also, given the lack of data, many health and environmental impacts are difficult to quantify. To add a further complexity to the mix, while a product may be benign and a good green option in one stage of its "life," at a later stage, it could be a bad option. This is the case with lead paint or asbestos, both of which can be extremely hazardous if they degrade or are in any way disturbed—but if left undisturbed, these materials have much smaller environmental and health impacts.

Yet another challenge can be timing. Some products are green in their design and/or production, but not in their operation, or vice versa. One key example was the installation of waterless urinals that required cumbersome maintenance, or the failure to train facility staff adequately to maintain these fixtures. This product may be a great green water-saving fixture, but it has a pungent odor if not maintained properly, and these urinals were therefore ripped out and replaced with less sustainable, water-using fixtures.

How would you define Life Cycle Assessment, and what do you forecast for this evaluation tool?

❯ Life-cycle issues broadly refer to phases of the process that lie upstream and downstream of the focus of the design; again, these phases are outside the boundary of the immediate design and hence can be missed unless explicitly accounted for. For example, sustainable design needs to consider the impact that the process will have not only during its life but also during its end-of-life. It is also often the case that the life-cycle impacts of acquisition and conversion of materials are much larger than the life cycle of the process that converts them into final products.

Thus, a best practice for sustainable process design is to consider all the phases of the life cycle. This requires tracing the inputs and outputs to the process upstream and downstream. It also requires that any products of the process be considered during their use phase and end-of-life phase as well as the impacts of the production of the inputs to the process.

Professor Matthew J. Realff, PhD, School of Chemical and Biomolecular Engineering, Georgia Institute of Technology

❯ Life Cycle Assessment is a tool for quantifying potential environmental impacts throughout the entire life cycle of a product or service, including raw material acquisition and processing, manufacturing, use and service, end-of-life management, and transportation. When I first learned about the concepts of LCA in an industrial ecology course at the University of Michigan, my entire perspective on choosing environmentally friendly products changed. The largest impacts are often invisible, e.g., the energy required to heat the water to clean your ceramic coffee mug. LCA is an important tool for product design by illustrating impacts of material choices, and a

helpful tool for consumer decision making to identify the major environmental impacts with alternative choices.

Melissa Vernon, LEED AP BD+C, director of sustainable strategy, InterfaceFLOR

❯ The initiative behind LCA is fantastic. For example, the idea that I can compare two products and make a recommendation that one product is more environmentally beneficial than the other is ideal, but the reality is that it's much more complex than this. Currently, there is no industry-wide accepted standard of which "environmental impacts" are truly important; these differences, along with lack of consistency, overall reliability of data inputs, etc., means that the end results can vary from one analysis to the next.

I think LCA could be an invaluable tool for use of evaluating products but we're not quite there yet, and I feel it needs to mature a bit more as a discipline before the market will begin to utilize it as a resource for overall decision making

Carlie Bullock-Jones , ASID, LEED AP BD+C & ID+C, owner, Ecoworks Studio

❯ LCA is a holistic view into your environmental impacts; it is a snapshot showing the details of the impact, where it occurs and what is the root cause. Can you imagine going in to see the doctor with a broken leg, and instead of the doctor taking an x-ray to see what is broken and where, and what needs to be done, he starts to treat it immediately? If he just started treatment without that initial examination, he might do more harm than good. In the same way, LCA provides information in order to treat your product's impacts in a manner that is appropriate and without hidden trade-offs.

Paul Firth, Manager, UL Environment

If we scale up this concept from a product (urinal) to a larger scale (a building) in which the design and construction process did good green practices , yet the operations phase of the building contributed to environmental harm, it is easy to see that the good and bad impacts can happen anywhere in the "life cycle" of the product or building. Therefore, it is important that a life-cycle perspective should be used for product or building evaluation, taking into account uncommon or unforeseen situations at all life stages.

Current Trends/Future of LCA

A recent big development in LCA was the addition of an LCA credit included within the current LEED Pilot Credit Library and anticipated to be in the next version of LEED.[37] This is an entry point for the life-cycle concept into the design industry so that practitioners such as architects, engineers, and interior designers may begin to include products based on their overall impact.

One example is cork or bamboo flooring. Cork is a rapidly renewable natural product that has a quick regrowth cycle, so that within less than ten years, it can regenerate to its original state. Does that sound like a great green product? It is. However, from a life-cycle perspective, raw materials in products such as cork often come from Spain, so the fossil fuels used to transport the materials large distances must be considered as a major green factor when weighing different product options.

While the selection of green materials during design is vital, there are other phases in a building's life that have impact.

Concrete Communications

STEVEN R. BAER, LEED AP BD+C

Senior Consultant

PE International Inc. & Five Winds Strategic Consulting

What was your education and experience path to becoming a sustainability specialist?

❯ I received my BS and MS in chemical engineering, then continued on professionally in the following areas: manufacturing management, product development, then marketing at a major building materials manufacturer. Overall, it's important to understand how business success can be linked to

sustainable behavior and to take a triple-bottom-line approach to decision making.

How do you evaluate a product in terms of its "green factor"?

❯ Utilizing a Life Cycle Assessment (LCA) that can be quantified in an Environmental Product Declaration (EPD) is a good way to evaluate a product's environmental impact.

If someone wanted to focus his or her career on green materials, what type of experience would you recommend?

Basic understanding of how businesses make money

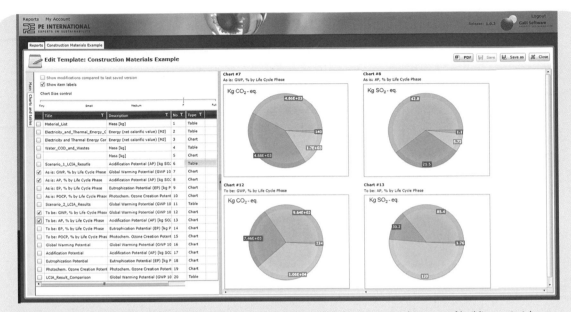

Example of PE International's GaBi i-report generated to assess the expected environmental impacts of building materials.
Image: PE INTERNATIONAL

Understanding of macroeconomics

Must understand consumer drivers, including regulatory

Understanding of LCA, including its benefits

Systems thinking—must understand how each product interacts with the system around it, and that no product exists alone (i.e., understanding automobiles requires a knowledge of tires or fuel combustion)

If you could give a few tips to someone pursuing the green materials specialist profession, what would they be?

Understand product systems.

Understand life-cycle implications of decision making.

Understand the triple-bottom-line concept.

Realize that decisions made in the abstract will not fly.

LIFE CYCLE ANALYSIS TOOL RESOURCES

The Athena Institute's EcoCalculator: www.athenasmi.org/tools/ecoCalculator/index.html

Carnegie Mellon University Green Design Institute Economic Input-Output Life Cycle Assessment (EIO-LCA): www.eiolca.net/

PE International GaBi Software:
    www.gabi-software.com/index.php?id=7427

Communication Tools

PAUL FIRTH

Manager

UL Environment

How do you describe LCA to someone who may be unfamiliar with the concept?

❯ For most outside of the sustainability space, LCA is quite foreign. However, when explaining it, I try to start with a product that I have in reach or a product that the person will easily understand. I then remind them that the product doesn't come from the store; rather it is manufactured somewhere. That manufacturing, particularly with plastics, starts with extracting resources, like oil, out of the ground. Then, those resources go through several manufacturing steps to produce a product. That product is then used by someone and ultimately disposed of. This disposal can be through some form of recycling or usually going to a landfill. Also, there is transportation involved throughout all of these steps. Now, throughout all of this product's life, from extraction through final disposal, impacts are occurring. The Life Cycle Assessment is a framework that allows you to account for all of those impacts that occur throughout the product's life cycle, from cradle to grave.

What are some of the pros/cons on both sides— product manufacturers and specifiers (designers/ architects) for EPD and LCA?

LCAs and Manufacturers:

❯ For manufacturers, the pros to performing LCAs seem to be widely discussed, with most of the benefit being internal knowledge gained. Many who hear that a manufacturer does LCA immediately believe that the manufacturer is more advanced and further along in sustainability than others. The cons are that

between the tool, group, or time involved, it ends up being a large commitment from a resource perspective, both of people and money (although the commitment isn't nearly as large as it was years ago). It also can be difficult to communicate and/or implement change if the practitioner is less experienced.

LCAs and Specifiers:

Most specifiers want to see that a manufacturer is performing LCAs for their products. However, trying to gain access to LCA information is a Catch-22. I used to receive requests weekly from specifiers to "send our LCA to them" as a part of their requests for proposals. Inevitably, I would end up on the phone asking what was really desired because most specifiers didn't understand that an LCA was a long report that they would not really understand all that well. These days, specifiers are much more knowledgeable, but the problem still persists. It's a great tool, but without consistency, structure, and peer review, the results are difficult to trust. I think the other issue that exists with LCA (and even EPDs) used in isolation is that they don't address performance. It's not a problem, but rather more of a misunderstanding. This is why a Type I and a Type III used in conjunction with one another is the best method.

EPDs:

EPDs address many of the "cons" associated with LCA and a lack of consistency and structure behind how the results are communicated. For simplicity, I'll bullet list a few talking points here that I often use:

It can serve as a management tool for manufacturers, purchasers, the procurement and purchasing functions of an organization, for product designers, and for marketing strategy—by monitoring the product data and applying the outcomes to improve environmental performance.

It is an evaluation/assessment tool for professionals, using the EPD for decision making and for benchmarking environmental information.

It is being discussed as a procurement tool for government, commercial, and institutional purchasers due to the consistency and credibility of the LCA results.

It is seen as an action tool for consumers and consumer groups by disseminating environmental information and product criteria.

Ultimately, it is a communication tool among manufacturers, suppliers, distributors, purchasers, contractors, specifiers, and any other users by functioning as a source of comprehensive environment information.

As with LCA, the one big "con" is that EPDs do not address performance by themselves. They are not meant to compete against EcoLabels, which do represent environmental preferability. As I mentioned, the greatest benefit is when you combine the environmental preferability with the life-cycle transparency (a Type I and a Type III), you get the best of both worlds: "I'm good and here's why I'm good."

Discuss EPP and EPD / LCA relative to your work as a product manufacturer.

❯ Understanding LCA is a critical need for people entering the sustainability field. We see this as a comprehensive, fundamental tool to help understand your product and process performance from multiple aspects and can provide keen insight into areas for continuous improvement.

When it comes to carpet, INVISTA supports a big-picture approach to understanding a product's true effect on our lives and the environment because we believe that products not designed for long-term performance ultimately impact our quality of life. Whether it's the hassles and cost associated with replacing products or the effect

on our planet, long term performance should not be compromised. INVISTA has achieved EPP (Environmentally Preferred Products) certification via SCS (Scientific Certification Systems) multiple times since 2002. This certification is based on Executive Order 13101 (replaced by Executive Order 13423), which recognizes products that have a lesser or reduced effect on health and the environment when compared with competing products that serve the same purpose. This certification is recognized by NSF-140 (Sustainable Carpet Assessment Standard) as an important attribute in carpet content evaluation.

Diane O'Sullivan, global director of marketing, INVISTA

Small Inspirations

DEBORAH DUNNING

Founder & CEO, Sphere-E LLC

Founder & President, The Green Standard

You have two key roles—founder and CEO of Sphere-E LLC, as well as founder and president of the Green Standard. How do these roles work together in your career?

❯ In these two roles, I work on the "ying" (helping manufacturers develop quality performance data) and on the "yang" (providing purchasers with efficient tools to select carefully the most environmentally benign products). It's a great adventure working with so many leaders committed to ensuring a healthy environment for us all.

The BRIGHT GREEN, BRIGHT FUTURE campaign launched the first EPD system in the United States. Why did you feel this was important? What are advantages to EPD?

❯ The Green Standard launched the first EPD program in the U.S. for building products in 2008, believing that an eco-label based on a standard developed by a body of global environmental experts and used around the world would be of value to manufacturers and purchasers of their products. That instinct is proving to be correct in that recently federal agencies are incorporating LCA into their procurement processes, and the U.S. Green Building Council has release a LEED Pilot credit for selecting products with LCAs and a double credit for those with EPDs.

How did the Green Standard decide to utilize the GaBi 4 tool (licensed from PE Americas) as the LCA tool of choice?

❯ The Green Standard has recommended use of GaBi software to develop product and service LCAs as it has the most comprehensive underlying database and is considered to be the most efficient LCA software in the world. These are important characteristics as the quality of the data is critical. "Garbage in, then garbage out" states the necessity to use high-quality tools to develop LCAs and use them to shape key decisions. PE International, the consulting firm that developed and maintains "GaBi" is considered the best firm in the world working on LCAs and EPDs.

LIFE-CYCLE RESOURCES

Athena Sustainable Materials Institute: http://athenasmi.org/index.html

The Green Standard: Environmental Product Declarations, Free Trial of GaBi 4: http://thegreenstandard.org/LCA_software.html

MATERIALS IN CONSTRUCTION

Contractors are critical in the procurement of the green materials, as they are the link between the design and the manufacturer and bring the entire picture into reality. So the contractor is weighing the pros/cons of several factors relative to green materials—meeting the design requirements of aesthetics/performance, cost, lead time, with a cross section of many green criteria such as recycled content, regional transportation considerations, and certifications. From new materials to waste materials. . . .

During construction, one key material impact is construction waste on-site and how to manage and divert it from the landfill to local recyclers, where applicable. This is especially important on renovation projects or when buildings are being demolished. The key best practices for a good construction waste management are:

Construction waste management (CWM) plan

Selected CWM hauler to pick up co-mingled waste or separate on-site

Educated construction team, from the superintendent to each subcontractor

Consistent tracking methodology

Another good material practice for contractors is to have a good network of resources such as sources for purchasing reused or refurbished materials and furniture.

MATERIALS IN OPERATIONS

After a building is completed, facilities managers purchase all the materials that go into the operations and management of a building. These products could be ongoing consumables such as paper towels and office paper, or they could include long-term purchases, called durable goods, such as furniture and equipment. Whatever the type of product, all purchases should be made with green best-practice processes in mind, such as third-party verification, as well as best management practices or ongoing programs such as recycling of lighting, equipment, and other waste streams.

GENERAL MATERIALS RESOURCES

Construction Materials Recycling Association: www.cdrecycling.org

Building Green, Inc.: Greenspec: www.buildinggreen.com

BuildingGreen, Inc., *Green Building Product Certifications: Getting What You Need* (published 2011)

Forest Stewardship Council, United States: www.fscus.org/green_building

Green Building Alliance's Green Product Labeling Grid

Interiors & Sources EcoLibrary Matrix

What is CARE?

❯ CARE is a nationwide organization of people committed to keeping used carpet out of the landfill. CARE members work together to reuse and recycle used carpet. By recycling carpet, we save valuable landfill space, and natural resources. Recycling carpet creates over 1,000 green jobs in local communities. CARE members are innovative entrepreneurs, successful businesspeople, and energetic and dynamic people!

What happens to the carpet in the recovery process? What kind of impact is CARE making by diverting carpet?

❯ Once a carpet reaches the end of its useful life, it is removed from homes and buildings. Carpet that is reclaimed is taken to a collector, where it is sorted by fiber type (i.e., Nylon 6, Nylon 6-6, PET, polypropylene, wool, etc.). Then the processing work begins. Through processes such as shredding and shearing, the carpet fiber (fuzzy side up) is separated from the backing. The carpet fiber is further cleaned and separated to remove as much of the ash and other nonfiber materials as pos-

sible. The next step is to pelletize the material. It is now ready to be recycled back into carpet, or used as an engineered resin for all types of consumer products. Did you know that the Ford Motor Company put more than four million pounds of recycled carpet into vehicles in 2009, by switching an engine part away from virgin material? The auto maker has been using cylinder head covers made with nylon derived from scrap carpet in four vehicles: the Escape, Fusion, Mustang, and F-150.

Our CARE members have diverted over two billion pounds of carpet from the landfill from 2002 to 2010. By diverting all of this carpet, CARE members have contributed to reducing our environmental impact, saving approximately ten million cubic yards of landfill space, enough BTUs to heat more than 111,000 homes for a year, and saving over six billion gallons of water. That is the kind of environmental savings that we can all be proud of.

Georgina Sikorski, executive director, Carpet America Recovery Effort (CARE)

Indoor Air Quality

The U.S. EPA reports that pollutant levels of indoor environments may run two to five times—and occasionally more than 100 times—higher than outdoor levels.[38] In particular, indoor air quality (IAQ) is significantly impacted by energy-producing emissions that create smog and other poor air-quality byproducts. Building materials also release emissions during manufacture, transportation, and even once fully installed. All of these emissions lead to poor air quality and thereby impact the health of those with asthma and breathing-related illness.

Classroom at Georgia Power Child Care Center Bright Generations (LEED NC Gold). Firm: Heery International. PHOTO: DAN GRILLET

Indoor air quality directly influences occupants' comfort and well-being. One of the key best practices in good air quality is to minimize pollutants entering the space via source control, improved ventilation or filtration. However, if materials in the building are emitting gases or volatile organic compounds (VOCs), there will likely be poor air quality inside the building.[39] Poor construction, including water infiltration via a leaky roof or building exterior, could also cause mold which can lead to occupant illness.[40] Poor air quality can also cause other more serious issues such as sick building syndrome (SBS). SBS is an illness from something in a building, which could be mold in the air ducts or high-emitting materials. The symptoms range from headaches to respiratory issues.[41] While premium air quality is optimum for reasons of health and lifestyle, poor air quality can also be a liability risk, so it makes sense at a business level to improve indoor air. On the core building team, mechanical engineers and contractors are involved in designing and constructing with good air quality in mind. There are also a number of specialists who focus on specific air quality issues. These experts include:

Air quality building site testers

Air quality product testers

Green housekeeping/cleaning product experts and testers

Toxicity experts

Inspirational Motives

DR. MARILYN BLACK

Founder

GREENGUARD Environmental Institute

What was your path to becoming a distinguished air quality specialist? Would you recommend the same path or resources to others? If not, what alternative(s) would you recommend?

❯ All of my degrees are in chemistry with a specialization in understanding the impact of chemicals on human health. My first job was the study of dioxin, and that opened my eyes to understanding how a chemical in such low levels could result in profound damage to human health. From then on, I dedicated myself to studying industrial chemicals, understanding their human health impact, and helping manufacturers reduce them or find alternatives—thus creating safer products for the marketplace. I chose chemistry instead of premed, and I would recommend this approach. It gave me greater depth and ability to understand chemicals and their mechanisms, better enabling me to find solutions to damaging chemical exposure.

How would you explain what you do? Can you describe a "typical" workday?

❯ As founder of both Air Quality Sciences and the GREENGUARD Environmental Institute, I have had many roles, from performing chemical analysis of products to studying the air quality in buildings. Like most entrepreneurs, I do what is needed. My typical day is filled with meetings helping our employees do their job

that include preparing proposals for manufacturers that want to become GREENGUARD certified or evaluate their products for toxicity, reviewing reports from our studies, helping prepare marketing materials that describe our services and their value proposition, or helping prepare training courses that explain the importance of good indoor air quality in buildings. Over 50 percent of my time is spent talking or visiting with manufacturers to help them understand how to create safer products, or speaking to organizations and at professional conferences about the importance of good indoor air quality and how to achieve it.

How does your work interface with others in the design and construction profession (e.g., architects, interior designers, engineers, green building consultants, etc.), and which of these team members most often engages your team?

❯ Every day we interact with architects, interior designers, building engineers, and green consultants—all of whom are engaged in achieving high-performance buildings through green or sustainable design. At the GREENGUARD Environmental Institute, we work primarily with architects, designers, and green consultants who are responsible for designing healthy buildings and specifying construction materials and furnishings to help achieve these goals. At AQS, we primarily work with building engineers and green consultants who want to know how to specify or find nontoxic materials and how to operate buildings for good indoor air quality.

What scares and inspires you most about air quality in buildings for the future?

❯ We help people breathe. Seeing mixtures of hundreds of different chemicals in the air that we and our families breathe and knowing that the makeup of this mixture changes frequently scares me. People spend more than 90 percent of their time indoors, and they expect the air quality to be safe and free of harm. We use industrial chemicals without fully understanding their indoor air quality impact. This, along with rapidly changing chemistries used to manufacture products and materials and the use of extensive global supply chains, brings unknown risks. We recognize the issue, and this brings inspirational motive for the work to be done for knowledge, change, and risk-management principles.

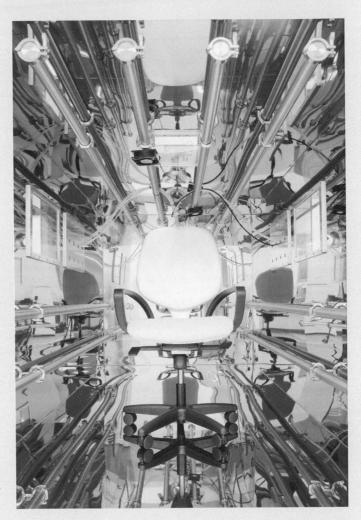

The intermediate chambers at AQS are used to evaluate both commercial and consumer products, such as furniture. PHOTO: RON BLUNT PHOTOGRAPHY FOR AIR QUALITY SCIENCE

AIR QUALITY BY BUILDING PHASES

One of the easiest and first main goals when creating good air quality is to prevent contaminants from entering the space in the first place. Often times, it can be something as simple as removing dirt on the bottom of people's shoes as they go into a building; in this case, the simple practice of installing foot grilles or walk-off mats to reduce pollutants can help produce good IAQ.

Then, if pollutants do get into the space, what is the best way to get rid of them? Three main processes of good air quality practices involve monitoring, filtering, and increasing ventilation/exhausting. Examples of this could include:

■ Carbon dioxide monitors

■ Opening windows for natural ventilation with monitoring controls

■ Mechanical ventilation controls that allow for increasing ventilation

■ Separation of pollutants in a closed-off space with separate exhausting

■ Finer filters on the HVAC equipment to catch the smaller particulates

Good air quality and daylighting practices occur in all three phases of design, construction, and operations of a building. Each phase is examined in detail in the following sections, in regards to additional best practices in indoor air quality.

AIR QUALITY IN DESIGN

The main focus during the design phase for green building professionals is to look at specified building materials in terms of reducing pollutants and potential toxins. Many of the certifications covered previously in the Materials section offer a variety of emissions testing and certifying options. In addition, good third-party certifications that focus solely on air quality are:

■ GREENGUARD Environmental Institute

■ Scientific Certification Systems Indoor Advantage

One standard in particular stands out in the industry, and that is California Section 01350, which serves as a solid reference for several certifications and rating systems. Overall, when considering air quality and emissions from products, a common term used is VOC, or volatile organic compounds that are emitted.[42] The "new car smell" or the pungent odor of a freshly painted room are signs that VOC emissions are likely at unhealthy levels. Luckily, the market has responded to the demand for low-VOC products, and many are readily available, such as low-VOC paint, carpeting, and furniture.

AIR QUALITY IN CONSTRUCTION

One of the key best practices for premium air quality during construction involves following the Sheet Metal and Air Conditioning Contractors' National Association (SMACNA) guidelines with an Indoor Air Quality Management Plan. The construction industry has responded to this based on criteria in LEED and other systems, so that many contractors practice this as "standard practice." The guidelines offer these five process steps:

HVAC protection during construction

Source control during construction

Pathway interruption during construction

Housekeeping during construction

Scheduling/phasing of materials during construction[43]

At the end of construction, it is important to do the final cleaning with green housekeeping products. One environmental operations strategy that focuses on air quality is to incorporate green housekeeping or green cleaning using low-emitting cleaning products and equipment. A good indoor air quality third-party certification for green cleaning products is Green Seal.

Green Seal Interview

CHARLOTTE PEYRAUD, LEED Green Associate

Marketing & Outreach Lead

Green Seal

How would you describe Green Seal?

❯ Green Seal is an independent, nonprofit organization founded in 1989 to identify, reward, and promote environmentally responsible products and services in the marketplace.

Green Seal's mission: Green Seal is a nonprofit environmental organization that uses science-based programs to empower consumers, purchasers, and companies to create a more sustainable world.

Why are standards such as ISO important in the field of green cleaning?

❯ Green Seal standards and certification meet ISO 14020 (Principles of Environmental Labeling) and 14024 (Principles and Procedures for Type I Ecolabels) requirements. This is important because it ensures important checks and balances are in place such as:

Avoidance of financial conflict of interest (certification must be earned, cannot be bought)

Certification based on standards with multiple criteria [Green Seal standards have criteria that are based on multiple environmental attributes (e.g., not just energy efficiency or biodegradability), which are based on a life-cycle evaluation of the category, including human health impacts, ecotoxicity, manufacturing sustainability, and packaging sustainability.]

Performance requirements (standards contain stringent criteria to ensure the effective functional performance of products)

On-site audit (verify the product/service actually complies with the standard)

Why are continuous monitoring, audits, and the overall process with Green Seal important?

❯ According to the U.S. EPA, any third-party certification should include an on-site audit of the manufacturing site or service facility to ensure that the product or service has actually met the requirements for certification.

Do you find that it is common to use an IAQ Management Plan on site? What kind of coordination of team members and resources is most helpful for successful execution of the IAQ Management Plan?

❭ As an interiors contractor we typically utilize Indoor Air Quality Management Plans as stipulated by the building management team and building engineers.

The basic steps within IAQ Management Plans should address the following:

   a. Identify all potential contaminants and pollutants

   b. Identify methods of protection and prevention
     - Existing conditions
     - Construction processes
     - Construction debris

   c. Material storage and handling

   d. Housekeeping

   e. Flush-out

   f. Air testing

Proper scheduling and project staging can assist in the completion of many IAQ tasks, and everyone involved with a project has the responsibility of sharing their knowledge and expertise to effectively protect the job-site environment both during and after construction.

Charles P. Sharitz, LEED Green Associate, vice president, Humphries & Company

If there are concerns about air quality at the end of construction and prior to occupancy, one of the strategies that can be employed is a "flush-out," whereby a large volume of outside air in a specific temperature and humidity range is flooded into the space for a predetermined duration of time. Optimally, the flush-out is done once all of the materials are installed, including the furniture. The process "airs out" the space and ideally flushes out all emissions. The alternative option would be to engage an air quality test specialist to test the air quality in the space with a monitor. Of note, sometimes even when the space has been designed with low-emitting materials, the facility can still fail the test due to unsuspected source emissions, such as common retail products like soap or furniture.

AIR QUALITY IN OPERATIONS

Once the building is occupied, another key to good indoor air quality is the practice of green environmental practices for daily maintenance or housekeeping. There are several good green maintenance practices, including:

   Using environmentally responsible snow and ice removal agents

   Integrated pest management (IPM)

When products are purchased or there are facility renovations or upgrades during the operations phase of a building (after all initial construction is complete), procedures should follow the guidance outlined in the Materials section in terms of third-party, independent, life-cycle-based purchasing decisions.

AIR QUALITY IN POST-OCCUPANCY

A key process that can be underutilized in the industry is post-occupancy surveys. These can be incredibly revealing, particularly in regards to both air quality and access to daylight, in which cases the comfort of occupants is very important for a number of reasons across all building types. Here are a few examples of ways in which a good interior environmental can help those who live and work there:

Corporate office — Workers are more productive and experience fewer sick days.

Schools — Students score better on tests and have less absenteeism.

Retail — Stores experience higher sales of merchandise.

Hospitality — Good Indoor Environmental Quality (IEQ) can mitigate risks due to mold and provide sound control benefits.

Health care — Good IEQ can reduce sick days and increase room turnover rate.

Studies confirm all of these examples, and the evidence can be further underscored by doing post-occupancy surveys.[44] The other advantage to these surveys is that it gives the facility manager feedback and the ability to adjust necessary building elements. For example, if certain spaces are too hot or too cold, better controls could be installed for occupants to use.

In addition, each of these examples links back to the financial triple bottom line. In 2009, the General Services Administration (GSA) produced a report titled *Energy Savings and Performance Gains in GSA Buildings: Seven Cost Effective Strategies.* One pertinent finding from this study was an example in which the GSA replaced HVAC filters on schedule and with a high performance filter. The cost savings is two-fold with better performing HVAC (financial) and higher satisfaction in the air quality of the occupants (social). This one strategy resulted in a 10.8 million kilowatt hour (kWh) savings of energy per year.[45]

GENERAL INDOOR AIR QUALITY RESOURCES

American Society of Heating, Refrigerating and Air-Conditioning Engineers: www.ashrae.org

California Department of Resources Recycling and Recovery, California Section 01350: www.calrecycle.ca.gov/greenbuilding/Specs/Section01350/#Criteria_

Center for the Built Environment: www.cbesurvey.org

GREENGUARD Environmental Institute: www.greenguard.org/en/indoorAirQuality.aspx

Green Seal: www.greenseal.org/

Scientific Certification Systems (SCS) Indoor Advantage: www.scscertified.com/gbc/indooradvantage.php

Sheet Metal and Air Conditioning Contractors' National Association, Inc. (SMACNA): www.smacna.org

South Coast Air Quality Management District (SCAQMD): www.aqmd.gov

U.S. Green Building Council Research on Occupant Satisfaction, Health, & Productivity: www.usgbc.org/DisplayPage.aspx?CMSPageID=77#occupant

U.S. Environmental Protection Agency, *Building Air Quality: A Guide for Building Owners and Facility Managers*: www.epa.gov/iaq/largebldgs/baqtoc.html

Whole Building Design Guide, Enhance Indoor Environmental Quality (IEQ): www.wbdg.org/design/ieq.php

NOTES

1. U.S. Environmental Protection Agency, "What Is an Urban Heat Island?" www.epa.gov/heatisland/about/index.htm, accessed October 14, 2011.

2. U.S. Environmental Protection Agency, "Buildings and Their Impact on the Environment: A Statistical Summary," Revised April 22, 2009, www.epa.gov/greenbuilding/pubs/gbstats.pdf, accessed October 14, 2011.

3. U.S. Environmental Protection Agency, "What is WaterSense?" www.epa.gov/watersense/about_us/what_is_ws.html, accessed October 14, 2011.

4. U.S. Environmental Protection Agency, "EPA WaterSense: Water Budget Tool Quick Start Guide," www.epa.gov/watersense/docs/water_budget_quick_start_final508.pdf, accessed October 14, 2011.

5. U.S. Environmental Protection Agency, "Why Build Green?" www.epa.gov/greenbuilding/pubs/whybuild.htm, accessed October 14, 2011.

6. BetterBricks, "Life-Cycle Cost Analysis versus Simple Payback – Why, When, How," www.betterbricks.com/graphics/assets/documents/BB_CostAnalysis_WWW.pdf, accessed October 14, 2011.

7. Richard Paradis, "Energy Analysis Tools," section B, "Match Tools to Task," Whole Building Design Guide, www.wbdg.org/resources/energyanalysis.php, accessed October 14, 2011.

8. Richard Paradis, "Energy Analysis Tools," sections C–G, Whole Building Design Guide, www.wbdg.org/resources/energyanalysis.php, accessed October 14, 2011.

9. Dana K. Smith and Alan Edgar, "Building Information Modeling (BIM)," Whole Building Design Guide, www.wbdg.org/bim/bim.php, accessed October 14, 2011.

10. Steve Jones, "New Report Discusses Convergence of Two Major Construction Industry Trends," AZoBuild, www.azobuild.com/news.asp?newsID=11609, accessed October 14, 2011.

11. McGraw-Hill Construction SmartMarket Report, *Green BIM: How Building Information Modeling is Contributing to Green Design and Construction, 2010,* http://images.autodesk.com/adsk/files/mhc_green_bim_smartmarket_report_(2010).pdf, accessed October 14, 2011.

12. National Institute of Building Sciences, Whole Building Design Guide, NIBS BIM Initiatives: "Building Smart Alliance Including International (IAI) Sites," June 26, 2010, www.wbdg.org/bim/nibs_bim.php, accessed October 14, 2011.

13. Whole Building Design Guide, "Daylighting," last updated August 29, 2011, www.wbdg.org/resources/daylighting.php, accessed March 1, 2012.

14. Environmental Protection Agency, ENERGY STAR, "Buildings & Plants," www.energystar.gov/index.cfm?c=business.bus_index, accessed October 3, 2011.

15. American Society of Heating, Refrigerating and Air-Conditioning Engineers, *Procedures for Commercial Building Energy Audits,* www.techstreet.com/cgi-bin/detail?product_id=1703613&utm_source=certification&utm_medium=BEAP&utm_campaign=procedures_cbea_firsted&ashrae_auth_token=, accessed October 3, 2011.16. ENERGY STAR, Joint Program of the U.S. Environmental Protection Agency and Department of Energy, "ENERGY STAR Overview of 2010 Achievements," www.energystar.gov/ia/partners/publications/pubdocs/2010%20CPPD%204pgr.pdf, accessed October 14, 2011.

17. ENERGY STAR, Joint Program of the U.S. Environmental Protection Agency and Department of Energy, "Portfolio Manager Overview," www.energystar.gov/index.cfm?c=evaluate_performance.bus_portfoliomanager, accessed October 14, 2011.

18. Ibid.

19. Ibid.

20. Whole Building Design Guide Project Management Committee, "Building Commissioning," last updated June 21, 2010, www.wbdg.org/project/buildingcomm.php, accessed October 3, 2011.

21. U.S. Department of Energy, "Net-Zero Energy Commercial Building Initiative," http://www1.eere.energy.gov/buildings/initiative.html, accessed October 14, 2011.

22. Energy Independence and Security Act (EISA) of 2007, Section 422, http://www1.eere.energy.gov/buildings/appliance_standards/commercial/pdfs/eisa_2007.pdf, accessed February 15, 2012.

23. Whole Building Design Guide, Executive Orders (EO): EO13514 Federal Leadership in Environmental, Energy, and Economic Performance (Part 7), October 8, 2009, www.wbdg.org/ccb/browse_doc.php?d=8151, accessed October 14, 2011.

24. Paul Schwer, "Carbon Neutral and Net Zero: The Case for Net Zero Energy Buildings," BetterBricks, www.betterbricks.com/design-construction/reading/carbon-neutral-and-net-zero, accessed October 14, 2011.

25. Architecture 2030, The 2030 Challenge, http://architecture2030.org/2030_challenge/the_2030_challenge, accessed October 14, 2011.

26. Architecture 2030, The 2030 Challenge: Adopters, http://architecture2030.org/2030_challenge/adopters, accessed October 14, 2011.

27. Paul Schwer, "Carbon Neutral and Net Zero: The Case for Net Zero Energy Buildings," BetterBricks, www.betterbricks.com/design-construction/reading/carbon-neutral-and-net-zero, accessed October 14, 2011.

28. U.S. Environmental Protection Agency, Green Building, Top Green Home Terms: Greenwashing, www.epa.gov/greenhomes/TopGreenHomeTerms.htm, accessed October 14, 2011.

29. U.S. Environmental Protection Agency, "Wastes - Resource Conservation - Reduce, Reuse, Recycle," www.epa.gov/epawaste/conserve/rrr/index.htm, accessed October 14, 2011.

30. International Organization for Standardization, "ISO 14021-1999 Environmental Labels and Declarations," www.iso.org/iso/catalogue_detail.htm?csnumber=23146, accessed October 14, 2011.

31. Code of Federal Regulations, Title 16–Commercial Practices, Chapter 1–Federal Trade Commission, Part 260–Guides for the Use of Environmental Marketing Claims, http://ecfr.gpoaccess.gov/cgi/t/

text/text-idx?c=ecfr&sid=b2333ddf96abf25788ef3037ffcfb40a&tpl=/ecfrbrowse/Title16/16cfr260_main_02.tpl, accessed October 14, 2011.

32. GREENGUARD Environmental Institute, "Health Impacts," www.greenguard.org/en/indoorAirQuality/iaq_healthImpacts.aspx, accessed October 14, 2011.

33. The Green Standard, "What are EPDs?" http://thegreenstandard.org/EPD_System.html, accessed October 16, 2011.

34. William McDonough and Michael Braungart, *Cradle to Cradle: Remaking the Way We Make Things,* New York: North Point Press, 2002, www.mcdonough.com/cradle_to_cradle.htm, accessed October 14, 2011.

35. U.S. Green Building Council, "Getting LCA into LEED: A Backgrounder on the First LCA Pilot Credit for LEED," November 2008, www.analyticawebplayer.com/GreenBuildings18/client/LCA%20credit%20backgrounder%20Nov13c11.pdf, accessed October 15, 2011.

36. William McDonough and Michael Braungart, *Cradle to Cradle: Remaking the Way We Make Things,* New York: North Point Press, 2002, www.mcdonough.com/cradle_to_cradle.htm, accessed October 14, 2011.

37. U.S. Green Building Council, LEED Pilot Credit Library, "Pilot Credit 1: Life Cycle Assessment of Building Assemblies and Materials," www.usgbc.org/ShowFile.aspx?DocumentID=6350, accessed October 15, 2011.

38. U.S. Environmental Protection Agency, "An Introduction to Indoor Air Quality (IAQ)," www.epa.gov/iaq/ia-intro.html, accessed October 15, 2011.

39. U.S. Environmental Protection Agency, "Glossary of Terms Definition of Volatile Organic Compound," http://www.epa.gov/iaq/glossary.html#V, accessed October 15, 2011.

40. U.S. Environmental Protection Agency, "The Key to Mold Control is Moisture Control," www.epa.gov/mold/index.html, accessed October 3, 2011.

41. U.S. Environmental Protection Agency, "Glossary of Terms: Sick Building Syndrome (SBS)," www.epa.gov/iaq/glossary.html#S, accessed October 3, 2011.

42. U.S. Environmental Protection Agency, "Glossary of Terms Definition of Volatile Organic Compound," http://www.epa.gov/iaq/glossary.html#V, accessed October 15, 2011.

43. Sheet Metal and Air Conditioning Contractors' National Association (SMACNA), *IAQ Guidelines for Occupied Buildings Under Construction,* 2nd Edition, 2007, www.smacna.org/bookstore/index.cfm?fuseaction=search_results&keyword=IAQ%20Guidelines%20for%20Occupied%20Buildings%20Under%20Construction%2C%202nd%20Edition, accessed October 15, 2011.

44. S. Abbaszadeh, L. Zagreus, D. Lehrer and C. Huizenga, "Occupant Satisfaction with Indoor Environmental Quality in Green Buildings," *Proceedings, Healthy Buildings 2006, Lisbon,* Vol. III, 365–370. Santa Cruz, CA: International Society of Indoor Air Quality and Climate, 2006, www.cbe.berkeley.edu/research/pdf_files/Abbaszadeh_HB2006.pdf, accessed October 15, 2011.

45. General Services Administration Public Building Service, Applied Research Program, "Energy Savings and Performance Gains in GSA Buildings: Seven Cost-Effective Strategies," March 2009, www.wbdg.org/research/energyefficiency.php?a=11, accessed October 15, 2011.

8 The Business of Green Buildings

There is no more strategic issue for a company, or any organization, than its ultimate purpose. For those who think business exists to make a profit, I suggest they think again. Business makes a profit to exist. Surely it must exist for some higher, nobler purpose than that.

—RAY ANDERSON *(Founder of Interface Carpet, author, known for industrial ecology and sustainability for business)*

THERE IS NOTHING SECONDARY about the economic discussion when it comes to the business of green buildings. As Patti Prairie, CEO of Brighter Planet, writes, "Against a backdrop of rather tepid near-term macroeconomic projections, market forecasters predict ongoing growth rates well into the double digits for corporate sustainability services, a market already valued in the billions of dollars. Sustainability is now big business in the US, and the way it evolves and matures over coming years will shape the way we all do business of any kind."[1]

Indeed, there is a whole host of signs that point to the rapid importance of the field and its rising place in world financial markets. There are new dedicated educational fields, career positions, risk mitigation, and economic investments—and these new areas of sustainable awareness are all being created at record speed.

This chapter delves into the fast-growing world of green business, looking at evolving careers in this area, such as chief sustainability officers and green financial experts, as well as the overall leadership matters that any green building professional should keep in mind when talking about the leadership, risks, and economic details behind sustainability.

What is missing from the green discussion?

❯ Money—and how it can be made for developers —is missing from the green buildings discussions.
Brian C. Small, LEED AP BD+C, city planner, City of Jacksonville

❯ That this is a human issue, not a left or right political issue. This is something that will have an effect on every single life on this planet. We all breathe, we all need water, and we all need nutritious soil to bear food. I hate it when people dismiss this and do not want to face this as a problem that we can conquer.

I think that financial objections are holding many people back from accepting this as a necessary step in our evolution. Green does not have to mean expensive. There are many inexpensive alternatives. Recycling is thought of before reusing. Antiques are the original "green" furnishings!
Stephanie Walker, interior designer, The Flooring Gallery

❯ What if we outlawed plastic bags everywhere? What if it were illegal to throw away a recyclable product? If I save my company money by saving paper, recycling, reducing waste, and I don't see an extra dime, where's the motivation? We need to answer these questions before we'll see greater successes.
Ryan R. Murphy, Associate AIA, CDT, LEED AP BD+C

❯ Frank conversations about social equity and diversity and what these mean for advocacy organizations and end users alike.
Katherine Darnstadt, AIA, LEED AP BD+C, CDT, NCARB, founder + principal architect, Latent Design

Feature stair at lunchroom area, APCO Worldwide Headquarters, Washington, DC. Firm: Envision Design. PHOTO: ERIC LAIGNEL

Chief Sustainability Officers

It all adds up to a corporate package that is becoming of great value in today's market. Says Eugene Linden, an author on climate change: "Chief sustainability officer sounds all crunchy granola and squishy.... But their rise shows that companies finally realize that sustainability and efficiency go hand in hand."[2]

Companies as diverse as Alaska Airlines, Ford, Starbucks, and Albertsons all have CSOs on board, and the list is growing. A recent study, *The State of the CSO: An Evolving Profile,* co-written and published by Eryn Emerich of Footprint Talent and William Paddock of WAP Sustainability Consulting, examined the green focus of over 250 major corporations and found that sustainability was ranked as a top ten strategic concern of over 65 percent of the responding businesses. Perhaps more tellingly, more than half of these businesses had someone with "sustainability" in his or her job title—and that number is projected to rise to over 80 percent in the next five years. Moreover, the vast majority of CSOs report directly to the CEO or board of directors, making the job one of executive leadership. CSOs set the vision for the corporation regarding the overall environmental impacts of building portfolio, transportation, supply chain, internal processes, and beyond.[3]

A chief sustainability officer, or director of sustainability, is fundamentally responsible for the environmental impact, programming, and footprint of a company. A chief sustainability officer (CSO) is responsible for a corporation's approach to environmental responsibility and for lessening the company's negative impact on the world's ecosystems. The CSO finds innovative ways for the corporation to meet its obligations as a responsible corporate citizen that is as concerned about the future as it is about today's profits.[4] Operating at the executive level, generally with the same corporate clout and corner office as the company's chief executive officer (CEO) and chief financial officer (CFO), CSOs are not employed by many of the largest companies in the world—including Google, Siemens, Johnson and Johnson, DuPont, and UPS.[5] "The emergence of the CSO title is indicative of the growing trend of Sustainability as a core business strategy," says Frank O'Brien-Bernini, CSO of Owens Corning. "Like all 'Chief' roles, it's critical that there is a distinct accountability for functional excellence...a high, wide and deep Sustainability perspective is integral to the executive leadership team where key decisions are made and strategic direction is set."[6] Taking both long- and short-term company goals into account, the CSO creates an overall vision of sustainability that incorporates green technical and communication skills across the entire breadth of the organization.

This increased recognition that sustainability needs executive-level leadership means that the CSO usually charts a course that helps comprehensively integrate green ideals into all areas of the company, including internal and external operations, financials, community and corporate social responsibility, public relations, investor relations, and

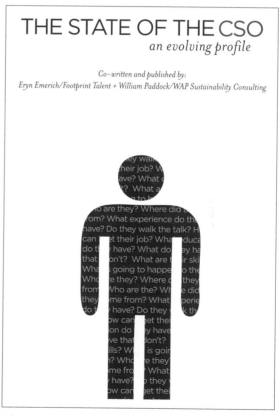

THE STATE OF THE CSO
an evolving profile

Co-written and published by:
Eryn Emerich/Footprint Talent + William Paddock/WAP Sustainability Consulting

White Paper: example of recent thought leadership from Footprint Talent. COPYRIGHT 2011, FOOTPRINT TALENT

O'Melveny: Reception desk with seating area in the background (LEED CI Gold). Firm: Gensler. PHOTO: DAVID JOSEPH

diversity. With similar education and training to other C-suite executives (MBAs, management-level training), the "new environmental chiefs...wield extraordinary power," notes the *New York Times*. "They are exploring partnerships with vendors and customers to create green products—and they have the power to close the deal. They are also getting a vote—often, the deciding vote—on product research and advertising campaigns."[7]

One of the first CSOs was Dupont's Linda J. Fischer, appointed to her position in 2004.[8] In 2007, the number of top corporate 500 companies with CSOs had increased to 5 percent, and within just one year, it doubled to 10 percent in 2008. As the mainstream market becomes more aware of environmental issues, it is clear that the demand for such positions will only increase. (For comparison, in the 1950s, only 5 percent of the corporate 500 had human resources departments.)[9]

ONE ROLE, MANY NAMES

Since the role of chief sustainability officer, or CSO, is so new, there is not an industry standard for the title. Here are a few examples of possible titles for the position:

- Chief sustainability officer
- Chief corporate social responsibility officer
- Senior vice president or vice president of sustainability
- Community and environmental responsibility officer
- Sustainable development officer
- Corporate social and environmental officer

The CSO Role

Among a company's executive officers, the CSO role will be customized based on each unique company's strategic goals. The CSO will be as focused on profit margins and business development, as is the entire company leadership, but the CSO will also thread sustainability into each decision. While the scope of work for the CSO varies, the overall role often includes key responsibilities such as the following:

- Assessment and reduction of environmental risk
- Reduction of waste (materials)
- Compliance with environmental regulations
- Resource conservation and management (carbon, energy, water)
- Product stewardship and lifecycle footprints
- New green product lines or services
- Community involvement and volunteerism
- Green communications, reporting, and marketing strategies
- Employee transportation plans and incentives

According to myfuture.com, the national salary average (as an average based on median level of pay) of a chief sustainability officer is approximately $160,000.[10] This site also showcases job growth and indicates which geographic areas have the highest growth. For companies that would like to move quickly toward sustainability, CSO is an important position to fill. If a company cannot afford a full-time CSO, they should consider hiring a sustainability consultant or green consultant to act in the interim.[11]

O'Melveny:
Lounge area
(LEED CI Gold).
Firm: Gensler.
PHOTO: DAVID
JOSEPH

Accountability as a Key Indicator

While the CSO is an increasing reality, one of the nation's leading corporate social responsibility recruiters, Ellen Weinreb, wrote a piece in 2010 entitled *The CSO Myth: Weinreb Group Defines the Chief Sustainability Officer*. Weinreb noted an increase in this role and analyzed the position judged on three key criteria: holds CSO title, relationship with strategic company leaders, and listing on the company's 10-K. The Form 10-K is required by the SEC (U.S. Securities and Exchange Commission) and provides information beyond the typical corporate annual report, showing accountability and including compensation and financial statements. Taking these criteria into consideration, she searched over 400 executives in terms of their CSO status, and discovered that only two executives actually held the final criterion. This is important to consider, especially in regards to the financial accountability component that denotes inclusion in strategic leadership decision making. Optimistically, however, Weinreb anticipates that more CSO titles will emerge, and once the position is officially integrated into corporate executive levels, it will be a large indicator that sustainability is understood as a core principle.[12]

CSO in the Built Environment

Specifically, what might a CSO do in terms of the building environment itself? The CSO usually oversees a company's building portfolio, which encompasses all of the structures a company owns and which may include corporate offices, warehouses, retail stores, and anything else with a physical presence. The CSO would manage and strategize with those who monitor how to balance maximum efficiency of these structures (heating, cooling, and all other energy considerations) with resources, cost savings, and overall employee and client satisfaction. Other roles might include managing the carbon footprint of a company; many large companies such as CB Richard Ellis (real estate owners, operators, and brokers) utilize the internationally recognized World Resource Institute (WRI) Greenhouse Gas Protocol that monitors historical data, shows progress, and sets future goals for carbon footprint reductions.[13] The CSO is also typically responsible for the corporate social responsibility report, a company record that surveys everything from company ethics and environmental stewardship to safety and governance.

Cooper Carry, Atlanta, GA: Waiting Area (LEED CI Platinum). Firm: Cooper Carry. PHOTO: GABRIEL BENZUR PHOTOGRAPHY

> As director of sustainability or chief sustainability officer for a major company, what are your greatest challenges and inspirations?

❯ As chief sustainability officer of Owens Corning, the challenges are many. We are focused on three key areas: greening our operations, greening our products, and accelerating energy efficiency and renewables penetration in the built environment. On the technical side, the challenges are around discovering and uncovering opportunities that are of sufficient scale to really move the needle—materially reducing our environmental footprint, significantly improving the relative greenness of our product offerings, and driving energy efficiency and renewables progress with our customers. On the leadership and change management side, the challenges revolve around mining the opportunities that will deliver value for our customers and shareholders today, while meeting the local and global needs of a sustainable today and tomorrow. There is nothing more inspirational to me than an engaged team with big ideas that lead to big decisions that lead to big actions that lead to big results that lead to proud employees, excited customers, happy shareholders, and communities that want us to grow in their neighborhoods.

Frank O'Brien-Bernini, vice president, chief sustainability officer, Owens Corning

Visionary Advocate

ERIN MEEZAN

Vice President, Sustainability

Interface

Note: Erin works for Interface, FLOR, InterfaceFLOR, and Bentley Prince Street—all Interface companies. For the purpose of this interview, all of these brands will be recognized as "Interface."

Your professional experience is diverse and includes prior positions as a lobbyist, director of energy and environment for the state of Georgia, and now a leader for sustainability at Interface, a global carpet manufacturer. How did each of these careers contribute to your current position?

❯ I guess I was always an advocate looking for a home—as a lobbyist and as a director in the energy office—and a big part of these jobs was being an advocate for sustainability and developing the ability to fight for what you need and convince others of the same. Another big and consistent part of those jobs is providing a perspective that is further down the road than where that organization or business is. This ability to peer into the future is critical at Interface—and I developed it as a lobbyist and at the Energy Office by understanding where we wanted to be. That futuristic view, as well as advocacy, are critical skills for me now; even though we are firmly committed at Interface to sustainability, I still fight for budgets, the time of our CEO, and the focus of our factory employees. Advocacy is a big part of the job.

Interestingly, your educational experience shows an environmental law degree. Verifiable metrics are becoming more and more important in the field of sustainability—how does your legal expertise support your work?

❯ The best thing about my legal training is probably the skills I learned related to making a good argument, making a good business case for something, and understanding how to communicate an idea. It might be different at an organization new to sustainability that is very focused on the metrics, but we are sort of using the metrics as a check-in—the bigger focus is what are the next three to five things we have to do to achieve our goals, how do we define that, make it happen and how to get buy-in to go there.

How would you describe your current role as vice president of sustainability? What does a "typical" day look like?

❯ I am sort of the chief cheerleader and advisor to our CEO on the next steps to take for the company to achieve its goals.

I spend a lot of time working with our CEO on strategic issues, but I also lead a team that works directly with our global businesses, so half the day is big picture, the other half is real on-the-ground projects that are geared toward achieving our goals on anything from energy to employee engagement. I have to know a lot about a lot and practice it about half the time.

What are three important characteristics you look for when hiring a team member for your internal Interface team?

❯ I am looking for new hires who are curious and willing to explore new ideas; we are creating the rules as it relates to sustainability, so we need explorers. I also look for someone with passion around the issue of sustainability, since that personal connection is what keeps a person focused, excited, and always willing to learn new things because they care about the topic. Lastly, I look for people who are willing to challenge others in a positive way; I always want to hire someone who will challenge me to think about my own ideas and strategies.

Please discuss Interface's key goals regarding global warming, carbon reductions, etc.

❯ The mission is huge—the company wants to become a sustainable company that does not take from the Earth and ultimately is restorative, and to be the first company that, by its deeds, shows the entire industrial world what sustainability is in all its dimensions, through people, process, product, place, and profits by 2020. By doing so, we will become restorative through the power of influence. To achieve that vision, we have established several goals: to have zero waste, to use 100 percent renewable energy, to eliminate all toxic emissions from our factories (including going fully carbon neutral for all facilities around the world), to operate our product manufacturing as a fully closed-loop system, to have sustainable transportation solutions, and to keep our employees connected and empowered to achieve this mission around the world. How we are doing on these goals is seen by the various metrics we measure and report at www.interfaceglobal.com/sustainability/Our-Progress.aspx.

What do you forecast for CSOs of the future?

❯ I think anyone who is really doing this now is either focusing on really creating organizational change, or they are just dabbling in a PR-type role. One day, we will realize that the people in these roles are the change agents and they are trying to make their organizations change through learning and empowering, so maybe the role will necessarily evolve to be about organizational change and they will be vice presidents of organizational learning or organizational change.

Truth Seeker

WILLIAM A. FRERKING

Vice President and Chief Sustainability Officer

Georgia-Pacific LLC

You have previously held roles as both general counsel and environmental attorney. How did these roles contribute to your current position? Would you recommend the same path or resources to others? If not, what alternative(s) would you recommend?

❯ I don't believe there's any single path that best prepares someone to lead sustainability efforts for a company. It depends on the nature of the business, the significance of sustainability to their industry, and what the company is trying to accomplish with sustainability.

At Georgia-Pacific, our executive leadership defined the CSO role and the traits they believed would make a candidate successful in the role. My experience as an environmental compliance attorney was seen as a benefit, as were my experiences working with, building, and leading legal teams, compliance and ethics capabilities, and government and public affairs capabilities for various businesses. Having experience applying GP's Market Based Management® philosophy was also a factor in my selection. With an emerging area like sustainability, being grounded in the fundamentals of how our businesses are run and the role capability and staff groups have in supporting those businesses has probably been as important as my other experiences.

What do you forecast for the CSOs of the future?

❯ I think the next generation of CSOs will be focused on driving competitive advantage. This will require several things:

- A close alignment with the strategies of the businesses
- A strong willingness to challenge conventional wisdom and be challenged for the positions they take
- The ability to work across large organizations with no direct-line authority and yet persuade and drive change
- The ability to balance the trade-offs in the three dimensions of sustainability (social, environmental, and economic) in a dynamic marketplace

Future CSOs will have the benefit of learning from the mistakes of their predecessors, but they may also face organizational and market hurdles because of some earlier failures and the perceived shortcomings of prior efforts.

If you could give some tips to someone pursuing the CSO profession, what would they be?

❯ Be a truth seeker and challenge the status quo—inside your organization and in what society generally accepts as most sustainable. Don't think that you can know what is most sustainable on a given issue; one size does not fit all. The market is dynamic, and change can turn the conventional thinking of today into something quite different tomorrow. Don't underestimate the complexity of a global economy or be too confident in your ability to understand secondary and tertiary impacts.

Thread of Understanding

PAUL MURRAY

VP, Sustainability and Environmental Affairs

Shaw Industries Group, Inc.

You have received degrees in both chemistry and management, and you serve on the boards of both the University of Michigan and Penn State, giving you a unique educational perspective. For those students who may want to embark on green building/sustainability–related professions, do you have any education recommendations?

❯ Although it is becoming possible to find college-level degree programs in sustainability, I still look for experience that shows a well-rounded individual who can fit into the team. The concepts can be learned, but a person with a well-balanced outlook in both education and personal activities is still what I look for. I think that a more basic science/engineering background enables this balanced outlook while maintaining the ability to grasp the science behind environmental performance. The exception would be someone who wants to lead efforts around corporate social responsibility. In that case, I might look for less science and more in the way of political science or another related type of degree. I will rarely, if ever, hire someone without a college degree; at a minimum, that is the barrier to entry to my department.

How did you increase your environmental knowledge along your path?

❯ My son's allergies to paint chemicals (I was a chemist working on the development of coatings) had just as big of an impact as that of Max DePree, the son of the founder of HMI, who as the CEO allowed us to form the first environmental steering committee at Herman Miller. I think students/future sustainability professionals need to realize that all their experiences should be focused on preparing them to make smart/balanced choices in their career and their job performance. The balance is the key to a good sustainability program.

How would you describe your current role as vice president of sustainability and environmental affairs? What is your "typical" day like?

❯ My job description is really broken into two distinct parts that are very connected in reality. The environmental affairs role is designed to make sure the company continues to meet and exceed any environmental regulatory program that concerns the design, manufacturing, and delivery of our product to the customer. The only way to ensure that this is done is to look for and find rules as they are being developed by various agencies and work with them to ensure that the rules are sustainable. The sustainable business part of my role is one in which I help ensure that Shaw makes money to stay in business while pushing the company's environmental and social aspects to new levels of performance. The balance I mentioned in the earlier question really comes into play here. I believe that my role is strategic in nature and helps create the thread of understanding between all roles of the business so that we consider as many of the known outcomes as possible and make the most balanced choice for the company.

If you could give one tip to someone pursuing a role such as yours, what would it be?

❯ Do not forget to have fun. If you act as if this is hard work, people will believe that the work we do is hard. I try to have fun and have really thrown some of my new work partners a curve by actually telling a joke or two in the middle of serious discussions. Life is too short to be sour. I have found my career, I love it, and I should act like that.

You represent a very important part of the green building community, the product manufacturers. Please explain how this industry in particular is unique compared to the specifiers and construction professionals.

❯ We make things, we use materials to do it, and we must get smarter in the way we do that. Specifiers can help by creating demand for materials that have been created with these principals in mind, while also paying attention to the idea that sometimes a simple improvement is better than requiring a leap of faith in technology only to have it not meet their requirements because of durability or other issues.

Outdoor patio at Herman Miller Los Angeles Showroom (LEED CI Platinum). Firm: tvsdesign. PHOTO: BRIAN GASSEL

Courageous Know-How

DAVID MICHAEL JEROME

Senior Vice President
Corporate Responsibility

Intercontinental Hotel Group (IHG)

You have held diverse positions in your prior professional career, including roles at InBev and GM, as well as a law practice. How have these roles contributed to your current position? Would you recommend a similar path or resources to others? If not, what alternative(s) would you recommend?

❯ The most important elements to success in corporate responsibility (CR) are: the passion to achieve, a willingness to learn/make mistakes, and some cross-functional business experience. CR is still being defined, and old mental models persist. But even at this early stage of development, it is clear that high-performing CR crosses traditional organizational silos and requires courage as business and its stakeholders work through its development while changing old paradigms. So I guess there is no one path.

How would you describe your current role as the senior vice president for corporate responsibility at IHG? What is your "typical" day like?

❯ We think of CR at IHG as a complex business issue. We consider the role of hotels in the twenty-first century, what makes a green hotel, and how to we optimize CR's benefits for both the business and the communities in which we operate. We then answer these questions by seeking to be innovative and collaborative in how we approach the environment and our communities. In the simplest terms, CR is about how we make our money, not about how we give it away.

What do you forecast for the CSO of the future?

❯ I think we all will be working with greater clarity as to what CR is and how it works. I think it will also be part of core business strategy, because done well, it can unlock tremendous value for business and society. We are lucky at IHG—we have senior executive and board-level support for our work, and this helps us to move more quickly into alignment with IHG's core business objectives.

Tell us about Green Engage and how it has been working within your hotels.

❯ Green Engage is an online system-wide program that guides our hotels in how they are designed, built, and operated. It is working well—it provides value for our owners and guests. It also future-proofs our business as it makes our hotels more efficient and valuable over time.

What challenges you the most in your work? What inspires you the most in your work?

❯ Old mental models are one of our biggest challenges, but then again, we love challenges. I also very much like the idea of how a little change at each hotel adds up to a big positive impact for our guests and our planet. For example, helping each one of our hotels to reduce their energy use by 15 percent equates to hundreds of millions of dollars and thousands of tons of carbon saved.

If you could give one tip to someone pursuing the CSO profession, what would it be?

❯ Think in terms of the HOW—how do we make our money? Once that is understood, then ask how we meet the needs of our guests and other stakeholders.

How is your operations background unique and influential within your current work at IHG?

❯ Because we know what it is like to have targets and other operational pressures, we are better able to develop solutions that are good for the business and our communities.

True Value

JEAN SAVITSKY, LEED AP BD+C

Managing Director/Chief Operating Officer (COO), Energy and Sustainability Services

Jones Lang LaSalle

Your educational background is in interior design. What was your path from interior design to your current role as COO at Jones Lang LaSalle (JLL)?

❯ My opportunity to work in energy and sustainability developed as a result of my role as project executive on the Bank of America Tower at One Bryant Park. I was given that opportunity as a result of my 25 plus years of construction project management experience. Bank of America Tower, One Bryant Park, was registered in the LEED NC pilot program, and it was Jones Lang LaSalle's first exposure/opportunity to green construction and certification. (The project was registered about ten years ago.) Our clients began requesting assistance in LEED project management, and JLL made a decision to develop a specific business line to deliver this service. I was asked to take the leadership of the LEED project management business as a result of my experience with managing the LEED certification requirements at One Bryant Park. Jones Lang LaSalle had a long-standing energy practice, including energy procurement, portfolio energy management, energy budgeting, and alternative energy solutions, and with the growth and interest in LEED certification from our clients, it was a natural direction to merge all of these individual business lines into an integrated solution for our clients. I was asked to take on the role of chief operating officer, since I had an understanding of the technical side of this work and had experience in managing and growing a business.

As someone with experience mentoring students, what would be your recommendation(s) for education and experience to students considering entering the green building field?

❯ An engineering background, specifically in either mechanical or electrical engineering, will help young professionals enter the field quickly. We are finding a lack of skilled professionals across the country with this expertise, and those candidates that have a technical background are hired quickly and at a premium. With the challenges in the economy, clients are more focused on projects that can present a quantifiable return on their investment and a tangible reduction in building operating costs. An energy expert that can run an energy model, walk through a building's plant and understand the equipment, etc., and have a basic understanding of accounting principles such as net present value and return on investment puts him/herself ahead of the competition. The other suggestion for students is to get as much experience as they can through internships and other volunteer opportunities in more tangible areas of sustainability (e.g., work on administration for LEED projects, spend time with other engineers during an energy audit, etc.). From what our clients are asking about, and where we see opportunities, it is less in the "softer" side of sustainability, i.e., policy, etc, although that is of importance as you need to set goals to be able to record successes. Instead, the focus in this challenging environment is more on a hard return for investments made and operating expense reductions.

How are green buildings unique to the real estate audience? What do you find is one of the most effective financial arguments?

The most effective financial argument for green buildings is a quantifiable, and easily understood,

Cooper Carry, Atlanta, GA: Board room (LEED CI Platinum). Firm: Cooper Carry. PHOTO: GABRIEL BENZUR PHOTOGRAPHY

expected return on investment from the "green" features, or associated capital improvements, such as increased rents, increased lease renewals, and higher value on an asset. An acceptable return on investment for a capital project is approximately 24 months, and possibly a rare exception of 36 months. If a retrofit or green project can be funded through achieved savings, that becomes a compelling discussion to have with an owner or investor.

How do you educate your clients/tenants on the benefits of green design? Once engaged, do you find that they are willing to invest a premium for green real estate properties?

❯ Many of our clients today are very savvy about green design and have some knowledge about LEED. Corporate real estate professionals have done a great deal to educate themselves on what they need to do to operate their buildings in a sus-

tainable and responsible manner and to educate their tenants in what they can do to participate in the efforts. What we try to do is increase our clients' awareness of other rating systems and options, such as green tenant assessments, Green Globes, and ENERGY STAR, for example. We sometimes encounter a misperception that achieving LEED certification is prohibitively expensive and that LEED certification does not make any difference to the occupants or owners. Achieving LEED certification, or LEED Silver certification, does not add any incremental cost to a project, and achieving LEED Gold certification only adds 10 percent. When these costs are presented and are supported by documented multiple-project examples, clients often change their minds and pursue LEED certification. As for rental rates, however, we see only a few clients that would consider paying a higher rental rate to be in a LEED-certified building. These clients are typically large corporate clients, with clearly defined corporate social responsibility statements and published sustainability goals. This is likely a direct impact of the challenging economy that we are currently experiencing.

What are three important characteristics you look for when hiring your internal JLL team?

❯ When hiring new team members, we look for candidates with experience in executing energy and LEED projects, with a technical education and background (preferably engineering, with credentials such as CEM, PE, and/or LEED AP), and who have strong presentation skills in order to be comfortable in front of clients and in order to participate in new business development activities.

If you could give one tip to someone pursuing the COO green profession, what would it be?

❯ The most important thing for anyone working in any aspect of the energy and sustainability business is to stay educated on what is new in the marketplace and what is coming. Be on top of upcoming regulations, legislation, rebates, and incentives. There is a great deal to learn and the information changes every day. Clients are looking to their energy and sustainability consultants not to bring them the current thinking and technology, but to help them understand the future, to help them wade through the volumes of information that are out there, and to share their thought leadership. At the end of the day, as much as building and operating real estate sustainably and conscientiously is the "right thing to do," it is the economic argument (i.e., payback and return on investment) that truly influences client decisions.

What advice would you give to others who want to follow in your footsteps?

❯ There is no straight-line career path to becoming a chief sustainability officer in a large company. Companies are at varied points along their path to sustainability, and this requires different skills and experiences at the top to accelerate progress. In the greening of Owens Corning, it has been a tremendous advantage to be technically deep in our processes, products, and customer applications. Having led our global R&D function prior to this role was great preparation. Having said that, my general suggestions to aspiring green professionals are: Be actively curious and hungry to gain relevant knowledge; be passionate, but listen more than you talk; know the details of what you are advocating, being able to get at least five-whys deep in discussions and debates, and finally; steer clear of the rigid rights and wrongs of sustainability—the science is evolving and it's your job to inject the right data/analysis at the right time to move corporate decision making toward more sustainable solutions.

Frank O'Brien-Bernini, vice president, chief sustainability officer, Owens Corning

> *Please explain how your role has changed over the last five years and what you forecast for the future.*

❭ The thing that has changed the most is the pull from the marketplace. Five or ten years ago, some of the leadership companies were pushing sustainability but there really wasn›t a pull from customers. Now, customers—both other companies and consumers—are looking to us to help provide more sustainable solutions. Very few are willing to pay more, but if you can provide a solution that both meets the performance needs and is more sustainable, customers will choose your product.

Dawn Rittenhouse, director of sustainable development, DuPont

Green Legal Advisors/Environmental Lawyers

As more developers and clients begin to understand—and request—green aspects to their buildings, misunderstandings about LEED and other certification codes have started to arise. Building developers claim and advertise LEED standards and ratings to prospective buyers, touting LEED rankings in marketing brochures before the process is even complete. Then, when LEED or other sustainable codes are not met, or a building underperforms, lawsuits are filed by developers and by buyers—as in the case of the Riverhouse litigation in Battery Park City (*Gidumal v. Site 16/17 Development LLC et al.*)[14] or an affordable house project in Chicago that was supposed to get LEED and didn't, so the owner took the architect to court (*Bain v. Vertex Architects*).[15] Other LEED-related cases have started to pop up, from an electrical contractor suing for not winning a bid based on his competitor's alleged lack of LEED experience to a class-action suit against the USGBC by Henry Gifford and others, alleging that LEED buildings are not any more energy-efficient than their conventional counterparts (*Gifford et al. v. USGBC*).[16]

"Many owners and landlords (or their attorneys) have failed to understand the intricacies of the LEED system and made improper representations about their projects' green features in offering plans, leases, and other legal documents," says Shari Shapiro, a LEED-accredited lawyer. "At least one other similar suit to Gidumal (in Canada) has been filed, and I expect that we will hear reports of other, similar suits by tenants and purchasers."[17] In addition, as states and local districts begin to implement their own green laws, challenges to those codes are being raised in court; City of Albuquerque in *AHRI v. City of Albuquerque* and the state of Washington in *BIA v. Washington* are just two recent examples.[18] And states themselves will begin to pass sustainable building measures, often coming up against other government bodies and private-sector opposition.

For all of these reasons, the importance of green lawyers or environmental lawyers will only continue to increase. With eco-credentials in hand, most of these lawyers offer a diverse set of services to legal clients that includes help with sustainable project financing, renewable energy transactions, consulting with contract drafting, regulatory permitting, land use approvals, and review of compliance issues and contracts, as well as litigation by drafting briefs, taking depositions, and otherwise managing court cases.

Donald Simon, partner at Wendel, Rosen, Black & Dean, created the following list of project team considerations that owners should consider on green or LEED building projects, as well as some suggested contract provisions.

Owner considerations for project team:

Assign project managers ("PM") with green building experience, such as LEED APs. Contractually prohibit parties from changing PMs without owner's prior consent. Consider liquidated damages for breach or where PM leaves their employ.

Consider requiring subcontractor workshops to educate key subs on green building attributes applicable to their scope of work and monitor compliance. This is especially important when the general contractor lacks significant green building experience.

Contract Provisions:

Use performance standards where applicable (like % construction waste that must be diverted from landfills).

Owners should include waiver language in contracts that prohibits designers or contractors from relying on compliance with green building/LEED requirements as a defense to traditional construction and design claims, such as where the contractor and/or architect attribute a roof failure to the added weight resulting from the owner's requirement that solar panels be installed on it. Instead, require designers and contractors to bring such issues to the owner's attention before the start of construction so that the liability is placed on them.[19]

> *Do you see any emerging trends in environmental law—in particular focused on green buildings?*

❯ One of the most common phone calls I receive in my law practice is from an exasperated property owner who is being inundated with stormwater from a neighboring development. But when developers or builders pay attention to LEED and other green building concepts, they take proper steps to control and treat their stormwater. This dramatically decreases the chances they will see me on the other side of the courtroom, because smart stormwater management won't flood or silt out your neighbor.

Jenny R. Culler, Esq., Stack & Associates, P.L.

Green Law

SUSAN CRAIGHEAD, J.D., LL.M., LEED GREEN ASSOCIATE

Craighead Law

Have you seen an increase in green building–related liability risk?

❯ To date there have been relatively few green building–related claims. However, green building professionals must recognize that the risks are increasing with the growing demand for green building and rapidly increasing state and local regulatory activity. Another area of concern that is often overlooked is the ownership and use of the intellectual property created in connection with such projects.

What is your advice to mitigate these risks?

❯ Understand what the risks are by discussing them with your legal counsel. Strong contract provisions should allocate risks among all of the project stakeholders by carefully defining the scope of work. You should also check your professional liability insurance policy for exclusion of claims arising out of warranties and guarantees. Your contracts should

Outdoor common space at Herman Miller Los Angeles Showroom (LEED CI Platinum). Firm: tvsdesign. PHOTO: BRIAN GASSEL

provide that signing LEED or other rating system credit submittal templates does not constitute a warranty or guarantee.

How have contracts changed in order to respond to these new potential risks? Provisions regarding disclaimers of liability and limitation of damages have become very specific to the industry. Contracts also have had to change to address the role of numerous stakeholders in such projects, including architects, engineers, builders, consultants, and owners.

Do you see any emerging trends in environmental law?

❯ The emphasis in environmental law has been shifting from cleaning up to sustainability. This is clearly demonstrated in the proliferation of green building codes and sustainability rating systems at national, state, and local levels. International law is also trending strongly in the direction of sustainable development law, i.e., the International Energy Conservation Code.

Eco-Legal

ROBERT C. NEWCOMER, ESQ./ LEED AP

The Lang Legal Group LLC

Have you seen an increase in green building–related liability risk?

❯ Yes, with the growth in green building there has been an increase in risk.

First, new materials, products, design techniques, technologies, or even familiar materials or products used in new applications do not have proven track records of actual performance in the field. In addition, the large amount of federal stimulus dollars committed to various projects in a very short period of time attracted a lot of bidding competition, and it will be difficult to maintain adequate oversight of these projects given the

shrinking budgets and resources available to regulatory authorities, especially at the local level.

Second, the adoption of government and contractual mandates and incentives introduces new standards that must be met, and with each and any new requirement, there is increased risk. Government mandates include, for example, building codes (but not policies such as those adopted by GSA or the City of Atlanta regarding the certification of their own [public] buildings).

Third, there is often a lot of excitement expressed about the benefits of green buildings. In many cases, this excitement is justified and the claims are clearly stated and may be supported by evidence, but in some cases the marketing hype may be, at least in part, inaccurate and if misleading can be the subject of an enforcement action by the

Federal Trade Commission (FTC) or can simply raise client expectations beyond a level that can actually be achieved, or that can only be achieved with future action (such as specific maintenance or operational requirements to achieve energy-efficiency targets).

These increased risks related to green buildings, however, do not appear to have resulted in any discernible increase in actual litigation. It is possible that the collaborative relationship inherent in green building might make it easier or at least more likely for parties to work out a dispute before it deteriorates to the point of actual litigation, or they may be more reluctant to initiate litigation. I have heard about an increase in insurance claims related to green building and, if true, that fact may be the most accurate indication of increased risk.

What is your advice to mitigate these risks?

❯ My advice in no particular order of priority is:

■ From a practical perspective, engage a qualified and experienced "green" team, including design and construction professionals and a green building consultant, early enough in the design and specification process for them to be effective and clearly define their roles and responsibilities throughout the project.

■ Engage legal counsel that understands green building and the specific roles and responsibilities of your green team, as well as how to identify and allocate risk in the contract documents to the party most able to control that risk during the project.

■ Manage client expectations by avoiding vague and misleading language in your advertising or marketing of products and services, and do not overstate the benefits of green buildings or the materials, products, or technologies used in the project and your ability to deliver that which you do not control (and specifically including actual performance over the life of the project).

■ Consider insurance coverage that protects design, construction, and other green building professionals from liability.

Legally Green™

CAROLYN S. KAPLAN

Counsel and Chief Sustainability Officer

Nixon Peabody LLP

What do you find are the greatest challenges and inspirations in your current roles at Nixon Peabody?

❯ Developing a sustainable workplace is not something that happens overnight—it's a long, sometimes arduous process requiring strong commitment from both management and personnel. It starts with incorporating sustainability into busi-

ness strategy, and eventually winds through every aspect of an organization's operations. Even when the commitment is there, competing needs for resources can slow down progress. So it's important to be both dedicated and patient.

I am continuously inspired by those of my colleagues who have incorporated sustainability into their being—it's simply part of who they are as people. As an example, these individuals consistently come up with innovative ways to do what they're already doing in a more sustainable manner. Their suggestions help us to reduce resources and challenge us to do better.

NixonPeabody: Reception. The rooms in the Conference Center are pulled away from the exterior glass, bringing light and views to all who visit. The space is filled with light and helps to tell the sustainable story with wool carpets, reclaimed orchard flooring, a recycled glass art wall, and tables made from salvaged wood (LEED CI Certified). Firm: Gensler. PHOTO: SHERMAN TAKATA

NixonPeabody: Breakout area seating at Conference Center. Moving the conference rooms off the perimeter affords the opportunity for breakout areas to have access to light and views (LEED CI Certified). Firm: Gensler. PHOTO: SHERMAN TAKATA

What advice would you give to others who want to follow in your footsteps?

❯ I'm not sure that the goal should be to train a regiment of CSOs. Rather, we'll really be making progress when sustainability is an aspect of each and every job description. I'd advise others to follow a path that enables them to "do what you like, like what you do" instead of simply focusing on becoming a "sustainability professional." What does that mean? Pursue a career that excites you and find a way to incorporate sustainability into everything you do. Take classes that interest you and attend your professor's office hours. Find an organization whose mission is important to you and get involved. Read everything, especially publications with which you disagree. Be willing to change direction quickly when opportunity knocks. That's what happened to me.

Nixon Peabody is one of the top 100 global law firms, and your position as CSO is the first for a law firm. How has this changed the tone internally, and what has been the response externally?

❯ By appointing me as CSO and launching our Legally Green™ initiative, our firm's management communicated that we are serious about incorporating sustainability into our operations and legal practice. Internally, we've seen a cultural shift; sustainability has become an integral part of our business, and we're constantly trying to raise the bar for ourselves. Externally, we've successfully shown our clients that we "walk the walk," and critically, that we understand how climate change and sustainability demands impact their business. Our Legally Green initiative has been positively received by our personnel and our clients. Some of the best evidence of our success is the frequency with which we are contacted by law firms, large and small, looking for guidance on how to implement their own sustainability initiatives.

GREEN LAW RESOURCES

American Institute of Architects (AIA) Guide for Sustainable Projects (free download)
http://info.aia.org/aia/sustainabilityguide.cfm

AIA Document B214-2007 Standard Form of Architects Services: LEED Certification

USGBC Legal Working Group: Lawyers who provide green building counsel

USGBC White Paper *The Legal Risk In "Building Green": New Wine in Old Bottles?* A
USGBC Panel Discussion in 2009:
www.seyfarth.com/dir_docs/publications/AttorneyPubs/White%20Paper_DBlake.pdf

Financials

Equally important to the "green" of the environment are the "greenbacks," or financials, in the green building professional's triple-bottom-line manner of decision making. There is good reason for this. While some project owners are motivated by the credo of "doing the right thing" for the environment, that same ethos of eco-idealism does not apply to everyone. As any manufacturer, facility manager, or business owner understands, resource-efficient design is smart design. Furthermore, the financial benefits of sustainability make it a profitable new engine for commerce and for cutting-edge innovative technologies waiting to be invented and manufactured, which will one day yield even more green jobs. Due to its importance, the ability to speak the language of fiscal sustainability is an important skill in any green building professional's repertoire.

Weather Channel: LED lights and studio light heating (LEED NC Gold). Firm: Vocon Architecture. PHOTO: DAN GRILLET

Big Concepts

Just as there are processes and tools that apply to all green building professionals regardless of specialty, so too are there global concepts that apply to financials. Many of these principles have been threaded throughout this book. The following section, however, brings into clearer focus the specifics and intricacies of the numbers when building green. In general, keeping things straightforward and understanding the return on investment over the life cycle of the building creates value the owner understands, and sets a vision for the entire project.

Keep It Simple

Often the best approach is the simplest. In the world of green building, there are some "low- or no-cost" strategies such as:

- Refrain from building.
- Re-purpose existing facilities.
- Keep it small—from the building footprint to the energy systems, keep things small and more efficient.
- Orient the building to maximize daylight and minimize heat gain.
- Select landscape materials that require minimal or no water.
- Specify ENERGY STAR equipment and appliances.
- Turn lights off.
- Check the utility bills.
- Schedule maintenance staff during daylight hours.

This basic list typically is a matter of course for a green building professional. Many of these materials, such as ENERGY STAR, are available at no additional cost. Other items may seem overly simplistic, such as the idea that people should look at their utility bills—but studies have shown that even such rudimentary actions will often reduce operational usage.

Others solutions might seem counterintuitive, such as the most fundamental idea that the best way to make a building green is to refrain from actually building. Martin Melaver, of Melaver Macintosh, created a company based on this concept. He relates that, "A number of years ago, Ray Anderson, who was on the board of Melaver, Inc., challenged us to envision a new type of real estate company: 'Wouldn't it be transformative,' he said, 'if we earned our living based on what we did not build.' Transformative indeed. Melaver McIntosh was founded in order to realize that radically simple principle."[20]

Fresh Systemic Approach

MARTIN MELAVER

Principal and Founder

Melaver McIntosh

How do you foresee a new way of doing eco-finance and a restructuring of capital markets for the future of green buildings?

❯ To start off, I'm less interested in building a building these days, even a green building, than I am in figuring out ways to integrate green building techniques into a more systemic or holistic approach to doing more with less within the built environment. And that means thinking less about what's happening on the footprint of a building and more about tapping into the variety of assets in close proximity to that building—energy and water infrastructure, economic/job development, multi-modal transportation, etc.

And this approach to systems-based thinking, as it turns out, has a lot to do with new approaches to finance. For the moment anyway, traditional approaches to financing are simply not so available. What IS available is a remarkable moment in time where a large segment of the American population over the next thirty years will be migrating back into cities that offer work/live/play, sustainable environments. Now, this upsurge in demand for urban living is occurring precisely at a time when most cities are reeling from decades of neglect and disinvestment in their urban infrastructure. High demand, woefully short supply. Which means that municipalities all across the country need to figure out quickly how to redevelop their urban core areas to meet demand. And that, in turn, calls for various innovative ap-

proaches to public/private partnerships. Cities have funding, but largely lack the developmental know-how. Private development companies have the know-how, but by and large lack the financial resources. Cities understand infrastructure. Developers understand buildings. It's a perfect time for public/private partnerships to develop in which cities can approach redevelopment more systematically. And it's also a perfect time for cities to create internal funding mechanisms, something like a CDC on steroids to create revolving loan mechanisms that enable continuous cycles of development while keeping financing fees within the community.

How do you think your perspective as a green building owner and developer gives you a unique outlook on the financials of green buildings?

❯ Again, my perspective on this question is going to follow along systems-thinking lines. Traditionally, developers have been known to approach cities with a long laundry list of demands about what they want in order to be "willing" to develop a project that a city might want or need. And cities have traditionally kowtowed to this form of suasion, if you can call it that. Now, the shoe is on the other foot. Developers need the financial resources that a city can bring to bear on a project. And that puts municipalities in the driver's seat in terms of ratcheting up their expectations about what a particular development must deliver. Maybe a particular development serves as its own district energy plant, maybe it provides tertiary treatment for water use for an entire part of town, maybe it enables some form of local job creation. In short, I think the perspective of a private green developer enables you to understand what it is a city could and should expect and demand from the stuff that gets built—on a whole different level than perhaps it once did.

In your book The Green Building Bottom Line: The Real Cost of Sustainable Building, *what are few key takeaways and the associated costs for someone new to green building?*

Although I probably never expressed this very succinctly, my fundamental working premise is that great ideas get funded, good ideas have to stand in line with all the other good ideas. If you are looking to "value-engineer" something that is innovative, you are probably going in the wrong direction. Market differentiation is a key ingredient with most anything in the capital marketplace—and the most innovative approaches of all, if executed well, will end up being not the most costly but the most remunerative.

Melaver McIntosh can assist clients with resource identification and alternative funding sources. How does this work?

We have something of a three-way test for taking on clients: (1) Does this project have the potential for significantly moving the needle for a municipality/region or an industry? (2) Does this project have the resources (not so much capital resources, but political, social, etc.) to give it a likely chance of success? (3) Is this a project that we will look back on twenty-five years from now and say, "That project made a big difference?" If we can satisfy ourselves about these three criteria, we feel reasonably confident that we have a "differentiate-able" project in hand, likely to be transformative, and so likely to be one that goes to the front of the queue when we are lining up tranches of financing.

RETURN

Some of the most straightforward financial concepts are those that we learned as children. Say that you loaned (or invested, in the case of particularly savvy siblings) five dollars to your kid sister. As a result, even as a child, you probably wanted to be paid back with something of equal or better value. As an adult, the same premise holds true: All clients want to be paid back, and green building is no exception. Generally, when considering returns, the financial picture can be assessed using methods of simple payback (SPB) or life cycle costing (LCC). On less complicated projects, using SPB means conducting an analysis of how long it will take the client to be paid back for their initial expenditure. For more complicated projects or more expensive investments, the LCC method may be more appropriate, as it takes a holistic view over the lifetime of the building. It looks at the first cost for design and construction of the building plus the operational costs against a backdrop of the benefits. In most cases, clients will have a number in mind of how long they are willing to wait for a return on their investment; this figure could be two years, or five years, or more. What timeframe the client envisions seeing a return on their investment is a good question for any green building professional to ask.

LIFE CYCLE COSTS

Over the lifetime of a building, there are numerous types of cost to be considered, from initial costs (design and construction) to operational costs (maintenance and upkeep) to replacement costs (rebuilding, renovations, or demolition). As with the life cycle analysis (LCA) discussion in Chapter 7, the same principle applies to cost strategies. Life cycle costs (LCC) look comprehensively at the original investment, and from that, deduce an approximate time it will take to realize a full return on investment—and, hopefully, also add on a certain amount of additional funds that will be realized over the lifetime of the project. There are several analysis tools that can assist a green building professional with life cycle costing.

Another consideration is the type of costs that occur across the life cycle "chain." There are both hard and soft costs. Hard costs refer to actual construction costs—the "bricks and sticks," or the materials that make the building. Soft costs are expenses such as professional fees.

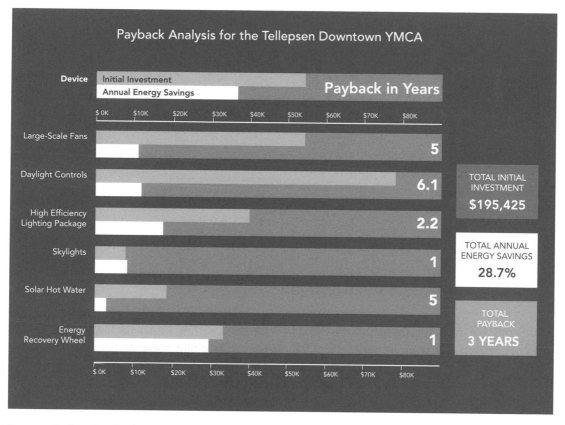

Energy payback analysis for the Downtown YMCA, Houston, Texas (LEED NC Gold). FIRM AND IMAGE: 2009 KIRKSEY

How would you describe life cycle cost?

> Life cycle cost is simply the total cost (not the initial cost) of something purchased, calculated over the life of its use.

Many people, using so-called first-cost analysis, would say that a piece of equipment that costs $100 is less expensive than a piece of equipment that costs $125. But that initial cost is not the full story. A heating/air-conditioning unit that costs $100, lasts for ten years, and costs $20 each year to run (because it's not very efficient) is actually more expensive than an alternative system that costs $125, also lasts for ten years, but costs $10 each year to run.

That example seems obvious to most of us. Less obvious, however, is comparing something like the purchase of a suburban house that requires an hour commute to work versus buying what appears to be a more expensive house in the city. Once you factor in wasted time in commuting, additional fuel costs, time away from family and friends, lack of time for exercise, leisure, cultural pursuits, probably higher medical costs, that so-called cheap suburban option turns out, based on life cycle analysis, to be something we pay dearly for.

Martin Melaver, principal and founder, Melaver McIntosh

> Life cycle cost analysis is a tool for selecting and evaluating components and systems used in a building. You compare the "total cost of ownership" (TCO) of two or more alternatives. Let's evaluate two 4-foot long fluorescent lamps for use in an office building. We need 1,000 lamps, and they operate 24 hours a day. Lamp "A" consumes 25 watts, has low mercury content, a rated life of 46,000 hours, and costs $5.00. Lamp "B" consumes 32 watts, has a rated life of 24,000 hours, and costs $2.52.

By selecting lamp "A," we need 40 percent fewer lamps. Over a ten-year investment horizon, we will need to buy 3,000 "A" lamps compared to 5,000 "B" lamps. This reduces the costs of purchasing, labor removal and replacement, and recycling. Lamp "A" uses 27 percent less energy than lamp "B"—this is important because energy is 90 percent or more of the TCO of a lighting system. In this case, the TCO of lamp "A" is $69,302 less than the TCO for lamp "B" on a present value basis. While lamp "A" initially costs $2.48 more per lamp to purchase (this is referred to as a "cost premium"), selecting this alternative saves $6.93 present value per lamp socket over ten years. That's a return on investment of 279 percent!

Since the break-even point or simple payback period is shorter than a year, it makes financial sense to start using the "A" lamp as soon as possible. The energy saved during that first year covers the cost of changing to lamp "A."

However, that is only part of the story. For every 3 watts of lighting energy saved, 1 watt of energy used by the building's HVAC system can be saved. Therefore, we can also reduce the size of the HVAC system to reflect the lower heat load, which reduces the building's first costs.

B. Alan Whitson, RPA, president, Corporate Realty, Design & Management Institute, chair, Model Green Lease Task Force

USGBC Headquarters: Open office, Washington, DC. Completed 2009 (LEED CI Platinum). Firm: Envision Design, PLLC. PHOTO: ERIC LAIGNEL

One of the common issues in green building finances is determining how the project funding is allotted. Typically, the design and construction of the building is a separate budget from operations. This is actually where some issues can arise because the design and construction may not incorporate a life cycle approach to operating expenses.

VALUE

Most American consumers see water as something that is either free or very low cost. Though this perception might place water on the low end of the economic value scale, water is actually one of the most valuable resources on the planet, required for all life and finite in its supply. When water becomes unavailable or is only in limited supply, as in the case of a drought or years of low rainfall, people begin to appreciate the value of water more, using less and conserving what they have. As water becomes scarcer on a global and constant level, people will start to see this natural resource as valuable, even though its actual cost may currently be low. This is a shift in paradigm.

One of the pivotal books for the green professional is *Natural Capitalism: Creating the Next Industrial Revolution*, by Paul Hawken, Amory Lovins, and L. Hunter Lovins. This book presents the premise that hundreds of companies have increased profitability by shifting their outlook on what is actually of value or is important. One of the key principles of natural capitalism is models based on natural systems.[21]

THE INVISIBLE BENEFITS

Many things in life are incredibly beneficial even though they cannot be seen. Take oxygen, for example, which is an essential element of life on Earth, yet is also invisible to the naked eye. In the same way, some of the byproducts of green design are very valuable, but the science of quantifying

that value is an art in itself. As just one example, several studies show that increased access to daylight and views yields:

- Increased office productivity
- Higher rate of retail sales
- Higher test scores for students[22]

Instead of just evaluating profit based on clear and actual numbers, a shift in direction toward value understanding would necessitate a clear look at the whole picture. In that way, a client who deliberately invests in a whole-value office, retail, or educational building will benefit from a better experience for occupants—which will "repay" any costs in the original design. One of the most frequently noted studies in this regard shows that the cost of design, construction, and operation is a combined 8 percent of a building initial cost, which pales in comparison to the salaries of the employees that occupy the building, at 92 percent over the lifetime of the building over thirty years.[23]

Cooper Carry, Atlanta, GA: The Town Center is the hub of Cooper Carry employee activity. Employees dine, meet, and relax here (LEED CI Platinum). Firm: Cooper Carry. PHOTO: GABRIEL BENZUR PHOTOGRAPHY

The Secret to Value

SCOTT MULDAVIN, CRE, FRICS

President, The Muldavin Company

Executive Director, Green Building Finance Consortium

Please provide a brief background on your education/experience and your current green building career.

❯ I am executive director of the Green Building Finance Consortium, a public service group whose mission is to improve sustainable valuation and underwriting practices to enable an assessment of sustainable properties from a financial perspective.

My path to becoming a green building valuation and finance professional relied upon my expertise in real estate finance and investment. I have been a consultant for over thirty years to many of the world's leading real estate companies while a lead real estate partner at Deloitte LLP and president of my own firm for thirteen years. I co-founded Guggenheim Real Estate, a $3+ billion private real estate investment company, served on the advisory board of Global Real Analytics, an advisor to $2 billion of REIT and CMBS funds, and completed over 300 consulting engagements involving real estate finance, mortgage lending, investment, valuation, securitization, and sustainability.

I lecture and speak throughout the world on real estate finance and sustainability. In addition to my foundational book, Value Beyond Cost Savings: How to Underwrite Sustainable Properties, I have authored 200 articles on real estate finance, investment, valuation, and sustainability. I am a graduate of UC Berkeley with a bachelor's in environmental studies and a master's in city and regional planning from Harvard University. I am both a Counselor of Real Estate (CRE) and a Fellow of the Royal Institute of Chartered Surveyors.

What is the Green Building Finance Consortium (GBFC)?

❯ In 2006, I founded the Green Building Finance Consortium (GBFC), a research and education initiative created to help fill the void of independent information, methods, and practices for the valuation and underwriting of sustainable properties and to forge greater connection between energy efficiency/sustainability specialists and capital providers.

BOMA International, the Urban Land Institute, the Pension Real Estate Association, the Mortgage Bankers Association, the National Association of Realtors, the Northwest Energy Efficiency Alliance (NEEA), and thirteen other organizations are founding members of the Consortium. Additionally, the Royal Institute of Chartered Surveyors, the Appraisal Institute, CoreNet Global, and other trade associations have provided board members, engaged in collaborative projects, and offered other support and assistance.

The Green Building Finance Consortium (GBFC) released Value Beyond Cost Savings: How to Underwrite Sustainable Properties in 2010, the first

book dedicated to enabling private owners and occupants to integrate the value of sustainable property investment into their decision making. The book is available for free as a public service of GBFC and has been distributed widely.

The Consortium's initial focus was to document how to identify, price (value), and mitigate sustainable property risk to enable financially based decision making. Value Beyond Cost Savings lays the foundation for such analysis. More recently, we are focusing our efforts on the application of our work to motivating value-based decision making and the development of financing options and scalable investment solutions.

Why do you think valuation and underwriting are so important to increasing sustainability/energy-efficiency investment?

❯ Value is a fundamental underpinning of investment. Loan to value ratios are one of the most important metrics used by lenders in making loans. Equity investors look at value and value creation as a basis for their investment decisions. Valuation is the analytic method that the real estate industry uses to capture the contribution of revenues, expenses, and risk from an investment. Sustainable property decision makers have historically limited investments to that which could be "justified" by energy cost savings over a short payback period. This was not a good practice historically, but with growing demand by regulators, tenants, and investors, and societal concern over carbon emissions, this practice is neither profit maximizing nor good for society.

Fortunately, underwriting and valuation methods for sustainable properties do not need to fundamentally change. However, we do need some additional knowledge and analytic techniques to better understand sustainable property performance. Once we understand the performance, we can then apply traditional market analysis techniques (talk to tenants and investors, analyze comparable properties, etc.) to assess the market's response to a particular property's sustainable performance.

The role of and importance of energy, and carbon emissions, have also undergone a dramatic shift during the last few years, requiring some adjustments to methods and practices. As governments, private companies, and individuals have begun to care about energy use and carbon emissions, the ability of private owners to "monetize" the public benefits they create has been substantially enhanced, requiring new knowledge and insights to properly analyze. The potential for health and productivity benefits from sustainable properties is another area of potential value that needs better underwriting practices.

› Why do you think sustainable properties have more value?

Actually, what I think is that there is a strong hypothesis supporting the general case for sustainable properties having higher value. I also think it is possible to test this hypothesis (this is what underwriters and appraisers do). The basic rationale for why sustainable properties have higher value is because they cost-effectively increase property cash flows while reducing cash-flow risk.

Sustainable property development costs are typically a bit higher than traditional properties (but not always). Higher initial development costs are offset by lower operating costs over the life of the development due to energy and water cost savings. Higher demand by regulators, tenants, and investors increases revenues. Higher tenant retention and improved property durability reduce capital expenditures and periodic tenant improvement and leasing commission costs. Finally, the "net" risks are positive as risk reduction due to integrated design, commissioning, and reduced risk of future tenant

and investor demand offset increased risks due to new design processes, service providers, contracts, products, and materials.

The value of sustainability to occupants (tenants or owner occupants) is driven by improved employee health and productivity, improved employee retention, reduced energy and water costs, reduced churning costs (cost of internal moves of staff), compliance with internal and external sustainability commitments, and other benefits.

The secret to capturing a property's potential value from sustainable investment is to understand that the value proposition stated is just a hypothesis and needs to be tested and proven for a specific property given its unique set of sustainability features, costs, tenants, investors, and market conditions. Value is maximized when the results of the testing of the value hypothesis are intelligently organized and presented in the financing request package.

The best way for owners/developers to maximize the value "potential" of sustainable properties is to design and build projects, or execute renovations and retrofits, with a clear predetermined understanding of the specific sustainable features and outcomes that regulators, tenants, and investors in your market value.

Risk mitigation is particularly important for attracting debt capital from lenders. Accordingly owners/developers should focus on following best practices relative to sustainable processes, features, and systems. Perhaps most important, financing request packages need to clearly and logically present the costs and benefits and how they translate to higher revenues and reduced risk (higher value). Capital reacts badly to over-reaching in conclusions, failure to disclose potential risks, and the application of data that have not been properly adjusted to the specific property under review.

Even if you do not believe in the value of sustainable investment today, the trends in demand for sustainability suggest that it would be prudent to develop a strategy to address potential changes in the market. For example, when you buy an existing building today, it is typically subject to leases that will roll over periodically in the future. Keeping buildings current and desirable for future tenants, or employees, is one of the most important jobs of asset managers. The risk of ignoring sustainability in real estate decisions also far exceeds the cost to consider and address sustainability as part of an organization's overall real estate strategy.

> *Do you believe that the green building movement has fully engaged the real estate market? If not, what do you think are the barriers/solutions?*

The green building movement has made remarkable inroads into the real estate markets during the last five years, but there is still significant work to do. To best answer this question you need to break the real estate property markets into at least the following three categories: (1) residential properties, (2) smaller commercial properties, and (3) larger commercial properties.

For example, penetration of sustainability investment into larger commercial properties owned by large corporations, pension funds, real estate investment trusts, and other large owners has been substantially better than for smaller properties, but the depth of investment has still been quite limited. More external forces have been driving the demand by larger property managers to investigate and consider sustainability investment—typically as part of a larger enterprise-level sustainability program. Key things that need to be done include better performance measurement and reporting, enhanced

Key Perspectives Based on Investor Type. TABLE COURTESY OF SCOTT MULDAVIN, *VALUE BEYOND COST SAVINGS: HOW TO UNDERWRITE SUSTAINABLE PROPERTIES,* EXPANDED CHAPTER II, EXHIBIT II-5.

Key Perspectives by Investor Type	
Investor Type	**Key Investment Perspectives**
Investor/Landlord	• If they take risks, they have the potential for substantial rewards. • Often longer-term perspective • What will tenants pay for? • Phasing of implementation—new vs. existing, which properties?
Space User	• If they take risks, they have the potential for substantial rewards. • Often longer-term perspective • Contribution to enterprise value—social license to operate • Potential health and productivity benefits
Spec Developer	• Exit/take-out risk • Initial costs-potential for project delays • Monetization of sustainable value in sales price • Impact on absorption rate • Government incentives
Tenant	• Contribution to enterprise value—social license to operate • Potential health and productivity benefits • Lease length—time to recoup value • Reduced occupancy costs (especially NNN costs)
Lender	• If risk taken, they lose if there are problems and do not share in rewards if successful • Mitigation of risk focus • Reliance on third party appraisers/other service providers

measurement and understanding of market performance and the value hypothesis, and improved risk mitigation and analysis.

One of your speech titles is "Sustainable Property Finance: How Money Thinks and How to Talk to It." Could you outline the highlights of the concepts discussed in your talk?

❯ One of the most important things you need to understand when seeking capital is what kind of money it is. For example, if you are going to a corporate CFO to get a sustainable project approved, you need to understand internal corporate hurdle rates, extreme reluctance to disrupt core mission operations, key drivers for the business (and how real estate and sustainability contribute to these drivers), and other factors not really related to the X's and O's of the sustainable investment. Equity capital comes in many different types based on the risk posture, return objectives, leverage goals, and other factors. Equity investors are also willing to take more risk than lenders because if a sustainability investment really works—and significantly increases demand or reduces energy costs—the equity investor can really benefit, while the lender just gets the mortgage payment. However, lenders take the hit if a project really

does not perform. It is not surprising they are so risk averse, demanding risks be mitigated.

While this question would require a long answer, another key thing about capital providers is that they are less interested in case studies and examples of hugely successful projects and more interested in what did not work and why their project is not like those that failed or underperformed.

Please suggest tools/resources that are good for those who may want to pursue green real estate or green finance related careers.

❯ *Value Beyond Cost Savings: How to Underwrite Sustainable Properties* is an excellent resource with a topical index and detailed table of contents to enable readers to find what interests them. The book is available for free online and is extensively hyperlinked to resources. The Consortium's website has a searchable research library and industry links section with thousands of documents and links coded using our research library index, which in itself is an excellent learning tool. We provide an annotated index for those who want to understand how documents and companies are coded (www. GreenBuildingFC.com).

Early Integration

As with any other aspect of building green, if the overall goal is to see a return on investment, an integrated design approach is the best solution. A truly integrated approach sees the cost synergies between various environmental strategies. A great resource for this is BuildingGreen's white paper *The Cost of LEED*, which demonstrates the paybacks from looking at costs comprehensively from the outset.[24] For example, the creation of a reduced-lighting energy system impacts a building's cooling needs—so that these two cost decisions should be considered in tandem. The result is that if green is integrated into the initial design phase, often the solution has proven to be low or no cost. While this guide is specific to the LEED Rating System it gives an framework for looking at common green building initiatives along with the estimated and itemized associated costs.

Eco-Real Estate

WILLIAM D. BROWNING

Founder

Terrapin/Bright Green, LLC

You were one of the authors of Green Development: Integrating Ecology and Real Estate. *If you could add a chapter today, what would it say?*

❯ Green Development was published in 1998, and it is still used as a text in a number of classes on green real estate. I would change the last chapter where we tell the story of a future development project that would successfully address a number of environmental and social issues. A project now ex-

ists that does all that, Dockside Green in Victoria, British Columbia. I would also add a chapter on biophilic design.

What would you say is the most misunderstood financial piece in the green discussion?

❯ We still hear people say that green buildings cost too much. When I hear that, I assume that the person does not have any real experience in green building and is looking for a convenient excuse not to change their practices. That said, given what we know about health and productivity benefits of green building and in particular with biophilic design, we should be willing to spend more on good buildings.

Productivity Pays

SAMUEL D. POBST, LEED AP, O+M, BD+C, ID+C

Principal and Founder

Eco Metrics, LLC

What are three key tips to successful cost estimating on a green building project?

❯ 1. Clearly identify the objective. An owner who wants a green building has specific objectives, and standard building practices are not a part of that mix.
2. Estimate using multiple approaches. Be prepared when implementing an unfamiliar technology or process. Utilize multiple

estimating strategies to check the veracity of the numbers. Means, Blue Book, square foot pricing, checking the Internet, and calling contractors are all tools that help to get a sense of what costs you should anticipate prior to receipt of bids.
3. Revise estimates as new information becomes available. It is an iterative process.

For those in or considering the field of construction/building science, what would you recommend in terms of resources to prepare them for discussing the financials of green building?

❯ The USGBC/Resources/GreenBuilding Research/ Research Staff Picks has the most current research on the economic studies for sustainable building regardless of the type of green buildings you work with. I am partial to the USGBC Paid-From-Savings Guide to Green Existing Buildings, which establishes the fundamental economics of financing sustainable building operations and maintenance.

Lake View Terrace Library, Lake View Terrace, CA. Firm: Fields Devereaux Architects & Engineers, James Weiner, AIA, LEED Fellow, design architect. The main reading room is oriented along the east/west axis between a courtyard to the north and a public park to the south. Light shelves at the south windows reflect light onto the vaulted ceiling, providing a low-glare reading environment. Acoustic panels lie between FSC-certified glu-lam beams to temper acoustics (LEED NC Platinum). PHOTO: © RMA PHOTOGRAPHY

When discussing green buildings and cost with a client, what process and tools do you commonly use?

❯ The language of commerce is vitally important to have mastered when talking to potential clients. Though many are interested in environmental standards, the economic impact drives most of the decision-making process. The economic case can be made for nearly every LEED best practice for every project. Weaving the disciplines of economy, ecology, and equity to validate the logic behind each of these best practices helps provide clients with new perspectives that may be beneficial to their business interests.

Much of our work is with LEED for building operations and maintenance. We are able to demonstrate on nearly every project that we can pay for the cost of certification within a time frame of their choosing with savings from gas, electric, and water use. Those three items can be quantified in BTUs, watts, or gallons, and calculations can be made to make the economic case.

Our buildings are responsible not only for shelter and comfort, but also to provide for health and productivity, which are intimately intertwined. Measuring air quality, light levels, and temperatures yields occupant satisfaction metrics that impact productivity. Statistics reported by EIA, DOE, and BOMA cite the average cost of energy per square foot in a building at $2.56. The average cost of operations and maintenance is $2.29 per square foot. The average cost of a salary is $282.23 per square

foot. A 1 percent gain in productivity pays for all of the energy costs of a building.

The real benefit to a green building owner comes from gains in productivity. Though it is difficult to assign a value to a potential gain, there is ample evidence that demonstrates that implementation of these operational best practices that affect occupant productivity will more than offset all of the energy costs of the building.

The client can base the decision to proceed on the hard facts of BTUs, watts, and gallons, but the icing on the cake is expressed after the fact with benefits provided to the occupants. Our studies and many others have validated these claims. Though the primary motive might be economic, we can convey the environmental and social benefits to fully engage all aspects of an organization.

Submarine Epiphany

B. ALAN WHITSON, RPA

President, Corporate Realty, Design & Management Institute

Chair, Model Green Lease Task Force

Please provide a brief background on your education/experience and your current green building career.

❯ I am the president of Corporate Realty, Design & Management Institute (CRDMI), which designs and delivers continuing education programs in design, construction, and operation of high-per-

formance and sustainable buildings. My firm was one of the first to tie economic issues together with a green building philosophy. CRDMI owns the federal trademark Turning Green into Gold®. In addition to live- and Web-based educational programs, CRDMI offers custom training and management consulting services to Fortune 1,000 corporations.

In 1972, I began my real estate career in Honolulu after leaving the U.S. Navy's nuclear submarine program. My experience encompasses over forty million square feet of facilities around the world, in the roles of asset manager, corporate facilities manager, construction manager, development manager, commercial real estate broker, and consultant.

The scope of my career has given me a keen insight into the real estate needs of today's corporation, and a unique understanding of the architecture, construction, and real estate industries. My interest in the built environment and its impact on human performance began in 1969 when assigned the responsibility for indoor air quality and operation and maintenance of oxygen generators, CO_2 scrubbers, and CO/H_2 burners aboard a nuclear submarine.

Your teaching focuses on the idea of the cost/value of green buildings. Could you give a few tips on how to have this discussion with a new client?

❯ First, let us address the cost issue. Many people mistakenly believe that a green building costs more than a traditional building. That is a perception that is simply not true. If a green building costs more than a traditional building, it is because somewhere in the process people decided to select more costly alternatives.

The value discussion depends upon who the client is. If the client is a real estate developer, the value proposition of a green building is the ability to attract tenants who can choose between multiple buildings that are both green and not green. This translates into filling the building faster with tenants, lower operating costs, and less vacancy over the life of the building.

If the client is the "user" of the building, the major benefit is how it affects worker productivity and health. More than 80 percent of the cost of doing business is salaries and benefits, while rent and utilities are 8 percent of the cost of doing business. While green buildings are known to have lower operating costs, people are still the number one asset.

How can green leases be more valuable to various parties—tenant, owner, facility manager, etc.?

❯ A valid lease requires four elements: the names of the parties, a description of the leased property, the lease term, and the consideration. Everything else in a lease document defines the rights and duties of the parties, and who pays for what. That is why the following real estate adage is so important: "If it's not in writing, you don't get it."

A well-crafted green lease, such as the Model Green Lease, is specific about the environmental performance of the building, the standards used, and the duties of the tenant, owner, employees, agents, contractors, and service providers. (A national task force of attorneys, real estate brokers, building owners, corporate tenants, interior architects, and LEED consultants wrote the Model Green Lease.) Here's an example: Office buildings are equipped with air filters to maintain good indoor air quality. A clause in the Model Green Lease requires the building's air filters comply with a national standard—ASHRAE 52.2 2007 (B) Appendix J. Without a requirement for Appendix J, a MERV-14 filter could be installed, even though it performs at a lower performance level than MERV 11. This would negatively affect indoor air quality. The testing requirement in the lease ensures that the building owner is buying and installing filters proven to perform in a manner expected by the building's tenants.

Being specific provides value to everyone. For the tenant, it ensures that the building is operated at the same environmental performance level if the building is sold or changes ownership during their lease term. For the owner, it defines the operational and environmental standard they will provide. For example, a well-crafted green lease will define the temperature and humidity range the building will maintain given specific weather and occupancy conditions. This is important to a building owner since tenants complaining about their space being "too hot or too cold" is the number-one headache in the daily operation of an office building. Because comfort is a subjective issue, dealing with a "hot and cold call" can create a no-win situation between a building owner and a tenant if the lease uses vague terms such as "reasonable" or "comparable to other class "A" office buildings in the area." However, by being specific, it takes the issue out of the subjective arena and allows direct measurable action to be taken.

The public learns about energy-efficient light bulb options in the exhibit tent at the U.S. Department of Energy Solar Decathlon 2011 at West Potomac Park in Washington, D.C.
PHOTO: STEFANO PALTERA/U.S. DEPARTMENT OF ENERGY SOLAR DECATHLON

What are some good financial green resources/tools?

❭ The Corporate Realty, Design and Management Institute's website (www.SquareFootage.net) has a number of articles and white papers that many find useful. The Institute offers half-day and full-day educational programs across North America. These programs meet the continuing educational requirement for such organizations as American Institute of Architects (AIA), American Society of Interior Designers (ASID), Building Owners & Managers Institute (BOMI), International Facilities Management Association (IFMA), and U.S. Green Building Council (USGBC). We have developed a unique finance program called Finance 101 for Facility and Property Managers. What makes the program valuable is the life cycle cost examples and formulas integral to maintaining a true green building included in an extensive workbook and USB data stick. Plus, instructors provide one year of online support.

Real Estate

Quite simply, real estate is the business of buying, selling, and leasing buildings and land. As such, a real estate professional's focus is on keeping buildings actively engaged through indicators such as tenant occupancy. From a financial viewpoint, the goal is to move property quickly and at the highest possible price the market will bear. For example, if looking at a basic apartment rental, any landlord would prefer to rent the space more quickly and at higher rental rates than those of the competition. By doing so, a landlord has an edge in the market, and therefore, increased profitability. Green buildings provide an additional leg up in the competitive market of real estate, as a number of studies have shown.

Indeed, a study by Piet Eichholtz, Nils Kok, and John M. Quigley on sustainability and the dynamics of green building provides new evidence on the financial performance of green office buildings. The study shows LEED-premium direct rental rates for LEED at 5.85 percent and

Microsoft West Campus, Redmond, WA (LEED NC Silver).
Firm: Callison. PHOTO: CALLISON/CHRIS EDEN 2011

ENERGY STAR buildings at 2.1 percent as compared to identical buildings taking into account quality and location with; effective rental rates at 5.9 percent for LEED and 6.6 percent for ENERGY STAR; and sales prices at 11.1 for LEED and 13.0 for Energy Star.[25] "In all markets, in respect to average rent per square foot, energy efficient buildings have performed slightly better than conventional," says Leanne Tobias, the founder and managing principal of Malachite LLC, a green real estate advisory services provider. "Generally speaking, green buildings are outperforming conventional buildings with regard to rental rates."[26] Moreover, in a February 2011 global study conducted by Jones Lang LaSalle and CoreNet, 50 percent of officers from commercial real estate companies said they would pay a premium for green even without energy cost savings, and an additional 23 percent said they would pay a premium if the rental premium were offset by energy cost reductions.[27] Says Tobias, "In this market, that is a significant advantage."[28]

Financing

While a real estate investor may be fully on board to finance a green building, the next step is convincing financial institutions of the value of such an investment. When searching for green financing, LEED-accredited lawyer and expert on green financing, Shari Shapiro of Cozen O'Connor, advises keeping the following rules in mind:

- Find a lender or bank that is committed to green projects.
- Make sure your green project pencils out so it actually is a wise investment.
- Provide as much information about the beneficial financial features as possible.[29]

The good news is that in September 2011, the largest single private-sector investment to date in commercial property energy retrofits and upgrades was made, in the amount of $650 million, so it is evident that there is indeed financing to be had.[30]

Aerial view of Music City Center roof, Nashville, TN. FIRM AND IMAGE: tvsdesign

> *What do you think are key points or, alternatively, points that are missing in the green discussion in terms of cost/investment and real estate—especially as they pertain to existing buildings?*

❯ In short, the *existing* built environment must be addressed in order to positively impact global climate impact, gas output, and material waste. We have done an excellent job of creating new and innovative strategies for building new buildings from renewable resources and materials and reducing their impact, but new buildings represent a tiny fraction of the actual building composition globally and always will. The problem exists in the past, not in the future. We must address what we have already built.

The purpose of Green Realty Trust is to acquire existing buildings and to retrofit or otherwise modify them to reduce their energy use and carbon output. We believe that this makes the greatest possible impact for the environment while at the same time providing the best available investment opportunity. By improving the overall efficiency of large-scale projects, one is essentially directly improving the net operating income of the project, which is the metric upon which all buildings are valued.

This issue of existing versus new buildings is too often lost because architects and politicians would rather stand in front of beautiful new buildings that look markedly different than the older buildings we all recognize. Everyone wants to *see* new not just hear about what is new. We have had and continue to have government incentives for new "green" buildings while the most impact (in terms of job creation, economic effect, carbon and waste reduction, etc.) is made in existing buildings. Making an existing building more energy efficient will make it more valuable and therefore generate a meaningful return on investment.

Rob Hannah, president, CEO, Insight Real Estate, LLC

357

Incentives

There are a multitude of federal, state, and local incentives available to help create good, green buildings that range beyond standard financial assistance. There are two major categories under which different types of incentives fall: framework incentives and financial incentives.

Framework incentives help put the overall conditions and process for a green building in place. This may include expedited building plan reviews by local code officials, which may be incredibly important on particularly fast-paced projects in which time is money.

Financial incentives come in many forms but can be grouped into two key methods of dissemination: tax credits and grants. The USGBC has an interactive tool where federal, state, local, higher education, and K–12 incentives can be searched by location and provide resources for funding. There are also specialized incentives for specific environmental initiatives such as renewable energy and energy efficiency.[31] In addition, the U.S. Department of Energy sponsors another interactive link called "DSIRE" where the user can search by state for this type of incentive.[32]

Another funding mechanism, grants are acquired once a proposal is submitted, then typically certain performance metrics must be met throughout the design and construction process in order to retain funding.

How to Have the "Money Talk"

When a green building professional is in a position to "sell" green building to someone outside the sustainable field, it is important to understand all of the principles described in this chapter so as to make a more convincing, and well-informed, argument. This type of discussion could be between a real estate professional and a bank lender or between a landlord and a tenant or even between an architect and an owner; no matter what green specialty may be your field of choice, everyone in the green building profession should be well informed on economic matters.

Navy Federal Credit Union (LEED NC Gold). Firm: ASD, Inc. CONTRACTOR AND FIRM: GREENHUT CONSTRUCTION COMPANY

As with any selling opportunity, it is important to know your audience and what drives them. Some potential motivators may include the following:

- Keeping ahead of regulations
- Reducing operating costs
- Increasing tenant sales
- Employee recruitment/retention/productivity
- Staying competitive
- Reducing liability risks
- Doing good

Once aware of the motive, you can craft your selling points to fit your audience's needs. Here are a few selling tools that can be used in an economic discussion of why to build green:

- Benchmarking — Find similar building types that demonstrate cost savings.

- Metrics of performance — A building that gives the owner more feedback on the green building performance will be tracked, measured, and verified. This could be via commissioning, building automation systems, sub-metering, etc.

- Be able to give a rough order of magnitude. Run enough numbers prior to the meeting so that you can delineate the potential costs and benefits of specific strategies.

- Often it is beneficial to have a contractor or cost estimator engaged in the process at this point in order to get more accurate local estimates.

Daylight in the lobby space of the Suntrust Plaza Garden Offices, the base building where Portman's architectural offices received LEED-CI Gold. Firm: John Portman and Associates. IMAGE COURTESY OF JOHN PORTMAN AND ASSOCIATES.

> **When discussing green buildings and cost with a client, what process and tools do you commonly use?**

❯ I generally get their attention by asking if they would like to know how to build their next building in a third less time, at a third less cost, have it cost a third less to operate, improve productivity, and be the most desired building of all their buildings to work in? I rarely get "NO," so I pull out a well-documented case study showing how a respected U.S.

company achieved those remarkable results. The key to their success was a collaborative design process involving owner, architect, major building systems/materials suppliers, and everyone's commitment to make decisions based on balancing three primary criteria: COST–FUNCTION–ENVIRONMENT.

Wes Evans, owner, Evergreen Consulting Services

When discussing green buildings and cost with a contractor, what process and tools do you commonly use?

❯ From the contractor's standpoint, sustainability is already a commonly required part of building within the commercial construction industry. Nearly 30 percent of all new commercial construction starts require LEED certification today. Implementing LEED is no more than putting in place a best practices methodology that can help in any construction situation. Site management of runoff, recycling, regional materials purchasing, recycled content of products, and low VOC paints and sealants are all items that can be managed at no additional cost and can help improve the overall quality of an installation. The contractor's time is affected by the documentation process, which is a little higher than what is normally expected; however, oftentimes the efficiencies of planning and installation that are put in place can reduce the number of change orders on a project because of the quality control measures that result because of LEED.

Tom Boeck, LEED AP, principal and founder, Sustainable Options

When discussing green buildings and costs with government, financial institutions, and other partners, what process and tools do you commonly use?

❯ We use the consensus *Green Value Score™*, which is the underwriting standard score from 25 to 100 for all properties documenting the presence of green building attributes that increase economic value.

Mike Italiano, president & CEO, The Institute for Market Transformation to Sustainability, founder, U.S. Green Building Council, director, Sustainable Furnishings Council, CEO, Capital Markets Partnership

What do you imagine will be the biggest shifts in the financial green building realm in the next five years?

❯ The biggest shift will be national green building financing since it's projected based on actual data, successful precedent, and Wall Street peer-reviewed due diligence released at the NYSE to:

Provide $1 trillion in private sector stimulus and create 8 million new jobs and $400 billion in new wages. Stop ongoing systemic financial market risks being caused by dangerous climate change in the insurance, government, agricultural, and fisheries sectors.

Mike Italiano, president & CEO, The Institute for Market Transformation to Sustainability, founder, U.S. Green Building Council, director, Sustainable Furnishings Council, CEO, Capital Markets Partnership

〉 I think the convergence of technology, science, and collaboration will have a powerful impact on our understanding of the real cost and financial benefit of designing, operating, and maintaining buildings. Today most decisions to build green buildings are based on financial comparisons of incremental costs and financial benefits in narrowly defined parameters such as energy savings, water savings, waste management, etc. Over the next five years, I believe more of what we know about the real cost of environmental impacts and potential financial benefits of minimizing them will be shared and integrated into easy-to-use technologies. Future BIM systems, for example, may provide building designers, owners, and operators valuable information needed to evaluate green building strategies based on expanded parameters including the financial impact they have on brand value, investor relations, employee attraction, retention, health, productivity, and public policy incentives & penalties

Wes Evans, owner, Evergreen Consulting Services

GREEN FINANCIAL AND LEADERSHIP RESOURCES

Natural Capitalism: Creating the Next Industrial Revolution, by Paul Hawken, Amory Lovins, and Hunter Lovins, Little Brown and Company, 1999

Small is Beautiful: Economics as if People Mattered, by E. F. Schumacker, Harper Perennial, 1989: www.amazon.com/Small-Beautiful-Economics-People-Mattered/dp/0060916303

Life Cycle Costing for Facilities, by Alphonse J. Dell'Isola and Stephen J. Kirk: www.amazon.com/Life-Cycle-Costing-Facilities-RSMeans/dp/0876297025/ref=sr_1_1?s=books&ie=UTF8&qid=1326074733&sr=1-1#_

U.S. Green Building Council (USGBC) Research Pubications – Cost Analysis of Whole Buildings:
www.usgbc.org/DisplayPage.aspx?CMSPageID=77#economic_analysis

EPA Green Building: Funding Opportunities:
www.epa.gov/greenbuilding/tools/funding.htm

U.S. Department of Energy, Federal Energy Management Program (FEMP):
Life-Cycle Cost (LCC) Analysis: www1.eere.energy.gov/femp/program/lifecycle.html

USGBC Public Policy Search:
www.usgbc.org/PublicPolicy/SearchPublicPolicies.aspx?PageID=1776

USGBC Occupant Satisfaction, Health & Productivity Studies:
www.usgbc.org/DisplayPage.aspx?CMSPageID=77#occupant

World Business Council for Sustainable Development:
www.wbcsd.org/plugins/DocSearch/details.asp?type=DocDet&ObjectId=MzQyMDY

As champions of sustainability, it is imperative that green building professionals understand the leadership and economic advantages for eco-construction, as well as the potential risks to long-term benefits. Though there are knowledgeable experts in each of these areas—including chief sustainability officers, environmental lawyers, and green financial experts—it is useful for all green building professionals to understand how these areas overlap and be conversant in each of the topics, both for their own practice and for better serving their clients. After all, a critical component of the future of green building is the ability to convince others of the value of sustainability.

NOTES

1. Patti Prairie, "The Four Keys to Corporate Sustainability in 2011," *Fast Company,* January 5, 2011, www.fastcompany.com/1714526/the-four-keys-to-corporate-sustainability-in-2011, accessed October 15, 2011.

2. Claudia H. Deutsch, "Companies Giving Green an Office," *The New York Times,* July 3, 2007, http://query.nytimes.com/gst/fullpage.html?res=9B02EFDD153EF930A35754C0A9619C8B63&pagewanted=all, accessed October 15, 2011.

3. Eryn Emerich and William Paddock, "The State of the CSO: An Evolving Profile," Footprint Sustainable Talent/WAP Sustainability, 2011, http://footprinttalent.wordpress.com/2011/03/09/the-state-of-the-cso-an-evolving-profile/, accessed October 15, 2011.

4. Terry Masters, "What Does a Chief Sustainability Officer Do?" wiseGEEK, Conjecture Corporation, Copyright 2003–2011, www.wisegeek.com/what-does-a-chief-sustainability-officer-do.htm, accessed October 15, 2011.

5. Johanna Sorrel, "The Rise of the CSO Chief Sustainability Officer," March 29, 2011, www.2degreesnetwork.com/blog/archives/90-The-Rise-of-the-CSO-Chief-Sustainability-Officer.html, accessed October 15, 2011.

6. Eryn Emerich and William Paddock, "The State of the CSO: An Evolving Profile," Footprint Sustainable Talent/WAP Sustainability," 2011, http://footprinttalent.wordpress.com/2011/03/09/the-state-of-the-cso-an-evolving-profile/, accessed October 15, 2011.

7. Claudia H. Deutsch, "Companies Giving Green an Office," *The New York Times,* July 3, 2007, http://query.nytimes.com/gst/fullpage.html?res=9B02EFDD153EF930A35754C0A9619C8B63&pagewanted=all, accessed October 15, 2011.

8. Johanna Sorrel, "The Rise of the CSO Chief Sustainability Officer," March 29, 2011, www.2degreesnetwork.com/blog/archives/90-The-Rise-of-the-CSO-Chief-Sustainability-Officer.html, accessed October 15, 2011.

9. "Corporate Sustainability Officers," eco-officiency, www.corporatesustainabilityofficers.com/, accessed October 15, 2011.

10. U.S. Department of Defense, myfuture.com, "Chief Sustainability Officers," http://myfuture.com/careers/overview/chief-sustainability-officers_11-1011.03, accessed October 15, 2011.

11. "Corporate Sustainability Officers," eco-officiency, http://www.corporatesustainabilityofficers.com/, accessed October 15, 2011.

12. Ellen Weinreb, "The CSO Myth – Weinreb Group Defines the Chief Sustainability Officer," May 23, 2010, http://weinrebgroup.com/category/insights/, accessed October 15, 2011.

13. CB Richard Ellis, "Environmental Stewardship Policy Effective May 31, 2007," www.cbre.com/en/aboutus/corporateresponsibility/pages/environment.aspx, accessed October 15, 2011.

14. Lloyd Alter, "Three Green Building Lawyer Bloggers Predict The Next Big Thing," *TreeHugger,* November 29, 2010, www.treehugger.com/files/2010/11/three-green-building-lawyer-bloggers.php, accessed October 15, 2011.

15. Stephen Del Percio, "Bain v. Vertex Architects: Firm 'Failed to Diligently Pursue and Obtain LEED for Homes Certification from USGBC,'" *Green Real Estate Law Journal,* March 18, 2011, www.greenrealestatelaw.com/2011/03/bain-v-vertex-architects-firm-failed-to-diligently-pursue-and-obtain-leed-for-homes-certification-from-usgbc/, accessed October 15, 2011.

16. Stephen Del Percio, "Class Action No More: Gifford-Led Plaintiffs File Amended Complaint Against USGBC," *Green Real Estate Law Journal,* February 8, 2011, www.greenrealestatelaw.com/2011/02/class-action-no-more-gifford-led-plaintiffs-file-amended-complaint-against-usgbc/, accessed October 15, 2011.

17. Lloyd Alter, "Three Green Building Lawyer Bloggers Predict The Next Big Thing," *TreeHugger,* November 29, 2010, www.treehugger.com/files/2010/11/three-green-building-lawyer-bloggers.php, accessed October 15, 2011.

18. Ibid.

19. Donald Simon Esq., partner at Wendel, Rosen, Black & Dean LLP, *Basic Green Building Liability Considerations,* USGBC-NCC, Silicon Valley Branch, August 10, 2010.

20. Ray Anderson, Melaver McIntosh, http://melaver-mcintosh.com/, accessed October 15, 2011.

21. Paul Hawken, Amory Lovins, and L. Hunter Lovins, *Natural Capitalism: Creating the Next Industrial Revolution,* Boston: Little Brown and Company, September 1999, www.natcap.org/, accessed October 15, 2011.

22. Heschong Mahone Group, "Daylighting and Productivity - CEC PIER: Daylight and Retail Sales - CEC PIER 2003," http://h-m-g.com/projects/daylighting/summaries%20on%20daylighting.htm#Skylighting_and_Retail_Sales%20-%20PG&E%201999, accessed October 15, 2011.

23. Joseph J. Romm, *Lean and Clean Management: How to Boost Profits and Productivity by Reducing Pollution,* New York: Kodansha International, 1994, http://openlibrary.org/books/OL1093491M/Lean_and_clean_management, accessed October 15, 2011.

24. Stephen Oppenheimer et al., "The Cost of LEED: A Report on Cost Expectations to Meet LEED-NC 2009," *BuildingGreen,* 2010, https://www.buildinggreen.com/ecommerce/cost-of-leed-whitepaper.cfm, accessed October 15, 2011.

25. Piet Eichholtz, Nils Kok, and John M. Quigley, Working Paper W10-003, "The Economics of Green Buildings," Institute of Business and Economic Research Program on Housing and Urban Policy Working Paper Series, April 2011, http://urbanpolicy.berkeley.edu/pdf/EKQ_041511_to_REStat_wcover.pdf, accessed October 15, 2011.

26. Susan Piperato, "Green Building Regulations: Carrots or Sticks?" *National Real Estate Investor,* September 19, 2011, http://nreionline.com/strategies/properties/green_building_carrots_sticks_09192011/, accessed October 15, 2011.

27. Jones Lang LaSalle and LaSalle Investment Management, 2010 CSR Report, http://www.joneslanglasalle.com/csr/SiteCollectionDocuments/CSR_full_report.pdf, accessed October 15, 2011.

28. Susan Piperato, "Green Building Regulations: Carrots or Sticks?" *National Real Estate Investor,* September 19, 2011, http://nreionline.com/strategies/properties/green_building_carrots_sticks_09192011/, accessed October 15, 2011.

29. Shari Shapiro, "The Top Ten Rules of Green Project Finance," Greenbiz.com, January 20, 2011, https://www.greenbiz.com/blog/2011/01/20/top-10-rules-green-project-finance?page=0%2C1, accessed October 15, 2011.

30. Randyl Drummer, "Fund Invests $650M In Emerging Market for Green Retrofits of Aging Buildings," CoStar, September 21, 2011, www.costar.com/News/Article/Fund-Invests-$650M-In-Emerging-Market-for-Green-Retrofits-of-Aging-Buildings/132198, accessed October 15, 2011.

31. U.S. Green Building Council, Green Building Incentive Strategies, www.usgbc.org/DisplayPage.aspx?CMSPageID=2078, accessed October 15, 2011.

32. U.S. Department of Energy, Database of State Incentives for Renewables & Efficiency (DSIRE), http://dsireusa.org/, accessed October 15, 2011.

9 The Future of Green Building

The future is something which everyone reaches at the rate of sixty miles an hour, whatever he does, whoever he is.

—C. S. LEWIS *(The* Times of London *ranked him eleventh on their list of "the 50 greatest British writers since 1945. Known for themes of common morality throughout humanity.)*

Forecast

The forecast is for sunny skies in our collective future. Though such a prediction may seem counterintuitive when reading messages about doom and gloom for the environment and the planet—it is really all in your perspective. Although there are certainly looming sustainable issues, there are also innumerable solutions and innovative thinkers working to build a regenerative future.

The following section includes the viewpoints of an array of building professionals, all of whom talk about their current careers and work—and their predictions for the future of sustainability.

In each case, three pertinent questions were asked:

- What is your background?
- How does your current work involve sustainability or green building?
- What do you predict for the future of green building?

Beginning with global forecasting, then narrowed down to U.S.-based professionals (both those at the end of their careers and those just starting out), this chapter aims to paint an overall picture of the current status of green building and where it is headed. Although these professionals come from diverse backgrounds and practice in a variety of fields, the common thread that runs throughout their answers is an underlying optimism, full of possibilities.

Solar farm beside green roof on the parking buildings. Energy Complex, Bangkok, Thailand (LEED CS Platinum). Firm: Architect 49. Owner: Energy Complex Co., Ltd. PHOTO: 2011, ENERGY COMPLEX

GLOBAL

There is a rapid movement afoot of green awareness within the global community that is beginning to take hold, even at a consumer level. There is also an increased understanding of the importance of our shared resources and how to mitigate the built environment's impact on our planet. If nothing else, the international community's awareness of global warming, and its response to the issue, have contributed to this growing eco-conscious vision. Each region has particular nuances that are specific to its climactic conditions, site terrain, and key environmental issues—yet despite the particularities of countries, cultures, and places, there is evidence of an emerging common language with a common goal of sustainability at its core.

International Perspectives

What is your background? How does your current work involve sustainability or green building? What do you predict for the future of green building in your country?

❯ Working with the Green Building Council of Australia [GBCA], and seeing the development of eighty other councils promoted by the World Green Building Council, I'm optimistic that new buildings will increasingly be designed and built to be energy efficient. One of the best examples is the Pixel Building in Melbourne, which has scored highest on the GBCA rating—and also LEED and BREEAM. Increasingly, governments and owners are realizing that the best investments are built green.

My current work involves promoting green building and development to reduce carbon emissions and introduce resilience to inevitable climate change. The Australian Sustainable Built Environment Council (ASBEC), of which I'm president, has task groups working on climate change and adaptation, cities, zero-carbon housing, green skills, and distributed energy.   At the same time, buildings that are currently the biggest contributors to Australia's greenhouse gas emissions are the quickest, easiest, and cheapest area for urgent reduction.

Combating climate change will produce lower carbon emissions and more resilient and comfortable buildings that aren't energy and water guzzlers.

The Honorable Tom Roper, president, Australian Sustainable Built Environment Council; board member, Climate Institute

❯ Currently I am responsible for growing Johnson Controls' Thailand business in energy performance and green building solutions projects by providing energy efficiency, renewable energy, and green consulting solutions to our Thailand customers.

Local engineers and academics in building engineering are trying to organize and put up local green building standards and certification processes. Nevertheless, LEED certification will still be the leading and most preferred green building certification due to its international flavor and acceptance, especially among multinational and internationally known local business enterprises.

Baldomero P. Din, LEED AP BD+C, sales manager for energy and green building solutions, Johnson Controls

❯ My career is to promote and develop sustainable building practice and strategies in China, covering design, construction, and building O&M (operation and maintenance).

I have been involved in the green building industry in China since 2005, and I can feel the outstanding changes here. LEED certification is a good demonstration of these changes. There were less than ten projects that adopted LEED certification before 2005, whereas over 300 projects applied for this green building certification from 2005 to 2010, and the trend keeps growing.

Joe Yang, LEED AP ID+C, general manager, East China, EMSI

UNITED STATES

Local Perspectives

What is your background? How does your current work involve sustainability or green building? What do you predict for the future of green building?

❯ The Living Building Challenge is the most exciting idea: buildings that can support themselves through their design. No need to pump in electricity and water when a building functions as an organism. This way of thinking will change everything.

I believe in the human capacity for wanting to learn, understand, do good things, and pay at-tention to important issues. If we don't get derailed by the idiocy of pop culture and its emphasis on stardom and material gains, we may have a chance on this Earth.

[People should] work hard to understand the human condition and what a compromised environment does to our physical and emotional selves. Be alert to all kinds of information. Expand your knowledge in culture, science, and literature—all the time-honored creative activities that make us human, and make us question ourselves.

Susan Szenasy, editor in chief, Metropolis *magazine*

Local Perspectives (Continued)

❯ Well before I heard about sustainable design (and frankly, before the term really existed), I began in a traditional-track architecture/engineering degree program at the University of Texas. In 1999, I went to work for William McDonough, and for the first time I felt that design could be based on a rational set of principles (and not just on personal taste) and that I could create a positive impact and profound value. I worked with Bill for most of the following decade and left in 2009 to write my next book, *The Shape of Green: Aesthetics, Ecology, and Design—or How Beauty Could Save the Planet.* (Ironically, this returns to the topic that made me impatient twenty years ago—that of aesthetics.) A year ago, I joined GreenBlue, a nonprofit (founded by Bill, though he's unaffiliated now) whose mission is to make products more sustainable.

GreenBlue works in a variety of industries and market sectors, so for the first time, I feel I'm in a position to work toward sustainability in a way that spans many scales of influence.

The next generation of the sustainability agenda in every field must focus on connecting the dots between physical resources (quantity of stuff) and well-being (quality of life). Imagine a day when we've perfectly solved the challenges of energy, resources, and emissions, and everything we do and make is clean, harmless, and infinitely renewable. Is that enough? Over the last few decades, the gross domestic product has risen steadily, but the number of Americans claiming to be "very happy" has fallen, while the incidence of clinical depression is now over ten times more prevalent than it was a century ago. We're richer in resources and poorer in spirit. The next phase of sustainability must expand its goals from merely making things harmless to begin promoting more fulfilling and uplifting lives.

Lance Hosey, president & CEO, GreenBlue

❯ I'm a founding partner, along with Hank Houser, of Houser Walker Architecture, an architecture and design firm focusing on cultural buildings and the culture of building.

As architects, we design the built environment, an activity that inherently involves matters of sustainability and ecology, whether they are explicitly addressed or not. We feel a strong moral imperative to be conservators of our common ecology and approach each project with a holistic process and outlook.

I'm also encouraged by how some sustainable design professionals are harnessing different communication platforms to spread real, concrete ideas companies can incorporate. And, finally, I'm hopeful that the "slow food" and "slow home" types of movements will continue to gain traction and ask all of us to reconsider fundamental questions of just "how much" is really enough.

Gregory Walker, AIA, LEED AP, Houser Walker Architecture

Interior of Toco Hill: Avis G. Williams Library. Firm: Houser Walker Architecture. PHOTO © BRIAN GASSELL, tvsdesign

❯ I was hired to teach interior design in a school of architecture; soon after, I was asked to teach drawing to both AR and ID students, and I then taught studio courses to both. I worked as a draftsman for local architects and sat in on architectural history classes. One professor had a great interest in vernacular Louisiana architecture and how heat and humidity were managed.

That introduction became a fascination with vernacular design and a realization that HVAC allowed any building type to be built in any location no matter how unsuitable it might appear or actually be. I developed a belief that HVAC was a blessing and a curse and needed to be understood. My early beliefs were driven by aesthetics and the Yom Kippur War of 1973, which made me realize that energy supplies were both vulnerable and expensive, and as I later realized, polluting. From this I began an interest in buildings conceived with climate constraints, as vernacular buildings are, that were also less fossil- or nuclear-fuel-reliant. From this I began a lifelong interest as to how we might live more gently on our world.

I am not an architect, nor a scientist, nor am I formally trained in any aspect of making a more sustainable or "greener" world. I do hold a humble but strong belief that we are living in a global warming era that is partially a geologic cyclical warming trend; remember that in geologic terms, the last ice age was a mere eye blink away, but one exacerbated by the massive carbon emissions that we rapidly reproducing human beings produce. When I was a teacher, I tried to be subtle in introducing ideas about what is now called sustainability long before that term become common. Being the son of a farmer can make one frugal. Perhaps it's a cliché, but I genuinely believed that ideas were better "planted" than preached.

Since I retired from teaching, I mainly design houses or additions and improvements to them. I now spend as much time trying to talk people out of wanting "space" as I used to spend creating it. I feel extremely fortunate to have traveled extensively in more densely populated parts of this world and use knowledge gained to convince people that "less is truly more" in the concept of what one needs in terms of volume to live a good life. I have recently overseen the installation of cisterns, use of gray water, better insulation and ventilation, and encouraged higher-efficiency appliances and HVAC units, but the simple use of space keeps coming to the forefront. Less size means less of all the above. As an old teacher, I try to teach people to use less stuff in a way that does not seem self-righteous, but it is really self-preservation for all of us. When we in any aspect of building design move a pencil or cursor, it is good to remember that we are expending materials and causing the future use of energy to be increased.

The future of all of this may be mayhem—we may fight for resources militarily or economically. Or it may be a gradual understanding that we need to move and live more gently on this planet. The key to me is Frederick Nietzsche's saying, "That which does not kill you makes you stronger." I would be so bold as to change that a bit and say instead that "it can make you stronger." It is not automatic to me; you must work for a genuine effort to produce sustainability. To improve the way we live could mean jobs, less reliance on nonrenewable resources, and a more interactive society. The prospects of that may seem daunting, but it can make us stronger as a species. Hopefully we will become more adept, more resilient, and stronger. I do not think we can remain reliant on dinosaurs [fossil fuels] forever. The potential for producing a sustainable world is enormous if we are wise enough to recognize it.

Gaines Thomas Blackwell, Emeritus Gresham Endowed and Alumni Professor, School of Architecture, Auburn University, Residential Design in Auburn, AL.

Local Perspectives (Continued)

❯ The American Institute of Architects is committed to the Architecture 2030 Challenge, which asks the architecture community to adopt aggressive efficiency targets through design to reduce fossil fuel and GHG emissions, resulting in carbon neutrality by 2030. Most of the education and communication we are putting out to architects today is balanced between sustainability and practice management in these perilous times—or more importantly, how do you keep an eye on sustainability when your firm is fighting to survive?

The good news is that most clients aren't asking if a project should be "green" or sustainable, they're asking, "How green can it be?" However, with the real estate market still perilous in so many parts of the country, good design decisions risk being "value engineered" out of buildings. For a while,

Neoterra Townhomes: Courtyard. FIRM AND PHOTO: GERDING COLLABORATIVE, LLC

new buildings are mostly going to be institutions who largely "get it" since they own and maintain the buildings for the long haul. Renovations will be more the norm than new construction, so the design and "green" industries need to get their arms around renovation and adaptive reuse.

Marci B. Reed, CFRE, MPA, executive director, AIA Georgia and Architecture Foundation of Georgia

❯ I focus my professional career on progressing the adoption of green technology as well as on opportunities to make our building stock more efficient. Whether I am working on a new product launch for energy efficiency or a policy change at a state legislature, my focus is always about moving the needle on clean or green technology/programs.

What I was doing just ten years ago was not completely mainstream and recognized, but today the tides have shifted and it is hard not to have some commonalities in the sustainability profession with companies that were not focused on green efforts some years ago. I, too, see that the younger generation is being exposed to sustainability issues at such a young age that as they grow up it will become a standard of life that we all seek.

Ben Taube, LEED AP, partner, Energy Fool and senior vice president, Evaporcool

❯ As practitioners of interior design, we believe that design solutions should promote environmental stewardship while advising clients of effective solutions that improve their facilities in an environmentally responsible way.

Whether a client chooses to pursue LEED certification or not, it is our goal to develop design solutions that implement sustainable principles that enhance the health and well-being of [those in] the work environment. Sustainability has become part of our daily lives.

Jennifer Treter, LEED AP ID+C, principal and owner, Hendrick Inc.

IDI View at small conference off reception area (LEED CI Gold). Firm: Hendrick. PHOTOGRAPHY BY BRIAN ROBBINS OF ROBBINS PHOTOGRAPHY INC.

❯ As I meet with prospective architecture students, one of the more popular questions is how sustainability is impacting the profession and how our institution, the University of Illinois, prepares students for it. Starting this year, I will teach our "Introduction to Architecture" course; as part of this introduction, students will learn about "green" from Re_home, our entry to the Solar Decathlon.

In my book, *Becoming an Architect,* 2nd edition, I highlighted "sustainability" as one of the future trends that is emerging in the profession.

While I never would want to predict the future, I do think that "sustainability" is here to stay. However, rather than being an add-on as it is now, sustainability will be commonplace. Clients will no longer need convincing that a "green" building is a good investment; instead, all buildings will be designed sustainable. In twenty or so years, architects will design buildings that address sustainability issues because it will be the right action to take.

Lee W. Waldrep, PhD, assistant director, School of Architecture, University of Illinois at Urbana-Champaign, author of Becoming an Architect: A Guide to Careers in Design, 2nd edition

Students from the University of Illinois at Urbana-Champaign speak with the Engineering Jury during judging at the U.S. Department of Energy Solar Decathlon 2011 in Washington, D.C. PHOTO: STEFANO PALTERA/U.S. DEPARTMENT OF ENERGY SOLAR DECATHLON

Local Perspectives (Continued)

❯ Our interest is in the creation of healthy environments—it is a broader term that encompasses a lot of competing definitions of "sustainability." When we say we are interested in the design of healthy, sustainable environments at all scales, two primary areas of focus emerge: projects at the urban scale such as highway corridors, Buford Highway, for example, and at the other end of the spectrum, domestic space, primarily houses, housing and interiors.

At the urban scale, the impact that the environment has on health can be directly measured, and research we have completed in conjunction with Georgia Tech on the Buford Highway Corridor is one of the foundational studies created by the CDC called "health impact assessments" (HIAs). These are pioneering studies that demonstrate direct relations between the composition of the built environment—namely auto-centric developments—and public health. We will all see instances in the future where HIAs figure into policy decisions about how to remediate settlements that are primarily designed around the automobile. HIAs will also be increasingly used to identify those areas with the highest concentrations of obesity; in so many newly developed areas today, city planning does not facilitate walking.

In 2006, we won a regional competition to design and build a low-cost, energy-efficient house sponsored by Southface Energy Institute and the Kendeda Foundation.   While the house was completed on a very tight budget, our work in low-cost design has been thwarted by the economic downturn. We continue researching higher-end houses, and Michael continues to co-teach a well subscribed interdisciplinary course at George Tech entitled "Zero Energy Housing." Students from various schools—engineering, architecture, business, construction—work with a number of professors and professionals to make design, construction, and financial proposals on in-town multifamily housing that seeks to be net-zero on the energy scale. This research is the foundation for a forthcoming book with the same name.

We anticipate a continuation of the trend we have seen over the last ten years towards more public awareness of the impact of our choices on the environment, more desire to implement sustainable strategies, and strong interest in being "off the grid" or "zero energy."

We share the expectation that everyone must embrace the principles of sustainable, healthy design, as it will soon become the standard expectation rather than a lofty goal. We also believe that the role of the green building professional will transition from educating clients about implementing sustainable practices to developing and promoting advancements in this field.

Lee Ann & Mike Gamble, principals, G+G Architects

Interior view of renovated ranch home. Firm: G+G Architects. PHOTO: JIM STODDART, 2010

Excerpt from Lori Dennis's book, *Green Interior Design*:

❯ "I am an interior designer who began practicing green behavior as a child, long before I knew it was a movement. Being raised by a struggling, single mother and a grandmother who lived through the Great Depression, I was taught to conserve energy, never waste, and recycle. My mother honored the Cherokee part of our heritage, and respect for the planet was a core value I also learned at a young age."

After graduating from the UCLA Interior Design program and as I started my career in interior design, it seemed logical to marry my agenda of green living with the concept of designing sustainably, and I've been extremely successful with it ever since. I've recently launched two new furniture lines featuring both classic and contemporary artisan pieces made in an eco-friendly way. In my years of doing green design, I've never quite found the right green/sustainable pieces that are made with impeccable manufacturing—so I went ahead and created them myself. Voila!

Sustainability will soon be the norm.

Lori Dennis ASID, LEED AP, Lori Dennis, Inc., author of **Green Interior Design**

❯ I was the environmental reporter for a daily newspaper and then the editor of Atlanta's alternative newsweekly. But the digital revolution has allowed me to create my own media organization focusing on my interest in the sustainable built environment. Sustainability and green building frames environmental issues in a positive, solutions-oriented way, which is very appealing to my optimistic nature. I'm the publisher and editor of RenewATL.com, an online media organization that informs and empowers the community of businesses and people who care about enhancing the sustainability of Atlanta's built environment.

As with most industries—especially those that include the world "building" in their names—the short-term outlook for green building is challeng

Students from the SCI-Arc/Caltech team designed an iPad app to control wirelessly the lights, shade, and entertainment system of their house at the U.S. Department of Energy Solar Decathlon 2011 in Washington, D.C. PHOTO: STEFANO PALTERA/U.S. DEPARTMENT OF ENERGY SOLAR DECATHLON

ing, even a bit scary. Over the long term, however, I have no doubt that sustainability and green building will be growth industries, because the environmental problems that need solving are becoming more pressing all the time.

Ken Edelstein, editor, GreenBuildingChronicle.com

❯ I spent fifteen years as an architect, but I didn't feel challenged anymore. I realized that my real talent was for hearing what someone was asking and then figuring out how to get a team from where we were at that moment to where we needed to be. So, I now use my skills and talents to help socially motivated businesses develop faster and better. We give them the tools they need to compete—and win—against businesses that are only motivated by the bottom line. Our goal is to help change the world through a wide variety of entrepreneurs.

Local Perspectives (Continued)

The design profession was uniquely situated to adapt to the concepts of sustainability. It uses a lot of materials of which quantities were already being tracked. In addition, the entire profession is built on thinking about new ways to do things and then convincing people to adopt those new ideas and behaviors. Now, if the profession as a whole can integrate this into the work (as opposed to a piece of their practice), I think there is potential for architects and designers to be recognized for their leadership in crafting a better world.

Michelle Morgan, founder, Hub Atlanta

❯ I published a book in 2009, *Fundamentals of Integrated Design for Sustainable Building*, with co-author Bill Burke. Published by Wiley & Sons, it was the first textbook for the U.S. university level. Chapters include: integrated design process, history of green building and green building legislation, basic principles of energy, energy use and standards, energy-efficient design, sustainable communities, and indoor air quality and human health.

For me it's all about the strides being made in sustainable design for health care.   But ever since Rachel Carson's efforts to ban DDT raised awareness (it was a struggle for her to gain credibility and acceptance) about synthetic chemical pesticides, we've slowly started to really take a look at the measured impacts of environmental chemicals: reproductive harm, respiratory disease, cancer, etc. Many buildings materials' chemicals are bioaccumulative toxins. These, and persistent organic pollutants, are banned in EU countries, but in North America we haven't made these regulations because of the predominance of chemical industry lobbies and our reluctance to rely on anything but mainstream industrial approaches to agriculture, food processing, water treatment, fertilization, pest control, building materials (you name it!). Now, with life spans growing shorter for the first time

in decades, the real pioneers of green buildings are the green building designers specializing in health-care facilities and their stakeholders (examples: Green Guide for Healthcare, Healthcare without Harm, LEED for Healthcare). Chemical management, health-care waste management, and green-cleaning practices are strategies we should incorporate in any building, regardless of building type or function. Taking these steps would improve air quality indoors and contribute to, rather than damage, human health.

Marian Keeler, Assoc. AIA, LEED AP BD+C, Simon & Associates, Inc.

❯ For so long I believed that there were certain thresholds in the progress of sustainability that we'd be able to cross, as industries and markets, and as makers and users of things. Those thresholds always had to do with changing behavior, with reshaping a status quo so that changes that had once seemed great would now be seen as a given. For example, that a certain percentage of recycled content in a flooring product would bump up demand, and change behaviors all of the way upstream. Or that some renewable-energy source would shoulder forward and suddenly everyone would agree that there was one right way to do things. The threshold crossed, other improvements could become incremental.

Wishful thinking, certainly. But also hopeful thinking.

What's happened instead is a shift in thinking—call it the playlist generation, call it an "App" approach—but the result is that we all believe the next big thing will be a million little things. We look for brilliant little innovations and believe that we can cluster them together around ourselves so that our cumulative impact is reduced.

It's true, of course—but it's also not. Because we judge everything purely on the basis of context and of relevance, rather than because it is patently good or patently bad. So sustainability is constantly in a place where it is in a crisis of relevance. There's always a mitigating factor, there's always a caveat. Everything is seen as an iteration.

For solutions, this is a wise approach. We should never think that we've arrived—or even that we've crossed a threshold where change can relax into the incremental.

But for problems, it's not a wise approach. The problems that sustainability seeks to address aren't small changes, or situational relevance. They're big, and deep and wide. So they still call for big action, and deep values, and wide collaboration. We can't settle for small changes.

The future of sustainability, it seems to me, will always rest with people who see this and act on it, people who want to do something big to make things better, and who are willing to let it cost them something. Because real benefit always has a cost; real change always requires a sacrifice. Why not let it cost my company, my project, my wallet? That's the only way things will move forward.

The beautiful part of being where we are is that everyone is asking: "Dear Green, what you did ten years ago was great, but what have you done for me lately?" It's not about where we've been, or even where we're headed. It's about where we are right now, and how we can do better today. So we're perfectly positioned for big thinking, again.

Caleb Ludwick, principal, 26 Tools llc

❯ After almost a decade of practice, I returned to academia to teach and to more rigorously research the structural form of space—in particular, its relationship to our experiences and perceptions within it.

My research seeks to give greater clarity in our understanding of how we describe space, use it, and/or perceive it, so that we can actually create viable, sustainable environments that don't necessitate constant revision.

In my opinion, professionals focused on sustainability or green building will, in the future, need to be the bridge that links all of the associated innovation and efforts between the disciplines of design and engineering. They will need to interconnect the efforts at the various scales—from interior to urban—facilitate communication across disciplines to ensure comprehensive design decisions, and in particular, coordinate all the varying regulations to orchestrate environmentally responsive communities.

S. Dawn Haynie, PhD candidate in the School of Architecture, Georgia Institute of Technology, part-time instructor of interior design, Georgia State University

Renaissance Schaumburg Convention Center, Schaumburg, IL. The water garden is an inventive solution to the challenge of reclaiming what was principally wetlands. Firm: John Portman & Associates. PHOTO: LEE HOGAN AERIALS

Local Perspectives (Continued)

❯ Through my academic work, local art installations, my architectural practice, and as the co-author and author of conference papers on reparative planning and solar accommodation in design, I continue to be fascinated by the endless opportunities and difficulties presented to us as inhabitants of this Earth.

The future of the green building profession is increasingly described to me in two divergent but not dissimilar ways:

1. "Green building will simply become 'good architecture' and will no longer be isolated as 'sustainable design.'" This attitude posits the role of the architect as one who is ethically bound to uphold the law and care for the health and welfare of individuals in the built environment. This parallels advancements in the energy code and other regulations to reduce resources used within building design, occupation, and operations. Additionally, the role of vernacular and place-based design strategies becomes elevated in this discussion to validate the fact that architecture and buildings can have intrinsic value as ecologically sensitive structures without being qualified or isolated as a particular "type" of practice or building.

   or

2. "Green building and sustainability will become a specialization with greater influence on design and construction processes." New positions and titles that now exist in many large architectural firms begin to provide evidence for this prediction. Titles like *director of sustainable strategies* or *green building analyst* begin to describe individuals in design firms who oversee multiple projects with the single task of making sure the performance and prescriptive goals set for a project do not get marginalized in the process of documentation, negotiation, and construction.

This attitude towards the future of sustainability holds an element of optimism and/or contention when it is voiced.

In either future, I feel that the green building profession will be primary to the design process.

Resource depletion, social awareness, professional ethics, strengthened regulations, and the realignment of cultural norms to limit consumption will ensure that no matter what the nomenclature, our processes for building must change to become more ecologically sensitive and reparative. I'm very optimistic for the future of our profession and the multiplicity of options that will constitute sustainable or green building practice. I'm not as optimistic about our resources and the environment's ability to endure the learning curve and realignment process that we simply must go through. I'm not sure we are moving fast enough, but at least there is movement in the right direction.

Ed Akins II, AIA, LEED AP, assistant professor of architecture, 3rd Year Design Studio coordinator, environmental technologies coordinator, Architecture Department, Southern Polytechnic State University

❯ Young designers. I just cannot believe how embedded sustainability is in their thinking. I've heard graduates (all under 28 years old) from Pratt, Harrington, SCAD, and universities throughout the country place sustainability as a natural part of their day-to-day thinking. It's like they can't imagine that anyone wouldn't have it wired into their thinking already. Couple that with the fact that more and more of these young designers are taking on product selection in their firms (in some ways attributable to the bloodletting of the last three years that has seen the middle ranks of A&D firms let go) then—by default—we should really start getting this right en masse.

One more thing: I think there's some acceptance to the idea that we need more architects that

Greenhaven Home Room (Energy Star and Earthcraft). Firm: Alejandra Dunphy, A|D Studio. PHOTO: ATTIC FIRE PHOTOGRAPHY

behave like rheumatologists and less like obstetricians. We have an entire world filled with existing and aging building stock. And while everyone likes new and shiny buildings, I hope there's a future where building professionals will be rewarded for applying green thinking to the taking care of and managing the aged stock, and not be so focused on delivering the new to the world.

Martin Flaherty, senior vice president of communications, SmartBIM

❯ In 2007 I founded a full-service design studio with a focus in sustainability and green living. The design studio offers interior design and product design solutions for residential, commercial, and hospitality projects. In 2008, a collection of sustainable textiles and accessories was launched. All items in the collection are hand-loomed using ancient weaving techniques, natural fibers, and eco-friendly dyes. This collaboration has given me the opportunity to work with talented artisans and promote their art and community. The whole process is socially responsible, sustainable, and organic.

New improvements in green technology, smarter building materials, and consumer education will lead the way to a more sustainable world.

Alejandra M. Dunphy, LEED AP, ASID, principal/design director, A|D Studio

❯ While I initially thought that it would be a ten-year venture before everything went mainstream, I'm seeing that due to the extensive inventory of existing buildings, along with the slowdown of the economy, that time frame may well go out another ten years or even twenty. Similar to the ADA standards, I believe that there may be a need for a small number of sustainability consulting firms to continue beyond that time, but not the number of firms that currently exists.

Tom Boeck, LEED AP, principal and founder, Sustainable Options

❯ I am a writer and a communications consultant, and at this time, I am director of communications for William McDonough + Partners. Bill McDonough was co-author of *Cradle to Cradle: Remaking the Way We Make Things*, a book that has been very influential in the sustainability movement in the U.S. and around the world, both for designers and for business. Bill is a masterful storyteller, and I have the privilege of helping facilitate that to a wide range of audiences. As the daughter of an architect and an interior designer, I think I will always be connected to the world of design, but my true passion is writing. I co-authored a book, *Women in Green: Voices of Sustainable Design*, with architect Lance Hosey, and that has led to an amazing ongoing conversation through articles, blog-

Local Perspectives (Continued)

ging, radio interviews, and panel discussions, and I hope to build on that and start a new book soon.

Today, I pair my work for the firm with a commitment to writing, and I'm proud be a contributing writer to *Metropolis* magazine and metropolismag. com. I hope to explore social media to find new ways to communicate and catalyze around green and women in green.

The best thing that could happen to this "movement," is that we stop labeling it "sustainability" or "green." This is hardly a new gripe, but I believe that it is increasingly important and increasingly clear during economic difficulty: Economic health is part of sustainability, but when green pursuits (buildings, jobs, etc.) are labeled "green," it's a license to segregate them as something separate from the intrinsic health of our economy and our society.

Kira Gould, AIA LEED AP, director of communications, William McDonough + Partners

❭ I think there is a lot to be optimistic about. The innovation and the pace of change, while not fast enough for many, is still moving forward even in a difficult economy. While many in the field believe it is too slow, the reality is that we are still progressing at a rapid pace from a historical perspective. I wish we could move faster, but then again, who doesn't wish that? We are still innovating with new products, new construction methods, better data to work with, more understanding by the broader community—the list could go on and on. I think that the biggest inspiration is knowing that we are doing this for more than just a paycheck. As our beloved Ray Anderson used to remind us, it's all for tomorrow's child. I don't have to look to tomorrow as I have four amazing kids right now. Their adoring faces are enough inspiration to keep me going for lifetimes to come.

Paul Firth, Manager, UL Environment

BEAUTY OF AGE

According to the Baby Boomer Headquarters, "The United States experienced an 'explosion' of births after American soldiers returned home from World War II. The sociologists define those born between (and including) 1946 and 1964 as 'baby boomers.' There are currently 76 million people considered as the baby boomers."[1]

> The economical impact of the baby boomers could not be ignored. In the United States alone, over 50% of the discretionary spending power rests with the baby boomers plus they are accountable for around half of all consumer spending. In the area of health care, baby boomers purchase 61% of non-prescription drugs and an unbelievable 77% of all prescription drugs. Even their vacation habits play a big role in the economy with boomers comprising around 80% of all leisure travel. With baby boomers start to age and approach and enter retirement, there are issues that their reduced spending capability might have a negative impact on the economy. As well as the baby boomers are aging. Roughly a baby boomer in the USA turns 50 every 8.5 seconds! It is obvious that these "Golden Boomers" are likely to affect all areas of American life now and for almost the next two decades,[2] says the Drake Labels website.

When considering the immediate future of green building, the baby boomer generation's needs are a natural consideration.

> ## How does universal design (or space design that is accessible for all) intersect with green design?

❯ This is an interesting question. Those of us who want to make a measurable contribution through interior design are drawn to both subjects, and there is definitely an intersection.

In my own house I have invisibly integrated over 200 green and universal features (www. AgingBeautifully.org/ranch). For example, we use active solar panels and passive solar greenhouses to provide most of our heat.

Many older and disabled people have reduced circulation and need higher ambient temperatures (up to 78°) but can't afford the higher cost. Our heating bills have averaged $69 per month, and we are at an altitude of 7,500 feet with temperatures as low as −20°.

We have insulation with high R-values, and we have tested for leaks using pressure and infrared measures. We added door bottoms which drop down to seal. This eliminates the need for thresholds, which are tripping hazards for older and disabled people. Our programmable thermostat reduces energy use and can be set from a laptop, a real advantage for wheelchair users and even those who are bedridden. It can be operated from anywhere you can get an Internet connection (including an airplane in case you forget to turn down your heat or need to preheat your house to accommodate reduced circulation).

In the summer, our evaporative cooler uses far less energy than air conditioning while making the house comfortable for older and disabled who cannot tolerate extremes of heat and cold. Our reversible ceiling fans also cool in the summer and draw heat up from the greenhouses in the winter.

In conclusion, I hope your readers will consider integrating these ideas on all their projects, not just those projects for older and disabled people. Universal and sustainable design is really just good design, not a special type of design for a special population.

Cynthia Leibrock, MA, ASID, Hon. IIDA, Easy Access to Health, LLC, author of **Design Details for Health: Making the Most Out of Interior Design's Healing Potential**

NEW LOOK

Looking at something with "new eyes," or a fresh perspective, will often yield insights that remained previously veiled. This type of outlook can come in a number of forms, from inexperience, to discussions with colleagues, to just stepping away from a project for a while. Once you have gained this novel standpoint, it is hard to go back to an old way of seeing things. Though everyone can gain this type of refreshing view, in many ways, the next generation has this approach built in, as they do not have past actions or experiences weighing on their future moves. In green building, a field in which many professionals seek to pass the sustainable torch on to their children (and children's children), this point of view is especially valuable.

🌐 *Who is leading the green movement now?*

❭ I think the young professionals are leading the green movement. Be it the Emerging Professionals or any other young leaders group, we are the ones who are going out into the community, being activists, and making a statement. We range from being radical anarchists to conscientious businessmen, and we reach into many facets of society.

Lisa Lin, LEED AP BD+C, ICLEI, Local Governments for Sustainability

❭ The green building movement has reached a tipping point where there is no one leader. The architecture and design community is versed in green building principles, contractors are bringing subcontractors up to speed on green construction, building owners are more receptive to the idea, and developers are recognizing the benefits of any premiums associated with building a LEED project.

Dana Mathews, IIDA, LEED AP ID+C, interior designer, Hickok Cole Architects

Reception area and national operation center at National Datacast Inc., Arlington, VA (LEED CI Silver). Firm: Envision Design. PHOTO: ERIC LAIGNEL

❭ Experts are great and necessary, but I think that great generalists are leading our industry today. Generalists have enough knowledge in a variety of areas that they are able to see the gaps in communication and strategy.

Brittany Grech, LEED AP + BD+C, O+M sustainability coordinator, YR&G Sustainability

❭ Green movement leaders are both grassroots community activists and industrial and corporate champions of sustainability. In order to achieve true sustainability, the solution to our environmental problems is interdisciplinary and intersocietal; we cannot deny participation of industry in the sustainability solution, because their input is invaluable. We cannot silence community leaders in voicing their concerns on behalf of families and neighborhoods, because we create communities for these very people. Through interdisciplinary, collaborative innovation and work, the green movement can and should be led by everyone on the planet.

Alessandra R. Carreon, PE, LEED AP O+M, ENVIRON

❭ The federal government has shown their support for LEED certification on nearly all new construction. With a budget as big as theirs, that's a welcome program that others should follow. The Army, Navy, GSA, and other federal agencies are really leading the effort, and possibly having the greatest overall effect in savings. Also, the individual. People have to take the initiative themselves to make an impact in their lives.

Ryan R. Murphy, Associate AIA, CDT, LEED AP BD+C

❭ Just in terms of scale and impact, I think large-scale and international firms like HOK are doing an amazing job shouldering the responsibility of being leaders. As an organization they really have a culture deeply rooted in the core tenets of sustainability—I mean, they literally wrote the book.

Ventrell Williams, Assoc. AIA, LEED AP O+M, Bank of America

❭ Younger people and students. I also see a lot of older people who were affected by the world wars and had to live conscientiously or who were growing up in the 1960s and 1970s when the environmental movement really began picking up steam. What I enjoy is when the two groups come together and bring their unique perspectives to solve an issue.

It reminds me that these are not new issues we are dealing with, just ones that we put on the back burner to chase the almighty dollar, forgetting that both could be achieved.

Heather Smith, City of Houston on the Green Office Challenge, VP of program development for veterans programs under the Bush Cares Project

❭ I think there are actually many interested groups leading the green movement now, which is great. USGBC is certainly a strong leader in our country and other parts of the world, but I would say college campuses are also one of the major hubs for sustainable activity, programs, and innovation. Other countries such as Sweden, Finland, and Germany are leaps and bounds ahead of the average U.S. state in regards to sustainable development. We should look to these innovative places for guidance, dialogue, and inspiration.

Stephanie Coble, RLA, ASLA, landscape architect, HagerSmith Design PA

❭ I think that overall, it is the everyday citizen who rides their bike around town, tries to create less waste by using items that can be reused and washed rather than thrown away, and thinks about every product they purchase, use, and consume. These people get others inspired to question their own actions.

Stephanie Walker, interior designer, The Flooring Gallery

❭ We are all leading the green building movement. It is not something that a single person, group, or organization can accomplish.

Edward Wansing, Associate AIA, LEED AP BD+C, project manager, Sustainable Design Assistance, Architectural Energy Corporation

What do you predict for the future of green building?

❭ I am a recent graduate of Auburn University's architecture school. After six-plus years of studying, I will graduate with a bachelor in architecture, bachelor in interior architecture, and a newly built thesis project.

As a naive architecture student, you start integrating "sustainable" materials into designs but it's hard to fathom the real impact these will have when designing theoretically, as we mostly do in architecture schools. It wasn't until my time at the Rural Studio [a groundbreaking program of the University's, http://apps.cadc.auburn.edu/rural-studio/Default. aspx] that I have begun to understand the scope of every choice that is made in building design. In its initial years, the Rural Studio became known for establishing an ethos of recycling, reusing, and remaking materials to construct beautiful homes and public structures for an underserved population. Today, the studio strives to define a balance between larger all-serving community projects and a desire to be aware of its own waste and consumption while consciously making locally oriented decisions.

I feel as though the primary lesson that has been instilled within me during the last two years is that good design relies on the power of place and a feeling of responsibility to that place. Good design can be for everyone, and green design should be for everyone, regardless of income—because good design has the ability to give people a higher quality of living and sometimes unknowingly inspire future generations.

Jamie Sartory, 2011 graduate of the School of Architecture, Auburn University, bachelor's degree in architecture and interior architecture, intern architect, Lake|Flato Architects in San Antonio, TX

THE END IS THE BEGINNING

A cross section of diverse voices in this book ranges from global to local, old to young, generalist to specialist—they all echo one clear voice that says green building is a pivotal profession for today and the distant future.

A common vision is created of structures that regenerate resources in their function as shelters to many souls. Regardless of your career decision, the core principles represented here can be integrated beyond buildings into any career—doctor, lawyer, or teacher. In the end, we are all empowered teachers and students even in the simple everyday acts for the next generation.

Lily and Cooper Johnson. THE BLINK LADY, BONNIE CERNIGLIA

NOTES

1. Baby Boomer Headquarters, "The Boomer Stats," www.bbhq.com/bomrstat.htm, accessed October 16, 2011.
2. Drake Labels, "Impact of Baby Boomers on the Economic Climate," http://drake.com/articledirectory/?impact-of-baby-boomers-on-the-economic-582, accessed October 16, 2011.

(APPENDIX)

Recommended Reading

BOOKS

Architecture

Waldrop, Lee S. *Becoming an Architect: A Guide to Careers in Design*. Hoboken, NJ: John Wiley & Sons, 2009.

Biomimicry

Benyus, Janine M. *Biomimicry: Innovation Inspired by Nature*. New York: HarperCollins, 2002.

Carson, Rachel. *Silent Spring*. New York, NY: Mariner Books, 2002.

Business

Anderson, Ray. *Mid-Course Correction: Toward a Sustainable Enterprise: The Interface Model*. Atlanta, GA: Peregrinzilla Press, 1999.

Anderson, Ray C., and White, Robin. *Business Lessons from a Radical Industrialist*. New York, NY: St. Martin's Griffin, 2011.

Career

Boldt, Laurence G. *Zen and the Art of Making a Living: A Practical Guide to Creative Career Design*. New York: Penguin, 1999.

de Morsella, Chris, and Tracey. *The Green Executive Recruiter Directory: The Most Complete Compilation of US Search Firms That Specialize in Renewable Energy, Green Building, Sustainability, Environmental, and Other Green Careers*. Seattle, WA: Green Growth Ventures LLC, 2011.

McClelland, Carol L. *Green Careers for Dummies*. Hoboken, NJ: John Wiley & Sons, 2010.

Education

Early, Sandra Leibowitz. *Educational Design and Building Schools: Green Guide to Educational Opportunities in the United States and Canada*. Oakland, CA: New Village Press, 2005.

Orr, David W. *Ecological Literacy*. New York: State University of New York Press, 1991.

Energy

Hertzog, Christine. *The Smart Grid Dictionary*. GreenSpring Marketing, LLC, 2009.

Engineering

Lechner, Norbert. *Heating, Cooling, Lighting: Sustainable Design Methods for Architects*. Hoboken, NJ: John Wiley & Sons, 2008.

Macaulay, David R., and McLennan, Jason F. *The Ecological Engineer, Volume 1: KEEN Engineering*. Bainbridge Island, WA: Ecotone Publishing, 2005.

Existing Buildings

Yudelson, Jerry. *Greening Existing Buildings*. New York, NY: McGraw-Hill Professional, 2009.

Financial

Dell'Isola, Alphonse, and Kirk, Stephen J. *Life Cycle Costing for Facilities*. Kingston, MA: Construction Publishers & Consultants, 2003.

Hawken, Paul. *The Ecology of Commerce: A Declaration of Sustainability*. New York, NY: Harper Business, 1994.

Hawken, Paul, with Lovins, Amory, and Lovins, L. Hunter. *Natural Capitalism: Creating the Next Industrial Revolution*. New York, NY: Back Bay Books, 2008.

Melaver, Martin, and Muehler, Phyllis. *The Green Building Bottom Line: The Real Cost of Sustainable Building*. New York, NY: McGraw-Hill Professional, 2008.

Muldavin, Scott. *Value Beyond Cost Savings: How to Underwrite Sustainable Properties*. San Rafael, CA: Green Building Finance Consortium, 2010.

Romm, Joseph J. *Lean and Clean Management: How to Boost Profits and Productivity by Reducing Pollution*. New York, NY: Kodansha American, Inc, 1994.

Shumaker, E. F. *Small is Beautiful: Economics as if People Mattered*. New York, NY: Harper Perennial, 1989.

General

Capra, Fritjof. *The Web of Life: A New Scientific Understanding of Living Systems.* New York, NY: Anchor Books, 1996.

Contributing authors. *Green Building: Project Planning and Cost Estimating.* Kingston, MA: Construction Publishers & Consultants, 2002.

Friedman, Thomas L. *Hot, Flat and Crowded: Why We Need a Green Revolution—And How It Can Renew America.* New York, NY: Farrar, Straus and Giroux, 2008.

Gould, Kira, and Hosey, Lance. *Women in Green: Voices of Sustainable Design.* Bainbridge Island, WA: Ecotone Publishing, 2007.

Johnson, Bart R., and Hill, Kristina. *Ecology and Design: Frameworks for Learning.* Washington, DC: Island Press, 2002.

Lyle, John Tillman. *Regenerative Design for Sustainable Development.* Hoboken, NJ: John Wiley & Sons, 1996.

McLennan, Jason F. *The Philosophy of Sustainable Design.* Kansas City, MO: Ecotone, 2004.

Wilson, Edward O. *The Future of Life.* New York: Alfred A. Knopf, 2002.

Yudelson, Jerry. *Green Building A to Z: Understanding the Language of Green Building.* British Columbia, Canada: New Society Publishers, 2007.

Yudelson, Jerry, and Fedrizzi, S. Richard. *The Green Building Revolution.* Washington, DC: Island Press, 2007.

Green Building Guidelines

Rider, Traci Rose. *Understanding Green Building Guidelines: For Students and Young Professionals.* New York, NY: W. W. Norton & Company, 2009.

Integrative Design

Macaulay, David R. *Integrated Design–MITHUN.* Bainbridge Island, WA: Ecotone Publishing, 2008.

Reed, Bill, and 7Group. *The Integrative Design Guide to Green Building: Redefining the Practice of Sustainability (Sustainable Design).* Hoboken, NJ: John Wiley & Sons, 2009.

Yudelson, Jerry. *Green Building Through Integrative Design.* New York, NY: McGraw-Hill Professional, 2008.

Interiors

Bonda, Penny, and Sosnowchik, Katie. *Sustainable Commercial Interiors.* Hoboken, NJ: John Wiley & Sons, 2006.

Dennis, Lori. *Green Interior Design.* New York, NY: Allworth Press, 2010.

Foster, Kari, Stelmack, Annette, and Hindman, Debbie. *Sustainable Residential Interiors.* Hoboken, NJ: John Wiley & Sons, 2006.

Landscape Architecture

Foster, Kelleann. *Becoming a Landscape Architect: A Guide to Careers in Design.* Hoboken, NJ: John Wiley & Sons, 2009.

Management

McElroy, Mark W., and van Engelen, Jo M. L. *Corporate Sustainability Management—The Art and Science of Managing Non-Financial Performance.* UK: Earthscan, 2011.

Materials

Calkins, Meg. *Materials for Sustainable Sites: A Complete Guide to Evaluation, Selection, and Use of Sustainable Construction Materials.* Hoboken, NJ: John Wiley & Sons, 2008.

McDonough, William, and Braungart, Michael. *Cradle to Cradle.* New York, NY: North Point Press, 2002.

Real Estate

Rocky Mountain Institute, Wilson, Alex, Uncapher, Jenifer L., McManigal, Lisa, Lovins, L. Hunter, Cureton, Maureen, and Browning, William D. *Green Development: Integrating Ecology and Real Estate.* Hoboken, NJ: John Wiley & Sons, 1998.

Urban Planning

Bayer, Michael, with Frank, Nancy, and Valerius, Jason. *Becoming an Urban Planner: A Guide to Careers in Planning and Urban Design.* Hoboken, NJ: John Wiley & Sons, 2010.

Farr, Douglas. *Sustainable Urbanism: Urban Design with Nature.* Hoboken, NJ: John Wiley & Sons, 2007.

Melaver, Martin, and Anderson, Ray. *Living Above the Store: Building a Business That Creates Value, Inspires Change, and Restores Land and Community—How One Family Business Transformed... Using Sustainable Management Practices.* White River Junction, VT: Chelsea Green Publishing, 2009.

DVD

Green is the Color of Money http://web.mac.com/sheddproductionsinc/SheddProductions%2CInc./Welcome.html

Water

Yudelson, Jerry. *Dry Run: Preventing the Next Urban Water Crisis.* British Columbia, Canada: New Society Publishers, 2010.

Volunteer—Get Involved

Arbor Day Foundation
www.arborday.org/programs/volunteers/

Clean Water Action
www.cleanwateraction.org/action_center/online_actions

Environmental Defense Fund
www.edf.org

GreenPlate
www.greenplate.org/volunteerform/

Healthy Child Healthy World
http://healthychild.org/get-involved/

Natural Resources Defense Council
www.nrdc.org

National Park Service
www.nps.gov/getinvolved/volunteer.htm

National Wildlife Federation
www.nwf.org/

Sierra Club
www.sierraclub.org/

The Clean Air Campaign
www.cleanaircampaign.org/

The Nature Conservancy
www.nature.org/

The Ocean Project
www.theoceanproject.org/

U.S. Green Building Council
www.usgbc.org

World Wildlife Fund
www.worldwildlife.org/how/index.html#takeAction

INDEX